# THE UNITED STATES ARMY IN
# WORLD WAR I
# GROUND UNITS, 1917-1919

## ©Richard A. Rinaldi

## Tiger Lily Publications LLC

### For

### www.orbat.com

### 2005

The title page illustrations are from the TrueTypes font "US Army"
(Iconian Fonts)

1st row:  First Army; I, II, III and V Army Corps; 1st and 2nd Divisions
2nd row:  3rd, 4th, 6th, 7th, 8th, 9th and 11th Divisions
3rd row:  14th, 28th, 31st, 32nd, 33rd, 34th and 35th Divisions
4th row:  40th, 77th 78th, 79th, 81st, 89th and 92nd Divisions

# Table of Contents

# Forward

The First World War may now seem so far in the past, and so outdated in its technology, as to be irrelevant to the student of military topics. At best it might be credited with introduction of the tank into warfare.

However, it's contributions to the US Army remain—even if overlooked—to this day. Many of the well-known Army bases (Forts Benning, Bragg, Dix, Gordon, Knox, and Jackson, for example) began as camps hastily constructed in World War I. Prior to 1914, the Army had no post large enough to house a division, or provide the grounds for training or maneuvering one.

In fact, the Army had no divisions before 1917, other than those created during a war and then disbanded. The first peacetime Regular divisions date from 1917, and the 1st, 2nd and 3rd Infantry Divisions have been continuously active since that date.[1] The basic numbering system for infantry divisions dates from 1917, and provided the general scheme for designations from then the period after World War II. Another result of the war was the loss of state designations in their National Guard units. With the rarest of exceptions, National Guard units reforming in the 1920s kept their wartime numbers, or adopted numbers consistent with the wartime system. Thus, the 69th Infantry, New York National Guard was reformed as the 165th Infantry and the 4th Infantry, Alabama National Guard, remained the 167th Infantry when it reformed.[2] The few regiments reformed with state designations lost them in 1940, and they now exist only as a parenthetical following the official designation: e.g., 123rd Armor (Second Kentucky).[3]

Another legacy of World War I is visible almost every time that you see a soldier in uniform. Although corps badges (generally worn on hats) were used in the Civil War, shoulder sleeve insignia ("shoulder patches") date from the First World War. The 81st Division is credited as being the first to use such a device, and many existing army, corps and division patches date directly from this period. Even the familiar three-colored triangle forming the basis for armored division patches dates from World War I.

---

[1] The National Guards of New York and Pennsylvania had organized a division in each state in 1898 and 1879, respectively; in 1917 these would become the 27th and 28th Divisions, and the 28th Infantry Division is still in existence as such.

[2] The two regiments had been on opposite sides in some of the same battles of the Civil War, and formed part of the 42nd Division, assembled from National Guard units from across the US. The 165th eventually got its old number back, becoming the 69th Infantry in 1963.

[3] The 2nd Kentucky had formed part of the wartime 149th Infantry, and was reformed following the war as the 149th Infantry.

The US participation might have been short compared to the European combatants, but it was costly as the fresh US divisions were used to defend against the German spring 1918 offensive, and then go over to the attack. Almost 37,000 men were killed in action, with another 14,000 died of wounds. Total casualties of the war were 224,000, with a single month (Oct 1918) responsible for almost 86,000 casualties, including nearly 13,000 killed in action. The total casualties represent over 11% of the AEF's strength the end of Oct 1918, and almost 21% of its actual combat strength that month. Marines serving in France had 1,465 killed in action and 991 died of wounds (equal to 10% of their 11 Nov 1918 strength.

## Purple Heart Certificate[4]

```
Purple heart No.  9867
           (copy)                          LBL 5/2
         WAR DEPARTMENT
     The Adjutant Generals office
              Washington
AG201 Rinaldi, Joseph D.

   Purple Heart           July 22,1932



   The Quatermaster General.



      1.  The Secretary of War directs that a Purple Heart,
engraved with the name of the recipient, be issued to

         Mr. Joseph D. Rinaldi,
            325 South Main Street,
              Taylor, Penna.


on account of wound received in action July 7,1918, while
serving as Private, Company B, 23 Infantry.




                                    Adjutant General.
Copy for Mr. Rinaldi
```

---

[4] The Purple Heart, as an award to individuals killed or wounded in action with an
enemy of the United States, was reestablished in 1932 and awarded retroactively.
During the war, those wounded received a wound chevron worn on the lower right
sleeve of the uniform.

vi

# Introduction

This book is a summary of the US Army's order of battle in World War I. (It is restricted to ground units, and so excludes the Air Service.) The beginning looks at the status of the Army in Apr 1917 when war was declared, and provides a summary of the mobilization and of the organization of divisions for combat.

The bulk of the work is a summary of Army units, beginning with headquarters (GHQ, army, and army corps) and proceeding through divisions to cavalry, infantry, machine gun units, field artillery, etc. Commanders are given for formations down to division level. Unit details are carried down to battalion level in the other sections. Information is given for place of organization and other stations in the US (though this is abbreviated, and ignores moves attendant on shipment to or from overseas, for example), date of movement overseas where applicable, and date of return to the US. For the most part it stops in 1919, although some details continue past that date (especially for American Forces in Germany). In the case of National Guard units, the sources for the World War I units are given.

The basic reference on this subject is *Order of Battle of the United States Land Forces in the World War (1917—19)*, published by the Army between 1931 and 1949 in three volumes. However, this has been supplemented as much as possible by other lineage data, and discrepancies between it and other sources are noted.

Language is a mixture of that in the *Order of Battle* volumes and more current lineage terminology. For example, those volumes refer to units as being skeletonized, and sometimes note the remainder as forming a record cadre. Today we would simply state that the units were reduced to cadre. Today, units are an element of larger organizations; at that time, they were components. Official Army lineages ignore such actions as reducing a unit to cadre, and also ignore assignments below division level. However, the World War I units were considered as components of the infantry and artillery brigades within divisions, and not just of the divisions themselves. The following are current lineage terms as used by the Army and also employed here, along with some modifications:

> CONSTITUTE. To place the designation of a new unit on the official rolls of the Army. I have also used, in places, the term "authorized." This plays a similar role in the *Order of Battle* volumes to the current term, "constitute."

CONVERT. To transfer a unit from one branch of the Army to another (for example, from cavalry to artillery). Such a move always requires a redesignation, with the unit adopting the names of its new branch; however, there is no break in the historical continuity of the unit. If the unit is active, it must also be reorganized under a new table of organization and equipment.

DEMOBILIZE. To remove the designation of a unit from the official rolls of the Army. If the unit is active, it must be inactivated. This term is used in unit lineages only when referring to the period during and immediately after World War I. Currently, the term "disband" is used.

ORGANIZE. To assign personnel and equipment to a unit and make it operative.

REDESIGNATE. To change a unit's official name or number or both. Redesignation is a change of title only. Depending on the reason for the change, an active unit might also have to be reorganized.

REORGANIZE. To change the structure of a unit in accordance with a new table of organization and equipment, or to change from one type of unit to another within the same branch of the Army.

In the US Army, the word "regiment" is no longer part of the official title of a regiment; it is regarded as "understood." Thus, the 15th Infantry or 7th Field Artillery instead of the 15th Infantry Regiment or 7th Field Artillery Regiment. The Marines did so informally (e.g., 5th Marines) when a regiment was formed, but the actual title was 5th Regiment Marines. The Corps at that time did not have permanent regiments.

## Mobilization and Organization

Within the Executive Branch of the government, the United States Army came under the War Department. The Secretary of War in 1917 was Newton D. Baker, who held the post from 1916 to 1921. The chief military position was Chief of Staff, a post created in 1903. This position was held by the following officers during the war:

| | |
|---|---|
| 16 Nov 1914 | Maj Gen Hugh L. Scott |
| 16 May 1917 | Maj Gen Tasker H. Bliss (acting)[5] |
| 17 Aug 1917 | Maj Gen Hugh L. Scott |
| 22 Sep 1917 | Maj Gen [Gen 6 Oct 1917][6] Tasker H. Bliss |
| 30 Oct 1917 | Maj Gen John Biddle (acting) |
| 17 Dec 1917 | Gen Tasker H. Bliss |
| 10 Jan 1918 | Maj Gen John Biddle (acting) |
| 4 Mar 1918 | Maj Gen [Gen 20 May 1918]Peyton C. March[7] |

Gen March would hold the position until 1921, when he was replaced by Gen Pershing. B oth Scott and Bliss were a year from compulsory retirement age and used to the routines of the small peacetime army. Gen March was brought back from France. The War Department itself was organized into various bureaus (such as Adjutant General, Chief of Engineers) in addition to the General Staff and personnel under the Chief of Staff. The bureaus were largely independent of the Chief of Staff.

The basic territorial organization of the Army was the department. At the beginning of 1917 there were four departments in the US and two overseas (Hawaiian and Philippine). However, on 1 May 1917 the US was reorganized into six departments:

    Northeastern Department (headquarters at Boston, MA)
    Eastern Department (headquarters at Governors' Island, NY)
    Southeastern Department (headquarters at Charleston, SC)
    Central Department (headquarters at Chicago, IL)
    Southern Department (headquarters at Ft. Sam Houston, TX)
    Western Department (headquarters at San Francisco, CA)

---

[5] Maj Gen Bliss was the Assistant to the Chief of Staff.

[6] The *Order of Battle* volumes show Pershing and Bliss promoted to Gen 8 Oct 1917 and March promoted 25 May 1918, while the comprehensive list of generals in The Army Almanac shows 6 Oct 1917 and 20 May 1918, respectively. I have followed the latter source.

[7] Acting to 20 May, when promoted to Gen.

The Army monograph on military mobilization indicates that the reason for the reorganization appeared more political than military. It was certainly ill-timed, since the departmental commanders would handle federalization of National Guard units and selection of cantonments for mobilization. On 26 Jun 1917 the Panama Canal Zone was separated from the Eastern Department; as the Panama Canal Department it joined the other two overseas commands. In addition to the departments, there were five coast artillery districts in the US: North Atlantic Coast Artillery District (aligned with the Northeastern Department), Middle Atlantic Coast Artillery District (aligned with the Eastern Department), South Atlantic Coast Artillery District (aligned with the Southeastern Department), and the North Pacific and South Pacific Coast Artillery Districts (aligned with the Western Department). There was also a Panama Coast Artillery District. For the commanding officers and some additional information on the departments, see Appendix 4.

*Strength and Mobilization of the Army*

The Army was small in 1917. With the exception of skirmishes in Mexico or along the border, it had last seen combat during the Spanish-American War and Philippine Insurrection. Organization above the level of regiment was largely theoretical, as was mobilization planning. The National Defense Act of 1916 made a number of changes in the organization of US military forces, but there was little time between its enactment in Jun 1916 and the declaration of war in Apr 1917. Operations along the Mexican border from 1911—and especially from 1915—led to the concentration of much of the Regular Army in that area. Almost all of the National Guard was called out in 1916 to support these operations. By early 1917 many of these units had been released, but nearly half of the Guard was still on duty in Apr 1917.

When the US declared war against Germany on 6 Apr 1917, the Regular Army had 127,588 personnel, along with 5,523 Philippine Scouts, for a total force of just over 133,000. This was about 13,000 men below the authorized strength. The major reserve force was the National Guard. With a total strength of 174,008, the Guard had 76,713 already federalized on that date and 97,295 still in state service. Beyond this, there was a Regular Army Reserve (former enlisted personnel) of 4,767 men; about another 3,000 had already been called to active duty in 1916 and the remainder were called 1 May 1917.[8] The Officers Reserve Corps had just over 900 the beginning of Mar 1917, with

---

[8] The Regular Army Reserve consisted of former enlisted personnel. It was distinct from the Enlisted Reserve Corps, which was intended to provide an additional reserve of enlisted men for the Engineers, Signal Corps, Quartermaster Corps, Ordnance Department, and Military Departments.

another 565 offered commissions. Increased recruiting led to 7,957 Reserve officers by mid May 1917, all of whom were called up and sent to Officers' Training Camps. There was also an Enlisted Reserve Corps, with fewer than 10,000 men in Apr 1917. The last reserve group was the Enlisted National Guard Reserve, with around 4400 personnel.

In summary, forces on duty (Regular Army, Philippine Scouts, and National Guard in federal service) totaled some 209,700 personnel, and there were around 122,000 reserve personnel (National Guard in state service, Regular Army Reserve, Officers Reserve Corps, Enlisted Reserve Corps, and Enlisted National Guard Reserve). This gave a total ground force of about 331,700 trained personnel.

Military and civilian planners determined in 1917 that the war could not be fought with volunteer enlistees only. The result was the Selective Service Act of 1917. By 11 Nov 1918, the Army raised over 4,100,000 personnel (2,800,000 were inducted under the Selective Service Act; the remainder either enlisted or were pre-war Regular, National Guard, or Reserve personnel). The pre-war Army (including National Guard) formed only about 7% of the total strength of the Army by the end of the war. In addition, the Marine Corps (which provided some units for France) had a Nov 1918 strength of just over 61,200. Just the number of officers commissioned during the war (more than 203,000) exceeded the entire pre-war Regular Army. Mobilizing the Army that would fight World War I was a major task, all the more impressive for the scarcity of trained personnel and the limited planning that had occurred beforehand.

The original troop basis for planning purposes was a 30-division program developed in summer and autumn 1917. This would produce an expeditionary force in Europe with five corps, 20 combat divisions, five corps replacement and school divisions, and five corps base and training divisions. By early 1918, the military situation led to a new plan, which was to have 80 divisions in France by 1919. A revision in Sep 1918 looked to 100 divisions in France and 12 in the US by Jun 1920. The Armistice in Nov 1918 rendered the new plan unnecessary before it was actually implemented. However, the 80-division plan did lead to organization of 62 infantry divisions by 1918, of which 41 were sent to France.[9] A cavalry division also existed in the US during 1917 and 1918, serving along the border with Mexico.

---

[9] In addition, another division was moving overseas at the time of the Armistice, and four infantry regiments (the infantry equivalent of a division) were with the French Army.

Divisions were allocated to the Regular Army, the National Guard, and the National Army. (The latter was a designation given to new units formed during the war and not allotted to either the Regular Army or NationalGuard.) Prior to 1918, personnel as well as units were allotted the same way, and even had different collar insignia. The transfer of draftees to fill units eroded the distinction among the three components, and Gen March finally decreed that there was only one army, the United States Army, and all personnel wore the collar insignia of the United States Army from 7 Aug 1918. However, divisions were still considered by their personnel, and recorded in histories, as belonging to the Regular Army, the National Guard, or the National Army.

Between Apr 1917 and Jan 1918, the 1st to 8th Divisions were organized in the Regular Army.[10] The 1st to 7th went overseas, and the 8th was in the process of moving to France when the war ended. The National Guard's 16 nominal divisions (see the next section) were organized into the 26th to 41st Divisions in Aug and Sep 1917, and a new 42nd (or "Rainbow") Division formed of units from various states across the nation. All of these divisions went overseas. In Aug 1917, 16 divisions (76th to 91st) were constituted and organized in the National Army. These were, at least initially, filled with personnel drawn from specific geographic areas for each division. All of these went overseas.

The next division formed, the 92nd in the National Army, reflected the fact that the Army (like much of the nation) was a segregated institution in 1917. Blacks were kept in separate units, whose officers were almost entirely white.[11] Most blacks went into service units, but the 92nd Division was organized in autumn 1917 from black draftees. This division served overseas as well. Black National Guard units and draftees formed an additional four infantry regiments; grouped as the 93rd Division (Provisional), these went overseas and served with units of the French Army. Another segregated group in the Army were Puerto Ricans. There were plans for a 94th Division to be formed in Puerto Rico, but only three infantry regiments were actually formed.

Note that while the nominal troop planning basis was for 30 divisions, 42 and parts of two others were actually organized by 1 Jan 1918. The move to an 80-division planning basis resulted in creation of two further groups of divisions in 1918. The 9th to 20th Divisions were formed during the summer. These 12 divisions were allotted to the Regular Army, although their components were a

---

[10] The 1st and 2nd Divisions were formed overseas, the remainder in the US. Only the 4th and 8th Divisions assembled and trained as such; the others came together only when shipped to Europe.

[11] The Army commissioned 639 blacks and approximately 700 Puerto Ricans during the war, all in the Infantry. This was out of over 203,000 officers commissioned during the war.

combination of Regular Army and National Army units. Finally, the 95th to 102nd Divisions were planned in the National Army. These were each to form one infantry brigade from existing pioneer infantry regiments (mostly in France) with the remaining divisional units to be newly-formed in the US. The 95th to 97th had begun to form some components when the war ended, but the remainder were little more than a small headquarters and a plan. They would have added a further 20 divisions to the 42 already noted.

It may be apparent from these notes that the different components had distinct groups of numbers. A decision in 1917 allotted division numbers 1 to 25, brigade numbers 1 to 50, and regimental numbers 1 to 100 to the Regular Army. The National Guard were to utilize division numbers 26 to 75, brigade numbers 51 to 150, and regimental numbers 101 to 300. The National Army was given division numbers beginning with 76, brigade numbers beginning with 151, and regimental numbers beginning with 301.[12] In the case of National Guard and National Army units, all numbers were new and were allotted in strict sequence in the divisions.[13] This numbering scheme continued into the post-war period, when National Army designations were reconstituted and given to the new Organized Reserve Corps units. In terms of divisions, the scheme largely continued to the present day.[14]

While it is convenient to look at numbers of divisions, the Army actually required many combat, combat support, and service units in order to operate in the field. And raising these forces was only one issue. Once raised, troops had to be shipped to Europe. Despite shipping losses to the German U-boats, the Allies managed to transport over 2,000,000 US soldiers to Europe by the end of Dec 1918. However, while the personnel were shipped, much of their armament and munitions were not. The First Army did not fire a single shell manufactured in America during its entire time in combat; except for four 14" naval guns it did not fire a single cannon made in America. The US purchased

---

[12] This strict separation fell down in the Field Artillery, Coast Artillery Corps, and Corps of Engineers. National Army regiments in the first two received numbers below 100, and National Army Engineer units could be found with numbers in any series.

[13] Both the numbering system and the need to accommodate new organizational tables led to the loss of state designations by National Guard units, and the conversion and scrambling of many others to form division components. A few regiments reclaimed their old numbers as an official designation following the war, but the new numbers became the norm.

[14] The 82nd Airborne and 101st Air Assault Divisions were Reserve divisions converted during World War II to airborne, and then allotted to the Regular Army following the war. The National Guard never used a division number higher than 45 before World War II and 51 afterwards, and some wartime divisions in World War II received numbers in the sequence from 61 to 75.

4,225 cannons from the French and 334 from the British, along with tanks (514 from the French), machine guns, automatic rifles, and mortars.  It also proved impossible to ship or procure the numbers of horses and mules required for the AEF, leaving units with about half of their authorized transportation.

The actual strength of the American Expeditionary Force (AEF) on 30 Nov 1918 was almost 1,930,000.[15]  Of this total, about 32% was in the Infantry and 15% in the Artillery (Field and Coast).  The Air Service was only about 3% of the total AEF. The Corps of Engineers were another 12.5% of the AEF, and there were significant numbers of Medical Department, Quartermaster Corps, Signal Corps, Ordnance Department, Military Police, and supply and ammunition trains personnel.

**Table 1. Strength of the AEF**

| Date | US Military Personnel in Europe | Actual Combat Strength[16] |
|---|---|---|
| 31 May 1917 | 1,308 | N/A |
| 30 Jun 1917 | 16,220 | N/A |
| 31 Jul 1917 | 20,120 | N/A |
| 31 Aug 1917 | 39,383 | N/A |
| 30 Sep 1917 | 61,927 | N/A |
| 31 Oct 1917 | 92,265 | N/A |
| 30 Nov 1917 | 129,623 | N/A |
| 31 Dec 1917 | 183,896 | N/A |
| 31 Jan 1918 | 224,665 | N/A |
| 28 Feb 1918 | 254,378 | N/A |
| 31 Mar 1918 | 329,005 | 406,844 |
| 30 Apr 1918 | 434,081 | N/A |
| 31 May 1918 | 667,119 | N/A |
| 30 Jun 1918 | 897,293 | N/A |
| 31 Jul 1918 | 1,210,703 | N/A |
| 31 Aug 1918 | 1,473,190 | 822,358 |
| 30 Sep 1918 | 1,783,955 | 999,602 |
| 30 Oct 1918 | 1,986,618 | 1,078,190 |
| 11 Nov 1918 | 2,057,675 | 1,078,222 |

[15] This was virtually all Army. However, there were about 18,400 Marines and 480 Navy Medical Department personnel in the total.

[16] These figures include only combat troops and exclude the troops in the SOS, headquarters, schools, hospitals, liaison service, and other special services. Except for 11 Nov 1918, the figures are from about the middle of each month rather than the last day.

In addition, the US Marine Corps 24,555 personnel with the AEF on 11 Nov 1918, and another 1,176 in France but not part of the AEF.

*Organization for Combat*

In 1905 the Army established the division, rather than the corps, as the basic combined arms unit. A division would have three brigades (each of two or more infantry regiments) along with artillery (provisional regiment), cavalry (regiment), engineers (battalion), and other support units. By 1910 the division was to include a field artillery brigade (two regiments) and additional support units. In addition, for the first time, divisions were to be numbered consecutively in order of formation. (In prior wars, there would be a 1$^{st}$ Division, First Corps; 1$^{st}$ Division, Second Corps; and so on.) There was also an organization for a cavalry division. In 1913 there was a plan to allot existing units to 1$^{st}$, 2$^{nd}$ and 3$^{rd}$ Divisions and a Cavalry Division. These were largely theoretical, as units (even where complete) were scattered among a number of posts and never concentrated as a division. In addition, the National Guard was organized 1914 into the 5$^{th}$ to 16$^{th}$ Divisions by grouping units in adjacent states; this was changed in early 1917 into the 5$^{th}$ to 20$^{th}$ Divisions and the groupings shifted.[17] The concentration of the Army along the border with Mexico in 1916 did not lead to creation of divisions. However, in Mar 1917 the 1$^{st}$, 2$^{nd}$ and 3$^{rd}$ Provisional Divisions were created (with their headquarters at Camp Wilson, TX, El Paso, TX, and Douglas, AZ, respectively), along with a 1$^{st}$ Provisional Cavalry Division (also headquartered at El Paso). These were all dissolved in Jun 1917. National Guard units federalized during 1916 and early 1917 were not mobilized or grouped by their nominal division structure.

For practical purposes, then, the Army existed only at the level of the regiment. Within the Regular Army, almost 16% of the personnel were in the Coast Artillery Corps, intended for defence of the seacoast and certain overseas locations in Hawaii, the Panama Canal Zone, and the Philippines. (The Coast Artillery Corps was more than twice the strength of the Field Artillery, and larger than any other branch except for the Infantry.) Line forces were organized into 38 infantry regiments (13 outside the US), 17 cavalry regiments

---

[17] Only New York (6$^{th}$ Division) and Pennsylvania (7$^{th}$ Division) had complete divisions within one state, and these both pre-dated the 1914 plan. The 1917 change allotted the 12$^{th}$ Division entirely to Illinois, instead of to Illinois and Indiana. Neither existing state division matched the organization specified for the (non-existent) Regular divisions. Governors in other states were not necessarily willing to create the support and service units necessary for divisions, as these would have no clear state role in normal times. However, many did begin to organize them. For example, a number of field artillery units were created, especially in 1916 and early 1917.

(three and a third overseas), nine field artillery regiments (three overseas), and three engineer regiments (one overseas). Some of these had only been organized in 1916, and were thus less than a year in existence when the war began.[18] The bulk of the line units in the US were in Texas and the Southwest. National Guard units were supposed to be moving towards congruence with the Regular organization tables. If all the artillery and engineers had been in the US, the Army could have formed three divisions; the remaining infantry was sufficient for an additional six divisions. The onset of war led to the formation of additional Regular Army field artillery and engineer regiments, and six divisions were formed with all-Regular components.[19]

The declaration of war in Apr 1917 required the Army to reconsider how its divisions ought to be organized, before it actually began to form them. The May 1917 division would have had just under 19,000 men and marked the first major change, with the infantry organized into two brigades of two regiments. (These four regiments, however, were individually larger than the nine regiments of the old division had been.) Artillery was still a brigade (but now three regiments) and the cavalry regiment was deleted. This is the first appearance of the "square" (four infantry regiment) division. Further studies and discussions with the British and French led to a much larger division, though on the same general lines. The divisions organized during 1917 would do so under the 8 Aug 1917 tables (see Chart 1, p. 14). This division had grown to 27,120 personnel. Changes from the May tables included the addition of three machine gun battalions (one for each brigade and one at division) as well as expansion of the engineers from a battalion to a regiment. The Aug 1917 division changed gradually based on actual experience in Europe, and the combat divisions in Nov 1918 were similar in structure but different from the 1917 division (see Chart 2, p. 15).

As noted in the previous section, the scheme for numbering divisions was changed to one allotting series of numbers to different components. Because of this, the nominal 5th to 20th Divisions from the National Guard became the more familiar 26th to 41st Divisions. Generally, each new division was organized at a single division camp. As divisions went overseas, those camps became available for the new divisions begun in 1918. When the war ended, the partially formed 1918 divisions were quickly demobilized and the camps

---

[18] The 31st to 38th Infantry were constituted 1 Jul 1916 in the Regular Army and organized Jul-Aug 1916 by transfer of personnel from existing units. The same was true of the 16th and 17th Cavalry and the 7th, 8th and 9th Field Artillery. The Engineers were battalions until expanded to regiments in 1916. Some additional units were authorized for the Regular Army in 1916 but not formed until 1917.
[19] For the purists, five-plus divisions, since one brigade in the 2nd Division was provided by the Marine Corps.

became available for units returning from Europe for demobilization. Demobilization was by units and not by individuals. Since the National Guard and National Army divisions still had some geographic coherence, an effort was made to send them to camps in the same general area their personnel were from.

A single cavalry division was formed, utilizing May 1917 tables (see Chart 3, p. 16). Apparently Gen Pershing (a former cavalryman) looked forward to having it in Europe, despite a lack of any role for cavalry by that point. The division spent its time patrolling along the Mexican border, never concentrated in one place, and was demobilized without other service in May 1918.

While pre-war planning had eliminated the corps and seen a field army as the command element for a grouping of divisions, the army corps was quickly introduced into planning. The thought was that each would control four combat divisions, and also have a corps replacement and school division along with a corps base and training division. Ultimately, handling replacements was separated from the army corps and handed over to the rear (Services of Supply). Six divisions (three each National Guard and National Army), were reorganized and redesignated on arrival as depot divisions, charged with handling new personnel as they arrived in the theater. Handling replacements went to replacement battalions rather than "replacement and school" divisions, although five divisions were skeletonized (what would now be termed reduced to cadre) after arrival in France to provide replacements for the heavy combat losses. The depot divisions themselves could be reduced to cadre, distributing their trained personnel, and then tasked to handle new arrivals. In addition, the idea of tying specific divisions to specific army corps was abandoned. Divisions could rotate in and out of combat and among the various army corps as needed.

While the corps became a flexible command element, there was a standardized "type" corps with certain combat, support and service units included. The nominal corps organization (and assigned strength) on 11 Nov 1918—a total of just about 25,000 personnel, not including any assigned divisions—is shown on page 12 below.[20]

---

[20] Taking out the two cavalry regiments—almost none were sent to Europe—produced a type corps of about 17,300 plus the assigned divisions.

### "Type" Corps Troops

| | |
|---|---:|
| Corps Headquarters | 504 |
| Pioneer Infantry Regiment | 3,551 |
| Cavalry Regiment | 3,804 |
| Cavalry Regiment | 3,804 |
| Corps Artillery | |
|     Artillery Brigade[21] | 3,555 |
|     240mm Trench Mortar Bn | 796 |
|     AA Machine Gun Bn | 766 |
|     Corps Artillery Park | 1,404 |
| Engineers | |
|     Engineer Regiment | 1,749 |
|     Engineer Train | 84 |
|     Pontoon Train | 174 |
| Field Signal Bn 488 | |
| Telegraph Bn | 222 |
| Corps Air Service | 1,725 |
| Military Police Coy | 205 |
| Trains and Services | 2,098 |

There were variations on this; in particular, the number of cavalry regiments shipped to Europe would not even have provided one regiment per corps. At one time the corps artillery brigade was to have been drawn from the replacement division assigned to the corps. When these were not established, it become necessary to make specific provision for the brigade. The corps design had originally included an AA battalion, but these were withdrawn and consolidated Apr 1918 under First Army and reorganized as AA sectors; in Oct 1918 the AA Service was shifted to direct control of the AEF.

There was also a "type" army troops. However, since for most of the war there was only First Army, the army command level was for tactical purposes little different from the GHQ level. Thus, AA units were concentrated into the AA Service, First Army, from Apr to Oct 1918, and the Railway Artillery Reserve was also under First Army until Oct 1918. Army Headquarters itself had a Nov 1918 strength of 911 personnel (compared with a planned strength of 3,250), along with an Army Artillery Headquarters of 318 personnel. A planned regiment of infantry as army traffic police and headquarters guard was replaced by four MP companies with formation of the Military Police Corps in Oct 1918.[22] A review of GHQ troops under the entry for First Army will give some

---

[21] One regiment with 4.7" guns and one with 6" guns.
[22] First Army Hq Regiment was formed from part of 1st Infantry, NH NG.

idea of the assigned army troops (at least in terms of artillery and engineers). Many other service and support units came under the control of the communications zone, whose final designation was Services of Supply.

*General Officer Ranks.*

In 1917, the US Army had (with one exception) no general officer rank higher than Major General. A 1916 act allowed "the senior major general of the line commanding the army" to be given the rank and pay of lieutenant general, and that officer could retire as a lieutenant general. The rank of general came into existence as a temporary rank for the duration of World War I under acts in 1917. In addition, acts passed in 1917 allowed the creation of lieutenant generals for the period of the war only, and two officers received these temporary promotions to lieutenant general. Following the war, an act of Sep 1919 appointed General John J. Pershing to the grade of General of the Armies of the United States, a title held by no other serving officer before or after. (Pershing continued to wear four stars on his uniform, and no actual insignia was specified for indicating this rank.) The rank of General lapsed following the war.

Since Major Generals were division commanders in other armies, creation of a tactical American field army in France required a higher rank. Accordingly, John J. Pershing and Tasker H. Bliss were promoted to General on 6 Oct 1917. Pershing was head of the American Expeditionary Force in France, and Bliss was the Army's Chief of Staff. The latter's promotion kept Pershing from outranking the Army's top uniformed position; the other promotion to general came in May 1918 when Peyton C. March replaced Bliss as Chief of Staff. There were no lieutenant generals in the Army until the last month of the war, when Robert L. Bullard and Hunter Liggett were so promoted. Liggett replaced Pershing in command of the First Army in Oct 1918, and Bullard was in command of the new Second Army.

In addition to these five men, there were 108 officers who served as major generals during the war. Six of them received their rank prior to the US declaration of war on 6 Apr 1917 and the remaining 102 were promoted after that date.

## Chart 1: Infantry Division, 8 Aug 1917[23]

| | |
|---|---:|
| Division Hq and Hq Troop | 164 |
| Infantry Brigade *x2* | 8,134 |
|     Brigade Hq | 23 |
|     Ordnance Department | 20 |
|     Infantry Regiment *x2* | 3,755 |
|         Hq and Hq Coy | 303 |
|         Infantry Bn *x3* | 1,026 |
|         MG Coy | 178 |
|         Supply Coy | 140 |
|         Medical and Chaplain | 56 |
|     Machine Gun Bn | 581 |
| Machine Gun Bn | |
|     769 | |
| Field Artillery Brigade | 5,105 |
|     Brigade Hq | 58 |
|     Ordnance Department | 37 |
|     Field Artillery Regiment [75mm] *x2* | 1,508 |
|         Hq and Hq By | 185 |
|         Field Artillery Bn *x2* | 596 |
|         Supply Bty | 102 |
|         Medical and Chaplain | 29 |
|     Field Artillery Regiment [155mm] | 1,806 |
|         Hq and Hq Bty | 231 |
|         Field Artillery Bn *x3* | 468 |
|         Supply Bty | 131 |
|         Medical and Chaplain | 40 |
|     Trench Mortar Bty | 188 |
| Engineer Regiment | 1,672 |
| Field Signal Bn 262 | |
| Division Trains | 2,880 |
|     Hq and MP Train | 342 |
|     Ammunition Train | 1,033 |
|     Supply Train | 472 |
|     Sanitary Train | 949 |
|     Engineer Train | 84 |
| | |
| Aggregate Personnel | 27,120 |

---

[23] There are some minor discrepancies between the version published in Wilson's *Maneuver and Firepower* volume (shown here) and that in the *Order of Battle* volumes. The latter gives a total of 27,123.

**Chart 2: Infantry Division, 1918[24]**

| | |
|---|---:|
| Division Hq | 304 |
| Infantry Brigade *x2* | 8,475 |
|     Brigade Hq | 25 |
|     Attached services | 151 |
|     Infantry Regiment *x2* | 3,770 |
|         Hq and Hq Coy | 349 |
|         Infantry Bn *x3* | 1,027 |
|         MG Coy | 178 |
|         Supply Coy | 162 |
|     Machine Gun Bn | 759 |
| Machine Gun Bn (motorized) | 395 |
| Field Artillery Brigade | 5,069 |
|     Brigade Hq | 79 |
|     Attached services | 161 |
|     Field Artillery Regiment [75mm or 3" gun] *x2* | 1,518 |
|     Field Artillery Regiment [155mm or 6" howitzer] | 1,616 |
|     Trench Mortar Bty | 177 |
| Engineer Regiment | 1,749 |
| Field Signal Bn | 488 |
| Division Trains | 3,150 |
| | |
| Aggregate Personnel | 28,105 |

Armament

| | |
|---|---:|
| Pistols | 11,913 |
| Rifles | 17,666 |
| Rifles, Automatic | |
|     768 | |
| Machine Guns, Heavy | 224 |
| Machine Guns, Antiaircraft | 36 |
| Trench Mortars | 36 |
| Guns, one-pounder | 12 |
| Guns, 75mm or 3" | 48 |
| Howitzers, 155mm or 6" | 24 |

---

[24] This represents the TOE in effect as of 11 Nov 1918, and shows the maximum authorized strength. With infantry companies cut from 250 to 175 enlisted personnel by Gen Pershing, the nominal full strength would have been around 24,500.

**Chart 3: Cavalry Division, 3 May 1917**[25]

| | |
|---|---:|
| Division Hq | 150 |
| Cavalry Brigade *x3* | 4,756 |
|     Brigade Hq | 19 |
|     Cavalry Regiment *x3* | 1,579 |
|         Hq and Hq Trp | 88 |
|         Cavalry Sqn *x3* | 434 |
|         MG Trp | 95 |
|         Supply Trp | 54 |
|         Medical and Chaplain | 40 |
| Field Artillery Regiment [horse] | 1,374 |
|     Hq and Hq Bty | 114 |
|     Field Artillery Bn *x3* | 392 |
|     Supply Bty | 44 |
|     Medical and Chaplain | 40 |
| Engineer Bn | 387 |
| Field Signal Bn | 259 |
| Aero Sqn | 173 |
| Division Trains | 1,553 |
|     Hq Train | 242 |
|     Ammunition Train | 263 |
|     Supply Train | 248 |
|     Sanitary Train | 715 |
|     Engineer Train | 85 |
| | |
| Aggregate Personnel | 18,164 |

Armament[26]

| | |
|---|---:|
| Pistols | 16,191 |
| Rifles | 13,337 |
| Machine guns | 84 |
| Guns, 3" | 24 |

---

[25] This shows TOE for a division with trains equipped with wagons. If division trains equipped with motorized vehicles (an alternate TOE), division trains increase to 1,565 and division aggregate personnel to 18,176. The only actual differences are in the ammunition train (299 instead of 263 personnel) and the supply train (224 personnel instead of 248).

[26] For a division with wagon-equipped trains. For the motor-equipped variant, the division would have 16,121 pistols (70 fewer) and 13,430 rifles (93 more). Both divisions included a spare 3" field gun in addition to the 24 in the artillery regiment.

# Headquarters[27]

**American Expeditionary Force (AEF)**      Headquarters, AEF was
organized 13 Jun 1917 in France. (Organization actually began late May 1917
in the US with selection of a staff, which landed in the UK 7 Jun 1917 and then
moved to France.) It was redesignated 17 Jan 1918 as General Headquarters,
AEF. GHQ AEF had overall control and direction of all US troops sent to
Europe (with the exception of the force sent to North Russia in 1918). It did
not exercise territorial or tactical command of units, responsibilities that
belonged to subordinate commands. However, it did supervise the
administration and deployment of US divisions. (Note that Gen Pershing also
served as commander of the First Army from 10 Aug to 15 Oct 1918.) GHQ
AEF was relieved of duties in Germany 3 Jul 1919 by American Forces in
Germany. Relieved of remaining responsibilities 1 Sep 1919 by American
Forces in France, it returned to the US. Established in Washington, DC, 13 Sep
1919, it was not discontinued until 31 Aug 1920.
Commander in Chief: 26 May 1917, Maj Gen [Gen 6 Oct 1917] John J.
Pershing
Chief of Staff: 26 May 1917 Lt Col James G. Harbord [promoted successively
31 Aug 1917 to Col and 8 Oct 1917 to Brig Gen], 6 May 1918, Maj Gen James
W. McAndrew, 27 May 1919 Maj Gen James G. Harbord [through 12 Aug
1919]

Units Assigned GHQ, AEF 11 Nov 1918
Engineers: Coy H 29th
Chemical Warfare Service: Two bns of 1st Gas Regt
Railway Arty Reserve:[28] 30th Brig CAC: Hq; 42nd, 43rd, 52nd, and 53rd CAC
      Regts; 40th Brig CAC: Hq; 73rd, 74th, and 75th CAC Regts. 1st, 2nd, 3rd,
      and 4th Railway Ordnance Repair Shops.
Tank Corps: Heavy Tank Bus: 301, 302, 303, 304, and 306. Light Tank Bns:
      328, 327, 328, 329, 330 332, 335, 336, 337, and 344. Tank Brig Hq:
      304th and 307th. Repair and Salvage Coys 307, 317, 318, and 321. 301st
      and 302nd Training Centers. Training and Replacement Coys (Light)
      302, 303, 378. 377, 378, 379, 380, 381.
As of 16 Oct 1918, the Anti-Aircraft Service, AEF, came under GHQ as well.

---

[27] The army and corps headquarters were all organized in the Regular Army.
[28] Until 10 Oct 1918, this had been Railway Artillery Reserve, First Army; on that date,
it became Railway Artillery Reserve, AEF.

**First Army**   Organized 10 Aug 1918 in France (organization began 4 Aug 1918). Beginning 25 Nov 1918, it administered training areas in France. First Army was demobilized 20 Apr 1919 in France.

Commanders: 10 Aug 1918, Gen John J. Pershing; 16 Oct 1918, Maj Gen [Lt Gen 16 Oct 1918][29] Hunter Liggett

Campaign participation credit: St. Mihiel, Meuse-Argonne

Composition 30 Aug – 16 Sep 1918 (including St. Mihiel operation)

Corps: I, IV, V, French II Colonial

Divisions: 1st, 2nd, 3rd, 4th, 5th, 26th, 33rd, 35th, 42nd, 78th, 80th, 82nd, 89th, 90th, French 2nd Dismounted Cavalry, French 15th Colonial

GHQ Units

> Artillery: Hq Army Arty, First Army;
>
> CAC: Hq 32nd Arty Brig, 42nd CA (24 cm), 43rd CA (19 cm) 44th CA (8" How), 51st CA (240 mm, 8" How), 52nd CA (32 cm), 53rd CA (19 cm, 340 mm, 400 mm), 57th CA (156 mm), 59th CA (8" How), 60th CA (l55 mm), 65th CA (9.2").
>
> French Artillery: 124th Field Arty (75 mm), 71st Heavy Arty (240 mm), 73rd Heavy Arty (270,293 mm), 74th Arty (19 cm railway), 76th Heavy Arty (305 mm), 77th Heavy Arty (340 mm), 78th Heavy Arty (82 cm, 370 mm), 82nd Heavy Arty (tractor, Coys 1, 9), 211th Arty (76 mm portee). Naval Btys: 1, 9, 13 (16cm)
>
> Anti-aircraft Arty: 1st Anti-Aircraft MG Bn; Coy A 2nd Anti-Aircraft MG Bn, Bty B 1st Anti-Aircraft Bn (CAC), 2nd Anti-Aircraft Bn (CAC), 7th Anti-Aircraft Bty (CAC)
>
> *French units:* Groups 19 and 23 (truck mounts), including Secs: 9, 17, 32, 38,72, 74, and 92. Semi-fixed Secs 48, 61, 65, 66, 67, 70, 72, 74, 119, 123, 126, 126,163,164, and 208. One MG Sec 146th Inf. 9th Searchlight Coy. Secs 2, 3, 9 (trailer mounts). French mobile repair unit 202.
>
> Miscellaneous Artillery: 66th FA Brig (41st Div) (155mm). First Army Arty Park. II Corps Arty Park. First Army Arty and Am Park. Hq Railway Arty First Army. Sound Ranging Secs 2 and 4. Flash Ranging Secs 1 and 2.
>
> Cavalry: 2nd Cav.
>
> Chemical Warfare: 1st Gas Regt.
>
> Engineers: 11th, 12th, 15th, 21st (all railway) Engrs; 22nd (Forestry), 23rd (Highway), 24th (Railway), 26th (Water Sup), 27th (Mining), 28th (Quarry), 37th (Elec & Mech), 56th (Searchlight), 464th (Pontoon). Service Bns: 505, 508, 524, 627, 628, 530, 537.

---

[29] Here, too, the date of rank in the *Order of Battle* volumes (1 Nov 1918)differs from *The Army Alamanac*.

602nd Engrs. Provisional Water Tns: 1st, 2nd. 51st, 52nd and 53rd Pion Inf Regts. 464th Pontoon Tn.

Tank Corps: 344th and 354th Bns.

Composition 26 Sep – 11 Nov 1918 (including Meuse-Argonne operation)

Corps: I, III, IV, V, French II Colonial, French XVII, French XXXIII; also VI and VII, which took no part in operations

Divisions: 1st, 2nd, 3rd, 4th, 5th, 6th, 7th, 26th, 28th, 29th, 32nd, 35th, 36th, 37th, 40th (Depot), 42nd, 77th, 78th, 79th, 80th, 81st, 82nd, 88th [took no part in operations], 89th, 90th, 92nd, French 2nd Dismounted Cavalry, French 6th Cavalry, French 10th Colonial, French 15th Colonial, French 18th, French 39th, French 73rd

GHQ Units

Artillery:[30] Hq Army Arty, First Army;

CAC: 31st Art Brig: Hq, 55th CA (155mm), 56th CA (155mm), 57th CA (155mm); 32nd Art Brig: Hq, 58th CA (8" How), 59th CA (8" How), 65th CA (9.2"); 39th Art Brig: Hq, 44th CA (8"), 51st CA (240mm, 8"), 60th (155mm). First Army Arty Park. First Army Provisional Park (52nd CA—32cm). 51st, 52nd, 53rd Am Tns (CA). Tractor Arty Replacement Bn (formerly 2nd Bn 54th CA). 2nd Section Range Finders.

Railway Arty: Hq; 30th Arty Brig (CAC): Hq; 42nd CA (240 mm), 43rd CA (19 cm), 52nd CA (32 cm), 63rd CA (19 cm, 840, 400mm). Naval Btys: 1, 2, 3, 4, and 5 (14"). First Provisional High Burst Ranging Sec. Detachment Railway Arty MTS. *French units:* 70th Heavy Arty: Btys 2, 19, and 31 (240mm). 7lst Heavy Arty: Btys 3, 6, and 7 (240 mm). 74th Heavy Arty: 2nd Bn (19 cm). 76th Heavy Arty: Bty 19 (306 mm). 76th Heavy Arty: Bty 20 (305 mm). 77th Heavy Arty: Bty 23 (340 mm). 78th Heavy Arty: Btys 4 and 26 (32 cm, 370 mm How).

Field Arty: 67th FA Brig (32nd Div [75, 155 mm]); 58th FA Brig (33rd Div [75, l55mm]); 66th FA Brig (41st Div [155 mm]); 166th FA Brig (91st Div [4.7", 155 mm]).

French Arty: 73rd Heavy Arty: 1st, 3rd, 7th, 8th, and 11th Bns (270, 293 mm). 81st Heavy Arty: A, B, and 1st Bns (155 mm). 82nd Heavy Arty (tractor), 1st Co. 86th Arty: A, B, C, and 3rd Bns (145, 155mm). 87th Heavy Arty: A, B, C, 4th, 5th, and 6th Bns (145, 155 mm). 151st Foot Arty. 156th Arty: Btys 2, 3, 4, 13, 14, 15, 21, 22. and 23. 176th Arty (TM): Hq; 1st, 2nd, 3rd, and 6th Bns, and Btys 23, 28, 35, 37, 38, 39, and 40. 203rd Arty: 3rd Bn (75

---

[30] Note that the Railway Artillery Reserve had been under First Army until 10 Oct 1918, and the Anti-Aircraft Service until 16 Oct 1918, when both were shifted to GHQ AEF.

mm). 211th Arty (75 mm). 247th Arty: 1st and 2nd Bns (75 mm). 282nd Heavy Arty: 1st, 2nd, 3rd, 4th, and 13th Bns (220 mm). 317th Heavy Arty: 2nd and 3rd Bus (155 mm). 420th Heavy Arty: 2nd Bn (155 mm). Naval Btys 6, 10, 11, 12, 16, 17, and 18 (16" Navy).

Anti Aircraft Arty: Hq; 1st Bn (3"), 2nd Bn, 5th Bty (3'), 7th Bty (3"), 1st MG Bn (Hotchkiss AA), 2nd MG Bn (Hotchkiss AA). *French units*: MG Cos: 44, 129, 143. 147, and 167. Semifixed Sections: 12, 27, 46, 48, 51, 63, 64, 55, 56, 57, 58, 59, 70, 119, 121, 123, 127, 131, 165, 162, 163, 164. 179, 195, 207, 208, 214, 300, 314, 315, 319, and 13th, 14th, and 19th Btys. Truck Mount Sections: 2, 3. 8, 9, 17, 19, 23, 32, 38, 56, 57, 60, 67. 68, 69, 72, 74, and 80. Trailer Mount Sections: 1, 2, 3, 4, 5, 6, 7, and 9. Trailer Mount Group 101, 102, 103.

Chemical Warfare: 1st Gas Regt. Army Gas Depots A, C, D, and E. British units serving with 1st Gas Regt: Special Coys, Royal Engrs: D, E, P, R, Z. and J.

Engineers: 11th, 12th, 14th , 15th, 16th, 21st, 22nd (all railway), 23rd (road), 24th (shop), 25th (construction), 26th (water supply), 27th (mining), 28th (quarry), 35th (railway shop), 37th (electrical and mechanical), 40th (camouflage), and 56th (searchlight Regts. Pion Inf Regts: 2, 3, 5, 6, 54. 56, 59, 801, 802, detachment of 804, 806, 806, 807, 808, 815, and 816. Service Bns: 505, 508, 522, 524, 527, 528, 530, 535, 537, 542 (Coy A), 544, 545, 546, 603, 604. Labor Bns: 17, 18, 313, 330, 839, and 344. Miscellaneous units: 114th Engrs. 801st Water Tank Tn. First Provisional Water Tn (311th Coy of the 103rd Mot Sup Tn). Second Provisional Water Tn (Truck Co No 3, 23rd Engrs). Third Provisional Water Tn (466th MT Coy—417th MST). Pontoon Trains 444 and 465. *French units*: 9/18 (Roads Service), D/27 (Depot), M/3T (Fortification), 6/1T Fortification), 13/2T (Fortification), 14/3T (Bridges and Bldgs), 20/5T (Bridges and Bldgs), 24/l (Supervision of Bridges), 25/2 (Fortification) , MD/22 (Shelter), MD/23 (Shelter). Pontoon Cos: 9/19, 15/18.

Tank Corps: 1st Brig Tank Corps: 344th and 345th Tank Bns, 316th and 321st Repair and Salvage Tank Cos. Det 9th Co 2nd Motor Mech Regt. 3rd Brig Tank Corps. *French units:* 504th Tank Regt, 505th Tank Regt, 4th Tank Group, 2 tank groups (St-Chamond) 1st Tank Group (Schneider): 14th and 17th Btys

**Second Army**        Organized 20 Sep 1918 in France.[31]  The Second Army took over a defensive sector in Lorraine formerly held by First Army. Following the Armistice, it became responsible for divisions in Luxembourg as well as its areas in France.  Second Army was demobilized 15 Apr 1919 in France.
Commander: 12 Oct 1918: Maj Gen [Lt Gen 16 Oct 1918][32] Robert L. Bullard
Campaign participation credit: Lorraine 1918


Composition 12 Oct—11 Nov 1918[33]
Corps: IV, VI, VII [for supply], French II Colonial, and French XVII
Divisions: 4th, 7th, 28th, 33rd, 35th, 37th, 79th, 88th (175th Inf Brig), 92nd, French 39th, French 2nd Dismounted Cavalry



**Third Army**    Organized 7—15 Nov 1918 in France.  Commanded the American occupation force in Germany (headquarters established Dec 1918 at Koblenz).  Demobilized 2 Jul 1919 in Germany (used to form Headquarters, American Forces in Germany).
Commander: 15 Nov 1918, Maj-Gen Joseph T. Dickman; 29 Apr 1919, Maj
        Gen Edward F. McGlachlin, Jr. (interim), 2 May 1919, Lt Gen Hunter
        Liggett


Composition for the occupation of Germany[34]
Corps: III, IV, VII
Divisions:  1st, 2nd, 3rd, 4th, 6th, 32nd, 33rd, 42nd, 89th, 90th



*Note on the Army Corps.*  A list of dates for the when the army corps in the AEF "were formed" in the *Order of Battle* volumes is discrepant both with their official lineages and with other material in those volumes.  That list has I Army Corps formed 20 Jan 1918 (which agrees with its official lineage); II, III and IV Army Corps on 25 Jun 1918; V, VI and VII Army Corps on 19 Aug 1919; and VIII and IX Army Corps on 29 Nov 1918.  The dates for VIII and IX are roughly consistent with their lineages; those for the II to VII bear no

---

[31] There is a discrepancy between the official lineage of Second Army (which shows 20 Sep 1918) and material in the *Order of Battle* volumes, which shows 10 Oct 1918 as when Second Army was "formed."  The latter date may be when the Army began to function as an operational unit.
[32] Per *The Army Almanac*; the *Order of Battle* volumes show 1 Nov 1918.
[33] GHQ units have been omitted given the limited service of Second Army. In addition, many of them were simply detachments of units serving with First Army.
[34] VI Corps came under command for a period in 1919, but its two divisions at that time (5th and 33rd) were in France and Luxembourg.

relationship to organization dates in the corps' lineages. That particular list may indicate when each of the army corps became operational as such, rather than the actual formation date.

**I Army Corps**          Organized 15-20 Jan 1918 in France. The corps moved to administer training areas in France following the Armistice. Demobilized 25 Mar 1919 in France.

Commanders: 20 Jan 1918, Maj Gen Hunter Liggett, 12 Oct 1918, Maj Gen Joseph T. Dickman, 13 Nov 1918, Maj Gen William M. Wright, 28 Feb 1919, Maj Gen Samuel D. Sturgis (interim), 14 Mar 1919, Maj Gen William M. Wright

Army assignments: 20 Jan 1918, GHQ; 21 Jun 1918, French Sixth Army; 13 Aug 1918, First Army; 22 Aug 1918, French Eighth Army; 30 Aug 1918, First Army; 18 Sep 1918, French Second Army; 22 Sep 1918, First Army

Campaign participation credit: Champagne-Marne, Aisne-Marne, St. Mihiel, Meuse-Argonne, Ile de France 1918, Champagne 1918, Lorraine 1918

Assigned Divisions

West of Chateau-Thierry (4-17 Jul 1918): 1st, 2nd, 3rd, 4th, 26th, 28th, French 167th

Aisne-Marne operation (18 Jul-6 Aug 1918): 3rd, 4th, 26th, 28th, 32nd, 42nd, French 62nd, French 167th

Vesle front (7-13 Aug 1918): 4th, 26th, 42nd, 77th, French 62nd

St. Mihiel operation (22 Aug-17 Sep 1918): 1st, 2nd, 5th, 35th, 78th, 82nd, 90th

Meuse-Argonne operation (21 Sep-10 Nov 1918): 1st, 6th, 28th, 35th, 36th, 42nd, 77th, 78th, 80th, 82nd, 91st, 92nd, French 5th Cavalry

**II Army Corps**          Organized 24 Feb 1918 in France. Served in the British sector, away from the rest of the US forces. Demobilized 1 Feb 1919 in France.

Commanders: 15 Jun 1918,[35] Maj Gen George W. Read

Army assignments: 24 Feb 1918, British GHQ; 27 Aug 1918, British Second Army; 3 Sep 1918, British GHQ; 20 Sep 1918, British Fourth Army; 14 Nov 1918, British Third Army; 16 Nov 1918, British GHQ

Campaign participation credit: Somme Offensive

---

[35] There was no commander prior to Maj Gen Read; the chief of staff acted from formation in Feb 1918.

Assigned Divisions
British front (Jul-Nov 1918): 27th, 30th, 33rd, 37th, 78th, 82nd, 91st, British 1st and 6th, Australian 2nd, 3rd and 5th

**III Army Corps**          Organized 30 Mar 1918 in France.  Moved into Germany for occupation duties following the Armistice (Headquarters established Dec 1918 at Neuwied).  Discontinued in Germany 1 Jul 1919 and returned to the US; demobilized 9 Aug 1919 at Camp Sherman, Ohio.
Commanders: 17 Jun 1918,[36] Maj Gen William M. Wright, 12 Jul 1918, Maj Gen John E. McMahon (interim), 14 Jul 1918, Maj Gen Robert L. Bullard, 12 Oct 1918, Maj Gen John L. Hines, 19 Feb 1919, Maj Gen Edward F. McGlachlin, Jr. (interim), 5 Mar 1919, Maj Gen John L. Hines, 29 Apr 1919, Maj Gen Edward F. McGlachlin, Jr. (interim), 11 May 1919, Maj Gen John L. Hines
Army assignments: 30 Mar 1918, GHQ; 13 Jul 1918, French Sixth Army; 16 Jul 1918, French Tenth Army; 24 Jul 1918, First Army; 4 Aug 1918, French Sixth Army; 8 Sep 1918, French Fifth Army; 10 Sep 1918, French Second Army; 22 Sep 1918, First Army; 17 Nov 1918, Third Army
Campaign participation credit: Aisne-Marne, Oise-Aisne, Meuse-Argonne, Champagne 1918, Lorraine 1918

Assigned Divisions
Aisne-Marne operation (4-6 Aug 1918): 3rd, 28th, 32nd, French 4th
Vesle front (7-17 Aug 1918): 3rd, 28th, 32nd, 77th, French 4th, French 164th
Oise-Aisne operation (18 Aug-9 Sep 1918): 28th, 32nd, 77th, French 62nd
Meuse-Argonne front and operation (14 Sep-11 Nov 1918): 1st, 3rd, 4th, 5th, 28th, 32nd, 33rd, 35th, 79th, 80th, 89th, 90th, 91st, French 157th
Post-Armistice: 1st, 2nd, 3rd, 4th, 32nd, 42nd, French 2nd Cavalry

**IV Army Corps**          Organized 20 Jun 1918 in France.  Moved into Germany for occupation duties following the Armistice (Headquarters established Dec 1918 at Cochem).  Demobilized 11 May 1919 in Germany.
Commanders: 18 Aug 1918, Maj Gen Joseph T. Dickman,[37] 12 Oct 1918, Maj Gen Charles H. Muir, 14 Apr 1919, Maj Gen Robert L. Howze (interim), 2 May 1919, Maj Gen Charles P. Summerall

---

[36] Maj Gen Wright was the first commander; prior to that date, the chief of staff acted.
[37] Maj Gen Dickman was the first commander; prior to that date, the chief of staff acted.

Army assignments: 19 Jun 1918, GHQ; 13 Aug 1918, French Eighth Army; 30
Aug 1918, First Army; 12 Oct 1918, Second Army; 17 Nov 1918,
Third Army
Campaign participation credit: St. Mihiel, Lorraine 1918

Assigned Divisions
St. Mihiel front and operation (20 Aug-16 Sep 1918): 1st, 2nd, 6th, 36th, 37th,
42nd, 78th, 79th, 82nd, 89th, 90th, 91st, 92nd
Toul sector and Thiaucourt zone (17 Sep-16 Nov 1918): 1st, 2nd, 4th, 5th, 7th,
28th, 33rd, 35th, 37th, 42nd, 77th, 78th, 79th, 82nd, 88th (one brigade), 89th,
90th, 92nd, French 69th
Post-Armistice: 1st, 3rd, 4th, part of 6th, 42nd

**V Army Corps**　　　　Organized 7-12 Jul 1918 in France.  Relocated to
control training areas following the Armistice.  Discontinued in France 5 Mar
1919.  Demobilized 2 May 1919 at Camp Funston, Kansas.
Commanders: 12 Jul 1918, Maj Gen William M. Wright, 21 Aug 1918, Maj
Gen George H. Cameron, 12 Oct 1918, Maj Gen Charles P. Summerall
[to 12 Feb 1919]
Army assignments: 12 Jul 1918, GHQ; 19 Aug 1918, First Army; 29 Aug 1918,
French Second Army; 30 Aug 1918, First Army; 17 Sep 1918, French
Second Army; 22 Sep 1918, First Army
Campaign participation credit: St. Mihiel, Meuse-Argonne, Lorraine 1918

Assigned Divisions
St. Mihiel front including operation (29 Aug-16 Sep 1918): 3rd, 4th, 26th, 33rd,
80th, French 2nd Dismounted Cavalry, French 15th Colonial
Meuse-Argonne operation (21 Sep-11 Nov 1918): 1st, 2nd, 3rd, 6th, 29th, 32nd,
37th, 42nd, 77th, 79th, 80th, 89th, 91st, French 73rd

**VI Army Corps**　　　　Organized 23 Jul—1 Aug 1918 in France.  Moved into
Luxembourg and Belgium Dec 1918.  Discontinued operations in Europe 11
Apr 1919.  Demobilized in May 1919 at Camp Devens, Massachusetts.
Commanders: 26 Aug 1918, Maj Gen Omar Bundy, 13 Sep 1918, vacant (chief
of staff acted), 23 Oct 1918, Maj Gen Charles C. Ballou, 10 Nov 1918,
Maj Gen Charles T. Menoher, 17 Dec 1918, Maj Gen Charles H.
Martin, 20 Dec 1918, Maj Gen George Bell, Jr.; 24 Dec 1918, Maj Gen
Robert L. Bullard (interim), 13 Jan 1919, Maj Gen Adelbert Cronkhite,
3 Feb 1919, Maj Gen George Bell, Jr. (interim), 18 Feb 1919, Maj Gen
Adelbert Cronkhite, 25 Mar 1919, Maj Gen George Bell, Jr. (interim),

27 Mar 1919, Maj Gen Adelbert Cronkhite, 10 Apr 1919, Maj Gen
George Bell, Jr. [to 11 Apr 1919]
Army assignments: 1 Aug 1918, GHQ; 12 Oct 1918, Second Army; 1 Apr
1919, Third Army
Campaign participation credit: Lorraine 1918
Assigned Divisions
Marbache sector (Lorraine) (23 Oct-13 Nov 1918): 7th, 88th, 92nd


**VII Army Corps** Organized 19 Aug 1918 in France. Did not
participate in combat during the war. Moved into Germany for occupation
duties following the Armistice (Headquarters established Dec 1918 at Wittlich).
Discontinued in Germany 11 May 1919. Demobilized 9-11 Jul 1919 at Camp
Upton, New York.
Commanders: 19 Aug 1918, Maj Gen William M. Wright, 6 Sep 1918, vacant
(chief of staff acted), 13 Sep 1918, Maj Gen Omar Bundy, 25 Oct
1918, vacant (chief of staff acted), 21 Nov 1918, Maj Gen William G.
Haan, 23 Apr 1919, Maj Gen Charles H. Martin (interim), 8 May 1919,
Maj Gen Henry T. Allen [to 11 May 1919]
Army assignments: 19 Aug 1918, GHQ; 8 Nov 1918, First Army; 22 Nov
1918, Third Army
Campaign participation credit: Streamer without inscription

Assigned Divisions
Post-Armistice: 5th, 6th, 29th, 33rd, 35th, 36th, 78th, 79th, 80th, 81st, 88th, 89th, 90th,
92nd


**VIII Army Corps** Organized 26-29 Nov 1918 in France. Took over
training of divisions withdrawn from the Meuse-Argonne. Demobilized 20 Apr
1919 in France.
Commanders: 26 Nov 1918, Maj Gen Henry T. Allen, 15 Apr 1919: Maj Gen
Walter H. Gordon
Army assignments: 26 Nov 1918, First Army


**IX Army Corps** Organized 25-29 Nov 1918 in France, initially taking
over part of Second Army zone. Demobilized 5 May 1919 in Europe.
Commanders: 26 Nov 1918, Maj Gen Adelbert Cronkhite, 13 Jan 1919, Lt Gen
Robert L. Bullard (interim), 18 Jan 1919, Maj Gen Joseph E. Kuhn
(interim), 26 Jan 1919, Maj Gen William Weigel (interim), 31 Jan
1919, Maj Gen Joseph E. Kuhn (interim), 28 Feb 1919, Maj Gen
Charles P. Summerall, 16 Apr 1919, Maj Gen Henry T. Allen, 21 Apr

1919, Maj Gen William Weigel (interim), 25 Apr 1919, Maj Gen
Charles J. Bailey (interim), 28 Apr 1919, Maj Gen Henry T. Allen
Army assignments: 26 Nov 1918, Second Army; 15 Apr 1919, First Army; 20
Apr 1919, GHQ

**AEF, North Russia**          Organized 9 Aug 1918 in England as
"Murmansk Expedition" with troops from 85th Division (339th Infantry, 1st Bn
310th Engineers, and medical units). Established 4 Sep 1918 at Archangel.
Redesignated 12 Sep 1918 as "American North Russia Expeditionary Forces."
Received final designation 9 Apr 1919. Archangel troops withdrawn Jun 1919;
two transportation companies at Murmansk withdrawn Aug 1919. Hq, AEF,
North Russia discontinued 5 Aug 1919.
Commanders: 4 Sep 1918: Col Charles E. Stewart, 9 Apr 1919, Brig Gen Wilds
P. Richardson

**AEF, Siberia**          US troops in the Philippines (27th and 31st Infantry)
and some support units sent to Siberia Aug 1918. Hq, AEF in Siberia activated
15 Aug 1918 in Siberia. Withdrawal began Jan 1920. Hq inactivated 1 Apr
1920 on departure from Siberia.
Commanders: 16 Aug 1918, Col Henry D. Stryer, 3 Sep 1918, Maj Gen
William S. Graves, 11 Jul 1919, Col Frederick H. Sargent (interim), 7
Sep 1919, Maj Gen William S. Graves

**American Forces in France**          Organized 1 Sep 1919 to control all
AEF forces in Europe not assigned to American Forces in Germany.
Discontinued 8 Jan 1920.
Commander: 1 Sep 1919, Brig Gen William D. Connor

**American Forces in Germany**          Established 2 Jul 1919 in Germany to
replace Third Army. The last division left Aug 1919 and the force fell below
10,000 personnel (organized into two brigades). Reduced in 1921 to one
brigade, which was demobilized Apr 1922. Handed over sector in Germany to
the French 27 Jan 1923 and demobilized ca. 21 Feb 1923.
Commanders: 3 Jul 1919, Maj Gen Edward F. McGlachlin, Jr. (interim), 8 Jul
1919, Maj Gen Henry T. Allen

**Services of Supply**          Established 5 Jul 1917 as Line of Communications in the AEF.  Redesignated 16 Feb 1918 as Service of the Rear.  Redesignated 13 Mar 1918 as Services of Supply.  This command was responsible for landing, supporting, and supplying the operational units of the AEF.  It also controlled divisions assigned depot and replacement duties. Following the Armistice, many of the training camps were taken over by the armies and corps in France, and SOS began the mission of repatriating the AEF back to the US.  It was abolished 1 Sep 1919 and responsibility for remaining AEF personnel outside of Germany transferred to American Forces in France. Commanders: 5 Jul 1917, Col David S. Stanley (interim); 25 Jul 1917, Brig Gen [Maj Gen 31 Aug 1917] Richard M. Blatchford; 2 Nov 1917, Brig Gen Mason M. Patrick (interim); 28 Nov 1917, Maj Gen Francis J. Kernan; 29 Jul 1918, Maj Gen James G. Harband; 27 May 1919, Brig Gen William D. Connor

The principal subordinate elements of SOS and its predecessors were:
Advance Section: established 4 Jul 1917 under GHQ, and placed under SOS 16 Feb 1918 (responsible for area behind the front). Discontinued 8 Oct 1919.
Intermediate Section: established 13 Aug 1917 (responsible for area between Advance Section and the base sections). Discontinued 25 Sep 1919.
Base Section No. 1: established 13 Aug 1917 with Hq at St. Nazaire; discontinued there 19 Jul 1919 and responsibility transferred to new Base Section No. 1 (Hq at Montour), which was discontinued 20 Oct 1919.
Base Section No. 2: established 13 Aug 1917 with Hq at Bordeaux; moved 4 Jul 1919 to St. Sulpice. Discontinued 30 Sep 1919.
Base Section No. 3 – see Base Section No. 4
Base Section No. 3: established 27 Nov 1917 in the UK to take over all installations there from the original Base Section No. 3. Discontinued 15 Jun 1919.
Base Section No. 4: established 13 Aug 1917 as Base Section No. 3 with Hq at Le Havre; also responsible for the UK until 27 Nov 1917 when restricted to France and renumbered. Discontinued 16 Apr 1919.
Base Section No. 5: established 10 Nov 1917 with Hq at Brest (taking part of the area from Base Section No. 1). Discontinued 4 Jan 1920.
Base Section No. 6: established 30 May 1918 with Hq at Marseilles. Discontinued 15 Jun 1919.
Base Section No. 7: established 28 Jun 1918 with Hq at La Pollice (taking part of the area from Base Section No. 2); Hq later moved to La Rochelle. Discontinued 25 Apr 1919.
Base Section No. 8: established 22 Oct 1918 with Hq at Padua to support American troops in Italy. Discontinued 20 May 1919.

Base Section No. 9: established 8 Apr 1919 with Hq at Antwerp to control troops and installations in Holland and Belgium in support of Third Army. Discontinued 15 Aug 1919 when American Forces in Germany took over this role.

District of Paris: established 3 Dec 1917 as US Troops in Paris (taking over role held by Provost Marshal); redesignated 6 May 1918 as District of Paris. Discontinued 7 Oct 1919.

## Infantry Divisions

**1ˢᵗ Division**     (Regular Army) Headquarters organized 8 Jun 1917 in New York, NY as Headquarters, 1ˢᵗ Expeditionary Division [redesignated 6 Jul 1917 in France as Headquarters, 1ˢᵗ Division]. Division elements moved overseas and the division was organized Jun-Dec 1917. Moved into Germany on occupation duties and established Dec 1918 at Montabaur. Returned to the US Aug-Sep 1919 and moved to Camp Taylor, KY.

Commanders: 8 Jun 1917: Brig Gen [Maj Gen 27 Jun 1917] William L. Sibert; 14 Dec 1917, Maj Gen Robert L. Bullard; 5 Apr 1918, Brig Gen Beaumont B. Buck (interim); 13 Apr 1918, Maj Gen Robert L. Bullard; 15 Jul 1918, Maj Gen Charles P. Summerall; 12 Oct 1918, Brig Gen Frank R. Bamford (interim); 18 Oct 1918, Brig Gen Frank Parker; 21 Nov 1918, Maj Gen Edward F. McGlachlin, Jr.; 10 May 1919, Brig Gen Francis C. Marshall (interim); 19 May 1919, Maj Gen Edward F. McGlachlin, Jr.; 29 Jun 1919, Brig Gen Frank E. Bamford (interim); 1 Jul 1919, Brig Gen Augustine McIntyre (interim); 4 Jul 1919, Maj Gen Edward F. McGlachlin, Jr.; 12 Jul 1919, Col Robert A. Brown (interim); 16 Jul 1919, Maj Gen Edward F. McGlachlin, Jr.; 21 Jul 1919, Brig Gen Frank E. Bamford (interim); 24 Jul 1919, Maj Gen Edward F. McGlachlin, Jr. [to 30 Aug 1919]

Assignments: 26 Jun 1917, GHQ; 14 Oct 1917, French IX Corps; 21 Nov 1917, French Eighth Army; 5 Jan 1918, French XXXII Corps; 3 Apr 1918, French Eighth Army; 5 Apr 1918, French Fifth Army 17 Apr 1918, French First Army; 21 Apr 1918, French VI Corps; 5 May 1918, French X Corps; 8 Jul 1918; French GAR (part) and French X Corps (part); 11 Jul 1918, French X Corps; 15 Jul 1918, French XX Corps; 23 Jul 1918, III Army Corps; 30 Jul 1918, French Eighth Army; 4 Aug 1918, French XXXII Corps; 22 Aug 1918, I Army Corps; 24 Aug 1918, First Army; 27 Aug 1918, IV Army Corps; 20 Sep 1918, III Army Corps; 29 Sep 1918, I Army Corps; 7 Oct 1918, V Army Corps; 12 Oct 1918, I Army Corps; 25 Oct 1918, V Army Corps; 12 Nov 1918, III Army Corps; 15 Nov 1918, French II Colonial Corps; 17 Nov 1918, IV Army Corps; 13 Dec 1918, III Army Corps; 2 Jul 1919, AF in G; 5 Aug 1919, SOS

Nickname: "The Big Red One"

Campaign participation credit: Montdidier-Noyon, Aisne-Marne, St. Mihiel, Meuse-Argonne, Lorraine 1917, Lorraine 1918, Picardy 1918

**2ⁿᵈ Division**     (Regular Army) Headquarters organized 26 Oct 1917 in France. Division formed Sep 1917 to Mar 1918 in France with both Army and Marine Corps elements. Moved into Germany on occupation duties and established Dec 1918 at Heddesdorf. Returned to the US Jul-Aug 1919 (and

Marine Brigade detached to Quantico); Army elements moved to Camp Travis, TX.

Commanders: 26 Oct 1917: Brig Gen Charles A. Doyen, USMC; 8 Nov 1917, Maj Gen Omar Bundy; 15 Jul 1918, Maj Gen James G. Harbord; 26 Jul 1918, Brig Gen James A. Lejeune, USMC (interim); 27 Jul 1918, Maj Gen James G. Harbord; 28 Jul 1918, Brig Gen [Maj Gen 1 Aug 1918] James A. Lejeune, USMC; 17 Jun 1919, Brig Gen Wendell C. Neville, USMC (interim); 22 Jun 1919, Maj Gen James A. Lejeune, USMC [to 3 Aug 1919]

Assignments: 26 Oct 1917, GHQ; 13 Mar 1918, French X Corps; 17 Apr 1918, French II Colonial Corps; 11 May 1918, French Second Army; 18 May 1918, French GAR; 30 May 1918, French Sixth Army; 31 May 1918, French VII Corps; 1 Jun 1918, French XXI Corps; 21 Jun 1918, French III Corps; 4 Jul 1918, I Army Corps; 16 Jul 1918, French Tenth Army; 18 Jul 1918, French XX Corps; 20 Jul 1918, French Tenth Army; 23 Jul 1918, III Army Corps; 30 Jul 1918, French Eighth Army; 4 Aug 1918, French XXXII Corps; 19 Aug 1918, First Army; 27 Aug 1918, I Army Corps; 18 Sep 1918, IV Army Corps; 27 Sep 1918, French GAC Reserve; 30 Sep 1918, French Fourth Army; 2 Oct 1918, French Fourth Army (part) and French XXI Corps (part); 3 Oct 1918, French XXI Corps; 10 Oct 1918, French Fourth Army (part) and French XXI Corps (part); 19 Oct 1918, French Fourth Army (part) and French IX Corps (part); 22 Oct 1918, V Army Corps; 14 Nov 1918, III Army Corps; 2 Jul 1919, AF in G; 5 Jul 1919; SOS

Nickname: "Indian Head Division"

Campaign participation credit: Aisne, Aisne-Marne, St. Mihiel, Meuse-Argonne, Ile de France 1918, Lorraine 1918


**3rd Division** (Regular Army) Headquarters organized 12 Nov 1917 at Camp Greene, NC; the division did not assemble as a unit before going overseas. Moved overseas Mar-Jun 1918. Moved into Germany on occupation duties and established Dec 1918 at Andernach. Returned to the US Aug 1919 and moved to Camp Pike, AR.

Commanders: 28 Nov 1917, Maj Gen Joseph T. Dickman; 11 Feb 1918, Brig Gen James A. Irons (interim); 13 Feb 1918, Maj Gen Joseph T. Dickman; 27 Feb 1918, Brig Gen James A. Irons (interim); 8 Mar 1918, Brig Gen Charles Crawford (interim); 10 Mar 1918, Brig Gen James A. Irons (interim); 19 Mar 1918, Brig Gen Charles Crawford (interim); 12 Apr 1919, Maj Gen Joseph T. Dickman; 18 Aug 1918, Brig Gen Fred W. Sladen (interim); 27 Aug 1918, Maj Gen Beaumont B. Buck; 18 Oct 1918, Brig Gen Preston Brown; 19 Nov 1918, Maj Gen Robert L. Howze; 11 May 1919, Brig Gen William M. Cruikshank (interim); 17 May 1919, Maj Gen Robert L. Howze; 3 Jun 1919, Brig

Gen Fred W. Sladen (interim); 13 Jun 1919, Maj Gen Robert L. Howze; 11 Jul 1919, Brig Gen Ora E. Hunt (interim); 17 Jul 1919, Maj Gen Robert L. Howze [to 23 JAug1919]

Assignments: 5 Apr 1918, GHQ; 13 Apr 1918, III Army Corps; 30 May 1918, French GAN; 31 May 1918, French XXXVIII Corps; 30 Jul 1918, French Sixth Army; 2 Aug 1918, French III Corps; 4 Aug 1918, III Army Corps (part) and French III Corps (part); 5 Aug 1918, III Army Corps; 16 Aug 1918, GHQ; 18 Aug 1918, First Army; 27 Aug 1918, V Army Corps; 3 Sep 1918, IV Army Corps; 16 Sep 1918, III Army Corps; 29 Sep 1918, V Army Corps; 12 Oct 1918, III Army Corps; 13 Nov 1918, VII Army Corps; 15 Nov 1918, IV Army Corps; 11 May 1919, III Army Corps; 17 Jun 1919, Third Army; 25 Jun 1919, III Army Corps; 2 Jul 1919, AF in G; 25 Jul 1919, SOS.

Nickname: "Marne Division"

Campaign participation credit: Aisne, Champagne-Marne, Aisne-Marne, St. Mihiel., Meuse-Argonne, Champagne 1918

**4th Division**    (Regular Army) Headquarters organized 10 Dec 1917 at Camp Greene, NC and the division formed there.  Moved overseas May-Jun 1918. Moved into Germany on occupation duties and established Dec 1918 at Bad Bertrich.  Returned to the US Jul-Aug 1919 and moved to Camp Dodge, IA.

Commanders: 10 Dec 1917: Brig Gen George H. Cameron; 11 Dec 1917: Col Benjamin W. Atkinson (interim); 13 Dec 1917, Brig Gen [Maj Gen 20 Dec 1917] George H. Cameron; 4 Feb 1918, Brig Gen Samuel W. Miller (interim); 6 Feb 1918, Maj Gen George H. Cameron; 26 Mar 1918, Brig Gen Frank D. Webster (interim); 27 Mar 1918, Maj Gen George H. Cameron; 14 Aug 1918, Brig Gen Benjamin A. Poore (interim); 27 Aug 1918, Maj Gen John L. Hines; 11 Oct 1918, Maj Gen George H. Cameron; 22 Oct 1918, Brig Gen Benjamin A. Poore (interim); 31 Oct 1918, Maj Gen Mark L. Hersey; 17 Nov 1918, Maj Gen Robert L. Howze; 19 Nov 1918, Maj Gen Mark L. Hersey; 3 Apr 1919, Brig Gen Benjamin A. Poore (interim); 7 Apr 1919, Maj Gen Mark L. Hersey; 11 May 1919, Brig Gen Augustine McIntyre (interim); 17 May 1919, Maj Gen Mark L. Hersey; 4 Jun 1919, Brig Gen Francis C. Marshall (interim); 14 Jun 1919, Maj Gen Mark L. Hersey; 31 Jun 1919, Brig Gen Augustine McIntyre (interim to 2 Aug 1919)

Assignments: 17 May 1918, GHQ; 18 May 1918, British First Army; 9 Jun 1918, French Sixth Army; 1 Jul 1918, French VII Corps (part) and French II Corps (part); 17 Jul 1918, French II Corps (part) and French VII Corps (part); 22 Jul 1918, French Sixth Army; 28 Jul 1918, I Army Corps; 13Aug 1918, French Sixth Army; 19 Aug 1918, GHQ; 21 Aug 1918, First Army; 27 Aug 1918, V Army Corps; 16 Sep 1918, III Army

Corps; 21 Oct 1918, First Army; 24 Oct 1918, IV Army Corps; 7 Nov 1918, III Army Corps; 9 Nov 1918, IV Army Corps; 1 May 1919, III Army Corps; 11 May 1919, SOS; 20 May 1919, Third Army; 28 Jun 1919, SOS.

Nickname: "Ivy Division"

Campaign participation credit: Aisne-Marne, St. Mihiel., Meuse-Argonne, Champagne 1918, Lorraine 1918

**5th Division** (Regular Army) Headquarters organized 11 Dec 1917 at Camp Logan, TX; the division did not assemble as a unit before going overseas. Moved overseas Mar-Jun 1918. Moved into Luxembourg following the armistice. Returned to the US Jul 1919 and moved to Camp Gordon, GA (less artillery, to Camp Bragg, NC).

Commanders: 11 Dec 1917, Maj Gen Charles H. Muir; 13 Dec 1917; Col William M. Morrow (interim); 1 Jan 1918, Brig Gen [Maj Gen 6 Feb 1918] John E. McMahon; 18 Oct 1918, Maj Gen Hanson E. Ely; 30 Jan 1919, Brig Gen Joseph C. Castner (interim); 3 Feb 1919, Maj Gen Hanson E. Ely; 1 Apr 1919, Brig Gen Thomas B. Dugan (interim); 15 Apr 1919, Maj Gen Hanson E. Ely [to 22 Jul 1919]

Assignments: 1 May 1918, III Army Corps; 31 May 1918, French XXXIII Corps; 23 Aug 1918, French Seventh Army; 27 Aug 1918, I Army Corps; 18 Sep 1918, IV Army Corps; 2 Oct 1918, III Army Corps; 16 Nov 1918, V Army Corps; 21 Nov 1918, VII Army Corps; 22 Nov 1918, Third Army; 12 Dec 1918, Second Army; 19 Dec 1918, VI Army Corps; 10 Apr 1919, VII Army Corps; 11 May 1919, SOS; 6 Jun 1919, Third Army; 28 Jun 1919, SOS

Nickname: "Red Diamond Division"

Campaign participation credit: St. Mihiel., Meuse-Argonne, Alsace 1918, Lorraine 1918

**6th Division** (Regular Army) Headquarters organized 26 Nov 1917 at Camp McClellan, AL; the division did not assemble as a unit before going overseas. Moved overseas Jun-Jul 1918. Returned to the US May-Jun 1919 and moved to Camp Grant, IL.

Commanders: 26 Nov 1917: Col Charles E. Tayman (interim); 29 Dec 1917, Brig Gen James B. Erwin; 28 Aug 1918, Maj Gen Walter H. Gordon; 27 Mar 1919, Brig Gen William R. Dashiell (interim); 29 Mar 1919, Brig Gen Lucius L. Durfee (interim); 10 Apr 1919, Maj Gen Walter H. Gordon; 18 Apr 1919, Brig Gen Lucius L. Durfee (interim); 21 Apr 1919, Maj Gen Walter H. Gordon [to 14 Jun 1919]

Assignments: 22 Jul 1918, GHQ; 25 Jul 1918, IV Army Corps; 12 Aug 1918, VI Army Corps; 27 Aug 1918, French XXXIII Corps; 4 Oct 1918, French I Corps; 13 Oct 1918, French Seventh Army; 26 Oct 1918, I

Army Corps; 10 Nov 1918, V Army Corps; 12 Nov 1918, French II Colonial Corps; 20 Nov 1918, VII Army Corps; 22 Nov 1918, First Army; 26 Nov 1918, VIII Army Corps; 20 Apr 1919, IX Army Corps; 30 Apr 1919, IV Army Corps (part) and IX Army Corps (part); 5 May 1919, GHQ (part) and Third Army (part); 8 May 1919, SOS.

Nickname: "Sight-Seeing Sixth"

Campaign participation credit: Meuse-Argonne, Alsace 1918

**7th Division**      (Regular Army) Headquarters organized 1 Jan 1918 at Camp Wheeler, GA; the division did not assemble as a unit before going overseas. Moved overseas Jul-Sep 1918.  Returned to the US May-Jun 1919 and moved to Camp Funston, KS.

Commanders: 1 Jan 1918: Brig Gen Charles H. Barth; 17 Feb 1918: Brig Gen Tiemann N. Horn (interim); 25 Feb 1918, Brig Gen Charles H. Barth; 7 Jun 1918, Brig Gen Tiemann N. Horn (interim); 21 Jun 1918, Brig Gen Charles H. Barth; 24 Oct 1918, Brig Gen Lutz Wahl (interim); 28 Oct 1918, Maj Gen Edmund Wittenmyer; 19 Jan 1919, Brig Gen Guy H. Preston (interim); 23 Jan 1919, Maj Gen Edmund Wittenmyer; 14 May 1919, Brig Gen Lutz Wahl (interim); 23 May 1919, Maj Gen Edmund Wittenmyer [to 20 Jun 1919]

Assignments: 11 Aug 1918, GHQ; 2 Sep 1918, VI Army Corps; 15 Sep 1918, First Army; 24 Sep 1918, IV Army Corps; 13 Nov 1918, VI Army Corps; 22 Dec 1917, Second Army; 12 Jan 1919, VI Army Corps; 1 Apr 1919, Second Army; 10 Apr 1919, IX Army Corps; 5 May 1919, GHQ; 8 May 1919, SOS.

Nickname: "Hourglass Division"

Campaign participation credit: Lorraine 1918

**8th Division**      (Regular Army) Headquarters organized 5 Jan 1918 at Camp Fremont, CA and the division formed there.  Moved overseas Nov 1918 (Headquarters and some elements only).  Returned to the US by elements Dec 1918-Sep 1919.  Demobilized 5 Sep 1919 at Camp Lee, VA.[38]

Commanders: 5 Jan 1918, Col Elmore F. Taggart (interim); 15 Feb 1918, Col George W. VanDeusen (interim); 25 Feb 1918, Brig Gen Joseph D. Leitch (interim); 10 Mar 1918, Maj Gen John F. Morrison; 18 Jun 1918, Brig Gen Joseph D. Leitch (interim); 18 Jul 1918, Maj Gen William S. Graves; 4 Aug 1918, Brig Gen Joseph D. Leitch (interim); 11 Aug 1918, Maj Gen William S. Graves; 12 Aug 1918, Brig Gen Joseph D. Leitch (interim); 2 Sep 1918, Maj Gen Eli A. Helmick; 20

---

[38] While Division Hq was demobilized Sep 1919, the bulk of the division had been demobilized during Feb 1919.

Nov 1918, Brig Gen John J. Bradley (interim); 26 Nov 1918, Maj Gen
Eli A. Helmick [to 10 Jul 1919]
Assignments: 9 Nov 1918, SOS.
Nickname: "Pathfinder Division"
Campaign participation credit: Streamer without inscription

**9th Division**      (Regular Army) Headquarters organized 18 Jul 1918 at Camp
Sheridan, AL and the division organized there.  Disbanded 15 Feb 1919 at
Camp Sheridan.
Commanders: 18 Jul 1918: Col Charles C. Clark; 27 Sep 1918, Maj Gen
Willard A. Holbrook; 29 Oct 1918, Brig Gen James A. Ryan (interim);
5 Nov 1918, Maj Gen Willard A. Holbrook; 16 Jan 1919, Brig Gen
James A. Ryan (interim); 20 Jan 1919, Maj Gen Willard A. Holbrook

**10th Division**      (Regular Army) Organized Jul 1918 at Camp Funston, KS.
Advanced detachment sent overseas Nov 1918.  Demobilized 18 Feb 1919 at
Camp Funston.
Commanders: 10 Aug 1918, Maj Gen Leonard Wood; 7 Jan 1919, Brig Gen
Howard R. Hickock (interim); 17 Jan 1919, Maj Gen Leonard Wood

**11th Division**      (Regular Army) Organized 5 Aug 1918 at Camp Meade, MD.
Scheduled to be a replacement and school division.  Advanced detachment sent
overseas Nov 1918.  Demobilized 5 Feb 1919 at Camp Meade.
Commanders: 5 Aug 1918, Brig Gen Joseph A. Gaston; 15 Aug 1918, Maj Gen
Jesse McI. Carter
Nickname: "Lafayette Division"

**12th Division**      (Regular Army) Organized 12 Jul 1918 at Camp Devens, MA.
Advanced detachment sent overseas Nov 1918.  Demobilized 18 Feb 1919
Camp Devens.
Commanders: 30 Jul 1918: Col George L. Byroade (interim); 13 Aug 1918, Col
Almon L. Parmerter (interim); 20 Aug 1918, Maj Gen Henry P.
McCain; 12 Feb 1919, Brig Gen John E. Woodward (interim); 15 Feb
1918, Maj Gen Henry P. McCain
Nickname: "Plymouth Division"

**13th Division**      (Regular Army) Organized 16 Jul 1918 at Camp Lewis, WA.
Demobilized 8 Mar 1919 at Camp Lewis.
Commanders: 17 Jul 1918, Col Edward N. Jones, Jr. (interim); 20 Aug 1918,
Brig Gen Cornelius Vanderbilt (interim); 11 Sep 1918, Brig Gen Frank
B. Watson (interim); 7 Oct 1918, Brig Gen [Maj Gen 12 Oct 1918]
Joseph D. Leitch
Nickname: "Lucky Thirteenth Division"

**14<sup>th</sup> Division**    (Regular Army) Organized Jul 1918 at Camp Custer, MI. Scheduled to be a base and training division.  Demobilized 19 Feb 1919 at Camp Custer.
Commanders: 29 Jul 1918: Col Samuel Burkhardt, Jr.; 5 Sep 1918, Brig Gen
Howard L. Laubauch; 19 Nov 1918, Maj Gen Grote Hutcheson
Nickname: "Wolverine Division"

**15<sup>th</sup> Division**    (Regular Army) Organized Aug 1918 at Camp Logan, TX. Demobilized 24 Feb 1919 at Camp Logan.
Commanders: 28 Aug 1918, Col David J. Baker, Jr.; 11 Sep 1918, Brig Gen Guy V. Henry

**16<sup>th</sup> Division**    (Regular Army) Organized Aug 1918 at Camp Kearny, CA. Demobilized 8 Mar 1919 at Camp Kearny.
Commanders: 19 Aug 1918, Col Llewellyn W. Oliver (interim); 21 Aug 1918,
Col Earle W. Tanner (interim); 23 Aug 1918, Col George B. Pritchard,
Jr. (interim); 26 Aug 1918, Col Sterling P. Adams (interim); 30 Aug
1918, Col Willis Uline (interim); 9 Sep 1918, Brig Gen Peter W.
Davison (interim); 20 Sep 1918, Maj Gen David C. Shanks; 27 Nov
1918, Brig Gen Peter W. Davison (interim); 3 Jan 1919, Brig Gen
Walter C. Short (interim); 25 Jan 1919, Brig Gen Peter W. Davison
(interim); 30 Jan 1919, Maj Gen Guy Carleton

**17<sup>th</sup> Division**    (Regular Army) Organized Aug 1918 at Camp Beauregard, LA.  Scheduled to be a replacement and school division. Demobilized 10 Feb 1919 at Camp Beauregard.
Commanders: 7 Aug 1918: Col Harold L. Jackson (interim); 1 Sep 1918, Col
James A. Irons (interim); 1 Nov 1918, Brig Gen Robert W. Mearns
(interim); 22 Dec 1918, Col Jack Hayes (interim); 9 Jan 1919, Maj Gen
Henry C. Hodges, Jr.; 30 Jan 1919, Brig Gen Robert W. Mearns
(interim); 5 Feb 1919, Maj Gen Henry C. Hodges, Jr.

**18<sup>th</sup> Division**    (Regular Army) Organized Aug 1918 at Camp Travis, TX. Demobilized 14 Feb 1919 at Camp Travis.
Commanders: 21 Aug 1918: Col James H. Frier (interim); 16 Sep 1918, Brig
Gen George H. Estes; 14 Oct 1918, Col James H. Frear (interim); 24
Oct 1918, Brig Gen Frederick P. Shaw (interim); 27 Oct 1918, Brig
Gen George H. Estes
Nickname: "Cactus Division"

**19<sup>th</sup> Division**    (Regular Army) Organized Aug 1918 at Camp Dodge, IA. Demobilized 14 Feb 1919 at Camp Dodge.

Commanders: 1 Sep 1918, Col William C. Bennett 26 Sep 1918, Col Armand
      A Lasseigne; 25 Oct 1918, Brig Gen Benjamin T. Simmons; 9 Feb
      1918, Maj Gen Charles C. Ballou

**20ᵗʰ Division**    (Regular Army) Organized Aug 1918 at Camp Sevier, SC.
Scheduled to be a base and training division.  Demobilized 25 Feb 1919 at
Camp Sevier.
Commanders: 12 Aug 1918: Col Louis J. Van Schaik (interim); 18 Aug 1918,
      Col Lawrence B. Simonds (interim); 27 Aug 1918, Col William F.
      Grote (interim); 30 Sep 1918, Brig Gen E. Leroy Sweetser; 3 Jan 1919,
      Maj Gen Harry F. Hodges; 26 Jan 1919, Brig Gen E. Leroy Sweetser
      (interim); 6 Feb 1919, Col Louis J. Van Schaik (interim); 13 Feb 1919,
      Maj Gen Harry F. Hodges; 20 Feb 1919, Col Louis J. Van Schaik
      (interim); 22 Feb 1919, Maj Gen Harry F. Hodges

**26ᵗʰ Division**    (National Guard) Headquarters organized 22 Aug 1917 near
Boston, MA; division organized from NG personnel from Connecticut, Maine,
Massachusetts, New Hampshire, Rhode Island, and Vermont.  The division
concentrated at various locations in New England and did not assemble or train
together before moving overseas. Moved overseas Sep 1917-Jan 1918.
Returned to the US Mar-Apr 1919. Demobilized 3 May 1919 at Camp Devens,
MA.
Commanders: 22 Aug 1917, Maj Gen Clarence R. Edwards; 12 Oct 1917, Brig
      Gen Peter E. Traub (interim); 22 Oct 1917, Brig Gen Charles H. Cole
      (interim); 31 Oct 1917, Brig Gen Peter E. Traub (interim); 11 Nov
      1917, Maj Gen Clarence R. Edwards; 25 Nov 1917, Brig Gen Peter E.
      Traub (interim); 1 Dec 1917, Maj Gen Clarence R. Edwards; 25 Oct
      1918, Brig Gen Frank E. Barnford; 19 Nov 1918, Maj Gen Harry C.
      Hale; 26 Apr 1919, Brig Gen George H. Shelton (interim)
Assignments: 23 Oct 1917, GHQ; 3 Feb 1918, French XI Corps; 18 Mar 1918,
      GHQ; 28 Mar 1918, French XXXII Corps; 29 Jun 1918, French Sixth
      Army; 3 Jul 1918, French III Corps; 4 Jul 1918, I Army Corps; 13 Aug
      1918, GHQ; 18 Aug 1918, First Army; 27 Aug 1918, V Army Corps;
      16 Sep 1918, French II Colonial Corps; 8 Oct 1918, First Army; 14 Oct
      1918, French XVII Corps; 6 Nov 1918, French II Colonial Corps; 14
      Nov 1918, VII Army Corps; 16 Nov 1918, First Army; 21 Nov 1918, V
      Army Corps; 25 Jan 1919, SOS.
Nickname: "Yankee Division"
Campaign participation credit: Champagne-Marne, Aisne-Marne, St. Mihiel,
      Meuse-Argonne, Ile de France 1918, Lorraine 1918

**27th Division** (National Guard) Headquarters, 6th Division [New York NG; called into federal service 16 Jul 1917 and drafted into federal service 5 Aug 1917] redesignated 1 Oct 1917 as Headquarters, 27th Division; division organized at Camp Wadsworth, SC with NG personnel from New York. Moved overseas May-Jul 1918. Returned to the US Feb-Mar 1919. Demobilized 1 Apr 1919 at Camp Upton, NY.

Commanders: 16 Jul 1917, Maj Gen John F. O'Ryan; 19 Sep 1917, Brig Gen Charles L. Phillips (interim); 6 Dec 1917, Maj Gen John F. O'Ryan; 23 Dec 1917, Brig Gen Charles L. Phillips (interim); 29 Dec 1917, Maj Gen John F. O'Ryan; 22 Feb 1918, Brig Gen Charles L. Phillips (interim); 1 Mar 1918, Maj Gen John F. O'Ryan; 16 Jun 1918, Brig Gen Palmer E. Pierce (interim); 18 Jun 1918, Maj Gen John F. O'Ryan; 14 Nov 1918, Brig Gen Palmer E. Pierce (interim); 23 Nov 1918, Maj Gen John F. O'Ryan

Assignments: 26 May 1918, British Fourth Army; 28 May 1918, British XIX Corps; 18 Jun 1918, British Third Army; 22 Jun 1918, British IV and V Corps; 30 Jun 1918, British Second Army; 3 Jul 1918, British XIX Corps; 4 Sep 1918, British GHQ; 20 Sep 1918, British Fourth Army; 22 Sep 1918, British III Corps; 25 Sep 1918, II Army Corps; 1 Feb 1919, SOS.

Nickname: "New York Division"

Campaign participation credit: Ypres-Lys, Somme Offensive

**28th Division** (National Guard) Headquarters, 7th Division [Pennsylvania NG; called into federal service 15 Jul 1917 and drafted into federal service 5 Aug 1917] redesignated 1 Sep 1917 as Headquarters, 28th Division; division organized at Camp Hancock, GA from NG personnel from Pennsylvania. Moved overseas Apr-Jun 1918. Returned to the US Apr 1919. Demobilized 17 May 1919 at Camp Dix, NJ.

Commanders: 15 Jul 1917: Maj Gen Charles M. Clement; 18 Sep 1918, Brig Gen William G. Price, Jr. (interim); 28 Oct 1917, Brig Gen Frederick W. Stillwell (interim); 4 Dec 1917, Maj Gen Charles M. Clement; 11 Dec 1918, Brig Gen Frederick W. Stillwell (interim); 15 Dec 1917, Maj Gen Charles H. Muir; 23 Oct 1918, Brig Gen Frank H. Albright (interim); 25 Oct 1918, Maj Gen William H. Hay; 16 Apr 1919, Maj Gen Charles H. Muir

Assignments: 17 May 1918, British Second Army; 9 Jun 1918, British First Army; 12 Jun 1918, French Tenth Army; 23 Jun 1918, French XXXVIII Corps; 8 Jul 1918, French III Corps; 17 Jul 1918, French III Corps (part) and French XXXVIII Corps (part); 20 Jul 1918, French XXXVIII Corps; 22 Jul 1918, I Army Corps (part) and French XXXVIII Corps (part); 25 Jul 1918, I Army Corps (part) and French III Corps (part); 26 Jul 1918, French XXXVIII Corps; 4 Aug 1918, III

Army Corps; 19 Sep 1918, French IX Corps; 21 Sep 1918, I Army
Corps; 10 Oct 1918, IV Army Corps; 17 Nov 1918, Second Army; 27
Nov 1918, VI Army Corps; 22 Dec 1918, Second Army; 10 Feb 1919,
IX Army Corps; 5 Mar 1919, SOS.

Nickname: "Keystone Division"

Campaign participation credit: Champagne-Marne, Aisne-Marne, Oise-Aisne,
Meuse-Argonne, Champagne 1918, Lorraine 1918

**29<sup>th</sup> Division** (National Guard) Headquarters organized 25 Aug 1917
at Camp McClellan, AL; division organized there with NG personnel from
Virginia, Maryland, Pennsylvania, and Washington, DC. (Delaware NG
personnel, originally assigned, were relieved from the division 8 Jan 1918.)
Moved overseas Jun-Jul 1918. Returned to the US May 1919. Demobilized 30
May 1919 at Camp Dix, NJ.

Commanders: 28 Jul 1917: Brig Gen Charles W. Barber; 25 Aug 1917: Maj
Gen Charles G. Morton; 24 Sep 1917, Brig Gen William C. Rafferty
(interim) ; 6 Dec 1917, Maj Gen Charles G. Morton; 11 Dec 1917, Brig
Gen William C. Rafferty (interim) ; 26 Dec 1917, Maj Gen Charles G.
Morton; 23 Mar 1918, Brig Gen William C. Rafferty (interim) ; 26 Mar
1918, Maj Gen Charles G. Morton; 11 Feb 1919, Brig Gen LaRoy S.
Upton (interim); 6 Mar 1919, Maj Gen Charles G. Morton; 19 Mar
1918, Brig Gen LaRoy S. Upton (interim), 22 Mar 1918, Maj Gen
Charles G. Morton; 13 Apr 1919, Brig Gen LaRoy S. Upton (interim),
20 Apr 1919, Maj Gen Charles G. Morton

Assignments: 28 Jun 1918, GHQ; 2 Jul 1918, IV Army Corps; 17 Jul 1918,
French Seventh Army; 18 Jul 1918, French XL Corps; 24 Sep 1918, V
Army Corps; 2 Oct 1918, French XVII Corps; 30 Oct 1918, V Army
Corps; 13 Nov 1918, VII Army Corps; 18 Nov 1918, First Army; 21
Nov 1918, V Army Corps; 11 Feb 1919, VIII Army Corps; 6 Apr 1919,
SOS.

Nickname: "Blue and Grey Division"

Campaign participation credit: Meuse-Argonne, Alsace 1918

**30<sup>th</sup> Division** (National Guard) Headquarters organized 28 Aug-12
Sep 1917 at Camp Sevier, SC; division organized there with NG personnel
from North Carolina, South Carolina and Tennessee. Moved overseas May-Jun
1918. Returned to the US Mar 1919. Demobilized 7 May 1919 at Camp
Jackson, SC.

Commanders: 28 Aug 1917, Maj Gen John F. Morrison; 19 Sep 1917, Brig Gen
William S. Scott (interim); 14 Oct 1917, Maj Gen Clarence P.
Townsley; 1 Dec 1917, Brig Gen Samson L. Faison (interim); 6 Dec
1917, Maj Gen Clarence P. Townsley; 17 Dec 1917, Brig Gen Samson
L. Faison (interim); 22 Dec 1917, Brig Gen Lawrence D. Tyson

(interim); 28 Dec 1917, Brig Gen George G. Gatley (interim); 1 Jan 1918, Brig Gen Samson L. Faison (interim); 30 Mar 1918, Brig Gen Lawrence D. Tyson (interim); 7 Apr 1918, Brig Gen Samson L. Faison (interim); 3 May 1918, Maj Gen George W. Read; 12 Jun 1918, Brig Gen Robert H. Noble (interim); 14 Jun 1918, Maj Gen George W. Read; 15 Jun 1918, Brig Gen Samson L. Faison (interim); 18 Jul 1918, Maj Gen Edward M. Lewis; 23 Dec 1918, Brig Gen Samson L. Faison (interim); 1 Jan 1919, Maj Gen Edward M. Lewis; 12 Jan 1919, Brig Gen Lawrence D. Tyson (interim); 15 Jan 1919, Maj Gen Edward M. Lewis; 12 Mar 1919, Brig Gen Samson L. Faison

Assignments: 24 May 1918, GHQ; 27 May 1918, British Second Army; 27 Jun 1918, British II Corps; 5 Sep 1918, British I Corps; 15 Sep 1918, British Third Army; 18 Sep 1918, British GHQ; 22 Sep 1918, Australian Corps; 25 Sep 1918, II Army Corps; 1 Feb 1919, SOS.

Nickname: "Old Hickory Division"

Campaign participation credit: Somme Offensive, Ypres-Lys, Flanders 1918

**31st Division**          (National Guard) Headquarters organized 25 Aug 1917 at Camp Wheeler, GA; division organized there with NG personnel from Alabama, Florida, and Georgia.  Moved overseas Sep-Nov 1918. Division (less field artillery) skeletonized on arrival and used as a replacement division. Returned to the US Dec 1918.  Demobilized 14 Jan 1919 at Camp Gordon, GA.

Commanders: 25 Aug 1917: Maj Gen Francis J. Kernan; 18 Sep 1917: Brig Gen John L. Hayden (interim); 21 Nov 1978, Brig Gen Walter A. Harris (interim); 23 Nov 1917, Brig Gen John L. Hayden (interim); 27 Dec 1917, Brig Gen Walter A. Harris (interim); 1 Jan 1918, Brig Gen John L. Hayden (interim); 15 Mar 1918, Maj Gen Francis H. French [reduced to Brig Gen 28 Mar 1918]; 15 May 1918: Maj Gen LeRoy S. Lyon; 18 Jul 1918, Brig Gen John L. Hayden (interim); 19 Jul 1918, Maj Gen LeRoy S. Lyon; 31 Jul 1918, Brig Gen Walter A. Harris (interim); 1 Aug 1918, Maj Gen LeRoy S. Lyon; 8 Sep 1918, Brig Gen Walter A. Harris  (interim); 14 Sep 1918, Maj Gen LeRoy S. Lyon; 28 Sep 1918, Brig Gen Walter A. Harris [to 14 Nov 1918]

Assignments: 15 Oct 1918, GHQ; 17 Oct 1918, SOS.

Nickname: "Dixie Division"

Campaign participation credit: Streamer without inscription

**32nd Division**          (National Guard) Headquarters organized 26 Aug 1917 at Camp MacArthur, TX; division organized there with NG personnel from Michigan and Wisconsin.  Moved overseas Jan-Mar 1918. (Served as replacement division for I Army Corps Feb-Apr 1918.) Moved into Germany on occupation duties and established Dec 1918 at Rengsdorf.  Returned to the US Apr-May 1919.  Demobilized 23 May 1919 at Camp Custer, MI.

Commanders: 26 Aug 1917, Maj Gen James Parker; 19 Sep 1917, Brig Gen
William G. Haan (interim); 7 Dec 1917, Maj Gen James Parker; 8 Dec
1917, Brig Gen [Maj Gen 7 Feb 1918] William G. Haan; 20 Nov 1918,
Maj Gen William Lassiter; 17 Feb 1919, Brig Gen Edwin B. Winans
(interim); 20 Feb 1919, Maj Gen William Lassiter; 23 Apr 1919, Maj
Gen William G. Haan

Assignments: 20 Feb 1918, GHQ; 14 May 1918, French XL Corps; 22 Jul
1918, French GHQ; 23 Jul 1918, III Army Corps; 26 Jul 1918, French
Sixth Army; 28 Jul 1918, French XXXVIII Corps; 4 Aug 1918, III
Army Corps; 23 Aug 1918, French Tenth Army; 27 Aug 1918, French
XXX Corps; 6 Sep 1918, French Tenth Army; 7 Sep 1918, French
Second Army; 10 Sep 1918, III Army Corps; 20 Sep 1918, V Army
Corps; 27 Oct 1918, III Army Corps; 8 Apr 1919, SOS.

Nickname: "Red Arrow Division"

Campaign participation credit: Aisne-Marne, Oise-Aisne, Meuse-Argonne,
Alsace 1918

**33rd Division**          (National Guard) Headquarters organized 27 Aug 1917
at Camp Logan, TX; division organized there with NG personnel from Illinois.
Moved overseas May-Jun 1918. Moved into Germany on occupation duties
and established Dec 1918 at Diekirch. Returned to the US May 1919.
Demobilized 6 Jun 1919 at Camp Grant, IL.

Commanders: 25 Aug 1917: Maj Gen George Bell, Jr.; 19 Sep 1917: Brig Gen
Henry D. Todd, Jr. (interim); 7 Dec 1917, Maj Gen George Bell, Jr.; 25
Jan 1919, Brig Gen Paul A. Wolf (interim); 26 Jan 1919, Brig Gen
Henry D. Todd, Jr. (interim); 29 Jan 1919, Maj Gen George Bell, Jr.; 4
Feb 1919, Brig Gen Henry D. Todd, Jr. (interim); 18 Feb 1919, Maj
Gen George Bell, Jr.; 28 Apr 1919, Brig Gen Henry D. Todd, Jr.
(interim); 3 May 1919, Maj Gen George Bell, Jr.

Assignments: 24 May 1918, GHQ; 25 May 1918, British Fourth Army; 27 May
1918, British XIX Corps; 21 Jun 1918, British III Corps; 17 Jul 1918,
British III Corps (part) and Australian Corps (part); 21 Aug 1918,
British Fourth Army; 25 Aug 1918, First Army; 27 Aug 1918, V Army
Corps; 5 Sep 1918, French XVII Corps; 14 Sep 1918, III Army Corps;
7 Oct 1918, French XVII Corps; 22 Oct 1918, French II Colonial
Corps; 6 Nov 1918, French XVII Corps; 13 Nov 1918, IV Army Corps;
17 Nov 1918, Second Army; 26 Nov 1918, IX Army Corps; 5 Dec
1918, Second Army; 12 Dec 1918, VII Army Corps; 17 Dec 1918,
Second Army; 19 Dec 1918, VI Army Corps; 11 Apr 1919, SOS.

Nickname: "Prairie Division"

Campaign participation credit: Somme Offensive, St. Mihiel, Meuse-Argonne,
Picardy 1918, Lorraine 1918

**34th Division** (National Guard) Headquarters organized 25 Aug 1917 at Camp Cody, NM; division organized there with NG personnel from North Dakota, South Dakota, Nebraska, Iowa and Minnesota. Moved overseas Sep-Oct 1918. Division (less field artillery) skeletonized on arrival and used as a replacement division. Returned to the US Dec 1918-Jan 1919. Demobilized 18 Feb 1919 at Camp Grant, IL.

Commanders: 25 Aug 1917: Brig Gen [Maj Gen 29 Aug 1917] Augustus P. Blocksom; 18 Sep 1917, Brig Gen Frank G. Mauldin (interim); 10 Dec 1917, Maj Gen Augustus P. Blocksom; 24 Dec 1917, Brig Gen Hubert A. Allen (interim); 27 Dec 1917, Maj Gen Augustus P. Blocksom [reduced to Brig Gen 19 Apr 1918]; 8 May 1918, Brig Gen Frank G. Mauldin (interim); 4 Jul 1918, Brig Gen John A. Johnston (interim); 24 Aug 1918, Brig Gen Hubert A. Allen (interim); 26 Aug 1918, Brig Gen John A. Johnston (interim); 22 Oct 1918, Maj Gen Beaumont B. Buck; 26 Oct 1918, Brig Gen John A. Johnston (interim)

Assignments: 29 Sep 1918, GHQ; 29 Oct 1918, SOS

Nickname: "Red Bull Division"

Campaign participation credit: Streamer without inscription

**35th Division** (National Guard) Headquarters organized 25 Aug 1917 at Camp Doniphan, OK; division organized there with NG personnel from Kansas and Missouri. Moved overseas Apr-Jun 1918. Returned to the US Apr 1919. Demobilized 26 May 1919 at Camp Funston, KS.

Commanders: 25 Aug 1917, Maj Gen William M. Wright; 18 Sep 1917, Brig Gen Lucien G. Berry (interim); 10 Dec 1917, Maj Gen William M. Wright; 25 Dec 1917, Brig Gen Lucien G. Berry (interim); 26 Dec 1917, Brig Gen Charles I. Martin (interim); 4 Jan 1918, Maj Gen William M. Wright; 15 Jun 1918, Brig Gen Nathaniel F. McClure; 20 Jul 1918, Maj Gen Peter E. Traub; 1 Nov 1918, Brig Gen Thomas B. Dugan (interim); 2 Nov 1918, Maj Gen Peter E. Traub; 25 Nov 1918, Brig Gen Thomas B. Dugan (interim); 7 Dec 1918, Maj Gen Peter E. Traub; 27 Dec 1918, Brig Gen Thomas B. Dugan; 31 Jan 1919, Brig Gen Lucien G. Berry (interim); 7 Feb 1919, Brig Gen Thomas B. Dugan; 26 Mar 1919, Maj Gen Peter E. Traub

Assignments: 11 May 1918, GHQ; 14 May 1918, British Fourth Army; 20 May 1918, British XIX Corps; 6 Jun 1918, French Seventh Army; 11 Jun 1918, French XXXIII Corps; 2 Sep 1918, I Army Corps; 18 Sep 1918, French Second Army; 19 Sep 1918, Group Mordacq; 20 Sep 1918, I Army Corps; 11 Oct 1918, French XXXIII Corps; 1 Nov 1918, French XVII Corps; 6 Nov 1918, French II Colonial Corps; 7 Nov 1918, III Army Corps; 8 Nov 1918, Second Army; 9 Nov 1918, French XVII Corps; 13 Nov 1918, IV Army Corps; 17 Nov 1918, Second Army; 26

Nov 1918, IX Army Corps; 10 Feb 1919, Second Army; 20 Feb 1919, SOS.

Nickname: "Sante Fe Division"

Campaign participation credit: Meuse-Argonne, Alsace 1918, Lorraine 1918

**36ᵗʰ Division** (National Guard) Headquarters organized 23 Aug 1917 at Camp Bowie, TX; division organized there with NG personnel from Texas and Oklahoma. Moved overseas Jul-Aug 1918. Returned to the US Jun 1919. Demobilized 18 Jun 1919 at Camp Bowie.

Commanders: 23 Aug 1917: Brig Gen [Maj Gen 31 Aug 1917] Edwin St. John Greble; 18 Sep 1917 Brig Gen George Blakely (interim); 6 Dec 1917, Maj Gen Edwin St. John Greble; 25 Dec 1917, Brig Gen George Blakely (interim); 2 Jan 1918, Maj Gen Edwin St. John Greble [reduced to Brig Gen 15 Mar 1918]; 8 Jul 1918, Brig Gen John A. Hulen (interim); 13 Jul 1918, Maj Gen William R. Smith; 25 Mar 1919, Brig Gen Pegram Whitworth (interim); 30 Mar 1919, Maj Gen William R. Smith; 4 May 1919, Brig Gen George H. Jamerson (interim); 14 May 1919, Maj Gen William R. Smith

Assignments: 30 Jul 1918, GHQ; 5 Aug 1918, IV Army Corps; 12 Aug 1918, VI Army Corps; 27 Aug 1918, GHQ; 2 Sep 1918, VI Army Corps; 15 Sep 1918, First Army; 23 Sep 1918, French GAC; 4 Oct 1918, French Fourth Army; 6 Oct 1918, French XXI Corps; 18 Oct 1918, French XI Corps; 28 Oct 1918, French Fourth Army; 30 Oct 1918, I Army Corps; 13 Nov 1918, VII Army Corps; 16 Nov 1918, First Army; 21 Nov 1918, I Army Corps; 25 Mar 1919, VIII Army Corps; 15 Apr 1919, SOS.

Nickname: "Texas Division"

Campaign participation credit: Meuse-Argonne

**37ᵗʰ Division** (National Guard) Headquarters organized 26 Aug 1917 at Camp Sheridan, AL; division organized there with NG personnel from Ohio. (Originally to include West Virginia as well, but that state transferred to 38ᵗʰ Division.) Moved overseas Jun-Jul 1918. Returned to the US Mar-Apr 1919. Demobilized 23 Jun 1919 at Camp Sherman, OH.

Commanders: 26 Aug 1917, Brig Gen William R. Smith; 3 Sep 1917, Maj Gen Charles G. Treat; 18 Sep 1917, Brig Gen William R. Smith (interim); 13 Nov 1917, Brig Gen William V. McMaken (interim); 18 Nov 1917, Brig Gen William R. Smith (interim); 5 Dec 1917, Maj Gen Charles G. Treat; 6 Dec 1917, Brig Gen William R. Smith (interim); 9 Dec 1917, Maj Gen Charles G. Treat; 29 Mar 1918, Brig Gen William R. Smith (interim); 1 Apr 1918, Brig Gen Joseph A. Gaston (interim); 4 Apr 1918, Maj Gen Charles G. Treat; 25 Apr 1918, Brig Gen Joseph A. Gaston (interim); 8 May 1918, Maj Gen Charles S. Farnsworth; 5 Dec

1918, Brig Gen William M. Fassett (interim); 10 Dec 1918, Maj Gen
Charles S. Farnsworth; 3 Mar 1919, Brig Gen Sanford B. Stanbery
(interim); 7 Mar 1919, Maj Gen Charles S. Farnsworth; 6 Apr 1919,
Col Robert S. Abernethy (interim); 12 Apr 1919, Col George W. Stuart
(interim)
Assignments: 22 Jun 1918, GHQ; 2 Jul 1918, IV Army Corps; 22 Jul 1918,
French VI Corps; 17 Sep 1918, French Second Army; 20 Sep 1918, V
Army Corps; 2 Oct 1918, IV Army Corps; 16 Oct 1918, Second Army;
22 Oct 1918, French GAF; 29 Oct 1918, French XXX Corps; 7 Nov
1918, French XXXIV Corps; 2 Dec 1918, French XXX Corps; 12 Jan
1919, II Army Corps; 1 Feb 1919, SOS.
Nickname: "Buckeye Division"
Campaign participation credit: Ypres-Lys, Meuse-Argonne, Lorraine 1918

**38th Division**          (National Guard) Headquarters organized 25 Aug 1917
at Camp Shelby, MS; division organized there with NG personnel from
Indiana, Kentucky, and West Virginia.  Moved overseas Sep-Oct 1918.
Division (less field artillery and engineers) skeletonized on arrival and used a s
replacement division.  Returned to the US Dec 1918. Demobilized 8 Mar 1919
at Camp Zachary Taylor, KY.
Commanders: 25 Aug 1917, Maj Gen William H. Sage; 19 Sep 1917, Brig Gen
Edward M. Lewis (interim); 8 Nov 1917, Brig Gen Henry H. Whitney
(interim); 12 Dec 1917, Maj Gen William H. Sage [reduced 15 Mar
1918 to Brig Gen]; 15 Apr 1918, Brig Gen William V. Judson
(interim); 10 Jul 1918, Brig Gen Frank M. Caldwell (interim); 12 Jul
1918, Brig Gen Augustine McIntyre (interim); 18 Jul 1918, Brig Gen
Frank M. Caldwell (interim); 30 Aug 1918, Maj Gen Robert L. Howze;
18 Oct 1918, Brig Gen Frank M. Caldwell (interim); 24 Oct 1918, Col
George T. Smith (interim); 27 Oct 1918, Maj Gen Robert L. Howze
Assignments: 11 Oct 1918, GHQ; 17 Oct 1918, SOS.
Nickname: "Cyclone Division"
Campaign participation credit: Streamer without inscription

**39th Division**          (National Guard) Headquarters organized 25 Aug 1917
at Camp Beauregard, LA; division organized there with NG personnel from
Louisiana, Mississippi and Arkansas.  Moved overseas Aug-Sep 1918.
Division (less field artillery, engineers, and 141st MG Bn) reorganized 22 Aug
1918 as 5th Depot Division. (5th Depot Division skeletonized 29 Oct 1918.)
Returned to the US Dec 1918.  Demobilized 23 Jan 1919 at Camp Beauregard.
Commanders: 25 Aug 1917, Maj Gen Henry C. Hodges, Jr.; 18 Sep 1917, Brig
Gen Ira A. Haynes (interim); 1 Oct 1918, Maj Gen Henry C. Hodges,
Jr.; 2 Nov 1917, Brig Gen Ira A. Haynes (interim); 18 Nov 1917, Maj
Gen Henry C. Hodges, Jr.; 27 Nov 1917, Brig Gen Ira A. Haynes

(interim); 25 Feb 1918, Maj Gen Henry C. Hodges, Jr.; 23 Mar 1918, Brig Gen Ira A. Haynes (interim); 27 Mar 1918, Maj Gen Henry C. Hodges, Jr.

Assignments: 27 Aug 1918, SOS

Campaign participation credit: Streamer without inscription

**40th Division** (National Guard) Headquarters organized 25 Aug 1917 at Camp Kearny, CA; division organized there with NG personnel from California, Nevada, Utah, Colorado, Arizona and New Mexico. Moved overseas Jul-Sep 1918. Division (less engineers) reorganized 28 Aug 1918 as 6th Depot Division. Tasked ca. Oct 1918 to serve as regional replacement depot for First Army. Returned to the US Feb-Mar 1919. Demobilized 20 Apr 1919 at Camp Kearny.

Commanders: 25 Aug 1917, Maj Gen Frederick S. Strong; 18 Sep 1917, Brig Gen George H. Cameron (interim); 19 Nov 1917, Brig Gen LeRoy S. Lyon (interim); 23 Nov 1917, Brig Gen George H. Cameron (interim); 6 Dec 1917, Brig Gen LeRoy S. Lyon (interim); 8 Dec 1917, Maj Gen Frederick S. Strong

Assignments: 20 Aug 1918, SOS.

Nickname: "Sunshine Division"

Campaign participation credit: Streamer without inscription

**41st Division** (National Guard) Headquarters organized 18 Sep 1917 at Camp Greene, NC; division organized there with NG personnel from Washington, Oregon, Montana, and Wyoming.[39] Moved overseas Nov 1917-Feb 1918. (Tasked as replacement division for I Army Corps 8 Dec 1917; changed 15 Jan 1918 to base and training division for I Army Corps; from 5 Mar 1918 also served as depot division for I Army Corps.) Division (less field artillery) reorganized 13 Jul 1918 as 1st Depot Division. 1st Depot Division abolished and 41st Division reassembled 26 Dec 1918. Returned to the US Feb 1919. Demobilized 22 Feb 1919 at Camp Dix, NJ.

Commanders: 18 Sep 1917 Maj Gen Hunter Liggett; 20 Sep 1917, Brig Gen Henry Jervey (interim); 12 Dec 1917, Brig Gen George LeR. Irwin (interim); 20 Dec 1917, Maj Gen Hunter Liggett; 18 Jan 1918, Brig Gen George LeR. Irwin (interim); 23 Jan 1918, Brig Gen Richard Coulter, Jr. (interim); 14 Feb 1918, Brig Gen Robert Alexander; 28 Feb 1918, Brig Gen Edward Vollrath (interim); 11 Mar 1918, Brig Gen Robert Alexander; 14 Apr 1918, Brig Gen Edward Vollrath (interim); 24 Apr 1918, Brig Gen Robert Alexander; 3 Aug 1918, Brig Gen

---

[39] The division was to have organized at Camp Fremont, CA; delays in preparing that camp led to organization at Camp Greene, NC, a site originally intended for the new 26th Division but available when that division organized at various locations in New England and was tasked for early shipment overseas.

Edward Vollrath (interim); 19 Aug 1918, Brig Gen William S. Scott;
21 Oct 1918, Maj Gen John E. McMahon; 24 Oct 1918, Brig Gen
Edward Vollrath (interim); 29 Oct 1918, Brig Gen Eli K. Cole, USMC;
27 Dec 1918, Brig Gen Edward Vollrath (interim); 29 Dec 1918, Maj
Gen Peter E. Traub

Assignments: 8 Jan 1918, GHQ; 20 Jan 1918, I Army Corps; 11 Apr 1918,
SOS.

Nickname: "Sunset Division"

Campaign participation credit: Streamer without inscription

**42nd Division** (National Guard) Headquarters organized 5 Sep 1917
at Camp Mills, NY; division organized with NG personnel from various parts
of the country (in part, units rendered surplus by the new divisional
organization). Moved overseas Oct-Dec 1917. Moved into Germany on
occupation duties and established Dec 1918 at Ahrweiler. Returned to the US
Apr-May 1919. Demobilized 9 May 1919 at Camp Dix, NJ.

Commanders: 5 Sep 1917, Maj Gen William A. Mann; 19 Dec 1917, Maj Gen
Charles T. Menoher; 10 Nov 1918, Brig Gen Douglas MacArthur; 22
Nov 1918, Maj Gen Clement A. F. Flagler; 28 Mar 1919, Brig Gen
George G. Gatley (interim); 10 Apr 1919, Maj Gen George W. Read

Assignments: 1 Nov 1917, GHQ; 16 Feb 1918, French VII Corps; 12 May
1918, French VI Corps;22 Jun 1918, French Eighth Army; 23 Jun
1918, French V Corps; 2 Jul 1918, French Fourth Army; 3 Jul 1918,
French XXI Corps; 18 Jul 1918, French Fourth Army; 20 Jul 1918,
French Sixth Army; 21 Jul 1918, I Army Corps; 17 Aug 1918, GHQ;
18 Aug 1918, IV Army Corps; 1 Oct 1918, First Army; 4 Oct 1918, V
Army Corps; 1 Nov 1918, I Army Corps; 10 Nov 1918, V Army
Corps; 14 Nov 1918, III Army Corps; 13 Dec 1918, IV Army Corps;
17 Mar 1919, Third Army; 1 Apr 1919, SOS.

Nickname: "Rainbow Division"

Campaign participation credit: Champagne-Marne, Aisne-Marne, St. Mihiel,
Meuse-Argonne, Champagne 1918, Lorraine 1918

**76th Division** (National Army) Headquarters organized 25 Aug 1917
at Camp Devens, MA; division organized with personnel from Maine, New
Hampshire, Vermont, Massachusetts, Rhode Island and Connecticut . Moved
overseas Jul-Aug 1918. Division (less field artillery, engineers, and 302nd
Infantry) reorganized 3 Aug 1918 as 3rd Depot Division. 3rd Depot Division
skeletonized 7 Nov 1918. Returned to the US Dec 1918. Demobilized 14 Jan
1919 at Camp Devens.

Commanders: 25 Aug 1917, Maj Gen Harry F. Hodges; 28 Nov 1917, Brig Gen
William Weigel (interim); 13 Feb 1918, Maj Gen Harry F. Hodges; 11
Jun 1918, Brig Gen Frank H. Albright (interim); 13 Jun 1918, Maj Gen

Harry F. Hodges; 22 Nov 1918, Lt Col Will D. Wills; 27 Nov 1918, Lt Col William C. Danks

Assignments: 14 Jul 1918, SOS.

Campaign participation credit: Streamer without inscription

**77th Division**　　　　(National Army) Headquarters organized 18 Aug 1917 at Camp Upton, NY; division organized with personnel from Metropolitan New York City. Moved overseas Mar-May 1918. Returned to the US Apr 1919. Demobilized 9 May 1919 at Camp Upton.

Commanders: 18 Aug 1917, Maj Gen J. Franklin Bell; 2 Dec 1917, Maj Gen George W. Read (interim); 4 Dec 1917, Brig Gen Evan M. Johnson (interim); 8 Mar 1918, Brig Gen Edmund Wittenmyer (interim); 9 Mar 1918, Brig Gen Evan M. Johnson (interim); 21 Mar 1918, Maj Gen J. Franklin Bell; 25 Mar 1918, Brig Gen Evan M. Johnson (interim); 8 May 1918, Maj Gen George B. Duncan; 20 Jul 1918, Brig Gen Evan M. Johnson (interim); 28 Jul 1918, Maj Gen George B. Duncan; 19 Aug 1918, Brig Gen Evan M. Johnson (interim); 27 Aug 1918, Maj Gen Robert Alexander; 14 Jan 1919, Brig Gen Michael J. Lenihan (interim); 24 Jan 1919, Maj Gen Robert Alexander; 17 Mar 1919, Brig Gen Michael J. Lenihan (interim); 25 Mar 1919, Maj Gen Robert Alexander; 10 Apr 1919, Brig Gen Michael J. Lenihan (interim); 16 Apr 1919, Maj Gen Robert Alexander

Assignments: 12 Apr 1918, GHQ; 15 Apr 1918, British Second Army [one brigade to British Third Army 14 May 1918]; 6 Jun 1918, French Eighth Army; 12 Jun 1918, French VI Corps; 4 Aug 1918, French Eighth Army; 6 Aug 1918, I Army Corps; 13 Aug 1918, III Army Corps; 9 Sep 1918, French XVI Corps; 16 Sep 1918, French Fifth Army; 17 Sep 1918, French Second Army; 18 Sep 1918, Group Mordacq; 20 Sep 1918, I Army Corps; 10 Nov 1918, V Army Corps; 21 Nov 1918, First Army; 26 Nov 1918, VIII Army Corps; 12 Feb 1919, SOS.

Nickname: "Statue of Liberty Division"

Campaign participation credit: Oise-Aisne, Meuse-Argonne, Champagne 1918, Lorraine 1918

**78th Division**　　　　(National Army) Headquarters organized 23 Aug 1917 at Camp Dix, NJ; division organized with personnel from New York and northern Pennsylvania. Moved overseas May-Jun 1918. Returned to the US May-Jun 1919. Demobilized 9 Jun 1919 at Camp Dix.

Commanders: 23 Aug 1917, Maj Gen Chase W. Kennedy; 28 Nov 1917, Brig Gen John S. Mallory (interim); 28 Dec 1917, Brig Gen James T. Dean (interim); 2 Jan 1918, Maj Gen Hugh L. Scott; 21 Feb 1918, Brig Gen James T. Dean (interim); 24 Feb 1918, Maj Gen Hugh L. Scott; 16 Mar

1918, Brig Gen James T. Dean (interim); 20 Apr 1918, Brig Gen [Maj Gen 30 Apr 1918] James H. McRae; 1 May 1918, Brig Gen James T. Dean (interim); 3 May 1918, Maj James H. McRae; 16 Feb 1919, Brig Gen James T. Dean (interim); 2 Mar 1919, Maj James H. McRae; 30 Mar 1919, Brig Gen Clint C. Hearn (interim); 2 Apr 1919, Brig Gen Otho B. Rosenbaum (interim); 4 Apr 1919, Maj James H. McRae; 9 Apr 1919, Brig Gen Otho B. Rosenbaum (interim); 11 Apr 1919, Brig Gen James T. Dean (interim); 12Apr 1919, Maj James H. McRae;

Assignments: 4 Jun 1918, British Second Army; 18 Jul 1918, British XVII Corps; 21 Aug 1918, GHQ; 25 Aug 1918, First Army; 27 Aug 1918, IV Army Corps; 3 Sep 1918, I Army Corps; 18 Sep 1918, IV Army Corps; 5 Oct 1918, I Army Corps; 10 Nov 1918, VII Army Corps; 15 Nov 1918, GHQ; 21 Nov 1918, I Army Corps; 25 Mar 1919, VIII Army Corps; 6 Apr 1919, SOS.

Nickname: "Lightning Division"

Campaign participation credit: St. Mihiel, Meuse-Argonne, Lorraine 1918

**79ᵗʰ Division** (National Army) Headquarters organized 25 Aug 1917 at Camp Meade, MD; division organized with personnel from southern Pennsylvania. Moved overseas Jul-Aug 1918. Returned to the US May 1919. Demobilized Jun 1919 at Camp Dix, NJ.

Commanders: 25 Aug 1917, Brig Gen [Maj Gen 29 Aug 1917] Joseph E. Kuhn; 26 Nov 1917, Brig Gen William J. Nicholson (interim); 17 Feb 1918, Maj Gen Joseph E. Kuhn; 15 Apr 1918, Brig Gen William J. Nicholson (interim); 16 Apr 1918, Maj Gen Joseph E. Kuhn; 22 May 1918, Brig Gen William J. Nicholson (interim); 8 Jun 1918, Maj Gen Joseph E. Kuhn; 28 Jun 1918, Brig Gen William J. Nicholson (interim); 23 Jul 1918, Maj Gen Joseph E. Kuhn; 29 Dec 1918, Brig Gen Evan M. Johnson (interim); 31 Dec 1918, Maj Gen Joseph E. Kuhn; 19 Jan 1919, Brig Gen Evan M. Johnson (interim); 2 Feb 1919, Brig Gen John S. Winn (interim); 3 Feb 1919, Brig Gen Andrew Hero, Jr. (interim); 9 Feb 1919, Brig Gen Evan M. Johnson (interim); 28 Feb 1919, Maj Gen Joseph E. Kuhn; 16 Mar 1919, Brig Gen Evan M. Johnson (interim); 30 Mar 1919, Maj Gen Joseph E. Kuhn; 4 May 1919, Brig Gen John S. Winn (interim); 8 May 1919, Maj Gen Joseph E. Kuhn

Assignments: 16 Jul 1918, GHQ; 27 Jul 1918, IV Army Corps; 12 Aug 1918, VI Army Corps; 9 Sep 1918, French Second Army; 12 Sep 1918, French XVII Corps; 14 Sep 1918, III Army Corps; 21 Sep 1918, V Army Corps; 30 Sep 1918, III Army Corps; 3 Oct 1918, French II Colonial Corps; 26 Oct 1918, French XVII Corps; 6 Nov 1918, French II Colonial Corps; 21 Nov 1918, VII Army Corps; 22 Nov 1918, First Army; 5 Dec 1918, IX Army Corps; 10 Apr 1919, SOS.

Nickname: "Lorraine Division"
Campaign participation credit: Meuse-Argonne, Lorraine 1918

**80th Division** (National Army) Headquarters organized 27 Aug 1917 at Camp Lee, VA; division organized with personnel from New Jersey, Virginia, Maryland, Delaware and District of Columbia. Moved overseas May-Jun 1918. Returned to the US May 1919. Demobilized 7 Jun 1919 at Camp Lee.

Commanders: 27 Aug 1917, Brig Gen Herman Hall (interim); 9 Sep 1917, Maj Gen Adlebert Cronkhite; 26 Nov 1917, Brig Gen Lloyd M. Brett (interim); 27 Dec 1917, Brig Gen Charles S. Farnsworth (interim); 28 Dec 1917, Brig Gen Wilds P. Richardson (interim); 6 Jan 1918, Brig Gen Gordon G. Heiner (interim); 7 Jan 1918, Brig Gen Charles S. Farnsworth (interim); 11 Jan 1918, Brig Gen Wilds P. Richardson (interim); 14 Jan 1918, Brig Gen Lloyd M. Brett (interim); 1 Mar 1918, Maj Gen Adlebert Cronkhite; 22 Nov 1918, Maj Gen Samuel D. Sturgis; 12 Apr 1919, Maj Gen Adlebert Cronkhite

Assignments: 31 May 1918, GHQ; 7 Jun 1918, British First Army; 28 Jun 1918, British Second Army; 4 Jul 1918, British Third Army; 23 Jul 1918, elements in line with British IV, V and VI Corps; 19 Aug 1918, British Third Army then GHQ; 27 Aug 1918, V Army Corps; 14 Sep 1918, III Army Corps; 22 Oct 1918, I Army Corps; 9 Nov 1918, V Army Corps; 13 Nov 1918, VII Army Corps; 16 Nov 1918, First Army; 21 Nov 1918, I Army Corps; 20 Mar 1919, SOS.

Nickname: "Blue Ridge Division"
Campaign participation credit: Somme Offensive, Meuse-Argonne

**81st Division** (National Army) Headquarters organized 25 Aug 1917 at Camp Jackson, SC; division organized with personnel from Tennessee, North Carolina and South Carolina. Moved overseas Jul-Aug 1918. Returned to the US Jun 1919. Demobilized 11 Jun 1919 at Hoboken, NJ.

Commanders: 25 Aug 1917, Brig Gen Charles H. Barth; 8 Oct 1917, Maj Gen Charles J. Bailey; 24 Nov 1917, Brig Gen Charles H. Barth (interim); 28 Dec 1917, Brig Gen George W. McIver (interim); 11 Mar 1918, Maj Gen Charles J. Bailey; 19 May 1918, Brig Gen George W. McIver (interim); 24 May 1918, Brig Gen Monroe McFarland (interim); 29 May 1918, Brig Gen George W. McIver (interim); 30 May 1918, Maj Gen Charles J. Bailey; 9 Jun 1918, Brig Gen George W. McIver (interim); 26 Jun 1918, Maj Gen Charles J. Bailey; 30 Jun 1918, Brig Gen George W. McIver (interim); 3 Jul 1918, Maj Gen Charles J. Bailey; 11 Apr 1919, Brig Gen George W. McIver (interim); 13 Apr 1919, Brig Gen Monroe McFarland (interim); 18 Apr 1919, Brig Gen Andrew Moses (interim); 20 Apr 1919, Brig Gen George W. McIver (interim); 23 Apr 1919, Maj Gen Charles J. Bailey; 27 Apr 1919, Brig Gen George W. McIver (interim); 2 May 1919, Maj Gen Charles J. Bailey; 23 May 1919, Brig Gen George W. McIver (interim); 25 May 1919, Brig Gen Monroe McFarland (interim)

Assignments: 16 Aug 1918, GHQ; 2 Sep 1918, VI Army Corps; 15 Sep 1918, French Second Army; 17 Sep 1918, French XXXIII Corps; 1 Oct 1918, French X Corps; 20 Oct 1918, French Seventh Army; 2 Nov 1918, French XVII Corps; 6 Nov 1918, French II Colonial Corps; 18 Nov 1918, First Army; 1 Dec 1918, VIII Army Corps; 20 Apr 1919, IX Army Corps; 2 May 1919, SOS.

Nickname: "Wild Cat Division"

Campaign participation credit: Meuse-Argonne, Lorraine 1918

**82nd Division**          (National Army) Headquarters organized 25 Aug 1917 at Camp Gordon, GA; division organized with personnel from Georgia, Alabama and Florida.  Moved overseas Apr-Jul 1918.  Returned to the US Apr-May 1919.  Demobilized 27 May 1919 at Camp Mills, NY.

Commanders: 25 Aug 1917, Maj Gen Eben Swift; 24 Nov 1917, Brig Gen James B. Erwin (interim); 27 Dec 1917, Brig Gen William P. Burnham (interim); 23 Mar 1918, Brig Gen Marcus D. Cronin (interim); 28 Mar 1918, Brig Gen [Maj Gen 23 May 1918] William P. Burnham; 4 Oct 1918, Maj Gen George B. Duncan; 17 Mar 1919, Brig Gen  Julian R. Lindsey (interim); 28 Mar 1919, Maj Gen George B. Duncan

Assignments: 7 May 1918, British GHQ; 16 May 1918, British Fourth Army; 20 May 1918, British XIX Corps; 11 Jun 1918, French GAE; 18 Jun 1918, French Eighth Army; 22 Jun 1918, French XXXII Corps; 10 Aug 1918, French Eighth Army; 14 Aug 1918, French XXXII Corps; 22 Aug 1918, I Army Corps; 18 Sep 1918, IV Army Corps; 20 Sep 1918, I Army Corps; 7 Nov 1918, GHQ; 21 Nov 1918, V Army Corps; 11 Feb 1919, SOS.

Nickname: "All American Division"

Campaign participation credit: St. Mihiel, Meuse-Argonne, Lorraine 1918

**83rd Division**          (National Army) Headquarters organized 25 Aug 1917 at Camp Sherman, OH; division organized with personnel from Ohio and West Virginia.  Moved overseas Jun-Aug 1918.  Division (less field artillery, engineers, and 332nd Infantry) reorganized 27 Jun 1918 as 2nd Depot Division. Returned to the US Jan 1919.  Demobilized 8 Oct 1919 at Camp Sherman.[40]

Commanders: 25 Aug 1917: Brig Gen [Maj Gen 7 Sep 1917] Edwin F. Glenn; 13 Jan 1918, Brig Gen Frederick Perkins (interim); 23 Mar 1918, Brig

---

[40] While Division Hq was demobilized in Oct 1919, the bulk of the division had been demobilized Feb-May 1919.

Gen Willard A. Holbrook (interim); 3 Apr 1918, Maj Gen Edwin F.
Glenn; 4 Jan 1919, Brig Gen Wilber E. Wilder (interim); 12 Jan 1919,
Maj Gen Edwin F. Glenn; 31 Jan 1919, Brig Gen Wilber E. Wilder
(interim); 6 Feb 1919, Brig Gen Louis C. Covell (interim); 10 Feb
1919, Maj Gen Edwin F. Glenn
Assignments: 17 Jun 1918, GHQ; 8 Jul 1918, SOS
Nickname: "Ohio Division"
Campaign participation credit: Streamer without inscription

**84th Division** (National Army) Headquarters organized 25 Aug 1917
at Camp Zachary Taylor, KY; division organized with personnel from Indiana
and Kentucky. Moved overseas Aug-Oct 1918. Division (less field artillery
and engineers) skeletonized 3 Oct 1918 and used as replacement division.
Returned to the US Jan 1919. Demobilized 26 Jul 1919 at Camp Zachary
Taylor.
Commanders: 25 Aug 1917: Col [Brig Gen 29 Aug 1917] Wilber E. Wilder
(interim); 6 Oct 1917, Maj Gen Harry C. Hale; 26 Nov 1917, Brig Gen
Wilber E. Wilder (interim); 13 Dec Brig Gen Daniel B. Devore
(interim); 15 Dec 1917, Brig Gen Wilber E. Wilder (interim); 1 Mar
1918, Maj Gen Harry C. Hale; 1 Jun 1918, Brig Gen Wilber E. Wilder
(interim); 5 Jun 1918, Maj Gen Harry C. Hale; 19 Jul 1918, Brig Gen
Wilber E. Wilder (interim); 21 Jul 1918, Maj Gen Harry C. Hale; 18
Oct 1918, Brig Gen Wilber E. Wilder (interim); 31 Oct 1918, Maj Gen
Harry C. Hale
Assignments: 25 Sep 1918, GHQ; 4 Oct 1918, SOS
Nickname: "Railsplitters"
Campaign participation credit: Streamer without inscription

**85th Division** (National Army) Headquarters organized 25 Aug 1917
at Camp Custer, MI; division organized with personnel from Michigan and
Wisconsin. Moved overseas Jul-Aug 1918. Division (less field artillery,
engineers, and 339th Infantry) reorganized 28 Jul 1918 as 4th Depot Division.
Tasked ca. Oct 1918 to serve as regional replacement depot for Second Army.
Returned to the US Mar 1919. Demobilized 18 Apr 1919 at Camp Custer.
Commanders: 25 Aug 1917, Maj Gen Joseph T. Dickman; 25 Nov 1917, Brig
Gen Samuel W. Miller (interim); 13 Dec 1918, Maj Gen James Parker;
21 Feb 1918, Brig Gen Benjamin C. Morse (interim); 27 Feb 1918,
Maj Gen Chase W. Kennedy; 3 Aug 1918, Brig Gen Thomas B. Dugan
(interim); 6 Aug 1918, Maj Gen Chase W. Kennedy; 14 Aug 1918,
Brig Gen Thomas B. Dugan (interim); 16 Aug 1918, Maj Gen Chase
W. Kennedy; 26 Oct 1918, Col Benjamin W. Atkinson (interim); 28
Oct 1918, Maj Gen Chase W. Kennedy; 23 Dec 1918, Brig Gen
George D. Moore (interim); 1 Jan 1919, Maj Gen Chase W. Kennedy;

1 Apr 1919, Brig Gen William C. Rivers (interim); 5 Apr 1919, Col Benjamin W. Atkinson (interim)

Assignments: 10 Aug 1918, SOS; 30 Oct 1918, Second Army; 13 Jan 1919, SOS

Nickname: "Custer Division"

Campaign participation credit: Streamer without inscription

**86<sup>th</sup> Division** (National Army) Headquarters organized 25 Aug 1917 at Camp Grant, IL; division organized with personnel from Illinois. Moved overseas Sep-Oct 1918. Division (less field artillery and engineers) skeletonized 3 Oct 1918 and used as replacement division. Returned to the US Jan 1919. Demobilized in Jan 1919 at Camp Grant.

Commanders: 25 Aug 1917, Maj Gen Thomas H. Berry; 16 Nov 1917, Brig Gen Lyman W. V. Kennon (interim); 15 Feb 1918, Maj Gen Thomas H. Berry ; 21 Mar 1918, Brig Gen Lyman W. V. Kennon (interim); 18 Apr 1918, Brig Gen [Maj Gen 30 Apr 1918] Charles H. Martin; 19 Oct 1918, Brig Gen Lincoln C. Andrews (interim); 24 Oct 1918, Col Guy G. Palmer (interim); 8 Nov 1918, Brig Gen Francis LeJ. Parker (interim); 9 Nov 1918, Brig Gen Lincoln C. Andrews (interim)

Assignments: 23 Sep 1918, GHQ; 4 Oct 1918, SOS

Nickname: "Black Hawk Division"

Campaign participation credit: Streamer without inscription

**87<sup>th</sup> Division** (National Army) Headquarters organized 27 Aug 1917 at Camp Pike, AR; division organized with personnel from Arkansas, Louisiana and Mississippi. Moved overseas Jun-Sep 1918. The division was broken up for laborers by the Services of Supply. Returned to the US Jan 1919. Demobilized 14 Feb 1919 at Camp Pike.

Commanders: 25 Aug 1917, Brig Gen [Maj Gen 28 Aug 1917] Samuel D. Sturgis; 13 Nov 1917, Brig Gen Robert C. Van Vliet (interim); 17 Nov 1917, Maj Gen Samuel D. Sturgis; 27 Nov 1917, Brig Gen Robert C. Van Vliet (interim); 10 Mar 1918, Maj Gen Samuel D. Sturgis; 2 Oct 1918, Brig Gen William F. Martin (interim); 23 Oct 1918, Maj Gen Samuel D. Sturgis; 22 Nov 1918, Brig Gen William F. Martin; 11 Jan 1919, Col Pearl M. Schaffer (interim); 20 Jan 1919, Brig Gen Marcus D. Cronin (interim); 21 Jan 1919, Brig Gen William F. Martin

Assignments: 9 Sep 1918, GHQ; 16 Sep 1918, SOS

Nickname: "Acorn Division"

Campaign participation credit: Streamer without inscription

**88ᵗʰ Division**          (National Army) 25 Aug 1917 at Camp Dodge, IA; division organized with personnel from Minnesota, Iowa, Nebraska, North Dakota and South Dakota. Moved overseas Aug-Sep 1918. Returned to the US May-Jun 1919. Demobilized 10 Jun 1919 at Camp Dodge.

Commanders: 25 Aug 1917 Maj Gen Edward H. Plummer; 27 Nov 1917, Brig
    Gen Robert N. Getty (interim); 19 Feb 1918, Maj Gen Edward H.
    Plummer; 15 Mar 1918, Brig Gen Robert N. Getty (interim); 24 May
    1918, Brig Gen William D. Beach (interim); 10 Sep 1918, Maj Gen
    William Weigel; 19 Jan 1919, Brig Gen Merch B. Stewart (interim);
    23 Jan 1919, Maj Gen William Weigel; 30 Mar 1918, Brig Gen
    William D. Beach (interim); 13 Apr 1919, Maj Gen William Weigel

Assignments: 2 Sep 1918, VI Army Corps; 15 Sep 1918, French Seventh
    Army; 22 Sep 1918, French XL Corps; 4 Nov 1918, French Seventh
    Army; 6 Nov 1918, Second Army (part) and IV Army Corps (part); 10
    Nov 1918, Second Army; 13 Nov 1918, VI Army Corps; 27 Nov 1918,
    Second Army; 5 Dec 1918, IX Army Corps; 26 Apr 1919, SOS

Campaign participation credit: Alsace 1918

**89ᵗʰ Division**          (National Army) Headquarters organized 13 Aug 1917 at Camp Funston, KS; division organized with personnel from Missouri, Kansas and Colorado. Moved overseas Jun-Jul 1918. Moved into Germany on occupation duties and established Dec 1918 at Kylburg. Returned to the US May 1919. Demobilized 12 Jun 1919 at Camp Funston.

Commanders: 27 Aug 1917, Maj Gen Leonard Wood; 6 Nov 1917, Brig Gen
    Frank L. Winn (interim); 12 Nov 1917, Maj Gen Leonard Wood; 26
    Nov 1917, Brig Gen Frank L. Winn (interim); 24 Dec 1917, Brig Gen
    Thomas G. Hanson (interim); 29 Dec 1917, Brig Gen Frank L. Winn
    (interim); 7 Jan 1918, Col James H. Reeves (interim); 10 Jan 1918,
    Brig Gen Frank L. Winn (interim); 12 Apr 1918, Maj Gen Leonard
    Wood; 1 Jun 1918, Brig Gen Frank L. Winn; 6 Sep 1918, Maj Gen
    William M. Wright; 12 Nov 1918, Maj Gen Frank L. Winn; 4 Feb
    1919, Brig Gen Hermann Hall (interim); 7 Feb 1919, Maj Gen Frank L.
    Winn; 29 Mar 1919, Brig Gen Edward T. Donnelly (interim); 31 Mar
    1919, Brig Gen Hermann Hall (interim); 2 Apr 1919, Maj Gen Frank
    L. Winn

Assignments: 21 Jun 1918, GHQ; 23 Jun 1918, IV Army Corps; 5 Aug 1918,
    French XXXII Corps; 20 Aug 1918, IV Army Corps; 8 Oct 1918, III
    Army Corps; 12 Oct 1918, V Army Corps; 21 Nov 1918, VII Army
    Corps; 25 Apr 1919, SOS

Nickname: "Middle West Division"

Campaign participation credit: St. Mihiel, Meuse-Argonne

**90<sup>th</sup> Division**          (National Army) Headquarters organized 25 Aug 1917 at Camp Travis, TX; division organized with personnel from Texas, Oklahoma, Arizona and New Mexico.  Moved overseas Jun -Jul 1918.  Moved into Germany on occupation duties and established Dec 1918 at Berncastel. Returned to the US Jun 1919.  Demobilized 17 Jun 1919 at Camp Bowie, TX.
Commanders: 25 Aug 1917 Maj Gen Henry T. Allen;  23 Nov 1917, Brig Gen
       Joseph A. Gaston (interim); 27 Dec 1917, Brig Gen William H.
       Johnston (interim); 1 Mar 1918, Maj Gen Henry T. Allen;  24 Nov
       1918, Brig Gen Joseph P. O'Neil (interim); 30 Dec 1918, Maj Gen
       Charles H. Martin
Assignments: 25 Jun 1918, GHQ; 2 Jul 1918, IV Army Corps; 18 Aug 1918,
       French XXXII Corps; 22 Aug 1918, I Army Corps; 18 Sep 1918, IV
       Army Corps; 12 Oct 1918, III Army Corps; 16 Nov 1918, V Army
       Corps; 21 Nov 1918, VII Army Corps; 6 May 1919, SOS
Nickname: "Tough 'Ombres"
Campaign participation credit: St. Mihiel, Meuse-Argonne, Lorraine 1918

**91<sup>st</sup> Division**          (National Army) Headquarters organized 26 Aug 1917 at Camp Lewis, WA; division organized with personnel from Washington, Oregon, California, Nevada, Utah, Idaho, Montana and Wyoming.  Moved overseas Jun-Jul 1918.  Returned to the US Apr 1919.  Demobilized 13 May 1919.
Commanders: 26 Aug 1917, Maj Gen Henry A. Greene; 24 Nov 1917, Brig
       Gen James A. Irons (interim); 25 Dec 1917, Brig Gen Frederick S.
       Foltz (interim); 3 Mar 1918, Maj Gen Henry A. Greene; 19 Jun 1918,
       Brig Gen Frederick S. Foltz (interim); 29 Aug 1918, Maj Gen William
       H. Johnston; 3 Feb 1919, Brig Gen John B. McDonald (interim); 4 Feb
       1919, Maj Gen William H. Johnston; 4 Mar 1919, Brig Gen John B.
       McDonald (interim); 6 Mar 1919, Maj Gen William H. Johnston; 22
       Apr 1919, Col Harry LaT. Cavenaugh (interim); 2 May 1919, Lt Col
       Clark Lynn (interim)
Assignments: 23 Jul 1918, GHQ; 28 Jul 1918, IV Army Corps; 12 Aug 1918,
       VI Army Corps; 12 Sep 1918, First Army; 13 Sep 1918, III Army
       Corps; 16 Sep 1918, French IX Corps; 20 Sep 1918, V Army Corps; 10
       Oct 1918, I Army Corps (part) and V Army Corps (part); 12 Oct 1918,
       I Army Corps; 16 Oct 1918, French GAF; 28 Oct 1918, French VII
       Corps; 8 Nov 1918, French XXX Corps; 17 Nov 1918, French VII
       Corps; 21 Nov 1918, French XXXIV Corps; 2 Dec 1918, French XXX
       Corps; 30 Dec 1918, II Army Corps; 1 Feb 1919, SOS
Nickname: "Wild West Division"
Campaign participation credit: Ypres-Lys, Meuse-Argonne, Lorraine 1918

**92<sup>nd</sup> Division**          (National Army) Headquarters organized 29 Oct 1917 at Camp Funston, KS. Division was formed at various locations with black enlisted personnel; it did not assemble or train as a division while in the US. Moved overseas Jun-Jul 1918. Returned to the US Feb 1919. Demobilized 7 Mar 1919 at Camp Upton, NY.

Commanders: 29 Oct 1917, Brig Gen Charles C. Ballou; 20 Nov 1917, Brig
          Gen John E. McMahon (interim); 29 Nov 1917, Brig Gen Malvern-Hill
          Barnum (interim); 1 Dec 1917, Brig Gen John E. McMahon (interim);
          3 Dec 1917, Maj Gen Charles C. Ballou; 19 Nov 1918, Maj Gen
          Charles H. Martin; 16 Dec 1918, Brig Gen James B. Erwin

Assignments: 19 Jun 1918, GHQ; 2 Jul 1918, IV Army Corps; 12 Aug 1918,
          French Seventh Army; 23 Aug 1918, French XXXIII Corps; 20 Sep
          1918, French Seventh Army and then I Army Corps; 30 Sep 1918,
          French XXXVIII Corps (part) and I Army Corps (part); 3 Oct 1918, I
          Army Corps; 4 Oct 1918, IV Army Corps; 23 Oct 1918, VI Army
          Corps; 19 Dec 1918, II Army Corps; 24 Dec 1918, SOS

Nickname: "Buffalo Division"

Campaign participation credit: Meuse-Argonne, Lorraine 1918

**93<sup>rd</sup> Division**          (National Army) Designation reserved for possible second division formed from black enlisted personnel. A small headquarters [93<sup>rd</sup> Division (Provisional)] was activated 5 Jan 1918 for administrative purposes only, and supervised formation of two brigade headquarters and four infantry regiments. (Three of the four regiments were from NG units organized with black enlisted personnel.) The provisional division moved overseas Dec 1917-Apr 1918. Division headquarters demobilized 15 May 1918 in France; the four regiments then served with the French Army.

Commander: 15 Dec 1917, Brig Gen Roy Hoffman

**94<sup>th</sup> Division**          (National Army) Designation reserved for possible division to be formed from Puerto Rican personnel (units except the field artillery brigade would be Spanish-speaking). The division was cancelled, but three regiments were formed Jul 1918 in Puerto Rico, with designations that would have belonged to a 94<sup>th</sup> Division, and assigned to a Provisional Tactical Brigade in Puerto Rico; it was demobilized Jan 1919.

**95<sup>th</sup> Division**          (National Army) Partially organized Sep 1918 at Camp Sherman, OH. Demobilized there 22 Dec 1918.

Commanders: 23 Sep 1918: Col Julien E. Gaujot; 26 Sep 1918: Col Edward Croft; 24 Oct 1918, Brig Gen Mathew C. Smith

**96<sup>th</sup> Division** (National Army) Partially organized Oct 1918 at Camp Wadsworth, NY. Demobilized there 7 Jan 1919.
Commanders: 20 Oct 1918, Maj Gen Guy Carleton; 5 Jan 1919, Col Fred W. Bugbee (interim)

**97<sup>th</sup> Division** (National Army) Partially organized Sep 1918 at Camp Cody, NM. Demobilized there 17 Jan 1919.
Commanders: 26 Sep 1918: Col Carl A. Martin; 25 Oct 1918, Brig Gen James R. Lindsay

**98<sup>th</sup> Division** (National Army) Division headquarters organized Oct 1918 at Camp McClellan, AL and demobilized 30 Nov 1918.
Commander: none appointed

**99<sup>th</sup> Division** (National Army) Division headquarters organized Oct 1918 at Camp Wheeler, GA and demobilized 30 Nov 1918.
Commander: none appointed

**100<sup>th</sup> Division** (National Army) Division headquarters organized Oct 1918 at Camp Bowie, TX and demobilized 30 Nov 1918.
Commander: none appointed

**101<sup>st</sup> Division** (National Army) Division headquarters organized Nov 1918 at Camp Shelby, MS and demobilized 30 Nov 1918.
Commander: none appointed

**102<sup>nd</sup> Division** (National Army) Division was to be organized Nov 1918 at Camp Dix, NJ but headquarters never organized and only small cadre assembled; demobilized 30 Nov 1918.
Commander: none appointed

## Cavalry Division

**15<sup>th</sup> Cavalry Division** (Regular Army) Organized Dec 1917 at Ft. Bliss, TX.[41] The division was intended for service in France, and also patrolled the

---

[41] When the numbers 1-25 were originally allotted for Regular Army divisions, numbers from 15 up were held for cavalry divisions. At that time, there were sufficient Regular Army infantry regiments available to form 14 divisions. Hence the seemingly odd designation of the 15<sup>th</sup> Cavalry Division. In Dec 1917, only the 1<sup>st</sup> to 8<sup>th</sup> Divisions had actually been constituted and were in the process of formation. After the cavalry division was demobilized in May 1918, infantry divisions were formed with numbers from 9 to 20, resulting in a double use of "15" during the war.

border with Mexico during formation. The assigned brigades and components were spread along the border and the division never assembled as such. Demobilized 12 May 1918 at Ft. Bliss, although the brigades remained active on border patrol.
Commanders: 10 Dec 1917, Maj Gen George W. Read; 30 Apr 1918, Brig Gen DeRosey C. Cabell

## Depot Divisions

| | |
|---|---|
| **1st Depot Division** | *See* 41st Division |
| **2nd Depot Division** | *See* 83rd Division |
| **3rd Depot Division** | *See* 76th Division |
| **4th Depot Division** | *See* 85th Division |
| **5th Depot Division** | *See* 39th Division |
| **6th Depot Division** | *See* 40th Division |

## Other Division

**1st Division, Philippine National Guard**      The Infantry Division of the PNG was concentrated at Camp Tomas Claudio 20 Nov 1918 and mustered into Federal service 2 Dec 1918. Designation changed 14 Dec 1918 from Philippine National Guard to Philippine Guard. The division was mustered out 19 Dec 1918, although training continued for another two months at which point this temporary formation was disbanded.
Commanders: 20 Nov 1918, Maj Gen Francis B. Harrison, PNG; 2 Dec 1918, Brig Gen Frederick R. Day

# Cavalry

*Cavalry Brigades*

**1$^{st}$ Cavalry Brigade**     Organized in Feb 1918 at Ft. Sam Houston, TX as component of 15$^{th}$ Cavalry Division; relieved from division 12 May 1918. [6$^{th}$ (to Mar 1918), 14$^{th}$, 16$^{th}$ Cav] Demobilized 14 Jul 1919 at Brownsville, TX.

**2$^{nd}$ Cavalry Brigade**     Organized 27 Dec 1917 at Ft. Bliss, TX as component of 15$^{th}$ Cavalry Division; relieved from division 12 May 1918. [5$^{th}$, 7$^{th}$, 8$^{th}$ Cav] Demobilized 9 Jul 1919 at Ft. Bliss, TX.

**3$^{rd}$ Cavalry Brigade**     Organized in Dec 1917 at Camp. Harry J. Jones, Douglas, AZ as component of 15$^{th}$ Cavalry Division; relieved from division 12 May 1918. [1$^{st}$, 15$^{th}$ (to Mar 1918), 17$^{th}$ Cav] Demobilized 15 Jul 1919 at Ft. Harry J. Jones.

*Regular Army Cavalry Regiments*

**1$^{st}$ Cavalry**     Stationed Camp Harry J. Jones, Douglas, AZ in Apr 1917. Assigned (less four troops) as divisional cavalry. 3$^{rd}$ Provisional Infantry Division 20 Mar 1917—May 1917. Moved to Ft. D. A. Russell, WY May 1917, and then returned Dec 1917 to Camp Harry J. Jones. Assigned 3$^{rd}$ Cavalry Brigade Dec 1917—Jul 1919.

**2$^{nd}$ Cavalry**     Stationed Ft. Ethan Allen, VT in Apr 1917. Moved overseas Mar 1918. Elements with I, III, IV Army Corps Jul-Nov 1918. Under First Army Sep 1918.[42] Detachments with Second Army post-Armistice. Regiment (less 2$^{nd}$ and 3$^{rd}$ Sqns) with Third Army in march to the Rhine; 1$^{st}$ Sqn with III Army Corps; one trp with IV Army Corps. Returned to the US Jun 1919 and moved to Ft. Riley, KS.

**3$^{rd}$ Cavalry**     Stationed Ft. Sam Houston, TX in Apr 1917. Assigned 20 Mar 1917—1 Jun 1917 to 1$^{st}$ Provisional Cavalry Brigade. Moved overseas Oct 1917.[43] Returned to the US Jun 1919 and moved to Ft. Myer, VA.

**4$^{th}$ Cavalry**     Stationed in the Territory of Hawaii; moved to the US Nov 1918 (Ft. Ringgold, TX).

**5$^{th}$ Cavalry**     Stationed Camp Stewart, TX in Apr 1917. Assigned 20 Mar 1917—1 Jun 1917 to 3$^{rd}$ Brigade, 1$^{st}$ Provisional Cavalry Division. Moved Oct 1917 to Ft. Bliss, TX. Assigned 2$^{nd}$ Cavalry Brigade Dec 1917—Jul 1919. Moved Sep 1919 to Marfa, TX.

---

[42] 2$^{nd}$ Cavalry received campaign participation credit for Aisne-Marne, St. Mihiel, and Meuse-Argonne.

[43] 3$^{rd}$ Cavalry received a streamer without inscription for World War I.

**6<sup>th</sup> Cavalry** Stationed Marfa, TX in Apr 1917. Assigned as divisional cavalry. 2<sup>nd</sup> Provisional Infantry Division 20 Mar 1917—1 Jun 1917. Moved Nov 1917 to Ft. Sam Houston, TX. Assigned 1<sup>st</sup> Cavalry Brigade Feb 1918—Mar 1918. Moved overseas Mar 1918.[44] Returned to the US Jun 1919 and moved to Ft. Oglethorpe, GA.

**7<sup>th</sup> Cavalry** Stationed Camp Stewart, TX in Apr 1917. Assigned 20 Mar 1917—1 Jun 1917 to 2<sup>nd</sup> Brigade, 1<sup>st</sup> Provisional Cavalry Division. Moved May 1917 to Ft. Bliss, TX. Assigned 2<sup>nd</sup> Cavalry Brigade Dec 1917—Jul 1919.

**8<sup>th</sup> Cavalry** Stationed Ft. Bliss, TX in Apr 1917. Assigned 20 Mar 1917—1 Jun 1917 to 1<sup>st</sup> Brigade, 1<sup>st</sup> Provisional Cavalry Division. Moved Oct 1917 to Marfa, TX. Assigned 2<sup>nd</sup> Cavalry Brigade Dec 1917—Jul 1919. Moved Oct 1919 to Ft. Bliss.

**9<sup>th</sup> Cavalry** Stationed in the Philippine Islands [regiment comprised black enlisted personnel].

**10<sup>th</sup> Cavalry** Stationed at Ft. Huachuca, AZ in Apr 1917 [regiment comprised black enlisted personnel]. Assigned (less one troop) as divisional cavalry. 3<sup>rd</sup> Provisional Infantry Division 20 Mar 1917—1 Jun 1917.

**11<sup>th</sup> Cavalry** Stationed Camp Stewart, TX in Apr 1917. Assigned 20 Mar 1917—May 1917 to 3<sup>rd</sup> Brigade, 1<sup>st</sup> Provisional Cavalry Division.Moved May 1917 to Ft. Oglethorpe, GA; Jan 1918 to Camp Forrest, GA; May 1918 to Ft. Oglethorpe; Sep 1918 to Ft. Myer, VA; and Jul 1919 to Presidio of Monterey, CA.

**12<sup>th</sup> Cavalry** Stationed Columbus, NM in Apr 1917. Attached (less 1<sup>st</sup> Sqn) to 2<sup>nd</sup> Provisional Infantry Division 20 Mar 1917—1 Jun 1917.

**13<sup>th</sup> Cavalry** Stationed Camp Stewart, TX in Apr 1917. Assigned (less one troop) 20 Mar 1917—May 1917 to 2<sup>nd</sup> Brigade, 1<sup>st</sup> Provisional Cavalry Division. Moved May 1917 to Ft. Riley, KS; Dec 1917 to Ft. Ringgold, TX; Jan 1918 to Bronsville, TX; Oct 1918 to Ft. Ringgold; and Dec 1918 to Ft. Clark, TX.

**14<sup>th</sup> Cavalry** Stationed Camp Del Rio, TX in Apr 1917. Assigned as divisional cavalry. 1<sup>st</sup> Provisional Infantry Division 20 Mar 1917—1 Jun 1917. Assigned 1<sup>st</sup> Cavalry Brigade Feb 1918—Jul 1919. Moved Apr 1918 to Ft. Sam Houston, TX; Jun 1918 to Camp Travis, TX; and Aug 1918 to Ft. Sam Houston, TX.

---

[44] 6<sup>th</sup> Cavalry received a streamer without inscription for World War I.

**15ᵗʰ Cavalry** Stationed in the Philippine Islands; returned to the US Oct 1917 (Camp Fremont, CA). Moved Dec 1917 to Camp Harry J. Jones, Douglas, AZ. Assigned 3ʳᵈ Cavalry Brigade Dec 1917— Mar 1918. Moved overseas Mar 1918.[45] Returned to the US Jun 1919 and moved to Ft. D. A. Russell, WY.

**16ᵗʰ Cavalry** Stationed Llano Gande, TX in Apr 1917. Assigned 20 Mar 1917—1 Jun 1917 to 1ˢᵗ Provisional Cavalry Brigade. Moved May 1917 to Mercedes, TX. Assigned 1ˢᵗ Cavalry Brigade Feb 1918— Jul 1919. Moved Jan 1919 to Brownsville, TX and Jun 1919 to Ft. Brown, TX.

**17ᵗʰ Cavalry** Stationed Ft. Bliss, TX in Apr 1917. Assigned 20 Mar 1917—1 Jun 1917 to 1ˢᵗ Brigade, 1ˢᵗ Provisional Cavalry Division. Moved May 1917 to Camp Harry J. Jones, Douglas, AZ. Assigned 3ʳᵈ Cavalry Brigade Dec 1917— Apr 1919. Moved to the Territory of Hawaii Apr 1919.

**18ᵗʰ Cavalry** Organized 13 Jun 1917 at Ft. Ethan Allen, VT. Converted and redesignated 1 Nov 1917 as 76ᵗʰ Field Artillery.

**19ᵗʰ Cavalry** Organized 23 May 1917 at Ft. Ethan Allen, VT. Converted and redesignated 1 Nov 1917 as 77ᵗʰ Field Artillery.

**20ᵗʰ Cavalry** Organized 1 Jun 1917 at Ft. Riley, KS. Converted and redesignated 18 Nov 1917 as 78ᵗʰ Field Artillery.

**21ˢᵗ Cavalry** Organized 1 Jun 1917 at Ft. Riley, KS. Converted and redesignated 1 Nov 1917 as 79ᵗʰ Field Artillery.

**22ⁿᵈ Cavalry** Organized 21 Jun 1917 at Ft. Oglethorpe, GA. Converted and redesignated 1 Nov 1917 as 80ᵗʰ Field Artillery.

**23ʳᵈ Cavalry** Organized 21 Jun 1917 at Ft. Oglethorpe, GA. Converted and redesignated 3 Nov 1917 as 81ˢᵗ Field Artillery.

**24ᵗʰ Cavalry** Organized 5 Jun 1917 at Ft. D. A. Russell, WY. Converted and redesignated 1 Nov 1917 as 82ⁿᵈ Field Artillery.

**25ᵗʰ Cavalry** Organized 5 Jun 1917 at Ft. D. A. Russell, WY. Converted and redesignated 1 Nov 1917 as 83ʳᵈ Field Artillery.

*National Guard Cavalry Regimens*[46]

**101ˢᵗ Cavalry** Organized Nov 1917 at Camp Hancock, GA and disbanded the same month.

---

[45] 15ᵗʰ Cavalry received a streamer without inscription for World War I.

[46] The National Guard actually had a number of cavalry regiments. However, as there was no perceived need for that arm, these units were largely broken up and converted. For example, the 1ˢᵗ Colorado Cavalry helped form the 157ᵗʰ Infantry and the 1ˢᵗ Wisconsin Cavalry formed the 120ᵗʰ Field Artillery.

*National Army Cavalry Regiments*

**301st Cavalry**
Organized 3 Feb 1918 at Camp Fremont, CA.  Broken up 27 Aug 1918 and elements converted and redesignated 46th and 47th Field Artillery and 16th Trench Mortar Bty.

**302nd Cavalry**
Organized 5 Feb 1918 at Camp Fremont, CA.  Broken up 26 Aug 1918 and elements converted and redesignated 46th and 64th Field Artillery and 29th Trench Mortar Bty.

**303rd Cavalry**
Organized 4 Feb 1918 at Camp Stanley, TX.  Broken up 14 Aug 1918 and elements converted and redesignated as 52nd and 53rd Field Artillery and 18th Trench Mortar Bty.

**304th Cavalry**
Organized 16 Feb 1918 at Camp Stanley, TX.  Broken up 15 Aug 1918 and elements converted and redesignated as 43rd and 54th Field Artillery and 25th Trench Mortar Bty.

**305th Cavalry**
Organized 3 Feb 1918 at Camp Stanley, TX.  Broken up 15 Aug 1918 and elements converted and redesignated as 44th and 45th Field Artillery and 15th Trench Mortar Bty.

**306th Cavalry**
Organized 6 Feb 1918 at Ft. Clark, TX.  Broken up 20 Aug 1918 and elements converted and redesignated as 49th and 50th Field Artillery and 17th Trench Mortar Bty.

**307th Cavalry**
Organized in Feb 1918 at Camp Del Rio, TX. Broken up 17 Aug 1918 and elements converted and redesignated as 51st and 55th Field Artillery and 27th Trench Mortar Bty.

**308th Cavalry**
Organized 24 Feb 1918 at Camp Harry J. Jones, AZ. Broken up 13 Sep 1918 and elements converted and redesignated as 65th and 66th Field Artillery and 22nd Trench Mortar Bty.

**309th Cavalry**
Organized 18 Feb 1918 at Ft. Sam Houston, TX. Broken up 18 Aug 1918 and elements converted and redesignated as 56th and 57th Field Artillery and 19th Trench Mortar Bty.

**310th Cavalry**
Organized 17 Feb 1918 at Ft. Ethan Allen, VT. Broken up 18 Oct 1918 and elements converted and redesignated as 56th and 59th Field Artillery and 20th Trench Mortar Bty.

**311th Cavalry**
Organized 15 Feb 1918 at Ft. Riley, KS.  Broken up 1 Sep 1918 and elements converted and redesignated as 67th and 68th Field Artillery and 23rd Trench Mortar Bty.

**312th Cavalry**
Organized 13 Mar 1918 at Ft. Meyer, VA; 12 Feb 1918 at Ft. Sheridan, IL; and 23 Mar 1918 at Ft. D. A. Russell, WY. Elements at Ft. Meyer converted and redesignated 13 Aug 1918 as 60th Field Artillery; elements at Ft. Sheridan converted and redesignated 14 Aug 1918 as 61st Field Artillery; and element at Ft. D. A. Russell converted and redesignated 14 Aug 1918 as 28th Trench Mortar Bty.

**313th Cavalry**        Organized 28 Mar 1918 at Del Rio, TX. Broken up 23 Aug 1918 and elements converted and redesignated as 69th and 70th Field Artillery and 26th Trench Mortar Bty.

**314th Cavalry**        Organized 6 Apr 1918 at Camp Owen Bierne, TX. Broken up 6 Oct 1918 and elements converted and redesignated as 62nd and 63rd Field Artillery and 21st Trench Mortar Bty.

***315th Cavalry***        Organized 30 Mar 1918 at Ft. D. A. Russell, WY. Broken up 19 Aug 1918 and elements converted and redesignated as 71st and 72nd Field Artillery and 24th Trench Mortar Bty.


# Infantry[47]

*Infantry Brigades*[48]

**1st Infantry Brigade**     Organized 8 Jun 1917 at New York as component of 1st Expeditionary Division [later 1st Division] and moved overseas. [16th and 18th Inf and 2nd MG Bn] Returned to the US Sep 1919 and moved to Camp Zachary Taylor, KY.

**2nd Infantry Brigade**     Organized 8 Jun 1917 at New York as component of 1st Expeditionary Division [later 1st Division] and moved overseas. [26th and 28th Inf and 3rd MG Bn] Returned to the US Sep 1919 and moved to Camp Zachary Taylor, KY.

**3rd Infantry Brigade**     Organized 11 Aug 1917 at Syracuse, NY as 1st Provisional Brigade and moved overseas  Redesignated 22 Sep 1917 as 3rd Infantry Brigade and assigned 2nd Division. [9th and 23rd Inf and 5th MG Bn] Returned to the US Aug 1919 and moved to Camp Travis, TX.

**4th Marine Brigade (Infantry)**     Organized 23 Oct 1917 in France as component of 2nd Division [5th and 6th Mar and 6th Mar MG Bn]. Returned to the US Aug 1919; detached from 2nd Division 8 Aug 1919 and moved to Quantico, VA; demobilization completed there 13 Aug 1919.[49]

**5th Infantry Brigade**     Organized Nov 1917 at Ft. Greene, NC as component of 3rd Division. [4th and 7th Inf and 8th MG Bn] Moved overseas Apr 1918. Returned to the US Aug 1919 and moved to Camp Pike, AR.

---

[47] In formal lineage terms, regiments are assigned to divisions. However, in this paper, the brigade to which the regiment was assigned is given.

[48] Officially, brigade lineages only apply to the headquarters element. The assignments units are shown in brackets.

[49] The Army would not form a 4th Infantry Brigade until Oct 1920.

**6<sup>th</sup> Infantry Brigade**   Organized 1 Dec 1917 at Ft. Greene, NC as component of 3<sup>rd</sup> Division. [30<sup>th</sup> and 38<sup>th</sup> Inf and 9<sup>th</sup> MG Bn]  Moved overseas Apr 1918.  Returned to the US Aug 1919 and moved to Camp Pike, AR.

**7<sup>th</sup> Infantry Brigade**   Organized Dec 1917 at Ft. Greene, NC as component of 4<sup>th</sup> Division. [39<sup>th</sup> and 47<sup>th</sup> Inf and 11<sup>th</sup> MG Bn] Moved overseas May 1918.  Returned to the US Jul 1919 and moved to Camp Dodge, IA.

**8<sup>th</sup> Infantry Brigade**   Organized Dec 1917 at Ft. Greene, NC as component of 4<sup>th</sup> Division. [58<sup>th</sup> and 59<sup>th</sup> Inf and 12<sup>th</sup> MG Bn]  Moved overseas May 1918.  Returned to the US Aug 1919 and moved to Camp Dodge, IA.

**9<sup>th</sup> Infantry Brigade**   Organized 1 Dec 1917 at Ft. Greene, NC as component of 5<sup>th</sup> Division. [6<sup>th</sup> and 11<sup>th</sup> Inf and 14<sup>th</sup> MG Bn] Moved overseas Apr 1918.  Returned to the US Jul 1919 and moved to Camp Gordon, GA.

**10<sup>th</sup> Infantry Brigade**   Organized 1 Jan 1918 at Chickamauga Park, GA as component of 5<sup>th</sup> Division. [60<sup>th</sup> and 61<sup>st</sup> Inf and 15<sup>th</sup> MG Bn] Moved overseas Apr 1918.  Returned to the US Jul 1919 and moved to Camp Gordon, GA.

**11<sup>th</sup> Infantry Brigade**   Organized 4 Dec 1917 at Camp Forrest, GA as component of 6<sup>th</sup> Division. [51<sup>st</sup> and 52<sup>nd</sup> Inf and 17<sup>th</sup> MG Bn] Moved overseas Jul 1918.  Returned to the US Jun 1919 and moved to Camp Grant, IL.

**12<sup>th</sup> Infantry Brigade**   Organized 29 Nov 1917 at Camp Forrest, GA as component of 6<sup>th</sup> Division. [53<sup>rd</sup> and 54<sup>th</sup> Inf and 18<sup>th</sup> MG Bn] Moved overseas Jul 1918.  Returned to the US Jun 1919 and moved to Camp Grant, IL.

**13<sup>th</sup> Infantry Brigade**   Organized 18 Dec 1917 at Chickamauga Park, GA as component of 7<sup>th</sup> Division. [35<sup>th</sup> and 55<sup>th</sup> Inf and 20<sup>th</sup> MG Bn] Moved overseas Aug 1918.  Returned to the US Jun 1919 and moved to Camp Funston, KS.

**14<sup>th</sup> Infantry Brigade**   Organized 20 Dec 1917 at Camp Bliss, TX as component of 7<sup>th</sup> Division. [56<sup>th</sup> and 64<sup>th</sup> Inf and 21<sup>st</sup> MG Bn] Moved overseas Aug 1918.  Returned to the US Jun 1919 and moved to Camp Funston, KS.

**15<sup>th</sup> Infantry Brigade**   *See* 17<sup>th</sup> Infantry Brigade

**15<sup>th</sup> Infantry Brigade**   Organized 5 Jan 1918 at Camp Fremont, CA as component of 8<sup>th</sup> Division. [8<sup>th</sup> and 12<sup>th</sup> Inf and 23<sup>rd</sup> MG Bn] Moved Nov 1918 to Camp Lee, VA. Demobilized 24 Feb 1919 at Camp Lee.

**16<sup>th</sup> Infantry Brigade**   Organized 8 Dec 1917 at Camp Fremont, CA and assigned 17 Dec 1917 to 8<sup>th</sup> Division. [13<sup>th</sup> and 62<sup>nd</sup> Inf and 24<sup>th</sup> MG Bn]  Moved overseas Oct 1918.  Demobilized 25 Nov 1918 in France.

**17<sup>th</sup> Infantry Brigade**   Organized 6 Dec 1917 at Camp Zachary Taylor, KY as 15<sup>th</sup> Infantry Brigade; redesignated 26 Dec 1917 as 17<sup>th</sup> Infantry Brigade and assigned 8 Jul 1918 to 9<sup>th</sup> Division. [45<sup>th</sup> and 67<sup>th</sup> Inf and 26<sup>th</sup> MG Bn] Demobilized 5 Feb 1919 at Camp Sheridan, AL.

**18<sup>th</sup> Infantry Brigade**   Organized 17 Jul 1918 at Camp Sheridan, AL as component of 9<sup>th</sup> Division and demobilized there 5 Feb 1919. [46<sup>th</sup> and 68<sup>th</sup> Inf and 27<sup>th</sup> MG Bn]

**19<sup>th</sup> Infantry Brigade**   Organized Aug 1918 at Camp Funston, KS as component of 10<sup>th</sup> Division and demobilized there Feb 1919. [41<sup>st</sup> and 69<sup>th</sup> Inf and 29<sup>th</sup> MG Bn]

**20<sup>th</sup> Infantry Brigade**   Organized Aug 1918 at Camp Funston, KS as component of 10<sup>th</sup> Division and demobilized there Feb 1919. [20<sup>th</sup> and 70<sup>th</sup> Inf and 30<sup>th</sup> MG Bn]

**21<sup>st</sup> Infantry Brigade**          Organized Aug 1918 at Camp Meade, MD as component of 11<sup>th</sup> Division and demobilized there Feb 1919. [17<sup>th</sup> and 71<sup>st</sup> Inf and 32<sup>nd</sup> MG Bn]

**22<sup>nd</sup> Infantry Brigade**   Organized Sep 1918 at Camp Meade, MD as component of 11<sup>th</sup> Division and demobilized there Feb 1919. [63<sup>rd</sup> and 72<sup>nd</sup> Inf and 33<sup>rd</sup> MG Bn]

**23<sup>rd</sup> Infantry Brigade**   Organized Aug 1918 at Camp Devens, MA as component of 12<sup>th</sup> Division and demobilized there Jan 1919. [36<sup>th</sup> and 73<sup>rd</sup> Inf and 35<sup>th</sup> MG Bn]

**24<sup>th</sup> Infantry Brigade**   Organized Aug 1918 at Camp Devens, MA as component of 12<sup>th</sup> Division and demobilized there Jan 1919. [42<sup>nd</sup> and 74<sup>th</sup> Inf and 36<sup>th</sup> MG Bn]

**25<sup>th</sup> Infantry Brigade**   Organized Aug 1918 at Camp Lewis, WA as component of 13<sup>th</sup> Division and demobilized there Mar 1919. [1<sup>st</sup> and 75<sup>th</sup> Inf and 38<sup>th</sup> MG Bn]

**26<sup>th</sup> Infantry Brigade**   Organized Aug 1918 at Camp Lewis, WA as component of 13<sup>th</sup> Division and demobilized there Mar 1919. [44<sup>th</sup> and 76<sup>th</sup> Inf and 39<sup>th</sup> MG Bn]

**27<sup>th</sup> Infantry Brigade**   Organized Jul 1918 at Camp Custer, MI as component of 14<sup>th</sup> Division and demobilized there Feb 1919. [10<sup>th</sup> and 77<sup>th</sup> Inf and 41<sup>st</sup> MG Bn]

**28<sup>th</sup> Infantry Brigade**   Organized Jul 1918 at Camp Custer, MI as component of 14<sup>th</sup> Division and demobilized there Feb 1919. [40<sup>th</sup> and 78<sup>th</sup> Inf and 42<sup>nd</sup> MG Bn]

**29th Infantry Brigade**   Organized Sep 1918 at Camp Logan, TX as component of 15th Division and demobilized there Feb 1919. [43rd and 79th Inf and 44h MG Bn]

**30th Infantry Brigade**   Organized Sep 1918 at Camp Logan, TX as component of 15th Division and demobilized there Feb 1919. [57th and 80th Inf and 45th MG Bn]

**31st Infantry Brigade**         Organized Sep 1918 at Camp Kearny, CA as component of 16th Division and demobilized there Feb 1919. [21st and 81st Inf and 47th MG Bn]

**32nd Infantry Brigade**   Organized Sep 1918 at Camp Kearny, CA as component of 16th Division and demobilized there Feb 1919. [32nd and 82nd Inf and 48th MG Bn]

**33rd Infantry Brigade**   Constituted as component of 17th Division but headquarters never organized. [5th and 83rd Inf and 50th MG Bn]

**34th Infantry Brigade**   Organized Jan 1919 at Camp Beauregard, LA as component of 17th Division and demobilized there Feb 1919. [29th and 84th Inf and 51st MG Bn]

**35th Infantry Brigade**   Organized Aug 1918 at Camp Travis, TX as component of 18th Division and demobilized there Feb 1919. [19th and 85th Inf and 53rd MG Bn]

**36th Infantry Brigade**   Organized Aug 1918 at Camp Travis, TX as component of 18th Division and demobilized there Feb 1919. [35th and 86th Inf and 54th MG Bn]

**37th Infantry Brigade**   Organized Oct 1918 at Camp Dodge, IA as component of 19th Division and demobilized there Jan 1919. [14th and 87th Inf and 56th MG Bn]

**38th Infantry Brigade**   Organized Oct 1918 at Camp Dodge, IA as component of 19th Division and demobilized there Jan 1919. [2nd and 88th Inf and 57th MG Bn]

**39th Infantry Brigade**   Organized Oct 1918 at Camp Sevier, SC as component of 20th Division and demobilized there Feb 1919. [48th and 89th Inf and 59th MG Bn]

**40th Infantry Brigade**   Organized Aug 1918 at Camp Sevier, SC as component of 20th Division and demobilized there Feb 1919. [50th and 90th Inf and 60th MG Bn]

**51st Infantry Brigade**         Organized Aug 1917 at Boston, MA as component of 26th Division (formed from Hq, 2nd Brigade, MA NG). [101st and 102nd Inf and 102nd MG Bn]  Moved overseas Sep 1917. Returned to the US Apr 1919 and demobilized at Camp Devens, MA.

**52<sup>nd</sup> Infantry Brigade**      Organized Aug 1917 at Westfield, MA as component of 26<sup>th</sup> Division. [103<sup>rd</sup> and 104<sup>th</sup> Inf and 103<sup>rd</sup> MG Bn] Moved overseas Sep 1917. Returned to the US Apr 1919 and demobilized at Camp Devens, MA.

**53<sup>rd</sup> Infantry Brigade**      Organized Oct 1917 at Camp Wadsworth, SC as component of 27<sup>th</sup> Division (redesignation of 1<sup>st</sup> Infantry Brigade, New York NG). [105<sup>th</sup> and 106<sup>th</sup> Inf and 105<sup>th</sup> MG Bn] Moved overseas May 1918. Returned to the US Mar 1919 and demobilized Apr 1919 at Camp Upton, NY.

**54<sup>th</sup> Infantry Brigade**      Organized Oct 1917 at Camp Wadsworth, SC as component of 27<sup>th</sup> Division (redesignation of 3<sup>rd</sup> Infantry Brigade, New York NG). [107<sup>th</sup> and 108<sup>th</sup> Inf and 106<sup>th</sup> MG Bn] Moved overseas May 1918. Returned to the US Mar 1919 and demobilized Apr 1919 at Camp Upton, NY.

**55<sup>th</sup> Infantry Brigade**      Organized Sep 1917 at Camp Hancock, GA as component of 28<sup>th</sup> Division (redesignation of 1<sup>st</sup> Infantry Brigade, Pennsylvania NG). [109<sup>th</sup> and 110<sup>th</sup> Inf and 108<sup>th</sup> MG Bn] Moved overseas May 1918. Returned to the US May 1919 and demobilized at Camp Dix, NJ.

**56<sup>th</sup> Infantry Brigade**      Organized Sep 1917 at Camp Hancock, GA as component of 28<sup>th</sup> Division (redesignation of 2<sup>nd</sup> Infantry Brigade, Pennsylvania NG). [111<sup>th</sup> and 112<sup>th</sup> Inf and 109<sup>th</sup> MG Bn] Moved overseas May 1918. Returned to the US Apr 1919 and demobilized May 1919 at Camp Dix, NJ.

**57<sup>th</sup> Infantry Brigade**      Organized Sep 1917 at Camp McClellan, AL as component of 29<sup>th</sup> Division (formed from Division Hq, NJ NG). [113<sup>th</sup> and 114<sup>th</sup> Inf and 111<sup>th</sup> MG Bn] Moved overseas Jun 1918. Returned to the US May 1919 and demobilized at Camp Dix, NJ.

**58<sup>th</sup> Infantry Brigade**      Organized Aug 1917 at Camp McClellan, AL as component of 29<sup>th</sup> Division. [115<sup>th</sup> and 116<sup>th</sup> Inf and 112<sup>th</sup> MG Bn] Moved overseas Jun 1918. Returned to the US May 1919 and demobilized at Camp Meade, MD.

**59<sup>th</sup> Infantry Brigade** Organized Sep 1917 at Camp Sevier, SC as component of 30<sup>th</sup> Division. [117<sup>th</sup> and 118<sup>th</sup> Inf and 114<sup>th</sup> MG Bn] Moved overseas May 1918. Returned to the US Mar 1919 and demobilized Apr 1919 at Ft. Oglethorpe, GA.

**60<sup>th</sup> Infantry Brigade**      Organized Sep 1917 at Camp Sevier, SC as component of 30<sup>th</sup> Division (formed from Brigade Hq, NC NG). [119<sup>th</sup> and 120<sup>th</sup> Inf and 115<sup>th</sup> MG Bn] Moved overseas May 1918. Returned to the US Apr 1919 and demobilized at Camp Jackson, SC.

**61st Infantry Brigade**      Organized Aug 1917 at Camp Wheeler, GA as component of 31st Division (formed from Brigade Hq, GA NG). [121st and 122nd Inf and 117th MG Bn] Moved overseas Oct 1918. Skeletonized Nov 1918. Returned to the US Dec 1918 and demobilized Jan 1919 at Camp Gordon, GA.

**62nd Infantry Brigade**      Organized Aug 1917 at Camp Wheeler, GA as component of 31st Division. [123rd and 124th Inf and 118th MG Bn] Moved overseas Oct 1918. Skeletonized Nov 1918. Returned to the US Dec 1918 and demobilized Jan 1919 at Camp Gordon, GA.

**63rd Infantry Brigade**      Organized Sep 1917 at Camp MacArthur, TX as component of 32nd Division (formed from Hq, 1st Infantry Brigade, MI NG). [125th and 126th Inf and 120th MG Bn] Moved overseas Feb 1918. Returned to the US May 1919 and demobilized at Camp Custer, MI.

**64th Infantry Brigade**      Organized Sep 1917 at Camp MacArthur, TX as component of 32nd Division (formed from Briade Hq, WI NG). [127th and 128th Inf and 121st MG Bn] Moved overseas Feb 1918. Returned to the US May 1919 and demobilized at Camp Grant, IL.

**65th Infantry Brigade**      Organized Aug 1917 at Camp Logan, TX as component of 33rd Division (formed from Hq, 2nd Infantry Brigade IL NG). [129th and 130th Inf and 123rd MG Bn] Moved overseas May 1918. Returned to the US May 1919 and demobilized at Camp Grant, IL.

**66th Infantry Brigade**      Organized Sep 1917 at Camp Logan, TX as component of 33rd Division (formed from Hq, 1st Infantry Brigade IL NG). [131st and 132nd Inf and 124th MG Bn] Moved overseas May 1918. R eturned to the US May 1919 and demobilized Jun 1919 at Camp Grant, IL.

**67th Infantry Brigade**      Organized Aug 1917 at Camp Cody, NM as component of 34th Division (formed from Hq, 1st Brigade, IA NG). [133rd and 134th Inf and 126th MG Bn] Moved overseas Sep 1918. Skeletonized Nov 1918. Returned to the US Jan 1919 and demobilized Feb 1919 at Camp Grant, IL.

**68th Infantry Brigade**      Organized Aug 1917 at Camp Cody, NM as component of 34th Division (formed from Hq, Brigade, MN NG). [135th and 136th Inf and 127th MG Bn] Moved overseas Oct 1918. Skeletonized Nov 1918. Returned to the US Jan 1919 and demobilized Feb 1919 at Camp Grant, IL.

**69th Infantry Brigade**      Organized Aug 1917 at Camp Doniphan, OK as component of 35th Division (formed from Hq, 1st Kansas Infantry Brigade, KS NG). [137th and 138th Inf and 129th MG Bn] Moved overseas May 1918. Returned to the US Apr 1919 and demobilized May 1919 at Camp Funston, KS.

**70<sup>th</sup> Infantry Brigade**    Organized Sep 1917 at Camp Doniphan, OK as component of 35<sup>th</sup> Division (formed from Hq, 1<sup>st</sup> Missouri Infantry Brigade, MO NG). [139<sup>th</sup> and 140<sup>th</sup> Inf and 130<sup>th</sup> MG Bn] Moved overseas Apr 1918. Returned to the US Apr 1919 and demobilized May 1919 at Camp Funston, KS.

**71<sup>st</sup> Infantry Brigade**    Organized Aug 1917 at Camp Bowie, TX as component of 36<sup>th</sup> Division (formed from Hq, 2<sup>nd</sup> Infantry Brigade TX NG). [141<sup>st</sup> and 142<sup>nd</sup> Inf and 132<sup>nd</sup> MG Bn] Moved overseas Jul 1918. Returned to the US Jun 1919 and demobilized at Camp Bowie.

**72<sup>nd</sup> Infantry Brigade**    Organized Sep 1917 at Camp Bowie, TX as component of 36<sup>th</sup> Division (formed from Hq, 1<sup>st</sup> Infantry Brigade TX NG). [143<sup>rd</sup> and 144<sup>th</sup> Inf and 133<sup>rd</sup> MG Bn] Moved overseas Jul 1918. Returned to the US Jun 1919and demobilized at Camp Bowie.

**73<sup>rd</sup> Infantry Brigade**    Organized Sep 1917 at Camp Sheridan, AL as component of 37<sup>th</sup> Division (formed from Hq, 2<sup>nd</sup> Infantry Brigade OH NG). [145<sup>th</sup> and 146<sup>th</sup> Inf and 135<sup>th</sup> MG Bn] Moved overseas Jun 1918. Returned to the US Mar 1919 and demobilized Apr 1919 at Camp Sherman, OH.

**74<sup>th</sup> Infantry Brigade**    Organized Sep 1917 at Camp Sheridan, AL as component of 37<sup>th</sup> Division (formed from Hq, 1<sup>st</sup> Infantry Brigade OH NG). [147<sup>th</sup> and 148<sup>th</sup> Inf and 136<sup>th</sup> MG Bn] Moved overseas Jun 1918. Returned to the US Mar 1919 and demobilized Apr 1919 at Camp Sherman, OH.

**75<sup>th</sup> Infantry Brigade**    Organized Sep 1917 at Camp Shelby, MS as component of 38<sup>th</sup> Division. [149<sup>th</sup> and 150<sup>th</sup> Inf and 138<sup>th</sup> MG Bn] Moved overseas Oct 1918. Skeletonized Nov 1918. Returned to the US Dec 1918 and demobilized Jan 1919 at Camp Zachary Taylor, KY.

**76<sup>th</sup> Infantry Brigade**    Organized Sep 1917 at Camp Shelby, MS as component of 38<sup>th</sup> Division (formed from Hq, 1<sup>st</sup> Brigade IN NG). [151<sup>st</sup> and 152<sup>nd</sup> Inf and 139<sup>th</sup> MG Bn] Moved overseas Oct 1918. Skeletonized Nov 1918. Returned to the US Dec 1918 and demobilized Jan 1919 at Camp Zachary Taylor, KY.

**77<sup>th</sup> Infantry Brigade**    Organized Aug 1917 at Camp Beauregard, LA as component of 39<sup>th</sup> Division. [153<sup>rd</sup> and 154<sup>th</sup> Inf and 141<sup>st</sup> MG Bn] Moved overseas Aug 1918. Skeletonized Nov 1918. Returned to the US Jan 1919 and demobilized at Camp Beauregard.

**78<sup>th</sup> Infantry Brigade**    Organized Aug 1917 at Camp Beauregard, LA as component of 39<sup>th</sup> Division. [155<sup>th</sup> and 156<sup>th</sup> Inf and 142<sup>nd</sup> MG Bn] Moved overseas Aug 1918. Skeletonized Nov 1918. Returned to the US Jan 1919 and demobilized at Camp Beauregard.

**79th Infantry Brigade**        Organized Aug 1917 at Camp Kearny, CA as component of 40th Division. [157th and 158th Inf and 144th MG Bn] Moved overseas Aug 1918. Returned to the US Apr 1919 and demobilized at Camp Kearny.

**80th Infantry Brigade**        Organized Aug 1917 at Camp Kearny, CA as component of 40th Division. [159th and 160th Inf and 145th MG Bn] Moved overseas Aug 1918. Returned to the US Apr 1919 and demobilized at Camp Kearny.

**81st Infantry Brigade**        Organized Sep 1917 at Camp Greene, NC as component of 41st Division. [161st and 162nd Inf and 147th MG Bn] Moved overseas Dec 1917. Returned to the US Mar 1919 and demobilized at Camp Dix, NJ.

**82nd Infantry Brigade**        Organized Sep 1917 at Camp Greene, NC as component of 41st Division. [163rd and 164th Inf and 148th MG Bn] Moved overseas Dec 1917. Returned to the US Feb 1919 and demobilized at Camp Dix, NJ.

**83rd Infantry Brigade**        Organized Aug 1917 at Camp Mills, NY as component of 42nd Division. [165th and 166th Inf and 150th MG Bn] Moved overseas Oct 1917. Returned to the US Apr 1919 and demobilized May 1919 at Camp Upton, NY.

**84th Infantry Brigade**        Organized Sep 1917 at Camp Mills, NY as component of 42nd Division. [167th and 168th Inf and 151st MG Bn] Moved overseas Nov 1917. Returned to the US Apr 1919 and demobilized May 1919 at Camp Dodge, IA.

**151st Infantry Brigade**        Organized Aug 1917 at Camp Devens, MA as component of 76th Division. [301st and 302nd Inf and 302nd MG Bn] Moved overseas Jul 1918. Skeletonized Nov 1918. Returned to the US Jan 1919 and demobilized Feb 1919 at Camp Devens.

**152nd Infantry Brigade**        Organized Aug 1917 at Camp Devens, MA as component of 76th Division. [303rd and 304th Inf and 303rd MG Bn] Moved overseas Jul 1918. Skeletonized Nov 1918. Returned to the US Jan 1919 and demobilized Feb 1919 at Camp Devens.

**153rd Infantry Brigade**        Organized Aug 1917 at Camp Upton, NY as component of 77th Division. [305th and 306th Inf and 305th MG Bn] Moved overseas Apr 1918. Returned to the US Apr 1919 and demobilized May 1919 at Camp Upton.

**154th Infantry Brigade**        Organized Aug 1917 at Camp Upton, NY as component of 77th Division. [307th and 308th Inf and 306th MG Bn] Moved overseas Apr 1918. Returned to the US Apr 1919 and demobilized May 1919 at Camp Upton.

**155<sup>th</sup> Infantry Brigade** Organized Aug 1917 at Camp Dix, NJ as component of 78<sup>th</sup> Division. [309<sup>th</sup> and 310<sup>th</sup> Inf and 308<sup>th</sup> MG Bn] Moved overseas May 1918. Returned to the US May 1919 and demobilized Jun 1919 at Camp Dix.

**156<sup>th</sup> Infantry Brigade** Organized Aug 1917 at Camp Dix, NJ as component of 78<sup>th</sup> Division. [311<sup>th</sup> and 312<sup>th</sup> Inf and 309<sup>th</sup> MG Bn] Moved overseas May 1918. Returned to the US May 1919 and demobilized at Camp Dix.

**157<sup>th</sup> Infantry Brigade** Organized Aug 1917 at Camp Meade, MD as component of 79<sup>th</sup> Division. [313<sup>th</sup> and 314<sup>th</sup> Inf and 311<sup>th</sup> MG Bn] Moved overseas Jul 1918. Returned to the US May 1919 and demobilized Jun 1919 at Camp Dix, NJ.

**158<sup>th</sup> Infantry Brigade** Organized Aug 1917 at Camp Meade, MD as component of 79<sup>th</sup> Division. [315<sup>th</sup> and 316<sup>th</sup> Inf and 312<sup>th</sup> MG Bn] Moved overseas Jul 1918. Returned to the US May 1919 and demobilized Jun 1919 at Camp Dix, NJ.

**159<sup>th</sup> Infantry Brigade** Organized Aug 1917 at Camp Lee, VA as component of 80<sup>th</sup> Division. [317<sup>th</sup> and 318<sup>th</sup> Inf and 314<sup>th</sup> MG Bn] Moved overseas May 1918. Returned to the US May 1919 and demobilized May 1919 at Camp Lee.

**160<sup>th</sup> Infantry Brigade** Organized Aug 1917 at Camp Lee, VA as component of 80<sup>th</sup> Division. [319<sup>th</sup> and 320<sup>th</sup> Inf and 315<sup>th</sup> MG Bn] Moved overseas May 1918. Returned to the US May 1919 and demobilized Jun 1919 at Camp Dix, NJ.

**161<sup>st</sup> Infantry Brigade** Organized Aug 1917 at Camp Jackson, SC as component of 81<sup>st</sup> Division. [321<sup>st</sup> and 322<sup>nd</sup> Inf and 317<sup>th</sup> MG Bn] Moved overseas Jul 1918. Returned to the US Jun 1919 and demobilized at Camp Jackson.

**162<sup>nd</sup> Infantry Brigade** Organized Aug 1917 at Camp Jackson, SC as component of 81<sup>st</sup> Division. [323<sup>rd</sup> and 324<sup>th</sup> Inf and 318<sup>th</sup> MG Bn] Moved overseas Jul 1918. Returned to the US Jun 1919 and demobilized at Camp Devens, MA.

**163<sup>rd</sup> Infantry Brigade** Organized Sep 1917 at Camp Gordon, GA as component of 82<sup>nd</sup> Division. [325<sup>th</sup> and 326<sup>th</sup> Inf and 320<sup>th</sup> MG Bn] Moved overseas Apr 1918. Returned to the US May 1919 and demobilized at Camp Mills, NY.

**164<sup>th</sup> Infantry Brigade** Organized Aug 1917 at Camp Gordon, GA as component of 82<sup>nd</sup> Division. [327<sup>th</sup> and 328<sup>th</sup> Inf and 321<sup>st</sup> MG Bn] Moved overseas May 1918. Returned to the US May 1919 and demobilized at Camp Mills, NY.

**165th Infantry Brigade**      Organized Aug 1917 at Camp Sherman, OH as component of 83rd Division. [329th and 330th Inf and 323rd MG Bn] Moved overseas Jun 1918. Returned to the US Feb 1919 and demobilized at Camp Sherman.

**166th Infantry Brigade**      Organized Aug 1917 at Camp Sherman, OH as component of 83rd Division. [331st and 332nd Inf and 324th MG Bn] Moved overseas Jun 1918. Returned to the US Jan 1919 and demobilized Feb 1919 at Camp Sherman.

**167th Infantry Brigade**      Organized Aug 1917 at Camp Zachary Taylor, KY as component of 84th Division. [333rd and 334th Inf and 326th MG Bn] Moved overseas Sep 1918. Skeletonized Nov 1918. Returned to the US Jan 1919 and demobilized Feb 1919 at Camp Zachary Taylor.

**168th Infantry Brigade**      Organized Aug 1917 at Camp Zachary Taylor, KY as component of 84th Division. [335th and 336th Inf and 327th MG Bn] Moved overseas Sep 1918. Skeletonized Nov 1918. Returned to the US Jan 1919 and demobilized Feb 1919 at Camp Zachary Taylor.

**169th Infantry Brigade**      Organized Aug 1917 at Camp Custer, MI as component of 85th Division. [337th and 338th Inf and 329th MG Bn] Moved overseas Jul 1918. Returned to the US Mar 1919 and demobilized Apr 1919 at Camp Custer.

**170th Infantry Brigade**      Organized Aug 1917 at Camp Custer, MI as component of 85th Division. [339th and 340th Inf and 330th MG Bn] Moved overseas Jul 1918. Returned to the US Apr 1919 and demobilized at Camp Custer.

**171st Infantry Brigade**      Organized Sep 1917 at Camp Grant, IL as component of 86th Division. [341st and 342nd Inf and 332nd MG Bn] Moved overseas Sep 1918. Skeletonized Nov 1918. Returned to the US Jan 1919 and demobilized at Camp Grant.

**172nd Infantry Brigade**      Organized Aug 1917 at Camp Grant, IL as component of 86th Division. [343rd and 344th Inf and 333rd MG Bn] Moved overseas Sep 1918. Skeletonized Nov 1918. Returned to the US Jan 1919 and demobilized at Camp Grant.

**173rd Infantry Brigade**      Organized Aug 1917 at Camp Pike, AR as component of 87th Division. [345th and 346th Inf and 335th MG Bn] Moved overseas Aug 1918. Returned to the US Jan 1919 and demobilized Feb 1919 at Camp Dix, NJ.

**174th Infantry Brigade**      Organized Aug 1917 at Camp Pike, AR as component of 87th Division. [347th and 348th Inf and 336th MG Bn] Moved overseas Aug 1918. Returned to the US Jan 1919 and demobilized at Camp Dix, NJ.

**175<sup>th</sup> Infantry Brigade**      Organized Sep 1917 at Camp Dodge, IA as component of 88<sup>th</sup> Division. [349<sup>th</sup> and 350<sup>th</sup> Inf and 338<sup>th</sup> MG Bn] Moved overseas Aug 1918. Returned to the US May 1919 and demobilized Jun 1919 at Camp Dodge.

**176<sup>th</sup> Infantry Brigade**      Organized Aug 1917 at Camp Dodge, IA as component of 88<sup>th</sup> Division. [351<sup>st</sup> and 352<sup>nd</sup> Inf and 339<sup>th</sup> MG Bn] Moved overseas Aug 1918. Returned to the US May 1919 and demobilized Jun 1919 at Camp Dodge.

**177<sup>th</sup> Infantry Brigade**      Organized Aug 1917 at Camp Funston, KS as component of 89<sup>th</sup> Division. [353<sup>rd</sup> and 354<sup>th</sup> Inf and 341<sup>st</sup> MG Bn] Moved overseas Jun 1918. Returned to the US May 1919 and demobilized Jun 1919 at Camp Funston.

**178<sup>th</sup> Infantry Brigade**      Organized Aug 1917 at Camp Funston, KS as component of 89<sup>th</sup> Division. [355<sup>th</sup> and 356<sup>th</sup> Inf and 342<sup>nd</sup> MG Bn] Moved overseas Jun 1918. Returned to the US May 1919 and demobilized Jun 1919 at Camp Zachary Taylor, KY.

**179<sup>th</sup> Infantry Brigade**      Organized Aug 1917 at Camp Travis, TX as component of 90<sup>th</sup> Division. [357<sup>th</sup> and 358<sup>th</sup> Inf and 344<sup>th</sup> MG Bn] Moved overseas Jun 1918. Returned to the US Jun 1919 and demobilized at Camp Pike, AR.

**180<sup>th</sup> Infantry Brigade**      Organized Aug 1917 at Camp Travis, TX as component of 90<sup>th</sup> Division. [359<sup>th</sup> and 360<sup>th</sup> Inf and 345<sup>th</sup> MG Bn] Moved overseas Jun 1918. Returned to the US Jun 1919 and demobilized at Camp Bowie, TX.

**181<sup>st</sup> Infantry Brigade**      Organized Sep 1917 at Camp Lewis, WA as component of 91<sup>st</sup> Division. [361<sup>st</sup> and 362<sup>nd</sup> Inf and 347<sup>th</sup> MG Bn] Moved overseas Jul 1918. Returned to the US Apr 1919 and demobilized at Camp Kearny, CA.

**182<sup>nd</sup> Infantry Brigade**      Organized Sep 1917 at Camp Lewis, WA as component of 91<sup>st</sup> Division. [363<sup>rd</sup> and 364<sup>th</sup> Inf and 348<sup>th</sup> MG Bn] Moved overseas Jul 1918. Returned to the US Apr 1919 and demobilized at Camp Lewis.

**183<sup>rd</sup> Infantry Brigade**      Organized Nov 1917 [with black enlisted personnel] at Camp Grant, IL as component of 92<sup>nd</sup> Division. [365<sup>th</sup> and 366<sup>th</sup> Inf and 350<sup>th</sup> MG Bn] Moved overseas Jun 1918. Returned to the US Feb 1919 and demobilized Mar 1919 at Camp Upton, NY.

**184<sup>th</sup> Infantry Brigade** Organized Nov 1917 [with black enlisted personnel] at Camp Upton, NY as component of 92<sup>nd</sup> Division. [367<sup>th</sup> and 368<sup>th</sup> Inf and 351<sup>st</sup> MG Bn] Moved overseas Jun 1918. Returned to the US Feb 1919 and demobilized Mar 1919 at Camp Meade, MD.

**185th Infantry Brigade**      Organized Dec 1917 [with black enlisted personnel] at Camp Jackson, SC; assigned Jan 1918 to 93rd Division (Provisional). [369th and 370th Inf] Moved overseas Apr 1918 and demobilized May 1918 in the AEF.

**186th Infantry Brigade**      Organized Dec 1917 [with black enlisted personnel] at Camp Jackson, SC; assigned Jan 1918 to 93rd Division (Provisional). [371st and 372nd Inf] Moved overseas Apr 1918 and demobilized May 1918 in the AEF.

[187th and 188th Infantry Brigades would have gone to the 94th Division had it been organized]

[189th Infantry Brigade was to be formed in France for 95th Division but never accomplished.]

[190th Infantry Brigade was constituted for 95th Division (379th and 380th Inf and 358th MG Bn) but Hq never organized]

[191st Infantry Brigade was to be formed in France for 96th Division but never accomplished.]

**192nd Infantry Brigade**      Organized Sep 1918 at Camp Wadsworth, SC as component of 96th Division and demobilized there Dec 1918. [383rd and 384th Inf and 363rd MG Bn]

[193rd Infantry Brigade was to be formed in France for 97th Division but never accomplished.]

[194th Infantry Brigade was constituted for 97h Division (387th and 388th Inf and 366th MG Bn) but Hq never organized]

[195th Infantry Brigade was to be formed in France for 98th Division but never accomplished.]

[196th Infantry Brigade was constituted for 98h Division but never organized]

[197th Infantry Brigade was to be formed in France for 99th Division but never accomplished.]

[198th Infantry Brigade was constituted for 99h Division but never organized]

[199th Infantry Brigade was to be formed in France for 100th Division but never accomplished.]

[200th Infantry Brigade was constituted for 100h Division but never organized]

[201st Infantry Brigade was to be formed in France for 101st Division but never accomplished.]

[202nd Infantry Brigade was constituted for 101st Division but never organized]

[203rd Infantry Brigade was to be formed in France for 102nd Division but never accomplished.]

[204th Infantry Brigade was constituted for 102nd Division but never organized]

**Provisional Tactical Brigade (Puerto Rican)**   Organized Oct 1918 at Camp Las Casas, PR and demobilized there Dec 1918.

**1ˢᵗ Hawaiian Brigade**  Organized Apr 1917 at Schofield Barracks, Territory of Hawaii and discontinued there Oct 1918.

**1ˢᵗ Infantry Brigade, Philippine National Guard**  Organized Nov 1918 at Camp Tomas Claudio, P.I. Released from federal service Dec 1918 and demobilized Feb 1919 at Camp Tomas Claudio.

**2ⁿᵈ Infantry Brigade, Philippine National Guard**  Organized Nov 1918 at Camp Tomas Claudio, P.I. Released from federal service Dec 1918 and demobilized Feb 1919 at Camp Tomas Claudio.

**3ʳᵈ Infantry Brigade, Philippine National Guard**  Organized Nov 1918 at Camp Tomas Claudio, P.I. Released from federal service Dec 1918 and demobilized Feb 1919 at Camp Tomas Claudio.

**1ˢᵗ Brigade, American Forces in Germany**  Organized Nov 1919 in Germany. Demobilized there Apr 1922.

**2ⁿᵈ Brigade, American Forces in Germany**  Organized Nov 1919 in Germany. Demobilized there Dec 1921.

*Regular Army Infantry Regiments*

**1ˢᵗ Infantry**  Apr 1917 station Territory of Hawaii. Returned to the US Jun 1918 and moved to Camp Lewis, WA. Assigned 25ᵗʰ Infantry Brigade 11 Sep 1918; relieved from 13ᵗʰ Division 8 Mar 1919.

**2ⁿᵈ Infantry**  Apr 1917 station Territory of Hawaii. Returned to the US Jul 1918 and moved to Camp Dodge, IA. Assigned 38ᵗʰ Infantry Brigade 27 Jul 1918; relieved from 19ᵗʰ Division 14 Feb 1919. Moved Nov 1919 to Camp Sherman, OH.

**3ʳᵈ Infantry**  Apr 1917 station Camp Eagle Pass, TX. Assigned 20 Mar 1917—1 Jun 1917 to 3ʳᵈ Brigade, 1ˢᵗ Provisional Infantry Division. Remained on duty patrolling the Mexican border.

**4ᵗʰ Infantry**  Apr 1917 station Brownsville, TX. Assigned 20 Mar 1917—1 Jun 1917 to 1ˢᵗ Brigade, 1ˢᵗ Provisional Infantry Division. Assigned 5ᵗʰ Infantry Brigade (3ʳᵈ Division) 1 Oct 1917 and moved to Camp Greene, NC. Moved overseas Apr 1918. Returned to the US Aug 1919 and moved to Camp Pike, AR.

**5ᵗʰ Infantry**  Apr 1917 station Panama CZ. Returned to the US Aug 1918, moving to Camp Beauregard, LA. Assigned 33ʳᵈ Infantry Brigade 27 Jul 1918; relieved from 17ᵗʰ Division 10 Feb 1919. Sent to Germany Oct 1919 and assigned Nov 1919 to 2ⁿᵈ Brigade, AF in G. Transferred Dec 1921 to 1ˢᵗ Brigade, AF in G. (1ˢᵗ Brigade, AF in G, demobilized Apr 1922.)

**6<sup>th</sup> Infantry** Apr 1917 station Camp Newton D. Baker, TX. Assigned 20 Mar 1917—May 1917 to 2<sup>nd</sup> Brigade, 2<sup>nd</sup> Provisional Infantry Division. Moved May 1917 to Chickamauga Park, GA. Assigned 10<sup>th</sup> Infantry Brigade (5<sup>th</sup> Division) 18 Nov 1917. Moved overseas Apr 1918. Returned to the US Jul 1919 and moved to Camp Gordon, GA.

**7<sup>th</sup> Infantry** Apr 1917 station Camp Fort Bliss, TX. Assigned 20 Mar 1917—1 Jun 1917 to 1<sup>st</sup> Brigade, 2<sup>nd</sup> Provisional Infantry Division. Moved Jun 1917 to Gettysburg, PA and Nov 1917 to Camp Greene, NC. Assigned 5<sup>th</sup> Infantry Brigade (3<sup>rd</sup> Division) 21 Nov 1917. Moved overseas Apr 1918. Returned to the US Aug 1919 and moved to Camp Pike, AR.

**8<sup>th</sup> Infantry** Apr 1917 station Philippine Islands. Returned to the US Sep 1917 and moved to Camp Fremont, CA. Assigned 16<sup>th</sup> Infantry Brigade (8<sup>th</sup> Division) 17 Dec 1917. Moved overseas Oct 1918. Remained in Europe and assigned Nov 1919 to 1<sup>st</sup> Brigade, AF in G.[50] (1<sup>st</sup> Brigade, AF in G, demobilized Apr 1922.)

**9<sup>th</sup> Infantry** Apr 1917 station Camp Wilson, TX. Assigned 20 Mar 1917—May 1917 to 2<sup>nd</sup> Brigade, 1<sup>st</sup> Provisional Infantry Division. Moved May 1917 to Syracuse, NY. Moved overseas Sep 1917 and assigned 3<sup>rd</sup> Infantry Brigade (2<sup>nd</sup> Division) 22 Sep 1917 in France. Returned to the US Jul 1919 and moved to Camp Travis, TX.

**10<sup>th</sup> Infantry** Apr 1917 station Panama CZ. Returned to the US May 1917 and moved to Ft. Benjamin Harrison, IN. Assigned 27<sup>th</sup> Infantry Brigade 5 Jul 1918 (and moved to Camp Custer, MI); relieved from 14<sup>th</sup> Division in Feb 1919.

**11<sup>th</sup> Infantry** Apr 1917 station Douglas, AZ. Assigned 20 Mar 1917—May 1917 to 2<sup>nd</sup> Brigade, 3<sup>rd</sup> Provisional Infantry Division. Moved May 1917 to Chickamauga Park, GA. Assigned 10<sup>th</sup> Infantry Brigade (5<sup>th</sup> Division) 17 Nov 1917. Moved overseas Apr 1918. Returned to the US Jul 1919 and moved to Camp Gordon, GA.

**12<sup>th</sup> Infantry** Apr 1917 station Nogales, AZ. Assigned 20 Mar 1917—May 1917 to 1<sup>st</sup> Brigade, 3<sup>rd</sup> Provisional Infantry Division. Moved May 1917 to Presidio of San Francisco, CA. Assigned 15<sup>th</sup> Infantry Brigade (8<sup>th</sup> Division) 17 Dec 1917 and moved Jan 1918 to Camp Fremont, CA. Moved Nov 1918 to Camp Stuart, VA; Oct 1919 to Ft. Jay, NY; and Nov 1919 to Camp Meade, MD.

---

[50] However, the 8<sup>th</sup> Infantry was officially assigned to the 8<sup>th</sup> Division until 1923 when switched to the 4<sup>th</sup> Division.

**13<sup>th</sup> Infantry**    Apr 1917 station Philippine Islands.  Returned to the US Aug 1917 and moved to Presidio of San Francisco, CA.  Assigned 16<sup>th</sup> Infantry Brigade (8<sup>th</sup> Division) 17 Dec 1917 and moved Jan 1918 to Camp Fremont, CA.  Moved Dec 1918 to Camp Merritt, NJ.

**14<sup>th</sup> Infantry**    Apr 1917 station Yuma, AZ.  Assigned (less 1<sup>st</sup> Bn) 20 Mar 1917—1 Jun 1917 to 1<sup>st</sup> Brigade, 3<sup>rd</sup> Provisional Infantry Division.  Moved Nov 1917 to Vancouver Barracks, WA; Jan 1918 to Ft. George Wright, WA; and Mar 1918 to Ft. Lawton, WA.  Assigned 37<sup>th</sup> Infantry Brigade 27 Jul 1918; relieved from 19<sup>th</sup> Division 14 Feb 1919.  Moved Dec 1918 to Camp Grant, IL and Nov 1919 to Camp Custer, MI.

**15<sup>th</sup> Infantry**    Apr 1917 station Tientsin, China.

**16<sup>th</sup> Infantry**    Apr 1917 station Camp Newton D. Baker, TX.  Assigned 20 Mar 1917—May 1917 to 2<sup>nd</sup> Brigade, 2<sup>nd</sup> Provisional Infantry Division.  Moved May 1917 to Ft. Bliss, TX.  Assigned 8 Jun 1917 to 1<sup>st</sup> Expeditionary Division [1<sup>st</sup> Infantry Brigade, 1<sup>st</sup> Division].  Moved overseas Jun 1917.  Returned to the US Sep 1919 and moved to Camp Zachary Taylor, KY.

**17<sup>th</sup> Infantry**    Apr 1917 station Ft. McPherson, GA.  Assigned 20 Mar 1917—1 Jun 1917 to 1<sup>st</sup> Brigade, 2<sup>nd</sup> Provisional Infantry Division.  Moved Aug 1917 to Chickamauga Park, GA; moved Mar 1918 to Charleston, SC; Jun 1918 to Camp Sevier, SC; and Jul 1918 to Camp Meade, MD.  Assigned 21<sup>st</sup> Infantry Brigade 5 Jul 1918; relieved from 11<sup>th</sup> Division in 1923 [sic].

**18<sup>th</sup> Infantry**    Apr 1917 station Camp Harry J. Jones, Douglas, AZ.  Assigned 20 Mar 1917—1 Jun 1917 to 2<sup>nd</sup> Brigade, 3<sup>rd</sup> Provisional Infantry Division.  Assigned 8 Jun 1917 to 1<sup>st</sup> Expeditionary Division [1<sup>st</sup> Infantry Brigade, 1<sup>st</sup> Division].  Moved overseas Jun 1917.  Returned to the US Sep 1919 and moved to Camp Zachary Taylor, KY.

**19<sup>th</sup> Infantry**    Apr 1917 station Ft. Sam Houston, TX.  Assigned 20 Mar 1917—1 Jun 1917 to 2<sup>nd</sup> Brigade, 1<sup>st</sup> Provisional Infantry Division.  Moved Jun 1918 to Camp Travis, TX.  Assigned 35<sup>th</sup> Infantry Brigade 29 Jul 1918; relieved from 18<sup>th</sup> Division 14 Feb 1919.  Moved Mar 1919 to Camp Harry J. Jones, Douglas, AZ.

**20<sup>th</sup> Infantry**    Apr 1917 station Camp Fort Bliss, TX.  Assigned 20 Mar 1917—May 1917 to 2<sup>nd</sup> Brigade, 2<sup>nd</sup> Provisional Infantry Division.  Moved May 1917 to Ft. Douglas, UT and Jun 1918 to Camp Funston, KS.  Assigned 20<sup>th</sup> Infantry Brigade 9 Jul 1918 (moved Dec 1918 to Ft. Leavenworth, KS); relieved from 10<sup>th</sup> Division 14 Feb 1919.  Moved Feb 1919 to Ft. Riley, KS and Jul 1919 to Ft. Crook, NE.

**21<sup>st</sup> Infantry**    Apr 1917 station San Diego, CA.  Assigned 31<sup>st</sup> Infantry Brigade 29 Jul 1918 (and moved Aug 1918 to Camp Kearny, CA); relieved from 16<sup>th</sup> Division 8 Mar 1919.  Moved Feb 1919 to Vancouver Barracks, WA and Mar 1919 to Ft. George Wright, WA.

**22nd Infantry**  Apr 1917 station Ft. Jay, NY. Assigned 20 Mar 1917—1 Jun 1917 to 2nd Brigade, 3rd Provisional Infantry Division. Remained in US, guarding installations in Eastern Department.

**23rd Infantry**  Apr 1917 station Camp Cotton, TX. Assigned 20 Mar 1917—May 1917 to 1st Brigade, 2nd Provisional Infantry Division. Moved May1917 to Syracuse, NY. Moved overseas Sep 1917. Assigned 22 Sep 1917 in France to 3rd Infantry Brigade (2nd Division). Returned to the US Aug 1919 and moved to Camp Travis, TX.

**24th Infantry**  Apr 1917 station Camp Furlong, NM [regiment formed with black enlisted personnel]. Assigned 20 Mar 1917—1 Jun 1917 to 3rd Brigade, 2nd Provisional Infantry Division.

**25th Infantry**  Apr 1917 station Hawaii [regiment formed with black enlisted personnel]. Returned to the US Oct 1918 and moved to Camp Stephen Little, AZ and assigned duties patrolling Mexican border.

**26th Infantry**  Apr 1917 station Harlingen, TX. Assigned 20 Mar 1917—1 Jun 1917 to 1st Brigade, 1st Provisional Infantry Division. Assigned 8 Jun 1917 to 1st Expeditionary Division [2nd Infantry Brigade, 1st Division]. Moved overseas Jun 1917. Returned to the US Sep 1919 and moved to Camp Zachary Taylor, KY.

**27th Infantry**  Apr 1917 station the Philippine Islands. Joined AEF, Siberia Jul 1918 and moved Aug 1918 to Vladivostok, Russia.[51] Left Russia 1920.

**28th Infantry**  Apr 1917 station Ft. Ringgold, TX. Assigned 20 Mar 1917—1 Jun 1917 to 1st Brigade, 1st Provisional Infantry Division. Assigned 8 Jun 1917 to 1st Expeditionary Division [2nd Infantry Brigade, 1st Division]. Moved overseas Jun 1917. Returned to the US Sep 1919 and moved to Camp Zachary Taylor, KY.

**29th Infantry**  Apr 1917 station Panama Canal Zone. Assigned 34th Infantry Brigade 29 Jul 1918; relieved from 17th Division 10 Feb 1919. Returned to the US Sep 1918 and moved to Camp Beauregard, LA. Moved Mar 1919 to Camp Shelby, MS and Oct 1919 to Camp Benning, GA.

**30th Infantry**  Apr 1917 station Camp Eagle Pass, TX. Assigned 20 Mar 1917—1 Jun 1917 to 3rd Brigade, 1st Provisional Infantry Division. Moved May 1917 to Syracuse, NY and Oct 1917 to Camp Greene, NC. Assigned 6th Infantry Brigade (3rd Division) 21 Nov 1917. Moved overseas Apr 1918. Returned to the US Aug 1919 and moved to Camp Pike, AR.

**31st Infantry**  Apr 1917 station the Philippine Islands. Joined AEF, Siberia Jul 1918 and moved Aug 1918 to Vladivostok, Russia.[52] Left Russia 1920.

---

[51] Entitled to Siberia 1918 and Siberia 1919 campaign participation credit.

[52] Entitled to Siberia 1918 and Siberia 1919 campaign participation credit.

**32<sup>nd</sup> Infantry** — Apr 1917 station Hawaii. Returned to the US Jul 1918 and moved to Camp Kearny, CA. Assigned 32<sup>nd</sup> Infantry Brigade 31 Jul 1918; relieved from 16<sup>th</sup> Division 8 Mar 1919.

**33<sup>rd</sup> Infantry** — Apr 1917 station Panama Canal Zone.

**34<sup>th</sup> Infantry** — Apr 1917 station Marfa, TX. Assigned 20 Mar 1917—May 1917 to 3<sup>rd</sup> Brigade, 2<sup>nd</sup> Provisional Infantry Division.Moved May 1917 to Camp Fort Bliss, TX. Assigned 14<sup>th</sup> Infantry Brigade (7<sup>th</sup> Division) 6 Dec 1917. Moved overseas Aug 1918. Returned to the US Jun 1919 and moved to Camp Funston, KS.

**35<sup>th</sup> Infantry** — Apr 1917 station Nogales, AZ. Assigned 20 Mar 1917—1 Jun 1917 to 1<sup>st</sup> Brigade, 3<sup>rd</sup> Provisional Infantry Division. Assigned 36<sup>th</sup> Infantry Brigade 7 Aug 1918; relieved from 18<sup>th</sup> Division 14 Feb 1919. Moved Aug 1918 to Camp Travis, TX and Nov 1918 to Camp Lewis, WA.

**36<sup>th</sup> Infantry** — Apr 1917 station Ft. Clark, TX. Assigned 20 Mar 1917—1 Jun 1917 to 3<sup>rd</sup> Brigade, 1<sup>st</sup> Provisional Infantry Division. Moved Jun 1917 to Ft. Snelling, MN. Assigned 23<sup>rd</sup> Infantry Brigade 5 Jul 1918; relieved from 12<sup>th</sup> Division 31 Jan 1919. Moved Aug 1918 to Camp Devens, MA.

**37<sup>th</sup> Infantry** — Apr 1917 station Ft. McIntosh, TX. Assigned 20 Mar 1917—1 Jun 1917 to 2<sup>nd</sup> Brigade, 1<sup>st</sup> Provisional Infantry Division.Remained on duty patrolling the Mexican border..

**38<sup>th</sup> Infantry** — Organized 1 Jun 1917 at Syracuse, NY. Assigned 6<sup>th</sup> Infantry Brigade (3<sup>rd</sup> Division) 1 Oct 1917. Moved overseas Mar 1918. Returned to the US Aug 1919 and moved to Camp Pike, AR.

**39<sup>th</sup> Infantry** — Organized 1 Jun 1917 at Syracuse, NY. Assigned 7<sup>th</sup> Infantry Brigade (4<sup>th</sup> Division) 19 Nov 1917. Moved overseas May 1918. Returned to the US Aug 1919 and moved to Camp Dodge, IA.

**40<sup>th</sup> Infantry** — Organized 20 Jun 1917 at Ft. Snelling, MN. Moved Jul 1918 to Camp Custer, MI. Assigned 28<sup>th</sup> Infantry Brigade 5 Jul 1918; relieved from 14<sup>th</sup> Division in Feb 1919. Moved Dec 1918 to Camp Sherman, OH.

**41<sup>st</sup> Infantry** — Organized 20 Jun 1917 at Ft. Snelling, MN. Moved Jun 1918 to Camp Funston, KS. Assigned 19<sup>th</sup> Infantry Brigade 9 Jul 1918; relieved from 10<sup>th</sup> Division 18 Feb 1919. Moved Nov 1919 to Camp Upton, NY.

**42<sup>nd</sup> Infantry** — Organized 24 Jun 1917 at Ft. Douglas, UT. Moved Nov 1918 to Camp Dodge, IA; Mar 1918 to Picatinny Arsenal, NJ; and Jul 1918 to Camp Devens, MA. Assigned 24<sup>th</sup> Infantry Brigade 5 Jul 1918; relieved from 12<sup>th</sup> Division 31 Jan 1919. Moved Dec 1918 to Camp Upton, NY.

**43<sup>rd</sup> Infantry**    Organized 1 Jun 1917 at Ft. Douglas, UT. Moved Nov 1917 to Camp Pike, AR ; Feb 1918 to New Orleans, LA and Jul 1918 to Camp Logan, TX. Assigned 29<sup>th</sup> Infantry Brigade 31 Jul 1918; relieved from 15<sup>th</sup> Division 18 May 1919. Moved Mar 1919 to Camp Travis, TX and Aug 1919 to Camp Lee, VA.

**44<sup>th</sup> Infantry**    Organized 11 Jun 1917 at Vancouver Barracks, WA. Moved Nov 1918 to Camp Lewis, WA and Dec 1918 to Presidio of San Francisco, CA. Assigned 26<sup>th</sup> Infantry Brigade 11 Sep 1918; relieved from 13<sup>th</sup> Division 8 Mar 1919.

**45<sup>th</sup> Infantry**    Organized 4 Jun 1917 at Ft. Benjamin Harrison, IN. Moved Nov 1917 to Camp Zachary Taylor, KY; Apr 1918 to Camp Gordon, GA and Jun 1918 to Camp Sheridan, AL. Assigned 17<sup>th</sup> Infantry Brigade 5 Jul 1918; relieved from 9<sup>th</sup> Division 15 Feb 1919. Moved Dec 1918 to Camp Gordon, GA and Sep 1919 to Camp Dix, NJ.

**46<sup>th</sup> Infantry**    Organized 4 Jun 1917 at Ft. Benjamin Harrison, IN. Moved Nov 1917 to Camp Zachary Taylor, KY; Apr 1918 to Camp Gordon, GA and May 1918 to Camp Sheridan, AL. Assigned 18<sup>th</sup> Infantry Brigade 5 Jul 1918; relieved from 9<sup>th</sup> Division 15 Feb 1919. Moved Mar 1919 to Ft. Oglethorpe, GA and Aug 1919 to Camp Jackson, SC.

**47<sup>th</sup> Infantry**    Organized 1 Jun 1917 at Syracuse, NY. Moved Oct 1917 to Camp Greene, NC. Assigned 7<sup>th</sup> Infantry Brigade (4<sup>th</sup> Division) 19 Nov 1917. Moved overseas May 1918. Returned to the US Jul 1919 and moved to Camp Dodge, IA.

**48<sup>th</sup> Infantry**    Organized 1 Jun 1917 at Syracuse, NY. Moved Sep 1917 to Camp Hill, VA and Dec 1917 to Camp Stuart, VA. Assigned 39<sup>th</sup> Infantry Brigade 31 Jul 1918; relieved from 20<sup>th</sup> Division 28 Feb 1919. Moved Aug 1918 to Camp Sevier, SC and Dec 1918 to Camp Jackson, SC.

**49<sup>th</sup> Infantry**    Organized 1 Jun 1917 at Syracuse, NY. Moved Sep 1917 to Camp Merritt, NJ. Moved overseas Jul 1918; joined the 83<sup>rd</sup> Division 12 Aug 1918 as an attached unit. (The 83<sup>rd</sup> Division was reorganized 27 Jun 1918 as 2<sup>nd</sup> Depot Division.) Returned to the US Jan 1919 and moved to Ft. Snelling, MN.

**50<sup>th</sup> Infantry**    Organized 1 Jun 1917 at Syracuse, NY. Moved Nov 1917 to Camp Greene, NC and Mar 1918 to Curtis Bay, MD. Assigned 40<sup>th</sup> Infantry Brigade 31 Jul 1918; relieved from 20<sup>th</sup> Division 28 Feb 1919. Moved Aug 1918 to Camp Sevier, SC and Dec 1918 to Camp Dix, NJ. Moved overseas Oct 1919 and assigned Nov 1919 to 2<sup>nd</sup> Brigade, AF in G. (Inactivated 31 Dec 1921 in Germany.)

**51<sup>st</sup> Infantry**          Organized 16 Jun 1917 at Chickamauga Park, GA. Assigned 11<sup>th</sup> Infantry Brigade (6<sup>th</sup> Division) 16 Nov 1917. Moved overseas Jul 1918. Returned to the US Jun 1919 and moved to Camp Grant, IL.

**52<sup>nd</sup> Infantry**          Organized 16 Jun 1917 at Chickamauga Park, GA. Assigned 11<sup>th</sup> Infantry Brigade (6<sup>th</sup> Division) 16 Nov 1917. Moved overseas Jul 1918. Returned to the US Jun 1919 and moved to Camp Grant, IL.

**53<sup>rd</sup> Infantry**          Organized 16 Jun 1917 at Chickamauga Park, GA. Assigned 12<sup>th</sup> Infantry Brigade (6<sup>th</sup> Division) 16 Nov 1917. Moved overseas Jul 1918. Returned to the US Jun 1919 and moved to Camp Grant, IL.

**54<sup>th</sup> Infantry**          Organized 16 Jun 1917 at Chickamauga Park, GA. Assigned 12<sup>th</sup> Infantry Brigade (6<sup>th</sup> Division) 16 Nov 1917. Moved overseas Jul 1918. Returned to the US Jun 1919 and moved to Camp Grant, IL.

**55<sup>th</sup> Infantry**          Organized 16 Jun 1917 at Chickamauga Park, GA.[53] Assigned 13<sup>th</sup> Infantry Brigade (7<sup>th</sup> Division) 16 Nov 1917. Moved overseas Aug 1918. Returned to the US Jun 1919 and moved to Camp Funston, KS.

**56<sup>th</sup> Infantry**          Organized 16 Jun 1917 at Ft. Oglethorpe, GA; moved Jul 1917 to Chickamauga Park, GA. Assigned 13<sup>th</sup> Infantry Brigade (7<sup>th</sup> Division) 16 Nov 1917. Moved overseas Aug 1918. Returned to the US Jun 1919 and moved to Camp Funston, KS.

**57<sup>th</sup> Infantry**          Organized 1 Jun 1917 at Camp Wilson, TX. Moved Jul 1917 to Camp Funston, TX; Oct 1917 to San Benito, TX; Nov 1917 to Brownsville, TX; Dec 1917 to Houston, TX; and May 1918 to Camp Logan, TX. Assigned 30<sup>th</sup> Infantry Brigade 31 Jul 1918; relieved from 15<sup>th</sup> Division 18 May 1919. Moved Dec 1918 to Camp Pike, AR and Nov 1919 to Camp Dix, NJ.

**58<sup>th</sup> Infantry**          Organized 5 Jun 1917 at Gettysburg National Park, PA. Moved Nov 1917 to Camp Greene, NC. Assigned 8<sup>th</sup> Infantry Brigade (4<sup>th</sup> Division) 19 Nov 1917. Moved overseas May 1918. Returned to the US Aug 1919 and moved to Camp Dodge, IA.

**59<sup>th</sup> Infantry**          Organized 8 Jun 1917 at Gettysburg National Park, PA. Moved Nov 1917 to Camp Greene, NC. Assigned 8<sup>th</sup> Infantry Brigade (4<sup>th</sup> Division) 19 Nov 1917. Moved overseas May 1918. Returned to the US Aug 1919 and moved to Camp Dodge, IA.

---

[53] Per Sawicki's lineage volume. The *Order of Battle* volume shows organization at Ft. McPherson, GA Jun 1917 and the moved to Chickamauga Park, GA Jul 1917.

**60th Infantry**    Organized 10 Jun 1917 at Gettysburg National Park, PA. Moved Nov 1917 to Camp Greene, NC. Assigned 9th Infantry Brigade (5th Division) 17 Nov 1917. Moved overseas Apr 1918. Returned to the US Jul 1919 and moved to Camp Gordon, GA.

**61st Infantry**    Organized 10 Jun 1917 at Gettysburg National Park, PA. Moved Nov 1917 to Camp Greene, NC. Assigned 9th Infantry Brigade (5th Division) 17 Nov 1917. Moved overseas Apr 1918. Returned to the US Jul 1919 and moved to Camp Gordon, GA.

**62nd Infantry**    Organized 1 Jun 1917 at the Presidio of San Francisco, CA. Assigned 15th Infantry Brigade 17 Dec 1917; relieved from 8th Division 5 Sep 1919. Moved Jan 1918 to Camp Fremont, CA; Oct 1918 to Camp Mills, NY; and Nov 1918 to Camp Lee, VA.

**63rd Infantry**    Organized 1 Jun 1917 at the Presidio of San Francisco, CA. Assigned 22nd Infantry Brigade 5 Jul 1918; relieved from 11th Division 29 Nov 1918. Moved Aug 1918 to Camp Meade, MD; Jan 1919 to East Potomac Park, DC; and Jun 1919 to Madison, Barracks, NY.

**64th Infantry**    Organized Jun 1917 at Camp Baker, TX and moved to Camp Fort Bliss, TX. Assigned 14th Infantry Brigade (7th Division) 16 Nov 1917. Moved overseas Aug 1918. Returned to the US Jun 1919 and moved to Camp Funston, KS.

[The numbers 65 and 66 were not used in World War I; "65" would be used in 1920 for the Puerto Rico Regiment of Infantry]

**67th Infantry**    Organized Jul 1918 at Camp Sheridan, AL and assigned 17th Infantry Brigade; relieved from 9th Division and demobilized 15 Feb 1919 at Camp Sheridan.

**68th Infantry**    Organized Jul 1918 at Camp Sheridan, AL and assigned 18th Infantry Brigade; relieved from 9th Division and demobilized 15 Feb 1919 at Camp Sheridan.

**69th Infantry**    Organized 10 Aug 1918 at Camp Funston, KS and assigned 19th Infantry Brigade; relieved from 10th Division and demobilized 13 Feb 1919 at Camp Funston.

**70th Infantry**    Organized 10 Aug 1918 at Camp Funston, KS and assigned 20th Infantry Brigade; relieved from 10th Division and demobilized 13 Feb 1919 at Camp Funston.

**71st Infantry**    Organized Aug 1918 at Camp Meade, MD and assigned 21st Infantry Brigade; relieved from 11th Division and demobilized 3 Feb 1919 at Camp Meade.

**72nd Infantry**    Organized Sep 1918 at Camp Meade, MD and assigned 22nd Infantry Brigade; relieved from 11th Division and demobilized 30 Jan 1919 at Camp Meade.

**73<sup>rd</sup> Infantry**   Organized Jul 1918 at Camp Devens, MA and assigned 23<sup>rd</sup> Infantry Brigade; relieved from 12<sup>th</sup> Division and demobilized 31 Jan 1919 at Camp Devens.

**74<sup>th</sup> Infantry**   Organized Jul 1918 at Camp Devens, MA and assigned 24<sup>th</sup> Infantry Brigade; relieved from 12<sup>th</sup> Division and demobilized 31 Jan 1919 at Camp Devens.

**75<sup>th</sup> Infantry**   Organized Aug 1918 at Camp Lewis, WA and assigned 25<sup>th</sup> Infantry Brigade; relieved from 13<sup>th</sup> Division and demobilized 27 Feb 1919 at Camp Lewis.

**76<sup>th</sup> Infantry**   Organized Aug 1918 at Camp Lewis, WA and assigned 26<sup>th</sup> Infantry Brigade; relieved from 13<sup>th</sup> Division and demobilized 5 Mar 1919 at Camp Lewis.

**77<sup>th</sup> Infantry** Organized Aug 1918 at Camp Custer, MI and assigned 27<sup>th</sup> Infantry Brigade; relieved from 14<sup>th</sup> Division and demobilized 18 Feb 1919 at Camp Custer.

**78<sup>th</sup> Infantry**   Organized Aug 1918 at Camp Custer, MI and assigned 28<sup>th</sup> Infantry Brigade; relieved from 14<sup>th</sup> Division and demobilized 18 Feb 1919 at Camp Custer.

**79<sup>th</sup> Infantry**   Organized Sep 1918 at Camp Logan, TX and assigned 29<sup>th</sup> Infantry Brigade; relieved from 15<sup>th</sup> Division and demobilized 18 Feb 1919 at Camp Logan.

**80<sup>th</sup> Infantry**   Organized Sep 1918 at Camp Logan, TX and assigned 30<sup>th</sup> Infantry Brigade; relieved from 15<sup>th</sup> Division and demobilized 18 Feb 1919 at Camp Logan.

**81<sup>st</sup> Infantry**   Organized Sep 1918 at Camp Kearny, CA and assigned 31<sup>st</sup> Infantry Brigade; relieved from 16<sup>th</sup> Division and demobilized 15 Feb 1919 at Camp Kearny.

**82<sup>nd</sup> Infantry**   Organized Sep 1918 at Camp Kearny, CA and assigned 32<sup>nd</sup> Infantry Brigade; relieved from 16<sup>th</sup> Division and demobilized 15 Feb 1919 at Camp Kearny.

**83<sup>rd</sup> Infantry**   Organized Aug 1918 at Camp Beauregard, LA and assigned 33<sup>rd</sup> Infantry Brigade; relieved from 17<sup>th</sup> Division and demobilized 31 Jan 1919 at Camp Beauregard.

**84<sup>th</sup> Infantry**   Organized Sep 1918 at Camp Beauregard, LA and assigned 34<sup>th</sup> Infantry Brigade; relieved from 17<sup>th</sup> Division and demobilized 31 Jan 1919 at Camp Beauregard.

**85<sup>th</sup> Infantry**   Organized Sep 1918 at Camp Travis, TX and assigned 35<sup>th</sup> Infantry Brigade; relieved from 18<sup>th</sup> Division and demobilized 13 Feb 1919 at Camp Travis.

**86<sup>th</sup> Infantry**   Organized Sep 1918 at Camp Travis, TX and assigned 36<sup>th</sup> Infantry Brigade; relieved from 18<sup>th</sup> Division and demobilized 13 Feb 1919 at Camp Travis.

**87th Infantry**     Organized Sep 1918 at Camp Dodge, IA and assigned 37th Infantry Brigade; relieved from 19th Division and demobilized 27 Jan 1919 at Camp Dodge.

**88th Infantry**   Organized Sep 1918 at Camp Dodge, IA and assigned 38th Infantry Brigade; relieved from 19th Division and demobilized 27 Jan 1919 at Camp Dodge.

**89th Infantry**     Organized Aug-Sep 1918 at Camp Sevier, SC and assigned 39th Infantry Brigade; relieved from 20th Division and demobilized 27-29 Mar 1919 at Ft. Oglethorpe, GA and Camp Sevier.

**90th Infantry**     Organized Aug-Sep 1918 at Camp Sevier, SC and assigned 40th Infantry Brigade; relieved from 20th Division and demobilized 13-22 Mar 1919 at Camp Wadsworth, SC, Camp Hancock, GA and Camp Greene, NC.

**Puerto Rico Regiment of Infantry**     Stationed in Puerto Rico. (Redesignated 14 Sep 1920 as 65th Infantry.)

*National Guard Infantry Regiments*[54]

**101st Infantry**     Organized 22 Aug 1917 (formed from 9th Infantry, MA NG and 5th Infantry (-), MA NG) at Framingham, MA and assigned 51st Infantry Brigade (26th Division). Moved overseas Sep 1917. Returned to the US Apr 1919. Demobilized 28 Apr 1919 at Camp Devens, MA.

**102nd Infantry**   Organized 20 Aug 1917 (formed from 2nd Infantry, CT NG and 1st Infantry, CT NG) at New Haven, CT and assigned 51st Infantry Brigade (26th Division). Moved overseas Sep 1917. Returned to the US Apr 1919. Demobilized 29 Apr 1919 at Camp Devens, MA.

**103rd Infantry**   Organized 21 Aug 1917 (formed from 2nd Infantry, ME NG, and 1st Infantry, NH NG) at Westfield, MA and assigned 52nd Infantry Brigade (26th Division). Moved overseas Sep 1917. Returned to the US Apr 1919. Demobilized 28 Apr 1919 at Camp Devens, MA.

**104th Infantry**     Organized 17 Aug 1917 (formed from 2nd Infantry, MA NG and personnel from 6th and 8th Infantry, MA NG) at Camp Bartlett, MA and assigned 52nd Infantry Brigade (26th Division). Moved overseas Sep 1917. Returned to the US Apr 1919. Demobilized 29 Apr 1919 at Camp Devens, MA.

---

[54] In some cases, existing National Guard regiments were simply redesignated with the new numbers and assigned to the new divisions; in other cases, the new regiments were formed from several existing units. For convenience, all are shown simply as organized the date they assumed the new numbers and division assignments. Where multiple NG regiments are shown, the first named is the most likely to have the World War I regiment in their official lineage.

**105th Infantry**  Organized 1 Oct 1917 (formed from 2nd Infantry, NY NG and personnel from 71st Infantry, NY NG) at Camp Wadsworth, SC and assigned 53rd Infantry Brigade (27th Division). Moved overseas May 1919. Returned to the US Mar 1919. Demobilized 1 Apr 1919 at Camp Upton, NY.

**106th Infantry**  Organized 1 Oct 1917 (formed from 23rd Infantry, NY NG and personnel from 14th Infantry, NY NG) at Camp Wadsworth, SC and assigned 53rd Infantry Brigade (27th Division). Moved overseas May 1919. Returned to the US Mar 1919. Demobilized 2 Apr 1919 at Camp Upton, NY.

**107th Infantry**  Organized 1 Oct 1917 (formed from 7th Infantry, NY NG and personnel from 1st and 12th Infantry, NY NG) at Camp Wadsworth, SC and assigned 54th Infantry Brigade (27th Division). Moved overseas May 1919. Returned to the US Mar 1919. Demobilized 2 Apr 1919 at Camp Upton, NY.

**108th Infantry**  Organized 1 Oct 1917 (formed from 3rd Infantry, NY NG and personnel from 12th and 74th Infantry, NY NG) at Camp Wadsworth, SC and assigned 54th Infantry Brigade (27th Division). Moved overseas May 1919. Returned to the US Mar 1919. Demobilized 31 Mar 1919 at Camp Upton, NY.

**109th Infantry**  Organized 11 Oct 1917 (formed from 13th and 1st Infantry, PA NG) at Camp Hancock, GA and assigned 55th Infantry Brigade (28th Division). Moved overseas May 1918. Returned to the US May 1919. Demobilized 20 May 1919 at Camp Dix, NJ.

**110th Infantry**  Organized 11 Oct 1917 (formed from 10th and 3rd Infantry, PA NG) at Camp Hancock, GA and assigned 55th Infantry Brigade (28th Division). Moved overseas May 1918. Returned to the US May 1919. Demobilized 24 May 1919 at Camp Dix, NJ.

**111th Infantry**  Organized 11 Oct 1917 (formed from 18th and 6th Infantry, PA NG) at Camp Hancock, GA and assigned 56th Infantry Brigade (28th Division). Moved overseas May 1918. Returned to the US Apr 1919. Demobilized 6-13 May 1919 at Camp Dix, NJ.

**112th Infantry**  Organized 11 Oct 1917 (formed from 16th and 8th (-) Infantry, PA NG) at Camp Hancock, GA and assigned 56th Infantry Brigade (28th Division). Moved overseas May 1918. Returned to the US Apr 1919. Demobilized 6 May 1919 at Camp Dix, NJ.

**113th Infantry**  Organized 11 Oct 1917 (formed from 1st, 2nd (-) and 4th (-) Infantry, NJ NG) at Camp McClellan, AL and assigned 57th Infantry Brigade (29th Division). Moved overseas Jun 1918. Returned to the US May 1919. Demobilized 28 May 1919 at Camp Dix, NJ.

**114th Infantry**        Organized 11 Oct 1917 (formed from 3rd (-) and 5th Infantry, NJ NG) at Camp McClellan, AL and assigned 57th Infantry Brigade (29th Division). Moved overseas Jun 1918. Returned to the US May 1919. Demobilized 14 May 1919 at Camp Dix, NJ.

**115th Infantry**        Organized 1 Oct 1917 (formed from 1st and elements 4th and 5th Infantry, MD NG) at Camp McClellan, AL and assigned 58th Infantry Brigade (29th Division). Moved overseas Jun 1918. Returned to the US May 1919. Demobilized 7 Jun 1919 at Camp Meade, MD.

**116th Infantry**        Organized 4 Oct 1917 (formed from 1st, 2nd and 4th (-) Infantry, VA NG) at Camp McClellan, AL and assigned 58th Infantry Brigade (29th Division). Moved overseas Jun 1918. Returned to the US May 1919. Demobilized 30 May 1919 at Camp Lee, VA.

**117th Infantry**        Organized 14 Sep 1917 (formed from 3rd Infantry, TN NG) at Camp Sevier, SC and assigned 59th Infantry Brigade (30th Division). Moved overseas May 1918. Returned to the US Mar 1919. Demobilized 17 Apr 1919 at Ft. Oglethorpe, GA.

**118th Infantry**        Organized 12 Sep 1917 (formed from 1st Infantry and 3rd Bn, 2nd Infantry, SC NG) at Camp Sevier, SC and assigned 59th Infantry Brigade (30th Division). Moved overseas May 1918. Returned to the US Mar 1919. Demobilized 1 Apr 1919 at Camp Jackson, SC.

**119th Infantry**        Organized 12 Sep 1917 (formed from 2nd Infantry, NC NG, and 1st Bn and other personnel 2nd Infantry, TN NG) at Camp Sevier, SC and assigned 60th Infantry Brigade (30th Division). Moved overseas May 1918. Returned to the US Apr 1919. Demobilized 17 Apr 1919 at Camp Jackson, SC.

**120th Infantry**        Organized 12 Sep 1917 (formed from 3rd Infantry, NC NG and personnel from 2nd Infantry, TN NG) at Camp Sevier, SC and assigned 60th Infantry Brigade (30th Division). Moved overseas May 1918. Returned to the US Apr 1919. Demobilized 17 Apr 1919 at Camp Jackson, SC.

**121st Infantry**  Organized 1 Oct 1917 (formed from 2nd Infantry (-), GA NG and three separate coys GA NG) at Camp Wheeler, GA and assigned 61st Infantry Brigade (31st Division). Moved overseas Oct 1918. (31st Division skeletonized upon arrival in Europe and served as a replacement division.) Returned to the US Dec 1918. Demobilized 14 Jan 1919 at Camp Gordon, GA.

**122nd Infantry**  Organized 1 Oct 1917 (formed from 5th Infantry, GA NG) at Camp Wheeler, GA and assigned 61st Infantry Brigade (31st Division). Moved overseas Oct 1918. (31st Division skeletonized upon arrival in Europe and served as a replacement division.) Returned to the US Dec 1918. Demobilized 14 Jan 1919 at Camp Gordon, GA.

**123$^{rd}$ Infantry**      Organized 18 Sep 1917 (formed from 1$^{st}$ Infantry, AL NG) at Camp Wheeler, GA and assigned 62$^{nd}$ Infantry Brigade (31$^{st}$ Division). Moved overseas Oct 1918. (31$^{st}$ Division skeletonized upon arrival in Europe and served as a replacement division.) Returned to the US Dec 1918. Demobilized 14 Jan 1919 at Camp Gordon, GA.

**124$^{th}$ Infantry**      Organized 1 Oct 1917 (formed from 2$^{nd}$ Infantry, FL NG) at Camp Wheeler, GA and assigned 62$^{nd}$ Infantry Brigade (31$^{st}$ Division). Moved overseas Oct 1918. (31$^{st}$ Division skeletonized upon arrival in Europe and served as a replacement division.) Returned to the US Dec 1918. Demobilized 14 Jan 1919 at Camp Gordon, GA.

**125$^{th}$ Infantry**      Organized 30 Sep 1917 (formed from 33$^{rd}$ Infantry and 1$^{st}$ Bn, 31$^{st}$ Infantry, MI NG and personnel from 3$^{rd}$, 4$^{th}$ and 5$^{th}$ Infantry, WI NG) at Camp MacArthur, TX and assigned 63$^{rd}$ Infantry Brigade (32$^{nd}$ Division). Moved overseas Feb 1918. Returned to the US May 1919. Demobilized 22 May 1919 at Camp Custer, MI.

**126$^{th}$ Infantry**      Organized 22 Sep 1917 (formed from 32$^{nd}$ Infantry and elements 31$^{st}$ Infantry, MI NG and personnel from 3$^{rd}$, 4$^{th}$ and 5$^{th}$ Infantry, WI NG) at Camp MacArthur, TX and assigned 63$^{rd}$ Infantry Brigade (32$^{nd}$ Division). Moved overseas Feb 1918. Returned to the US May 1919. Demobilized 24 May-2 Jun 1919 at Camp Custer, MI.

**127$^{th}$ Infantry**      Organized 24 Sep 1917 (formed from elements 1$^{st}$ and 2$^{nd}$ Infantry, WI NG) at Camp MacArthur, TX and assigned 64$^{th}$ Infantry Brigade (32$^{nd}$ Division). Moved overseas Feb 1918. Returned to the US May 1919 . Demobilized 18 May 1919 at Camp Grant, IL.

**128$^{th}$ Infantry**      Organized 24 Sep 1917 (formed from elements 1$^{st}$ and 2$^{nd}$ Infantry, WI NG) at Camp MacArthur, TX and assigned 64$^{th}$ Infantry Brigade (32$^{nd}$ Division). Moved overseas Feb 1918. Returned to the US May 1919. Demobilized 19 May 1919 at Camp Grant, IL.

**129$^{th}$ Infantry**      Organized 12 Oct 1917 (formed from 3$^{rd}$ Infantry, IL NG) at Camp Logan, TX and assigned 65$^{th}$ Infantry Brigade (33$^{rd}$ Division). Moved overseas May 1918. Returned to the US May 1919. Demobilized 6 Jun 1919 at Camp Grant, IL.

**130$^{th}$ Infantry**      Organized 10 Oct 1917 (formed from 4$^{th}$ Infantry, IL NG) at Camp Logan, TX and assigned 65$^{th}$ Infantry Brigade (33$^{rd}$ Division). Moved overseas May 1918. Returned to the US May 1919. Demobilized 31 May 1919 at Camp Grant, IL.

**131$^{st}$ Infantry**      Organized 12 Oct 1917 (formed from 1$^{st}$ Infantry, IL NG) at Camp Logan, TX and assigned 66$^{th}$ Infantry Brigade (33$^{rd}$ Division). Moved overseas May 1918. Returned to the US May 1919. Demobilized 6 Jun 1919.

**132<sup>nd</sup> Infantry**      Organized 12 Oct 1917 (formed from 2<sup>nd</sup> Infantry, IL NG) at Camp Logan, TX and assigned 66<sup>th</sup> Infantry Brigade (33<sup>rd</sup> Division). Moved overseas May 1918. Returned to the US May 1919. Demobilized 31 May 1919 at Camp Grant, IL.

**133<sup>rd</sup> Infantry**      Organized 1 Oct 1917 (formed from 1<sup>st</sup> Infantry and 3<sup>rd</sup> Bn, 2<sup>nd</sup> Infantry, IA NG and troop 1<sup>st</sup> Sqn Cavalry, IA NG) at Camp Cody, NM and assigned 67<sup>th</sup> Infantry Brigade (34<sup>th</sup> Division). Moved overseas Oct 1918. (34<sup>th</sup> Division skeletonized upon arrival in Europe and served as a replacement division.) Returned to the US Jan 1919. Demobilized 18 Feb 1919 at Camp Grant, IL.

**134<sup>th</sup> Infantry**      Organized 1 Oct 1917 (formed from 1<sup>st</sup> Infantry, NE NG) at Camp Cody, NM and assigned 67<sup>th</sup> Infantry Brigade (34<sup>th</sup> Division). Moved overseas Oct 1918. (34<sup>th</sup> Division skeletonized upon arrival in Europe and served as a replacement division.) Returned to the US Jan 1919. Demobilized 18 Feb 1919 at Camp Grant, IL.

**135<sup>th</sup> Infantry**      Organized 1 Oct 1917 (formed from 1<sup>st</sup> Infantry, MN NG) at Ft. Snelling, MN and assigned 68<sup>th</sup> Infantry Brigade (34<sup>th</sup> Division). Moved overseas Oct 1918. (34<sup>th</sup> Division skeletonized upon arrival in Europe and served as a replacement division.) Returned to the US Jan 1919. Demobilized 18 Feb 1919 at Camp Grant, IL.

**136<sup>th</sup> Infantry**      Organized 1 Oct 1917 (formed from 2<sup>nd</sup> Infantry, MN NG) at Camp Cody, NM and assigned 68<sup>th</sup> Infantry Brigade (34<sup>th</sup> Division). Moved overseas Oct 1918. (34<sup>th</sup> Division skeletonized upon arrival in Europe and served as a replacement division.) Returned to the US Jan 1919. Demobilized 18 Feb 1919 at Camp Grant, IL.

**137<sup>th</sup> Infantry**      Organized 1 Oct 1917 (formed from 1<sup>st</sup> and 2<sup>nd</sup> Infantry, KS NG) at Camp Doniphan, OK and assigned 69<sup>th</sup> Infantry Brigade (35<sup>th</sup> Division). Moved overseas Apr 1918. Returned to the US Apr 1919. Demobilized 26 May 1919 at Camp Funston, KS.

**138<sup>th</sup> Infantry**      Organized 1 Oct 1917 (formed from 1<sup>st</sup> and 5<sup>th</sup> Infantry, MO NG) at Camp Doniphan, OK and assigned 69<sup>th</sup> Infantry Brigade (35<sup>th</sup> Division). Moved overseas May 1918. Returned to the US Apr 1919. Demobilized 12 May 1919 at Camp Funston, KS.

**139<sup>th</sup> Infantry**      Organized 1 Oct 1917 (formed from 4<sup>th</sup> Infantry, MO NG and 3<sup>rd</sup> Infantry, KS NG) at Camp Doniphan, OK and assigned 70<sup>th</sup> Infantry Brigade (35<sup>th</sup> Division). Moved overseas Apr 1918. Returned to the US Apr 1919. Demobilized 9-11 May 1919 at Ft. Riley, KS.

**140<sup>th</sup> Infantry**      Organized 1 Oct 1917 (formed from 3<sup>rd</sup> and 6<sup>th</sup> Infantry, MO NG) at Camp Doniphan, OK and assigned 70<sup>th</sup> Infantry Brigade (35<sup>th</sup> Division). Moved overseas Apr 1918. Returned to the US Apr 1919. Demobilized 12-13 May 1919 at Ft. Riley, KS.

**141st Infantry**  Organized 12 Oct 1917 (formed from 1st and 2nd Infantry, TX NG) at Camp Bowie, TX and assigned 71st Infantry Brigade (36th Division). Moved overseas Jul 1918. Returned to the US Jun 1919. Demobilized 3 Jul 1919 at Camp Travis, TX.

**142nd Infantry**  Organized 15 Oct 1917 (formed from 7th Infantry, TX NG and 1st Infantry, OK NG) at Camp Bowie, TX and assigned 71st Infantry Brigade (36th Division). Moved overseas Jul 1918. Returned to the US Jun 1919. Demobilized 17 Jun 1919

**143rd Infantry**  Organized 15 Oct 1917 (formed from 3rd (-) and 5th Infantry, TX NG) at Camp Bowie, TX and assigned 72nd Infantry Brigade (36th Division). Moved overseas Jul 1918. Returned to the US Jun 1919. Demobilized 13 Jun 1919 at Camp Bowie, TX.

**144th Infantry**  Organized 15 Oct 1917 (formed from 4th and 6th Infantry, TX NG) at Camp Bowie, TX and assigned 72nd Infantry Brigade (36th Division). Moved overseas Jul 1918. Returned to the US Jun 1919. Demobilized 21 Jun 1919 at Camp Bowie, TX.

**145th Infantry**  Organized 25 Sep 1917 (formed from 4th Infantry and elements 2nd Infantry, OH NG) at Camp Sheridan, AL and assigned 73rd Infantry Brigade (37th Division).[55] Moved overseas Jun 1918. Returned to the US Mar 1919. Demobilized 22 Apr 1919 at Camp Sherman, OH.

**146th Infantry**  Organized 15 Sep 1917 (formed from 8th and elements 1st, 2nd and 6th Infantry, OH NG) at Camp Sheridan, AL and assigned 73rd Infantry Brigade (37th Division). Moved overseas Jun 1918. Returned to the US Mar 1919. Demobilized 19-21 Apr 1919 at Camp Sherman, OH.

**147th Infantry**  Organized 25 Oct 1917 (formed from 5th and elements 2nd and 6th Infantry, OH NG) at Camp Sheridan, AL and assigned 74th Infantry Brigade (37th Division). Moved overseas Jun 1918. Returned to the US Mar 1919. Demobilized 19 Apr 1919 at Camp Sherman, OH.

**148th Infantry**  Organized 15 Sep 1917 (formed from 3rd Infantry, OH NG) at Camp Sheridan, AL and assigned 74th Infantry Brigade (37th Division). Moved overseas Jun 1918. Returned to the US Mar 1919. Demobilized 21 Apr 1919 at Camp Sherman, OH.

---

[55] There are inconsistencies between the lineages in Sawicki and the material from the Militia Bureau in the *Order of Battle* volumes for the Ohio infantry regiments. The Militia Bureau information has been used for the 145th to 148th and 166th Infantry.

**149th Infantry**    Organized 1 Oct 1917 (formed from 2nd and 3rd (-) Infantry, KY NG) at Camp Shelby, MS and assigned 75th Infantry Brigade (38th Division). Moved overseas Oct 1918. (38th Division skeletonized upon arrival in Europe and served as a replacement division.) Returned to the US Dec 1918. Demobilized Jan 1919 at Camp Zachary Taylor, KY.

**150th Infantry**    Organized 19 Sep 1917 (formed from 1st Bn, 1st Infantry ad 2nd Infantry, WV NG) at Camp Shelby, MS and assigned 75th Infantry Brigade (38th Division). Moved overseas Oct 1918. (38th Division skeletonized upon arrival in Europe and served as a replacement division.) Returned to the US Dec 1918. Demobilized 5 Jan 1919 at Camp Zachary Taylor, KY.

**151st Infantry**    Organized 1 Oct 1917 (formed from 1st Infantry, IN NG and troop, Sqn Cavalry, IN NG) at Camp Shelby, MS and assigned 76th Infantry Brigade (38th Division). Moved overseas Oct 1918. (38th Division skeletonized upon arrival in Europe and served as a replacement division.) Returned to the US Dec 1918. Demobilized 8 Mar 1919 at Camp Zachary Taylor, KY.[56]

**152nd Infantry**    Organized 1 Oct 1917 (formed from 2nd Infantry, IN NG and two troops, Sqn Cavalry, IN NG) at Camp Shelby, MS and assigned 76th Infantry Brigade (38th Division). Moved overseas Oct 1918. (38th Division skeletonized upon arrival in Europe and served as a replacement division.) Returned to the US Dec 1918. Demobilized 8 Mar 1919 at Camp Zachary Taylor, KY.

**153rd Infantry**    Organized 27 Sep 1917 (formed from 1st Infantry, AR NG) at Camp Pike, AR [and then moved Nov 1917 to Camp Beauregard, LA] and assigned 77th Infantry Brigade (39th Division). Moved overseas Aug 1918. (39th Division reorganized Aug 1918 as 5th Depot Division.) Returned to the US Dec 1918. Demobilized 23 Jan 1919 at Camp Beauregard, LA.

**154th Infantry**    Organized 27 Sep 1917 (formed from 3rd (-) Infantry, AR NG, plus personnel from 1st Infantry, LA NG and 1st Bn, 2nd Infantry, MS NG) at Camp Beauregard, LA and assigned 77th Infantry Brigade (39th Division). Moved overseas Aug 1918. (39th Division reorganized Aug 1918 as 5th Depot Division.) Returned to the US Dec 1918. Demobilized 23 Jan 1919 at Camp Beauregard, LA.

---

[56] The Sawicki lineages show Mar 1919 demobilization for the 151st and 152nd Infantry, while the *Order of Battle* volumes show Jan 1919. The latter would seem more likely, but the units were only cadres in any case.

**155<sup>th</sup> Infantry**  Organized 27 Sep 1917 (formed from 1<sup>st</sup> Infantry, MS NG) at Camp Beauregard, LA and assigned 78<sup>th</sup> Infantry Brigade (39<sup>th</sup> Division). Moved overseas Aug 1918. (39<sup>th</sup> Division reorganized Aug 1918 as 5<sup>th</sup> Depot Division.) Returned to the US Dec 1918 . Demobilized 23 Jan 1919 at Camp Beauregard, LA.

**156<sup>th</sup> Infantry**  Organized 27 Sep 1917 (formed from elements 1<sup>st</sup> Infantry, LA NG) at Camp Beauregard, LA and assigned 78<sup>th</sup> Infantry Brigade (39<sup>th</sup> Division). Moved overseas Aug 1918. (39<sup>th</sup> Division reorganized Aug 1918 as 5<sup>th</sup> Depot Division.) Returned to the US Dec 1918. Demobilized 23 Jan 1919 at Camp Beauregard, LA.

**157<sup>th</sup> Infantry**  Organized 24 Sep 1917 (formed from 1<sup>st</sup> and 2<sup>nd</sup> Separate Infantry Bns, Colorado NG) at Camp Kearny, CA[57] and assigned 79<sup>th</sup> Infantry Brigade (40<sup>th</sup> Division). Moved overseas Aug 1918. (40<sup>th</sup> Division reorganized Aug 1918 as 6<sup>th</sup> Depot Division.) Returned to the US Apr 1919. Demobilized 27 Apr 1919 at Ft. D. A. Russell, WY.

**158<sup>th</sup> Infantry**  Organized 3 Oct 1917 (formed from 1<sup>st</sup> Infantry, AZ NG) at Camp Kearny, CA and assigned 79<sup>th</sup> Infantry Brigade (40<sup>th</sup> Division). Moved overseas Aug 1918. (40<sup>th</sup> Division reorganized Aug 1918 as 6<sup>th</sup> Depot Division.) Returned to the US Apr 1919. Demobilized 3 May 1919 at Camp Kearny, CA.

**159<sup>th</sup> Infantry**  Organized 25 Sep 1917 (formed from 5<sup>th</sup> and elements 2<sup>nd</sup> Infantry, CA NG) at Camp Kearny, CA and assigned 80<sup>th</sup> Infantry Brigade (40<sup>th</sup> Division). Moved overseas Aug 1918. (40<sup>th</sup> Division reorganized Aug 1918 as 6<sup>th</sup> Depot Division.) Returned to the US Apr 1919. Demobilized 1 May 1919 at the Presidio, San Francisco, CA.

**160<sup>th</sup> Infantry**  Organized 25 Sep 1917 (formed from 7<sup>th</sup> and Bn, 2<sup>nd</sup> Infantry, CA NG) at Camp Kearny, CA and assigned 80<sup>th</sup> Infantry Brigade (40<sup>th</sup> Division). Moved overseas Aug 1918. (40<sup>th</sup> Division reorganized Aug 1918 as 6<sup>th</sup> Depot Division.) Returned to the US Mar 1919. Demobilized 7 May 1919 at Camp Kearny, CA.

**161<sup>st</sup> Infantry**  Organized 19 Sep 1917 (formed from 2<sup>nd</sup> Infantry, WA NG and elements 3<sup>rd</sup> Infantry, DC NG) at Camp Murray, WA and assigned 81<sup>st</sup> Infantry Brigade (41<sup>st</sup> Division). Moved overseas Dec 1917. (41<sup>st</sup> Division reorganized Jul 1918 as 1<sup>st</sup> Depot Division.) Returned to the US Feb 1919. Demobilized 1-8 Mar 1919 at Camp Dix, NJ and Camp Dodge, IA.

---

[57] 1<sup>st</sup> Cavalry, Colorado NG consolidated with 157<sup>th</sup> Infantry 13 Oct 1917. The *Order of Battle* volume shows the original unit as 1<sup>st</sup> Infantry, CO NG, rather than as two separate battalions.

**162<sup>nd</sup> Infantry**　　　Organized 2 Oct 1917 (formed from 3<sup>rd</sup> Infantry, OR NG and 2<sup>nd</sup> Bn, 3<sup>rd</sup> Infantry, DC NG) at Camp Greene, NC and assigned 81<sup>st</sup> Infantry Brigade (41<sup>st</sup> Division). Moved overseas Dec 1917. (41<sup>st</sup> Division reorganized Jul 1918 as 1<sup>st</sup> Depot Division.) Returned to the US Feb 1919. Demobilized 1-8 Mar 1919 at Camp Dix, NJ.

**163<sup>rd</sup> Infantry**　　　Organized 19 Sep 1917 (formed from 1<sup>st</sup> Infantry, MN NG and 3<sup>rd</sup> Bn, 3<sup>rd</sup> Infantry, DC NG) at Camp Greene, NC and assigned 82<sup>nd</sup> Infantry Brigade (41<sup>st</sup> Division). Moved overseas Dec 1917. (41<sup>st</sup> Division reorganized Jul 1918 as 1<sup>st</sup> Depot Division.) Returned to the US Feb 1919. Demobilized 21 Feb 1919 at Camp Dix, NJ.

**164<sup>th</sup> Infantry**　　　Organized 4 Oct 1917 (formed from 1<sup>st</sup> Infantry and five companies 2<sup>nd</sup> Infantry, ND NG) at Camp Greene, NC and assigned 82<sup>nd</sup> Infantry Brigade (41<sup>st</sup> Division). Moved overseas Dec 1917. (41<sup>st</sup> Division reorganized Jul 1918 as 1<sup>st</sup> Depot Division.) Returned to the US Feb 1919. Demobilized 28 Feb 1919 at Camp Dix, NJ.

**165<sup>th</sup> Infantry**　　　Organized 25 Jul 1917 (formed from 69<sup>th</sup> Infantry, NY NG) at Camp Mills, NY and assigned 83<sup>rd</sup> Infantry Brigade (42<sup>nd</sup> Division). Moved overseas Oct 1917. Returned to the US Apr 1919. Demobilized 7 May 1919 at Camp Upton, NY.

**166<sup>th</sup> Infantry**　　　Organized 20 Aug 1917 (formed from 3<sup>rd</sup> Infantry, Ohio NG) at Camp Perry, OH and assigned 83<sup>rd</sup> Infantry Brigade (42<sup>nd</sup> Division). Moved overseas Oct 1917. Returned to the US Apr 1919. Demobilized 17 May 1919 at Camp Sherman, OH.

**167<sup>th</sup> Infantry**　　　Organized 1 Aug 1917 (formed from 4<sup>th</sup> Infantry, AL NG) at Camp Sheridan, AL and assigned 84<sup>th</sup> Infantry Brigade (42<sup>nd</sup> Division). Moved overseas Nov 1917. Returned to the US Apr 1919. Demobilized 19 May 1919 at Camp Shelby, MS.

**168<sup>th</sup> Infantry**　　　Organized 16 Aug 1917 (formed from 3<sup>rd</sup> Infantry, IA NG) at Des Moines, IA and assigned 84<sup>th</sup> Infantry Brigade (42<sup>nd</sup> Division). Moved overseas Nov 1917. Returned to the US Apr 1919. Demobilized 17 May 1919 at Camp Dodge, IA.

*National Army Infantry Regiments*

**301<sup>st</sup> Infantry**　　　Organized 29 Aug 1917 at Camp Devens, MA and assigned 151<sup>st</sup> Infantry Brigade (76<sup>th</sup> Division). Moved overseas Jul 1918. (76<sup>th</sup> Division reorganized Aug 1918 as 3<sup>rd</sup> Depot Division.) Returned to the US Jan 1919. Demobilized 1-20 Jan 1919 at Camp Devens.

**302nd Infantry**      Organized 29 Aug 1917 at Camp Devens, MA and assigned 151st Infantry Brigade (76th Division). Moved overseas Jul 1918. (76th Division reorganized Aug 1918 as 3rd Depot Division but 302nd Infantry withheld.) Returned to the US Jan 1919. Demobilized 14-20 Jan 1919 at Camp Devens.

**303rd Infantry**      Organized 29 Aug 1917 at Camp Devens, MA and assigned 152nd Infantry Brigade (76th Division). Moved overseas Jul 1918. (76th Division reorganized Aug 1918 as 3rd Depot Division.) Returned to the US Jan 1919. Demobilized 20 Jan 1919 at Camp Devens.

**304th Infantry**      Organized 29 Aug 1917 at Camp Devens, MA and assigned 151st Infantry Brigade (76th Division). Moved overseas Jul 1918. (76th Division reorganized Aug 1918 as 3rd Depot Division.) Returned to the US Jan 1919. Demobilized 14-20 Jan 1919 at Camp Devens.

**305th Infantry**      Organized 26-29 Aug 1917 at Camp Upton, NY and assigned 153rd Infantry Brigade (77th Division). Moved overseas Apr 1918. Returned to the US Apr 1919. Demobilized 9 May 1919 at Camp Upton.

**306th Infantry**      Organized 26 Aug 1917 at Camp Upton, NY and assigned 153rd Infantry Brigade (77th Division). Moved overseas Apr 1918. Returned to the US Apr 1919. Demobilized 9 May 1919 at Camp Upton.

**307th Infantry**      Organized 26 Aug 1917 at Camp Upton, NY and assigned 154th Infantry Brigade (77th Division). Moved overseas Apr 1918. Returned to the US Apr 1919. Demobilized 9 May 1919 at Camp Upton.

**308th Infantry**      Organized in Sep 1917 at Camp Upton, NY and assigned 154th Infantry Brigade (77th Division). Moved overseas Apr 1918. Returned to the US Apr 1919. Demobilized in May 1919 at Camp Upton.

**309th Infantry**      Organized 29 Aug 1917 at Camp Dix, NJ and assigned 155th Infantry Brigade (78th Division). Moved overseas May 1918. Returned to the US May 1919. Demobilized 30 May-6 Jun 1919 at Camp Dix and at Camp Upton, NY.

**310th Infantry**      Organized 6-10 Sep 1917 at Camp Dix, NJ and assigned 155th Infantry Brigade (78th Division). Moved overseas May 1918 . Returned to the US May 1919. Demobilized 6 Jun 1919 at Camp Dix.

**311th Infantry**      Organized 6-10 Sep 1917 at Camp Dix, NJ and assigned 156th Infantry Brigade (78th Division). Moved overseas May 1918. Returned to the US May 1919. Demobilized 30 May-5 Jun 1919 at Camp Dix.

**312th Infantry**  Organized Aug-Sep 1917 at Camp Dix, NJ and assigned 156th Infantry Brigade. (78th Division). Moved overseas May 1918. Returned to the US May 1919. Demobilized 26 May 1919 at Camp Dix.

**313th Infantry**  Organized 26 Aug 1917 at Camp Meade, MD and assigned 157th Infantry Brigade (79th Division). Moved overseas Jul 1918. Returned to the US May 1919. Demobilized 9-10 Jun 1919 at Camp Meade.

**314th Infantry**  Organized 26 Aug 1917 at Camp Meade, MD and assigned 157th Infantry Brigade (79th Division). Moved overseas Jul 1918. Returned to the US May 1919. Demobilized 29 May 1919 at Camp Meade.

**315th Infantry**  Organized 29 Aug 1917 at Camp Meade, MD and assigned 158th Infantry Brigade (79th Division). Moved overseas Jul 1918. Returned to the US May 1919. Demobilized 31 May 1919 at Camp Meade.

**316th Infantry**  Organized in Aug 1917 at Camp Meade, MD and assigned 158th Infantry Brigade (79th Division). Moved overseas Jul 1918. Returned to the US May 1919. Demobilized in May 1919 at Camp Meade.

**317th Infantry**  Organized 23-27 Aug 1917 at Camp Lee, VA and assigned 159th Infantry Brigade (80th Division). Moved overseas May 1918. Returned to the US Jun 1919. Demobilized 13-14 Jun 1919 at Camp Lee.

**318th Infantry**  Organized 22-27 Aug 1917 at Camp Lee, VA and assigned 159th Infantry Brigade (80th Division). Moved overseas May 1918. Returned to the US May 1919. Demobilized 1-5 Jun 1919 at Camp Lee.

**319th Infantry**  Organized 27 Aug 1917 at Camp Lee, VA and assigned 160th Infantry Brigade (80th Division). Moved overseas May 1918. Returned to the US Jun 1919. Demobilized 10 Jun-Jul 1919 at Camp Lee.

**320th Infantry**  Organized Aug-Sep 1917 at Camp Lee, VA and assigned 160th Infantry Brigade (80th Division). Moved overseas May 1918. Returned to the US May 1919. Demobilized 7 Jun 1919 at Camp Lee.

**321st Infantry**  Organized 29 Aug 1917 at Camp Jackson, SC and assigned 161st Infantry Brigade (81st Division). Moved overseas Jul 1918. Returned to the US Jun 1919. Demobilized 28 Jun 1919 at Camp Lee, VA.

**322nd Infantry**      Organized 31 Aug 1917 at Camp Jackson, SC and assigned 161st Infantry Brigade (81st Division). Moved overseas Jul 1918. Returned to the US Jun 1919. Demobilized 22 Jun 1919 at Camp Lee, VA.

**323rd Infantry**      Organized 29 Aug 1917 at Camp Jackson, SC and assigned 162nd Infantry Brigade (81st Division). Moved overseas Jul 1918. Returned to the US Jun 1919. Demobilized 17-30 1919 at Camp Lee, VA.

**324th Infantry**      Organized Sep 1917 at Camp Jackson, SC and assigned 162nd Infantry Brigade (81st Division). Moved overseas Aug 1918. Returned to the US Jun 1919. Demobilized 17 1919 at Camp Lee, VA.

**325th Infantry**      Organized 1 Sep 1917 at Camp Gordon, GA and assigned 163rd Infantry Brigade (82nd Division). Moved overseas Apr 1918. Returned to the US May 1919. Demobilized 18-25 May 1919 at Camp Upton. NY.

**326th Infantry**      Organized 2 Sep 1917 at Camp Gordon, GA and assigned 163rd Infantry Brigade (82nd Division). Moved overseas Apr 1918 . Returned to the US Jun 1919. Demobilized 3-11 Nov 1919 at Camp Upton. NY.[58]

**327th Infantry**      Organized 17 Sep 1917 at Camp Gordon, GA and assigned 164th Infantry Brigade (82nd Division). Moved overseas May 1918. Returned to the US May 1919. Demobilized 26 May 1919 at Camp Upton. NY.

**328th Infantry**      Organized Sep 1917 at Camp Gordon, GA and assigned 164th Infantry Brigade (82nd Division). Moved overseas May 1918. Returned to the US May 1919. Demobilized 27-29 May 1919 at Camp Upton. NY.

**329th Infantry**      Organized 30 Aug 1917 at Camp Sherman, OH and assigned 165th Infantry Brigade (83rd Division). Moved overseas Jun 1918. (83rd Division reorganized Jun 1918 as 2nd Depot Division.) Returned to the US Jan 1919. Demobilized 15 Feb 1919 at Camp Sherman.

**330th Infantry**      Organized 30 Aug 1917 at Camp Sherman, OH and assigned 165th Infantry Brigade (83rd Division). Moved overseas Jun 1918. (83rd Division reorganized Jun 1918 as 2nd Depot Division.) Returned to the US Jan 1919. Demobilized 13 Feb-10 Apr 1919 at Camp Sherman.

---

[58] Sawicki's lineages shows Nov 1919 demobilization; the *Order of Battle* volumes show Jun 1919, which seems more likely.

**331<sup>st</sup> Infantry**      Organized 30 Aug 1917 at Camp Sherman, OH and assigned 166<sup>th</sup> Infantry Brigade (83<sup>rd</sup> Division). Moved overseas Jun 1918. (83<sup>rd</sup> Division reorganized Jun 1918 as 2<sup>nd</sup> Depot Division.) Returned to the US Jan 1919. Demobilized 8-9 Feb 1919 at Camp Sherman.

**332<sup>nd</sup> Infantry**      Organized 30 Aug 1917 at Camp Sherman, OH and assigned 166<sup>th</sup> Infantry Brigade (83<sup>rd</sup> Division). Moved overseas Jun 1918. (83<sup>rd</sup> Division reorganized Jun 1918 as 2<sup>nd</sup> Depot Division; however, 332<sup>nd</sup> Infantry detached and sent to Italy.[59]) Returned to the US Apr 1919. Demobilized 1 Jul 1919 at Camp Sherman.

**333<sup>rd</sup> Infantry**      Organized 25 Aug 1917 at Camp Zachary Taylor, KY and assigned 167<sup>th</sup> Infantry Brigade (84<sup>th</sup> Division). Moved overseas Sep 1918. (84<sup>th</sup> Division skeletonized Oct 1918.) Returned to the US Jan 1919. Demobilized 24-31 Jan 1919 at Camp Zachary Taylor.

**334<sup>th</sup> Infantry**      Organized 25 Aug 1917 at Camp Zachary Taylor, KY and assigned 167<sup>th</sup> Infantry Brigade (84<sup>th</sup> Division). Moved overseas Sep 1918. (84<sup>th</sup> Division skeletonized Oct 1918.) Returned to the US Jan 1919. Demobilized 18 Feb 1919 at Camp Zachary Taylor.

**335<sup>th</sup> Infantry**      Organized 26 Aug 1917 at Camp Zachary Taylor, KY and assigned 168<sup>th</sup> Infantry Brigade (84<sup>th</sup> Division). Moved overseas Sep 1918. (84<sup>th</sup> Division skeletonized Oct 1918.) Returned to the US Jan 1919. Demobilized 18 Feb 1919 at Camp Zachary Taylor.

**336<sup>th</sup> Infantry**      Organized 25 Aug 1917 at Camp Zachary Taylor, KY and assigned 168<sup>th</sup> Infantry Brigade (84<sup>th</sup> Division). Moved overseas Sep 1918. (84<sup>th</sup> Division skeletonized Oct 1918.) Returned to the US Jan 1919. Demobilized 18 Feb 1919 at Camp Zachary Taylor.

**337<sup>th</sup> Infantry**      Organized 30 Aug 1918 at Camp Custer, MI and assigned 169<sup>th</sup> Infantry Brigade (85<sup>th</sup> Division). Moved overseas Jul 1918. (85<sup>th</sup> Division reorganized Jul 1918 as 4<sup>th</sup> Depot Division.) Returned to the US Apr 1919. Demobilized 23 Apr 1919 at Camp Custer.

**338<sup>th</sup> Infantry**      Organized 30 Aug 1918 at Camp Custer, MI and assigned 169<sup>th</sup> Infantry Brigade (85<sup>th</sup> Division). Moved overseas Jul 1918. (85<sup>th</sup> Division reorganized Jul 1918 as 4<sup>th</sup> Depot Division.) Returned to the US Apr 1919. Demobilized 14 Apr 1919 at Camp Custer.

---

[59] Entitled to Vittoria-Veneto and Venetia 1918 campaign participation credit.

**339th Infantry**     Organized 30 Aug 1918 at Camp Custer, MI and assigned 170th Infantry Brigade (85th Division). Moved overseas Jul 1918. (85th Division reorganized Jul 1918 as 4th Depot Division; however, 339th Infantry detached and later served in North Russia.[60]) Returned to the US Jul 1919. Demobilized 18-22 Jul 1919 at Camp Custer.

**340th Infantry**     Organized Aug-Sep 1918 at Camp Custer, MI and assigned 170th Infantry Brigade (85th Division). Moved overseas Jul 1918. (85th Division reorganized Jul 1918 as 4th Depot Division.) Returned to the US Apr 1919. Demobilized 21 Apr 1919 at Camp Custer.

**341st Infantry**     Organized 5 Sep 1917 at Camp Grant, IL and assigned 171st Infantry Brigade (86th Division). Moved overseas Sep 1918. (86th Division skeletonized Oct 1918.) Returned to the US Jan 1919. Demobilized 17 Feb 1919 at Camp Grant.

**342nd Infantry**     Organized 26 Aug-4 Sep 1917 at Camp Grant, IL and assigned 171st Infantry Brigade (86th Division). Moved overseas Sep 1918. (86th Division skeletonized Oct 1918.) Returned to the US Jan 1919. Demobilized 17 Feb 1919 at Camp Grant.

**343rd Infantry**     Organized 26 Aug 1917 at Camp Grant, IL and assigned 172nd Infantry Brigade (86th Division). Moved overseas Sep 1918. (86th Division skeletonized Oct 1918.) Returned to the US Jan 1919. Demobilized 17 Feb 1919 at Camp Grant.

**344th Infantry**     Organized in Sep 1917 at Camp Grant, IL and assigned 172nd Infantry Brigade (86th Division). Moved overseas Sep 1918. (86th Division skeletonized Oct 1918.) Returned to the US Jan 1919. Demobilized in Jan 1919 at Camp Grant.

**345th Infantry**     Organized 1 Sep 1917 at Camp Pike, AR and assigned 173rd Infantry Brigade (87th Division). Moved overseas Aug 1918. Returned to the US Jan 1919. Demobilized 10 Mar 1919 at Camp Upton, NY.

**346th Infantry**     Organized 4 Sep 1917 at Camp Pike, AR and assigned 173rd Infantry Brigade (87th Division). Moved overseas Aug 1918. Returned to the US Mar 1919. Demobilized 6-8 Mar 1919 at Camp Dix, NJ.

**347th Infantry**     Organized 1 Sep 1917 at Camp Pike, AR and assigned 174th Infantry Brigade (87th Division). Moved overseas Aug 1918. Returned to the US Dec 1918. Demobilized 22 Jan-4 Feb 1919 at Camp Dix, NJ.

---

[60] Entitled to Russia campaign participation credit.

**348<sup>th</sup> Infantry** Organized in Sep 1917 at Camp Pike, AR and assigned 174<sup>th</sup> Infantry Brigade (87<sup>th</sup> Division).  Moved overseas Aug 1918.  Returned to the US Mar 1919.  Demobilized in Mar 1919 at Camp Dix, NJ.

**349<sup>th</sup> Infantry** Organized 30 Aug 1917 at Camp Dodge, IA and assigned 175<sup>th</sup> Infantry Brigade (88<sup>th</sup> Division).  Moved overseas Aug 1918.  Returned to the US May 1919.  Demobilized 12 Jun 1919 at Camp Dodge.

**350<sup>th</sup> Infantry** Organized 27 Aug 1917 at Camp Dodge, IA and assigned 175<sup>th</sup> Infantry Brigade (88<sup>th</sup> Division) . Moved overseas Aug 1918.  Returned to the US May 1919.  Demobilized 5-8 Jun 1919 at Camp Dodge.

**351<sup>st</sup> Infantry** Organized 30 Aug 1917 at Camp Dodge, IA and assigned 176<sup>th</sup> Infantry Brigade (88<sup>th</sup> Division).  Moved overseas Aug 1918.  Returned to the US May 1919.  Demobilized 7 Jun 1919 at Camp Dodge.

**352<sup>nd</sup> Infantry** Organized Sep 1917 at Camp Dodge, IA and assigned 176<sup>th</sup> Infantry Brigade (88<sup>th</sup> Division).  Moved overseas Aug 1918.  Returned to the US Jun 1919.  Demobilized in Jun 1919 at Camp Dodge.

**353<sup>rd</sup> Infantry** Organized 27 Aug 1917 at Camp Funston, KS and assigned 177<sup>th</sup> Infantry Brigade (89<sup>th</sup> Division).  Moved overseas Jun 1918.  Returned to the US May 1919.  Demobilized 2 Jun 1919 at Camp Funston.

**354<sup>th</sup> Infantry** Organized 27 Aug 1917 at Camp Funston, KS and assigned 177<sup>th</sup> Infantry Brigade (89<sup>th</sup> Division).  Moved overseas Jun 1918.  Returned to the US May 1919.  Demobilized 2-3 Jun 1919 at Camp Funston.

**355<sup>th</sup> Infantry** Organized 27 Aug 1917 at Camp Funston, KS and assigned 178<sup>th</sup> Infantry Brigade (89<sup>th</sup> Division).  Moved overseas Jun 1918.  Returned to the US May 1919.  Demobilized 1-3 Jun 1919 at Camp Funston.

**356<sup>th</sup> Infantry** Organized 27 Aug 1917 at Camp Funston, KS and assigned 178<sup>th</sup> Infantry Brigade (89<sup>th</sup> Division).  Moved overseas Jun 1918.  Returned to the US May 1919.  Demobilized 11 Jun 1919 at Camp Funston.

**357<sup>th</sup> Infantry** Organized 25 Aug 1917 at Camp Travis, TX and assigned 179<sup>th</sup> Infantry Brigade (90<sup>th</sup> Division).  Moved overseas Jun 1918.  Returned to the US Jun 1919.  Demobilized 18-21 Jun 1991 at Camp Pike, AR.

**358<sup>th</sup> Infantry** Organized 25 Aug 1917 at Camp Travis, TX and assigned 179<sup>th</sup> Infantry Brigade (90<sup>th</sup> Division). Moved overseas Jun 1918. Returned to the US Jun 1919. Demobilized 22 Jun 1991 at Camp Pike, AR.

**359<sup>th</sup> Infantry** Organized 5 Sep 1917 at Camp Travis, TX and assigned 180<sup>th</sup> Infantry Brigade (90<sup>th</sup> Division). Moved overseas Jun 1918. Returned to the US Jun 1919. Demobilized 24 Jun 1991 at Camp Bowie, TX.

**360<sup>th</sup> Infantry** Organized Sep 1917 at Camp Travis, TX and assigned 180<sup>th</sup> Infantry Brigade (90<sup>th</sup> Division). Moved overseas Jun 1918. Returned to the US Jun 1919. Demobilized in Jun 1991 at Camp Bowie, TX.

**361<sup>st</sup> Infantry** Organized 4-6 Sep 1917 at Camp Lewis, WA and assigned 181<sup>st</sup> Infantry Brigade (91<sup>st</sup> Division). Moved overseas Jul 1918. Returned to the US Apr 1919. Demobilized 22-30 Apr 1919 at Camp Lewis.

**362<sup>nd</sup> Infantry** Organized 4 Sep 1917 at Camp Lewis, WA and assigned 181<sup>st</sup> Infantry Brigade (91<sup>st</sup> Division). Moved overseas Jul 1918. Returned to the US Apr 1919. Demobilized 3 May 1919 at Ft. D. A. Russell, WY.

**363<sup>rd</sup> Infantry** Organized 4 Sep 1917 at Camp Lewis, WA and assigned 182<sup>nd</sup> Infantry Brigade. (91<sup>st</sup> Division). Moved overseas Jul 1918. Returned to the US Apr 1919. Demobilized 2 May 1919 at the Presidio, San Francisco, CA.

**364<sup>th</sup> Infantry** Organized in Sep 1917 at Camp Lewis, WA and assigned 182<sup>nd</sup> Infantry Brigade (91<sup>st</sup> Division). Moved overseas Jul 1918. Returned to the US Apr 1919. Demobilized in Apr 1919 at Camp Lewis.

**365<sup>th</sup> Infantry** Organized 26 Oct 1917 at Camp Grant, IL with black enlisted personnel and assigned 183<sup>rd</sup> Infantry Brigade (92<sup>nd</sup> Division). Moved overseas Jun 1918. Returned to the US Feb 1919. Demobilized 31 Mar 1919 at Camp Lee, VA.

**366<sup>th</sup> Infantry** Organized Nov 1917 at Camp Dodge, IA with black enlisted personnel and assigned 183<sup>rd</sup> Infantry Brigade (92<sup>nd</sup> Division). Moved overseas Jun 1918. Returned to the US Feb 1919. Demobilized 25 Mar 1919 at Ft. Oglethorpe, GA.

**367<sup>th</sup> Infantry** Organized 3 Nov 1917 at Camp Upton, NY with black enlisted personnel and assigned 184<sup>th</sup> Infantry Brigade (92<sup>nd</sup> Division). Moved overseas Jun 1918. Returned to the US Feb 1919. Demobilized 8-9 Mar 1919 at Camp Upton and Camp Meade, MD.

**368th Infantry**        Organized 25 Oct 1917 at Camp Meade, MD with black enlisted personnel and assigned 184th Infantry Brigade (92nd Division). Moved overseas Jun 1918. Returned to the US Feb 1919. Demobilized 27 Feb-7 Mar 1919 at Camp Meade.

**369th Infantry**        15th Infantry, NY NG [formed with black enlisted personnel] redesignated 1 Mar 1918 as 369th Infantry and assigned 93rd Division, Provisional. Moved overseas Dec 1917 (served with the French Army). Returned to the US Feb 1919. Demobilized 28 Feb 1919 at Camp Upton, NY.

**370th Infantry**        8th Infantry, IL NG [formed with black enlisted personnel] redesignated 1 Dec 1917 as 370th Infantry and assigned 93rd Division, Provisional. Moved overseas Apr 1918 (served with the French Army). Returned to the US Feb 1919. Demobilized 11 Mar 1919 at Camp Grant, IL.

**371st Infantry**        1st Provisional Infantry Regiment [organized 31 Aug 1917 at Camp Jackson, SC with black enlisted personnel] redesignated 1 Dec 1917 as 371st Infantry and assigned 93rd Division, Provisional. Moved overseas Apr 1918 (served with the French Army). Returned to the US Feb 1919. Demobilized 28 Feb 1919 at Camp Jackson.

**372nd Infantry**        Organized in Jan 1918 at Camp Stewart, VA from existing NG units [all formed with black enlisted personnel: Sep Inf Bn, DC NG; Sep Coy Inf, CT NG; Sep Coy Inf, MA NG; Sep Inf Coy, MD NG, and Sep Coy Inf, TN NG] and assigned 93rd Division, Provisional. Moved overseas Mar 1918 (served with the French Army). Returned to the US Feb 1919. Demobilized 6 Mar 1919 at Camp Sherman, OH.

**373rd Infantry**        Organized during Jul 1918 at Camp La Casas, San Juan, PR with Puerto Rican enlisted personnel and assigned Provisional Division, Puerto Rico. Demobilized 10 Jan 1919 at Camp la Casas.

**374th Infantry**        Organized 16 Jul 1918 at Camp La Casas, San Juan, PR with Puerto Rican enlisted personnel and assigned Provisional Division, Puerto Rico. Demobilized 10 Jan 1919 at Camp la Casas.

**375th Infantry**        Organized 16 Jul 1918 at Camp La Casas, San Juan, PR with Puerto Rican enlisted personnel and assigned Provisional Division, Puerto Rico. Demobilized 10 Jan 1919 at Camp la Casas.

**376th Infantry**        Constituted Jun 1918 as element of Provisional Division, Puerto Rico but not organized. Disbanded 11 Jan 1919.

**377th Infantry**        Constituted 5 Sep 1918 and assigned 95th Division. (Was to be organized in France from personnel of 1st Pioneer Infantry but never accomplished.) Disbanded 22 Dec 1918.

**378th Infantry**        Constituted 5 Sep 1918 and assigned 95th Division. (Was to be organized in France from personnel of 2nd Pioneer Infantry but never accomplished.) Disbanded 22 Dec 1918.

**379<sup>th</sup> Infantry**    Organized 24 Sep 1918 at Camp Sherman, OH as element of 95<sup>th</sup> Division.  Demobilized 10-20 Dec 1918 at Camp Sherman.

**380<sup>th</sup> Infantry**    Organized 26 Sep 1918 at Camp Sherman, OH as element of 95<sup>th</sup> Division.  Demobilized 17 Dec 1918 at Camp Sherman.

**381<sup>st</sup> Infantry**    Constituted 5 Sep 1918 and assigned 96<sup>th</sup> Division. (Was to be organized in France from personnel of 3<sup>rd</sup> Pioneer Infantry but never accomplished.)  Disbanded 7 Jan 1919.

**382<sup>nd</sup> Infantry**    Constituted 5 Sep 1918 and assigned 96<sup>th</sup> Division. (Was to be organized in France from personnel of 4<sup>th</sup> Pioneer Infantry but never accomplished.)  Disbanded 7 Jan 1919.

**383<sup>rd</sup> Infantry**    Organized 27 Sep 1918 at Camp Wadsworth, SC as element of 96<sup>th</sup> Division.  Demobilized 7 Jan 1919 at Camp Wadsworth.

**384<sup>th</sup> Infantry**    Organized 27 Sep 1918 at Camp Wadsworth, SC as element of 96<sup>th</sup> Division.  Demobilized 7 Jan 1919 at Camp Wadsworth.

**385<sup>th</sup> Infantry**    Constituted 5 Sep 1918 and assigned 97<sup>th</sup> Division. (Was to be organized in France from personnel of 5<sup>th</sup> Pioneer Infantry but never accomplished.)  Disbanded 22 Dec 1918.

**386<sup>th</sup> Infantry**    Constituted 5 Sep 1918 and assigned 97<sup>th</sup> Division. (Was to be organized in France from personnel of 51<sup>st</sup> Pioneer Infantry but never accomplished.)  Disbanded 22 Dec 1918.

**387<sup>th</sup> Infantry**    Organized 1 Oct 1918 at Camp Cody, NM as element of 97<sup>th</sup> Division.  Demobilized 11 Dec 1918 at Camp Cody.

**388<sup>th</sup> Infantry**    Organized in Oct 1918 at Camp Cody, NM as element of 97<sup>th</sup> Division.  Demobilized in Dec 1918 at Camp Cody.

**389<sup>th</sup> Infantry**    Constituted 23 Jul 1918 and assigned 98<sup>th</sup> Division. (Was to be organized in France from personnel of 52<sup>nd</sup> Pioneer Infantry but never accomplished.)  Disbanded 30 Nov 1918.

**390<sup>th</sup> Infantry**    Constituted 23 Jul 1918 and assigned 98<sup>th</sup> Division. (Was to be organized in France from personnel of 53<sup>rd</sup> Pioneer Infantry but never accomplished.)  Disbanded 30 Nov 1918.

**391<sup>st</sup> Infantry**    Constituted 23 Jul 1918 and assigned 98<sup>th</sup> Division. Disbanded 30 Nov 1918.

**392<sup>nd</sup> Infantry**    Constituted 23 Jul 1918 and assigned 98<sup>th</sup> Division. Disbanded 30 Nov 1918.

**393<sup>rd</sup> Infantry**    Constituted 23 Jul 1918 and assigned 99<sup>th</sup> Division. (Was to be organized in France from personnel of 54<sup>th</sup> Pioneer Infantry but never accomplished.)  Disbanded 30 Nov 1918.

**394<sup>th</sup> Infantry**    Constituted 23 Jul 1918 and assigned 99<sup>th</sup> Division. (Was to be organized in France from personnel of 55<sup>th</sup> Pioneer Infantry but never accomplished.)  Disbanded 30 Nov 1918.

**395<sup>th</sup> Infantry** Constituted 23 Jul 1918 and assigned 99<sup>th</sup> Division. Disbanded 30 Nov 1918.

**396<sup>th</sup> Infantry** Constituted 23 Jul 1918 and assigned 99<sup>th</sup> Division. Disbanded 30 Nov 1918.

**397<sup>th</sup> Infantry** Constituted 23 Jul 1918 and assigned 100<sup>th</sup> Division. (Was to be organized in France from personnel of 56<sup>th</sup> Pioneer Infantry but never accomplished.) Disbanded 30 Nov 1918.

**398<sup>th</sup> Infantry** Constituted 23 Jul 1918 and assigned 100<sup>th</sup> Division. (Was to be organized in France from personnel of 57<sup>th</sup> Pioneer Infantry but never accomplished.) Disbanded 30 Nov 1918.

**399<sup>th</sup> Infantry** Constituted 23 Jul 1918 and assigned 100<sup>th</sup> Division. Disbanded 30 Nov 1918.

**400<sup>th</sup> Infantry** Constituted 23 Jul 1918 and assigned 100<sup>th</sup> Division. Disbanded 30 Nov 1918.

**401<sup>st</sup> Infantry** Constituted 23 Jul 1918 and assigned 101<sup>st</sup> Division. (Was to be organized in France from personnel of 58<sup>th</sup> Pioneer Infantry but never accomplished.) Disbanded 30 Nov 1918.

**402<sup>nd</sup> Infantry** Constituted 23 Jul 1918 and assigned 101<sup>st</sup> Division. (Was to be organized in France from personnel of 59<sup>th</sup> Pioneer Infantry but never accomplished.) Disbanded 30 Nov 1918.

**403<sup>rd</sup> Infantry** Constituted 23 Jul 1918 and assigned 101<sup>st</sup> Division. Disbanded 30 Nov 1918.

**404<sup>th</sup> Infantry** Constituted 23 Jul 1918 and assigned 101<sup>st</sup> Division. Disbanded 30 Nov 1918.

**405<sup>th</sup> Infantry** Constituted 23 Jul 1918 and assigned 102<sup>nd</sup> Division. (Was to be organized in France from personnel of 60<sup>th</sup> Pioneer Infantry but never accomplished.) Disbanded 30 Nov 1918.

**406<sup>th</sup> Infantry** Constituted 23 Jul 1918 and assigned 102<sup>nd</sup> Division. (Was to be organized in France from personnel of 61<sup>st</sup> Pioneer Infantry but never accomplished.) Disbanded 30 Nov 1918.

**407<sup>th</sup> Infantry** Constituted 23 Jul 1918 and assigned 102<sup>nd</sup> Division. Disbanded 30 Nov 1918.

**408<sup>th</sup> Infantry** Constituted 23 Jul 1918 and assigned 102<sup>nd</sup> Division. Disbanded 30 Nov 1918.

**1<sup>st</sup> Provisional Infantry Regiment** *See* 371<sup>st</sup> Infantry

*Pioneer Infantry Regiments*[61]

**1st Pioneer Infantry** — Organized Jan 1918 at Camp Wadsworth, SC as corps troops unit (formed from balance of 1st Infantry, NY NG). Moved overseas Jul 1918. Served with I Army Corps Jul-Aug 1918; III Army Corps Aug-Nov 1918. Slotted for conversion to 377th Infantry but war ended before that occurred. With Third Army on Rhine occupation. Returned to the US Jul 1919 and demobilized at Camp Zachary Taylor, KY.

**2nd Pioneer Infantry** — Organized Jan 1918 at Camp Wadsworth, SC as army troops unit (formed from balance of 14th Infantry, NY NG). Moved overseas Jun 1918. Served with First Army Sep-Nov 1918. Slotted for conversion to 378th Infantry but war ended before that occurred. Returned to the US Oct 1919 and demobilized Nov 1919 at Camp Dix, NJ.

**3rd Pioneer Infantry** — Organized Feb 1918 at Camp Greene, NC as army troops unit (formed from balance of 5th Infantry, MA NG). Moved overseas Aug 1918. Served with First Army Sep-Nov 1918. Slotted for conversion to 381st Infantry but war ended before that occurred. Returned to the US Jul 1919 and demobilized at Camp Dodge, IA.

**4th Pioneer Infantry** — Organized Feb 1918 at Camp Greene, NC as corps troops unit (formed from balance of 6th Infantry, MA NG). Moved overseas Sep 1918. Slotted for conversion to 382nd Infantry but war ended before that occurred. Returned to the US Feb 1919 and demobilized at Camp Hill, VA.

**5th Pioneer Infantry** — Organized Feb 1918 at Camp Greene, NC [but moved to Camp Wadsworth, SC] as corps troops unit (formed from balance of 8th Infantry, MA NG). Served with First Army Sep-Nov 1918.[62] Slotted for conversion to 385th Infantry but war ended before that occurred. Demobilized Jan 1919 at Camp Wadsworth.

**6th Pioneer Infantry** — Organized Oct 1918 at Camp Sherman, OH as corps troops unit and demobilized there Feb 1919.

---

[61] Most of the original pioneer infantry regiments were formed from surplus NG infantry regiments. An indication of "balance of" indicates that the regiment formed, or contributed, to a different unit as well. This is separate from whether the successor unit has the service as a pioneer infantry regiment in its official lineage. The 16 regiments with black enlisted personnel (801st to 816th) were organized to replace white units slated for conversion to infantry regiments to help form new divisions.

[62] So shown under First Army in the *Order of Battle* volumes, but the listing under Infantry does not show that the 5th Pioneer Infantry went overseas. Given the date of formation it would seem that it could have. However, the First Army list also shows the 6th Pioneer Infantry but that seems quite unlikely.

**51st Pioneer Infantry**          Organized Jan 1918 at Camp Wadsworth, SC as corps troops unit (formed from 10th Infantry, NY NG). Moved overseas Jul 1918. Served with IV Army Corps Aug-Sep 1918. Served with First Army Sep 1918. Served with IV and VI Army Corps Sep-Nov 1918. Slotted for conversion to 386th Infantry but war ended before that occurred. With Third Army on Rhine occupation. Returned to the US Jul 1919 and demobilized at Camp Upton, NY.

**52nd Pioneer Infantry**          Organized Jan 1918 at Camp Wadsworth, SC as corps troops unit (formed from balance of 12th Infantry, NY NG). Moved overseas Aug 1918. Served with First Army Sep 1918. Served with V Army Corps Sep-Nov 1918. Slotted for conversion to 389th Infantry but war ended before that occurred. Returned to the US Apr 1919 and demobilized at Camp Dix, NJ.

**53rd Pioneer Infantry**          Organized Jan 1918 at Camp Wadsworth, SC as corps troops unit (formed from 47th Infantry, NY NG). Moved overseas Aug 1918. Served with First Army Sep 1918. Served with III Army Corps Aug-Sep 1918; I Army Corps Sep-Nov 1918. Slotted for conversion to 390th Infantry but war ended before that occurred. Returned to the US May 1919 and demobilized at Camp Upton, NY.

**54th Pioneer Infantry**          Organized Jan 1918 at Camp Wadsworth, SC as army troops unit (formed from balance of 71st Infantry, NY NG). Moved overseas Aug 1918. Served with First Army Sep-Nov 1918. Slotted for conversion to 393rd Infantry but war ended before that occurred. With Third Army on Rhine occupation. Returned to the US Jun 1919 and demobilized Jul 1919 at Camp Grant, IL.

**55th Pioneer Infantry**          Organized Jan 1918 at Camp Wadsworth, SC as army troops unit (formed from balance of 74th Infantry, NY NG). Moved overseas Sep 1918. Slotted for conversion to 394th Infantry but war ended before that occurred. Returned to the US Feb 1919 and demobilized at Camp Hill, VA.

**56th Pioneer Infantry**          Organized Feb 1918 at Camp Greene, NC as army troops unit (formed from the bulk of 1st Heavy Field Artillery, ME NG). Moved overseas Aug 1918. Served with First Army Sep-Nov 1918. Slotted for conversion to 397th Infantry but war ended before that occurred. With Third Army on Rhine occupation. Returned to the US Jun 1919 and demobilized Jul 1919 at Camp Dix, NJ.

**57th Pioneer Infantry**          Organized Feb 1918 at Camp Greene, NC as army troops unit (formed from balance of 1st Infantry, VT NG). Moved overseas Sep 1918. Slotted for conversion to 398th Infantry but war ended before that occurred. Returned to the US Feb 1919 and demobilized at Camp Devens, MA.

**58<sup>th</sup> Pioneer Infantry**       Organized Feb 1918 at Camp Greene, NC [but moved to Camp Wadsworth, SC] as army troops unit (formed from personnel from 1<sup>st</sup> Infantry, CT NG). Slotted for conversion to 401<sup>st</sup> Infantry but war ended before that occurred. Demobilized Jan 1919 at Camp Wadsworth.

**59<sup>th</sup> Pioneer Infantry**       Organized Jan 1918 at Camp Dix, NJ as army troops unit (formed from 1<sup>st</sup> Infantry, DE NG). Moved overseas Aug 1918. Served with First Army Sep-Nov 1918. Slotted for conversion to 402<sup>nd</sup> Infantry but war ended before that occurred. Returned to the US Jul 1919 and demobilized at Camp Dix.

**60<sup>th</sup> Pioneer Infantry**       Organized Jul 1918 at Camp Wadsworth, SC as army troops unit. Slotted for conversion to 405<sup>th</sup> Infantry but war ended before that occurred. Demobilized Jan 1919 at Camp Wadsworth.

**61<sup>st</sup> Pioneer Infantry**       Organized Jul 1918 at Camp Wadsworth, SC as corps troops unit. Slotted for conversion to 406<sup>th</sup> Infantry but war ended before that occurred. Demobilized Jan 1919 at Camp Wadsworth.

**62<sup>nd</sup> Pioneer Infantry**       Organized Jul 1918 at Camp Wadsworth, SC as corps troops unit. Demobilized Jan 1919 at Camp Wadsworth.

**63<sup>rd</sup> Pioneer Infantry**       Organized Oct 1918 at Camp Dix, NJ as corps troops unit. Demobilized Jan 1919 at Camp Dix.

**64<sup>th</sup> Pioneer Infantry**       Organized Oct 1918 at Camp Zachary Taylor, KY as corps troops unit. Demobilized Feb 1919 at Camp Zachary Taylor.

**65<sup>th</sup> Pioneer Infantry**       Organized Oct 1918 at Camp Funston, KS as corps troops unit. Demobilized Dec 1918 at Camp Funston.

**801<sup>st</sup> Pioneer Infantry**       Organized Jun 1918 at Camp Zachary Taylor, KY with black enlisted personnel as corps troops unit. Moved overseas Sep 1918. Served with First Army Sep-Nov 1918. Returned to the US Jun 1919 and demobilized at Camp Zachary Taylor.

**802<sup>nd</sup> Pioneer Infantry**       Organized Jul 1918 at Camp Sherman, OH with black enlisted personnel as army troops unit. Moved overseas Aug 1918. Served with First Army Sep-Nov 1918. Returned to the US Jul 1919 and demobilized at Camp Gordon, GA.

**803<sup>rd</sup> Pioneer Infantry**       Organized Jul 1918 at Camp Grant, IL with black enlisted personnel as army troops unit. Moved overseas Sep 1918. Served with Second Army Oct-Nov 1918. Returned to the US Jul 1919 and demobilized at Camp Grant.

**804th Pioneer Infantry**     Organized Jul 1918 at Camp Dodge, IA with black enlisted personnel as corps troops unit.  Moved overseas Sep 1918.  Served with VI Army Corps Oct-Nov 1918.  Returned to the US Jul 1919 and demobilized at Camp Gordon, GA.

**805th Pioneer Infantry**     Organized Jun 1918 at Camp Funston, KS with black enlisted personnel as army troops unit.  Moved overseas Sep 1918.  Served with First Army Sep-Nov 1918.  Returned to the US Jun 1919 and demobilized Jul 1919 at Camp Shelby, MS.

**806th Pioneer Infantry**     Organized Jul 1918 at Camp Funston, KS with black enlisted personnel as army troops unit.  Moved overseas Sep 1918.  Served with First Army Sep-Nov 1918.  Returned to the US Jun 1919 and demobilized Jul 1919 at Camp Shelby, MS.

**807th Pioneer Infantry**     Organized Jul 1918 at Camp Dix, NJ with black enlisted personnel as army troops unit.  Moved overseas Sep 1918.  Served with First Army Sep-Nov 1918.  Returned to the US Jul 1919 and demobilized at Camp Jackson, SC.

**808th Pioneer Infantry**     Organized Jul 1918 at Camp Meade, MD with black enlisted personnel as army troops unit.  Moved overseas Aug 1918.  Served with First Army Sep-Nov 1918.  Returned to the US Jun 1919 and demobilized at Camp Lee, VA.

**809th Pioneer Infantry**     Organized Aug 1918 at Camp Dodge, IA with black enlisted personnel as corps troops unit.  Moved overseas Sep 1918.  Returned to the US Jul 1919 and demobilized at Camp Sherman, OH.

**810th Pioneer Infantry**     Organized Sep 1918 at Camp Greene, NC with black enlisted personnel as corps troops unit.  Demobilized Dec 1918 at Camp Greene.

**811th Pioneer Infantry**     Organized Aug 1918 at Camp Dix, NJ with black enlisted personnel as corps troops unit.  Moved overseas Oct 1918.  Returned to the US Jul 1919 and demobilized at Camp Dix.

**812th Pioneer Infantry**     Organized Aug 1918 at Camp Grant, IL with black enlisted personnel as corps troops unit.  Demobilized Jan 1919 at Camp Grant.

**813th Pioneer Infantry**     Organized Aug 1918 at Camp Sherman, OH with black enlisted personnel as army troops unit.  Moved overseas Sep 1918.  Served with Second Army Oct-Nov 1918.  Returned to the US Jul 1919 and demobilized at Camp Dix, NJ.

**814th Pioneer Infantry**     Organized Aug 1918 at Camp Zachary Taylor, KY with black enlisted personnel as corps troops unit.  Moved overseas Oct 1918.  Returned to the US Dec 1918 and demobilized at Camp Zachary Taylor.

**815<sup>th</sup> Pioneer Infantry**     Organized Sep 1918 at Camp Funston, KS
  with black enlisted personnel as corps troops unit. Moved overseas Oct
  1918. Served with First Army Oct-Nov 1918. Returned to the US Jul
  1919 and demobilized at Camp Travis, TX.

**816<sup>th</sup> Pioneer Infantry**     Organized Sep 1918 at Camp Funston, KS
  with black enlisted personnel as army troops unit. Moved overseas Oct
  1918. Served with First Army Oct-Nov 1918. Returned to the US Aug
  1919 and demobilized at Camp Shelby, MS.

[817<sup>th</sup> Pioneer Infantry authorized but never organized]

*Marines in 2<sup>nd</sup> Division*[63]

**5<sup>th</sup> Marines**     Organized 7 Jun 1917 at the Navy Yard, Philadelphia, PA.
  Attached 9 Jun 1917 to 1<sup>st</sup> Expeditionary Division [later 1<sup>st</sup> Division].
  Moved overseas Jun 1917. Relieved 23 Sep 1917 from attachment to
  1<sup>st</sup> Division. Assigned 23 Oct 1917 to 4<sup>th</sup> Marine Brigade (Infantry).
  Returned to the US Aug 1919 and moved to Quantico, VA where
  demobilized 13 Aug 1919.

**6<sup>th</sup> Marines**     Organized 4 Aug 1917 at Quantico, VA. Moved overseas Sep
  1917-Feb 1918 (arriving by echelons). Assigned 23 Oct 1917 to 4<sup>th</sup>
  Marine Brigade (Infantry). Returned to the US Aug 1919 and moved
  to Quantico where demobilized 13 Aug 1919.

**6<sup>th</sup> Machine Gun Bn, Marines** Organized 17 Aug 1917 at Quantico, VA as 1<sup>st</sup>
  MG Bn, Marines (renumbered 20 Jan 1918). Moved overseas Sep-Nov
  1917 and assigned 23 Oct 1917 to 4<sup>th</sup> Marine Brigade (Infantry).
  Returned to the US Aug 1919 and moved to Quantico where
  demobilized 13 Aug 1919.

*Hawaiian Infantry*

**1<sup>st</sup> Hawaiian Infantry**   1<sup>st</sup> Infantry, NG of Hawaii drafted into Federal service
  1 Jun 1918 in the Territory of Hawaii and redesignated. Demobilized
  31 Jul 1919.

---

[63] The Marines later formed a 5<sup>th</sup> Brigade as well (11<sup>th</sup> and 13<sup>th</sup> Marines and 5<sup>th</sup> Brigade Machine Gun Bn), which arrived in France Sep-Nov 1918. Its units never served together as a brigade, and were scattered at camps and posts in the Services of Supply all over France. Duties included, among others, such assignments as provost guard, hospital center guard, camp guards, railroad transportation officers, commanding dock guard, dock guard, unloading ships, military police, warehouse guards, convoying of, railroad trains, and special guards for shipments of commissary supplies. The brigade returned to the US Aug 1919 and was demobilized 13 Aug 1919 at Quantico, VA.

**2nd Hawaiian Infantry** 2nd Infantry, NG of Hawaii drafted into Federal service 1 Jun 1918 in the Territory of Hawaii and redesignated.. Demobilized 14 Feb 1919.

*Philippine Infantry*[64]

**1st Philippine Infantry (Provisional)**    Formed Apr 1918 in Philippine Islands (absorbed 1st and 6th Bns, Philippine Scouts).

**2nd Philippine Infantry (Provisional)**    Organized 5 Apr 1918 in Philippine Islands (absorbed 4th and 10th Bns, Philippine Scouts).[65]

**3rd Philippine Infantry (Provisional)**    Formed Apr 1918 in Philippine Islands (absorbed 3rd and 7th Bns, Philippine Scouts).

**4th Philippine Infantry (Provisional)**    Formed Apr 1918 in Philippine Islands (absorbed 8th and 9th Bns, Philippine Scouts).

**1st Bn, Philippine Scouts**    Stationed in Philippine Islands. Absorbed Apr 1918 by 1st Philippine Infantry (Provisional).

**2nd Bn, Philippine Scouts**    Stationed in Philippine Islands.

**3rd Bn, Philippine Scouts**    Stationed in Philippine Islands. Absorbed Apr 1918 by 3rd Philippine Infantry (Provisional).

**4th Bn, Philippine Scouts**    Stationed in Philippine Islands. Absorbed Apr 1918 by 2nd Philippine Infantry (Provisional).

**5th Bn, Philippine Scouts**    Stationed in Philippine Islands.

**6th Bn, Philippine Scouts**    Stationed in Philippine Islands. Absorbed Apr 1918 by 1st Philippine Infantry (Provisional).

**7th Bn, Philippine Scouts**    Stationed in Philippine Islands. Absorbed Apr 1918 by 3rd Philippine Infantry (Provisional).

**8th Bn, Philippine Scouts**    Stationed in Philippine Islands. Absorbed Apr 1918 by 4th Philippine Infantry (Provisional).

**9th Bn, Philippine Scouts**    Stationed in Philippine Islands. Absorbed Apr 1918 by 4th Philippine Infantry (Provisional).

**10th Bn, Philippine Scouts**    Stationed in Philippine Islands. Absorbed Apr 1918 by 2nd Philippine Infantry (Provisional).

**11th Bn, Philippine Scouts**    Stationed in Philippine Islands. Absorbed Apr 1918 by 1st Philippine Field Artillery (Provisional) (Mountain).

---

[64] The provisional infantry regiments became the 45th, 57th and 62nd Infantry (Philippine Scouts) in 1921 [former 1st, 2nd and 4th, respectively]. The 3rd was probably used to form the 43rd Infantry (Philippine Scouts) the same year, but the lineage of the 43rd does not reflect that.

[65] According to the lineage, formed from 4th, 10th and 15th Bns and the 72nd, 73rd, 74th and 75th Coys, Philippine Scouts. However, the *Order of Battle* volumes only listed battalions of Philippine Scouts.

**12<sup>th</sup> Bn, Philippine Scouts**    Stationed in Philippine Islands. Absorbed Apr 1918 by 1<sup>st</sup> Philippine Field Artillery (Provisional) (Mountain).

**13<sup>th</sup> Bn, Philippine Scouts**    Stationed in Philippine Islands.

[14<sup>th</sup> Bn, Philippine Scouts was authorized but never organized]

**1<sup>st</sup> Infantry, Philippine NG**    Organized Dec 1918 (component of 1<sup>st</sup> Infantry Brigade, PNG) and demobilized the same month.[66]

**2<sup>nd</sup> Infantry, Philippine NG**    Organized Dec 1918 (component of 1<sup>st</sup> Infantry Brigade, PNG) and demobilized the same month.

**3<sup>rd</sup> Infantry, Philippine NG**    Organized Dec 1918 (component of 1<sup>st</sup> Infantry Brigade, PNG) and demobilized the same month.

**4<sup>th</sup> Infantry, Philippine NG**    Organized Dec 1918 (component of 2<sup>nd</sup> Infantry Brigade, PNG) and demobilized the same month.

**5<sup>th</sup> Infantry, Philippine NG**    Organized Dec 1918 (component of 2<sup>nd</sup> Infantry Brigade, PNG) and demobilized the same month.

**6<sup>th</sup> Infantry, Philippine NG**    Organized Dec 1918 (component of 2<sup>nd</sup> Infantry Brigade, PNG) and demobilized the same month.

**7<sup>th</sup> Infantry, Philippine NG**    Organized Dec 1918 (component of 3<sup>rd</sup> Infantry Brigade, PNG) and demobilized the same month.

**8<sup>th</sup> Infantry, Philippine NG**    Organized Dec 1918 (component of 3<sup>rd</sup> Infantry Brigade, PNG) and demobilized the same month.

**9<sup>th</sup> Infantry, Philippine NG**    Organized Dec 1918 (component of 3<sup>rd</sup> Infantry Brigade, PNG) and demobilized the same month.

## Machine Gun Units

*Regular Army Machine Gun Battalions*

**1<sup>st</sup> Machine Gun Bn**    Organized Nov 1917 in the AEF as component of 1<sup>st</sup> Division. Moved to the US Sep 1919 and moved to Camp Zachary Taylor, KY.

**2<sup>nd</sup> Machine Gun Bn**    Organized Jan 1918 in the AEF as component of 1<sup>st</sup> Division (1<sup>st</sup> Infantry Brigade). Moved to the US Sep 1919 and moved to Camp Zachary Taylor, KY.

**3<sup>rd</sup> Machine Gun Bn**    Organized Jan 1918 in the AEF as component of 1<sup>st</sup> Division (2<sup>nd</sup> Infantry Brigade). Moved to the US Sep 1919 and moved to Camp Zachary Taylor, KY.

---

[66] Since the brigades of the PNG were in existence from Nov 1918 to Feb 1919 (but only in federal service Nov-Dec 1918), these dates from the Order of Battle volumes must reflect only the period of federal service.

**4th Machine Gun Bn**      Organized Oct 1917 at Gettysburg, PA as component of 2nd Division. Moved overseas Dec 1917. Returned to the US Aug 1919 and moved to Camp Travis, TX.

**5th Machine Gun Bn**      Organized Jan 1918 in the AEF as component of 2nd Division (3rd Infantry Brigade). Moved to the US Aug 1919 and moved to Camp Travis, TX.

[6th Machine Gun Bn formed from USMC companies and assigned 4th Marine Brigade of 2nd Division]

**7th Machine Gun Bn**      Organized Nov 1917 at Camp Greene, NC as component of 3rd Division. Moved overseas Apr 1918. Detached 1919 and joined American Forces in Germany, and under 1st Brigade, AF in G in 1920. Demobilized later.

**8th Machine Gun Bn**      Organized Nov 1917 at Camp Greene, NC as component of 3rd Division (5th Infantry Brigade). Moved overseas Apr 1918. Returned to the US Aug 1919 and moved to Camp Pike, AR.

**9th Machine Gun Bn**      Organized Nov 1917 at Camp Greene, NC as component of 3rd Division (6th Infantry Brigade). Moved overseas Apr 1918. Returned to the US Aug 1919 and moved to Camp Pike, AR.

**10th Machine Gun Bn**  Organized Nov 1917 at Camp Greene, NC as component of 4th Division. Moved overseas May 1918. Returned to the US Jul 1919 and moved to Camp Dodge, IA.

**11th Machine Gun Bn**  Organized Dec 1917 at Camp Greene, NC as component of 4th Division (7th Infantry Brigade). Moved overseas May 1918. Returned to the US Jul 1919 and moved to Camp Dodge, IA.

**12th Machine Gun Bn**  Organized Dec 1917 at Camp Greene, NC as component of 4th Division (8th Infantry Brigade). Moved overseas May 1918. Returned to the US Jul 1919 and moved to Camp Dodge, IA.

**13th Machine Gun Bn**  Organized Nov 1917 at Ft. Sam Houston, TX as component of 5th Division. Moved overseas Apr 1918. Returned to the US Jul 1919 and moved to Camp Gordon, Ga.

**14th Machine Gun Bn**  Organized Dec 1917 at Camp Greene, NC as component of 5th Division (9th Infantry Brigade). Moved overseas Apr 1918. Returned to the US Jul 1919 and moved to Camp Gordon, Ga.

**15th Machine Gun Bn**  Organized Jan 1918 at Camp Forrest, GA as component of 5th Division (10th Infantry Brigade). Moved overseas Apr 1918. Returned to the US Jul 1919 and moved to Camp Gordon, GA.

**16th Machine Gun Bn**  Organized Jan 1918 at Camp Forrest, GA as component of 6th Division. Moved overseas Jul 1918. Returned to the US Jun 1919 and moved to Camp Grant, IL.

**17th Machine Gun Bn**  Organized Dec 1917 at Camp Forrest, GA as component of 6th Division (11th Infantry Brigade). Moved overseas Jul 1918. Returned to the US Jun 1919 and moved to Camp Grant, IL.

**18<sup>th</sup> Machine Gun Bn**   Organized Dec 1917 at Camp Forrest, GA as component of 6<sup>th</sup> Division (12<sup>th</sup> Infantry Brigade).  Moved overseas Jul 1918.  Returned to the US Jun 1919 and moved to Camp Grant, IL.

**19<sup>th</sup> Machine Gun Bn**   Organized Jan 1918 at Camp Forrest, GA as component of 7<sup>th</sup> Division.  Moved overseas Aug 1918.  Returned to the US Jun 1919 and moved to Camp Funston, KS.

**20<sup>th</sup> Machine Gun Bn**   Organized Jan 1918 at Camp Forrest, GA as component of 7<sup>th</sup> Division (13<sup>th</sup> Infantry Brigade).  Moved overseas Aug 1918.  Returned to the US Jun 1919 and moved to Camp Funston, KS.

**21<sup>st</sup> Machine Gun Bn**   Organized Jan 1918 at Camp Fort Bliss, TX as component of 7<sup>th</sup> Division (14<sup>th</sup> Infantry Brigade).  Moved overseas Aug 1918.  Returned to the US Jun 1919 and moved to Camp Funston, KS.

**22<sup>nd</sup> Machine Gun Bn**   Organized Mar 1918 at Camp Fremont, CA as component of 8<sup>th</sup> Division.  Moved Nov 1918 to Camp Lee, VA and demobilized there Feb 1919.

**23<sup>rd</sup> Machine Gun Bn**   Organized Feb 1918 at Camp Fremont, CA as component of 8<sup>th</sup> Division (15<sup>th</sup> Infantry Brigade).  Moved Nov 1918 to Camp Lee, VA and demobilized there Feb 1919.

**24<sup>th</sup> Machine Gun Bn**   Organized Jan 1918 at Camp Fremont, CA as component of 8<sup>th</sup> Division (16<sup>th</sup> Infantry Brigade).  Moved Nov 1918 to Camp Lee, VA and demobilized there Feb 1919.

**25<sup>th</sup> Machine Gun Bn**   Organized Aug 1918 Camp Sheridan, AL as component of 9<sup>th</sup> Division.  Demobilized Feb 1919 at Camp Sheridan.

**26<sup>th</sup> Machine Gun Bn**   Organized Dec 1917 Camp Zachary Taylor, KY as component of 9<sup>th</sup> Division (17<sup>th</sup> Infantry Brigade).  Moved Jun 1918 to Camp Sheridan, AL and demobilized there Feb 1919.

**27<sup>th</sup> Machine Gun Bn**   *See* 29<sup>th</sup> Machine Gun Bn

**27<sup>th</sup> Machine Gun Bn**   Organized Jul 1918 at Camp Sheridan, AL as component of 9<sup>th</sup> Division (18<sup>th</sup> Infantry Brigade).  Demobilized Feb 1919 at Camp Sheridan.

**28<sup>th</sup> Machine Gun Bn**   Organized Aug 1918 at Camp Funston, KS as component of 10<sup>th</sup> Division.  Demobilized Feb 1919 at Camp Funston.

**29<sup>th</sup> Machine Gun Bn**   Organized Dec 1917 at Ft. Sam Houston, TX as 27<sup>th</sup> MG Bn, a component of 9<sup>th</sup> Division (18<sup>th</sup> Infantry Brigade).  Redesignated Jul 1918 as 29<sup>th</sup> MG Bn, moved to Camp Funston, KS, and assigned 10<sup>th</sup> Division (19<sup>th</sup> Infantry Brigade).  Demobilized Feb 1919 at Camp Funston.

**30<sup>th</sup> Machine Gun Bn**   Organized Aug 1918 at Camp Funston, KS as component of 10<sup>th</sup> Division (20<sup>th</sup> Infantry Brigade).  Demobilized Feb 1919 at Camp Funston.

**31st Machine Gun Bn**  Organized Sep 1918 at Camp Meade, MD as
component of 11th Division.  Demobilized Jan 1919 at Camp Meade.

**32nd Machine Gun Bn**  Organized Sep 1918 at Camp Meade, MD as
component of 11th Division (21st Infantry Brigade).  Demobilized Jan
1919 at Camp Meade.

**33rd Machine Gun Bn**  Organized Sep 1918 at Camp Meade, MD as
component of 11th Division (22nd Infantry Brigade).  Demobilized Jan
1919 at Camp Meade.

**34th Machine Gun Bn**  Organized Jul 1918 at Camp Devens, MA as
component of 12th Division.  Demobilized Jan 1919 at Camp Devens.

**35th Machine Gun Bn**  Organized Jul 1918 at Camp Devens, MA as
component of 12th Division (23rd Infantry Brigade).  Demobilized Jan
1919 at Camp Devens.

**36th Machine Gun Bn**  Organized Jul 1918 at Camp Devens, MA as
component of 12th Division (24th Infantry Brigade).  Demobilized Jan
1919 at Camp Devens.

**37th Machine Gun Bn**  Organized Sep 1918 at Camp Lewis, WA as
component of 13th Division.  Demobilized Feb 1919 at Camp Lewis.

**38th Machine Gun Bn**  Organized Sep 1918 at Camp Lewis, WA as
component of 13th Division (25th Infantry Brigade).  Demobilized Feb
1919 at Camp Lewis.

**39th Machine Gun Bn**  Organized Sep 1918 at Camp Lewis, WA as
component of 13th Division (26th Infantry Brigade).  Demobilized Feb
1919 at Camp Lewis.

**40th Machine Gun Bn**  Organized Sep 1918 at Camp Custer, MI as component
of 14th Division.  Demobilized Feb 1919 at Camp Custer.

**41st Machine Gun Bn**  Organized Sep 1918 at Camp Custer, MI as component
of 14th Division (27th Infantry Brigade).  Demobilized Feb 1919 at
Camp Custer.

**42nd Machine Gun Bn**  Organized Sep 1918 at Camp Custer, MI as component
of 14th Division (28th Infantry Brigade).  Demobilized Feb 1919 at
Camp Custer.

**43rd Machine Gun Bn**  Organized Nov 1918 at Camp Logan, TX as
component of 15th Division.  Demobilized Feb 1919 at Camp Logan.

**44th Machine Gun Bn**  Organized Nov 1918 at Camp Logan, TX as
component of 15th Division (29th Infantry Brigade).  Demobilized Feb
1919 at Camp Logan.

**45th Machine Gun Bn**  Organized Nov 1918 at Camp Logan, TX as
component of 15th Division (30th Infantry Brigade).  Demobilized Feb
1919 at Camp Logan.

[46th Machine Gun Bn          Constituted as component of 16th Division but
never organized]

**47<sup>th</sup> Machine Gun Bn**  Organized Sep 1918 at Camp Kearny, CA as component of 16<sup>th</sup> Division (31<sup>st</sup> Infantry Brigade).  Demobilized Feb 1919 at Camp Kearny.

**48<sup>th</sup> Machine Gun Bn**  Organized Sep 1918 at Camp Kearny, CA as component of 16<sup>th</sup> Division (32<sup>nd</sup> Infantry Brigade).  Demobilized Feb 1919 at Camp Kearny.

**49<sup>th</sup> Machine Gun Bn**  Organized Sep 1918 at Camp Beauregard, LA as component of 17<sup>th</sup> Division.  Demobilized Jan 1919 at Camp Beauregard.

**50<sup>th</sup> Machine Gun Bn**  Organized Sep 1918 at Camp Beauregard, LA as component of 17<sup>th</sup> Division (33<sup>rd</sup> Infantry Brigade).  Demobilized Jan 1919 at Camp Beauregard.

**51<sup>st</sup> Machine Gun Bn**  Organized Oct 1918 at Camp Beauregard, LA as component of 17<sup>th</sup> Division (34<sup>th</sup> Infantry Brigade).  Demobilized Jan 1919 at Camp Beauregard.

**52<sup>nd</sup> Machine Gun Bn**  Organized Oct 1918 at Camp Travis, TX as component of 18<sup>th</sup> Division.  Demobilized Feb 1919 at Camp Travis.

**53<sup>rd</sup> Machine Gun Bn**  Organized Oct 1918 at Camp Travis, TX as component of 18<sup>th</sup> Division (35<sup>th</sup> Infantry Brigade).  Demobilized Feb 1919 at Camp Travis.

**54<sup>th</sup> Machine Gun Bn**  Organized Oct 1918 at Camp Travis, TX as component of 18<sup>th</sup> Division (36<sup>th</sup> Infantry Brigade).  Demobilized Feb 1919 at Camp Travis.

**55<sup>th</sup> Machine Gun Bn**  Organized Oct 1918 at Camp Dodge, IA as component of 19<sup>th</sup> Division.  Demobilized Jan 1919 at Camp Dodge.

**56<sup>th</sup> Machine Gun Bn**  Organized Oct 1918 at Camp Dodge, IA as component of 19<sup>th</sup> Division (37<sup>th</sup> Infantry Brigade).  Demobilized Jan 1919 at Camp Dodge.

**57<sup>th</sup> Machine Gun Bn**  Organized Oct 1918 at Camp Dodge, IA as component of 19<sup>th</sup> Division (38<sup>th</sup> Infantry Brigade).  Demobilized Jan 1919 at Camp Dodge.

**58<sup>th</sup> Machine Gun Bn**  Organized Oct 1918 at Camp Sevier, SC as component of 20<sup>th</sup> Division.  Demobilized Jan 1919 at Camp Sevier.

**59<sup>th</sup> Machine Gun Bn**  Organized Sep 1918 at Camp Sevier, SC as component of 20<sup>th</sup> Division (39<sup>th</sup> Infantry Brigade).  Demobilized Feb 1919 at Camp Sevier.

**60<sup>th</sup> Machine Gun Bn**  Organized Oct 1918 at Camp Sevier, SC as component of 20<sup>th</sup> Division (40<sup>th</sup> Infantry Brigade).  Demobilized Jan 1919 at Camp Sevier.

*National Guard Machine Gun Battalions*

**101st Machine Gun Bn**    Organized Sep 1917 at Niantic, CT as component of 26th Division (formed from 1st Sqn Cavalry, CT NG and personnel from 1st Infantry, VT NG). Moved overseas Oct 1917. Returned to the US Apr 1919 and demobilized at Camp Devens, MA.

**102nd Machine Gun Bn**    Organized Aug 1917 at Framingham, MA as component of 26th Division (51st Infantry Brigade) (formed from three troops, 1st Sqn Cavalry, MA NG and personnel from 1st Infantry, VT NG). Moved overseas Sep 1917. R eturned to the US Apr 1919 and demobilized at Camp Devens, MA.

**103rd Machine Gun Bn**    Organized Aug 1917 at Westfield, MA as component of 26th Division (52nd Infantry Brigade) (formed from MG Trp, Cavalry NH NG, 1st Separate Sqn Cavalry (-), RI NG, and personnel from 1st Infantry, VT NG). Moved overseas Oct 1917. Returned to the US Apr 1919 and demobilized at Camp Devens, MA.

**104th Machine Gun Bn**    Organized Oct 1917 at Camp Wadsworth, SC as component of 27th Division (formed form six troops and additional personnel, 1st Cavalry, NY NG). Moved overseas May 1918. Returned to the US Mar 1919. Demobilized Apr 1919 at Camp Upton, NY.

**105th Machine Gun Bn**    Organized Oct 1917 at Camp Wadsworth, SC as component of 27th Division (53rd Infantry Brigade) (formed from Sqn A Cavalry and Separate MG Trp, NY NG and personnel from 1st Cavalry, NY NG). Moved overseas May 1918. Returned to the US Mar 1919. Demobilized Apr 1919 at Camp Upton, NY.

**106th Machine Gun Bn**    Organized Oct 1917 at Camp Wadsworth, SC as component of 27th Division (54th Infantry Brigade) (formed from thee troops and additional personnel, 1st Cavalry, NY NG). Moved overseas May 1918. Returned to the US Mar 1919. Demobilized Apr 1919 at Camp Upton, NY.

**107th Machine Gun Bn**    Organized Oct 1917 at Camp Hancock, GA as component of 28th Division (formed from 2nd Bn, 4th Infantry, PA NG). Moved overseas May 1918. Returned to the US Apr 1919. Demobilized May 1919 at Camp Dix, NJ.

**108th Machine Gun Bn**    Organized Oct 1917 at Camp Hancock, GA as component of 28th Division (55th Infantry Brigade) (formed from two companies, 4th Infantry, PA NG and MG Trp, 1st Cavalry, PA NG). Moved overseas May 1918. Returned to the US May 1919 and demobilized at Camp Dix, NJ.

**109th Machine Gun Bn**    Organized Oct 1917 at Camp Hancock, GA as component of 28th Division (56th Infantry Brigade) (formed from three companies, 4th Infantry, PA NG). Moved overseas May 1918. Returned to the US May 1919 and demobilized at Camp Dix, NJ.

**110th Machine Gun Bn**    Organized Sep 1917 at Camp McClellan, AL as component of 29th Division (formed from MG Coys of 5th Infantry, MD NG, 4th Infantry, NJ NG, and 1st Infantry, VA NG). Moved overseas Jun 1918. Returned to the US May 1919. Demobilized Jun 1919 at Camp Meade, MD.

**111th Machine Gun Bn**    Organized Sep 1917 at Camp McClellan, AL as component of 29th Division (57th Infantry Brigade) (formed from two companies 2nd Infantry and MG Coy, 3rd Infantry, MD NG). Moved overseas Jun 1918. Returned to the US May 1919 and demobilized at Camp Dix, NJ.

**112th Machine Gun Bn**    Organized Oct 1917 at Camp McClellan, AL as component of 29th Division (58th Infantry Brigade) (formed from company, 1st Infantry and MG Coy, 4th Infantry, MD NG and two companies, 4th Infantry, VA NG). Moved overseas Jun 1918. Returned to the US May 1919 and demobilized at Camp Stuart, VA.

**113th Machine Gun Bn**    Organized Sep 1917 at Camp Sevier, SC as component of 30th Division (formed from MG Coys from 1st Infantry, NC NG, 2nd Infantry, SC NG, 1st and 2nd Infantry, TN NG and additional personnel 2nd Infantry, TN NG). Moved overseas May 1918. Returned to the US Apr 1919 and demobilized at Ft. Oglethorpe, GA.

**114th Machine Gun Bn**    Organized Sep 1917 at Camp Sevier, SC as component of 30th Division (59th Infantry Brigade) (formed from 1st Sqn Cavalry (-), TN NG). Moved overseas May 1918. Returned to the US Mar 1919. Demobilized Apr 1919 at Ft. Oglethorpe, GA.

**115th Machine Gun Bn**    Organized Sep 1917 at Camp Sevier, SC as component of 30th Division (60th Infantry Brigade) (formed from two troops, 1st Sqn Cavalry and MG Trp, NC NG). Moved overseas May 1918. Returned to the US Mar 1919. Demobilized Apr 1919 at Camp Jackson, SC.

**116th Machine Gun Bn**    Organized Sep 1917 at Camp Wheeler, GA as component of 31st Division (formed from MG Coys from 2nd Infantry, AL NG and 1st Infantry, FL NG, and two companies, 1st Infantry, GA NG). Moved overseas Oct 1918. Skeletonized Nov 1918. Returned to the US Dec 1918 and demobilized Jan 1919 at Camp Gordon, GA.

**117th Machine Gun Bn**    Organized Sep 1917 at Camp Wheeler, GA as component of 31st Division (61st Infantry Brigade) (formed from three companies, 1st Infantry, GA NG and some personnel 1st Infantry, FL NG). Moved overseas Oct 1918. Skeletonized Nov 1918. Returned to the US Dec 1918 and demobilized Jan 1919 at Camp Gordon, GA.

**118<sup>th</sup> Machine Gun Bn** Organized Oct 1917 at Camp Wheeler, GA as component of 31<sup>st</sup> Division (62<sup>nd</sup> Infantry Brigade) (formed from MG Trp, 1<sup>st</sup> Cavalry, AL NG, two companies, 1<sup>st</sup> Infantry, GA NG, and personnel from 1<sup>st</sup> Infantry, FL NG). Moved overseas Oct 1918. Skeletonized Nov 1918. Returned to the US Dec 1918 and demobilized Jan 1919 at Camp Gordon, GA.

**119<sup>th</sup> Machine Gun Bn** Organized Oct 1917 at Camp MacArthur, TX as component of 32<sup>nd</sup> Division (formed from personnel from 4<sup>th</sup>, 5<sup>th</sup> and 6<sup>th</sup> Infantry, WI NG). Moved overseas Feb 1918. Returned to the US May 1919. Demobilized Jun 1919 at Camp Grant, IL.

**120<sup>th</sup> Machine Gun Bn** Organized Sep 1917 at Camp MacArthur, TX as component of 32<sup>nd</sup> Division (63<sup>rd</sup> Infantry Brigade) (formed from personnel from 31<sup>st</sup> and 33<sup>rd</sup> Infantry, MI NG). Moved overseas Feb 1918. Returned to the US May 1919 and demobilized at Camp Custer, MI.

**121<sup>st</sup> Machine Gun Bn** Organized Oct 1917 at Camp MacArthur, TX as component of 32<sup>nd</sup> Division (64<sup>th</sup> Infantry Brigade) (formed from personnel from 3<sup>rd</sup> and 5<sup>th</sup> Infantry, WI NG). Moved overseas Feb 1918. Returned to the US May 1919 and demobilized at Camp Grant, IL.

**122<sup>nd</sup> Machine Gun Bn** Organized Oct 1917 at Camp Logan, TX as component of 33<sup>rd</sup> Division (formed from three companies, 5<sup>th</sup> Infantry and MG Coy, 7<sup>th</sup> Infantry, IL NG). Moved overseas May 1918. Returned to the US May 1919 and demobilized at Camp Grant, IL.

**123<sup>rd</sup> Machine Gun Bn** Organized Oct 1917 at Camp Logan, TX as component of 33<sup>rd</sup> Division (65<sup>th</sup> Infantry Brigade) (formed from three companies, 5<sup>th</sup> Infantry, IL NG). Moved overseas May 1918. Returned to the US May 1919 and demobilized at Camp Grant, IL.

**124<sup>th</sup> Machine Gun Bn** Organized Oct 1917 at Camp Logan, TX as component of 33<sup>rd</sup> Division (66<sup>th</sup> Infantry Brigade) (formed from three companies, 5<sup>th</sup> Infantry, IL NG). Moved overseas May 1918. R eturned to the US May 1919 and demobilized at Camp Grant, IL.

**125<sup>th</sup> Machine Gun Bn** Organized Oct 1917 at Camp Cody, NM as component of 34<sup>th</sup> Division (formed from 1<sup>st</sup> Bn, 2<sup>nd</sup> Infantry, IA NG, troop, 1<sup>st</sup> Sqn Cavalry, IA NG, and MG Coy, 3<sup>rd</sup> Infantry, MN NG). Moved overseas Sep 1918. Skeletonized Nov 1918. Returned to the US Jan 1919. Demobilized Feb 1919 at Camp Grant, IL.

**126<sup>th</sup> Machine Gun Bn** Organized Oct 1917 at Camp Cody, NM as component of 34<sup>th</sup> Division (67<sup>th</sup> Infantry Brigade) (formed from 2<sup>nd</sup> Bn, 2<sup>nd</sup> Infantry, IA NG and MG Coy, 6<sup>th</sup> Infantry, NE NG) . Moved overseas Sep 1918. Skeletonized Nov 1918. Returned to the US Jan 1919. Demobilized Feb 1919 at Camp Grant, IL.

**127<sup>th</sup> Machine Gun Bn**       Organized Oct 1917 at Camp Cody, NM as component of 34<sup>th</sup> Division (68<sup>th</sup> Infantry Brigade) (formed from 2<sup>nd</sup> Sqn, 1<sup>st</sup> Cavalry, SD NG). Moved overseas Oct 1918. Skeletonized Nov 1918. Returned to the US Jan 1919. Demobilized Feb 1919 at Camp Grant, IL.

**128<sup>th</sup> Machine Gun Bn**       Organized Oct 1917 at Camp Doniphan, OK as component of 35<sup>th</sup> Division (formed from 1<sup>st</sup> Bn and MG Coy, 2<sup>nd</sup> Infantry, MO NG). Moved overseas Apr 1918. Returned to the US Apr 1919. Demobilized May 1919 at Camp Funston, KS.

**129<sup>th</sup> Machine Gun Bn**       Organized Oct 1917 at Camp Doniphan, OK as component of 35<sup>th</sup> Division (69<sup>th</sup> Infantry Brigade) (formed from 2<sup>nd</sup> Bn, 2<sup>nd</sup> Infantry, MO NG). Moved overseas Apr 1918. Returned to the US Apr 1919. Demobilized May 1919 at Camp Funston, KS.

**130<sup>th</sup> Machine Gun Bn**       Organized Oct 1917 at Camp Doniphan, OK as component of 35<sup>th</sup> Division (70<sup>th</sup> Infantry Brigade) (formed from 3<sup>rd</sup> Bn, 2<sup>nd</sup> Infantry, MO NG). Moved overseas Apr 1918. Returned to the US Apr 1919. Demobilized May 1919 at Camp Funston, KS.

**131<sup>st</sup> Machine Gun Bn**       Organized Oct 1917 at Camp Bowie, TX as component of 36<sup>th</sup> Division (formed from MG Coys of 1<sup>st</sup> Infantry, OK NG and 3<sup>rd</sup> and 4<sup>th</sup> Infantry, TX NG). Moved overseas Jul 1918. Returned to the US Jun 1919 and demobilized at Camp Bowie.

**132<sup>nd</sup> Machine Gun Bn**       Organized Oct 1917 at Camp Bowie, TX as component of 36<sup>th</sup> Division (71<sup>st</sup> Infantry Brigade) (formed from MG Coy, 1<sup>st</sup> Infantry, TX NG). Moved overseas Jul 1918. Returned to the US Jun 1919 and demobilized at Camp Bowie.

**133<sup>rd</sup> Machine Gun Bn**       Organized Oct 1917 at Camp Bowie, TX as component of 36<sup>th</sup> Division (72<sup>nd</sup> Infantry Brigade) (formed from MG Trp, 1<sup>st</sup> Cavalry, TX NG and one company each 3<sup>rd</sup> and 6<sup>th</sup> Infantry, TX NG). Moved overseas Jul 1918. Returned to the US Jun 1919 and demobilized at Camp Bowie.

**134<sup>th</sup> Machine Gun Bn**       Organized Sep 1917 at Camp Sheridan, AL as component of 37<sup>th</sup> Division (formed from six companies, 10<sup>th</sup> Infantry, OH NG). Moved overseas Jun 1918. Returned to the US Mar 1919. Demobilized Apr 1919 at Camp Sherman, OH.

**135<sup>th</sup> Machine Gun Bn**       Organized Sep 1917 at Camp Sheridan, AL as component of 37<sup>th</sup> Division (73<sup>rd</sup> Infantry Brigade) (formed from MG Coy, 6<sup>th</sup> Infantry and two companies, 10<sup>th</sup> Infantry, OH NG). Moved overseas Jun 1918. Returned to the US Mar 1919. Demobilized Apr 1919 at Camp Sherman, OH.

**136th Machine Gun Bn**        Organized Sep 1917 at Camp Sheridan, AL as component of 37th Division (74th Infantry Brigade) (formed from four companies, 10th Infantry and some personnel from 1st Infantry, OH NG). Moved overseas Jun 1918. Returned to the US Mar 1919. Demobilized Apr 1919 at Camp Sherman, OH.

**137th Machine Gun Bn**        Organized Oct 1917 at Camp Shelby, MS as component of 38th Division (formed from 1st Bn and MG Coy, 1st Infantry, WV NG). Moved overseas Oct 1918. Skeletonized Nov 1918. Returned to the US Dec 1918. Demobilized Jan 1919 at Camp Zachary Taylor, KY.

**138th Machine Gun Bn**        Organized Oct 1917 at Camp Shelby, MS as component of 38th Division (75th Infantry Brigade) (formed from MG Coy, 1st Infantry and three companies, 3rd Infantry, KS NG). Moved overseas Oct 1918. Skeletonized Nov 1918. Returned to the US Dec 1918. Demobilized Jan 1919 at Camp Zachary Taylor, KY.

**139th Machine Gun Bn**        Organized Oct 1917 at Camp Shelby, MS as component of 38th Division (76th Infantry Brigade) (formed from MG Coys from 3rd and 4th Infantry, IN NG). Moved overseas Oct 1918. Skeletonized Nov 1918. Returned to the US Dec 1918. Demobilized Jan 1919 at Camp Zachary Taylor, KY.

**140th Machine Gun Bn**        Organized Nov 1917 at Camp Beauregard, LA as component of 39th Division (formed from 3rd Bn and two companies, 2nd Infantry, MS NG and MG Trp, 1st Separate Sqn Cavalry, MS NG). Moved overseas Aug 1918. Skeletonized Nov 1918. Returned to the US Jan 1919 and demobilized at Camp Beauregard.

**141st Machine Gun Bn**        Organized Oct 1917 at Camp Beauregard, LA as component of 39th Division (77th Infantry Brigade) (formed from 3rd Bn, 3rd Infantry and MG Coy, 2nd Infantry, AR NG). Moved overseas Aug 1918. Detached for training in AA MG role. Returned to the US Jan 1919 and demobilized at Camp Beauregard.

**142nd Machine Gun Bn**        Organized Oct 1917 at Camp Beauregard, LA as component of 39th Division (78th Infantry Brigade) (formed from two companies, 1st Infantry, LA NG). Moved overseas Aug 1918. Skeletonized Nov 1918. Returned to the US Jan 1919 and demobilized at Camp Beauregard.

**143rd Machine Gun Bn** Organized Oct 1917 at Camp Kearny, CA as component of 40th Division (formed from 1st and 2nd Bns, 1st Infantry, NM NG). Moved overseas Aug 1918. Returned to the US Apr 1919 and demobilized at Camp Grant, IL.

**144th Machine Gun Bn**        Organized Oct 1917 at Camp Kearny, CA as component of 40th Division (79th Infantry Brigade) (formed from 3rd Bn and MG Coy, 1st Infantry, NM NG). Moved overseas Aug 1918. Returned to the US Apr 1919 and demobilized at Camp Grant, IL.

**145th Machine Gun Bn**        Organized Oct 1917 at Camp Kearny, CA as component of 40th Division (80th Infantry Brigade) (formed from 1st Separate Sqn, Cavalry (-) and MG Trp, Cavalry, CO NG).  Moved overseas Aug 1918. R eturned to the US May 1919 and demobilized at the Presidio of San Francisco, CA.

**146th Machine Gun Bn**        Organized Sep 1917 at Camp Greene, NC as component of 41st Division (formed from 3rd Bn, 2nd Infantry, ND NG, MG Coy, 4th Infantry, SD NG, and MG Coy, 3rd Infantry, WY NG).  Moved overseas Jan 1918.  Returned to the US Feb 1919.  Demobilized Apr 1919 at Camp Funston, KS.

**147th Machine Gun Bn**        Organized Oct 1917 at Camp Greene, NC as component of 41st Division (81st Infantry Brigade) (formed from MG Coy, 3rd Infantry, DC NG, MG Coy, 2nd Infantry, ID NG, company, 2nd Infantry, ND NG, and MG Trp, Cavalry, WA NG).  Moved overseas Jan 1918.  Returned to the US Feb 1919. Demobilized Mar 1919 at Camp Upton, NY.

**148th Machine Gun Bn**        Organized Oct 1917 at Camp Greene, NC as component of 41st Division (82nd Infantry Brigade) (formed from three companies, 4th Infantry, SD NG).  Moved overseas Jan 1918.  Returned to the US Feb 1919.  Demobilized Mar 1919 at Camp Dodge, IA.

**149th Machine Gun Bn**        Organized Aug 1917 at Lancaster, PA as component of 42nd Division (formed from 3rd Bn, 4th Infantry, PA NG).  Moved overseas Nov 1917.  Returned to the US Apr 1919.  Demobilized May 1919 at Camp Dix, NJ.

**150th Machine Gun Bn**        Organized Aug 1917 at Camp Douglas, WI as component of 42nd Division (83rd Infantry Brigade) (formed from three companies, 2nd Infantry, WI NG).  Moved overseas Oct 1917.  Returned to the US Apr 1919.  Demobilized May 1919 at Camp Grant, IL.

**151st Machine Gun Bn**        Organized Aug 1917 at Camp Harris, GA as component of 42nd Division (84th Infantry Brigade) (formed from three companies, 2nd Infantry, GA NG).  Moved overseas Oct 1917.  Returned to the US Apr 1919.  Demobilized May 1919 at Camp Gordon, GA.

*National Army Machine Gun Battalions*

**301st Machine Gun Bn**        Organized Aug 1917 at Camp Devens, MA as component of 76th Division.  Moved overseas Jul 1918.  Skeletonized Nov 1918.  Returned to the US Jan 1919 and demobilized at Camp Devens.

**302ⁿᵈ Machine Gun Bn**   Organized Aug 1917 at Camp Devens, MA as component of 76th Division (151st Infantry Brigade). Moved overseas Jul 1918. Skeletonized Nov 1918. Returned to the US Jan 1919. Demobilized Feb 1919 at Camp Devens.

**303ʳᵈ Machine Gun Bn**   Organized Aug 1917 at Camp Devens, MA as component of 76th Division (152nd Infantry Brigade). Moved overseas Jul 1918. Skeletonized Nov 1918. Returned to the US Jan 1919. Demobilized Feb 1919 at Camp Devens.

**304ᵗʰ Machine Gun Bn**   Organized Sep 1917 at Camp Upton, NY as component of 77th Division. Moved overseas Apr 1918. Returned to the US May 1919 and demobilized at Camp Upton.

**305ᵗʰ Machine Gun Bn**   Organized Sep 1917 at Camp Upton, NY as component of 77th Division (153rd Infantry Brigade). Moved overseas Mar 1918. Returned to the US Apr 1919. Demobilized May 1919 at Camp Upton.

**306ᵗʰ Machine Gun Bn**   Organized Sep 1917 at Camp Upton, NY as component of 77th Division (154th Infantry Brigade). Moved overseas Apr 1918. Returned to the US Apr 1919. Demobilized May 1919 at Camp Upton.

**307ᵗʰ Machine Gun Bn**   Organized Sep 1917 at Camp Dix, NJ as component of 78th Division. Moved overseas May 1918. Returned to the US May 1919 and demobilized at Camp Dix.

**308ᵗʰ Machine Gun Bn**   Organized Sep 1917 at Camp Dix, NJ as component of 78th Division (155th Infantry Brigade). Moved overseas May 1918. Returned to the US May 1919 and demobilized at Camp Dix.

**309ᵗʰ Machine Gun Bn**   Organized Sep 1917 at Camp Dix, NJ as component of 78th Division (156th Infantry Brigade). Moved overseas May 1918. Returned to the US May 1919 and demobilized at Camp Dix.

**310ᵗʰ Machine Gun Bn**   Organized Sep 1917 at Camp Meade, MD as component of 79th Division. Moved overseas Jul 1918. Returned to the US May 1919 and demobilized at Camp Dix, NJ.

**311ᵗʰ Machine Gun Bn**   Organized Sep 1917 at Camp Meade, MD as component of 79th Division (157th Infantry Brigade). Moved overseas Jul 1918. Returned to the US May 1919 and demobilized at Camp Dix, NJ.

**312ᵗʰ Machine Gun Bn**   Organized Sep 1917 at Camp Meade, MD as component of 79th Division (158th Infantry Brigade). Moved overseas Jul 1918. Returned to the US May 1919. Demobilized Jun 1919 at Camp Dix, NJ.

**313th Machine Gun Bn**        Organized Sep 1917 at Camp Lee, VA as component of 80th Division. Moved overseas May 1918. Returned to the US Jun 1919 and demobilized at Camp Dix, NJ.

**314th Machine Gun Bn**        Organized Sep 1917 at Camp Lee, VA as component of 80th Division (159th Infantry Brigade). Moved overseas May 1918. Returned to the US Jun 1919 and demobilized at Camp Dix, NJ.

**315th Machine Gun Bn**        Organized Sep 1917 at Camp Lee, VA as component of 80th Division (160th Infantry Brigade). Moved overseas May 1918. Returned to the US May 1919. Demobilized Jun 1919 at Camp Dix, NJ.

**316th Machine Gun Bn**        Organized Sep 1917 at Camp Jackson, SC as component of 81st Division. Moved overseas Jul 1918. Returned to the US Jun 1919 and demobilized at Camp Upton, NY.

**317th Machine Gun Bn**        Organized Sep 1917 at Camp Jackson, SC as component of 81st Division (161st Infantry Brigade). Moved overseas Jul 1918. Returned to the US Jun 1919 and demobilized at Camp Upton, NY.

**318th Machine Gun Bn**        Organized Sep 1917 at Camp Jackson, SC as component of 81st Division (162nd Infantry Brigade). Moved overseas Jul 1918. Returned to the US Jun 1919 and demobilized at Camp Upton, NY.

**319th Machine Gun Bn**        Organized Sep 1917 at Camp Gordon, GA as component of 82nd Division. Moved overseas May 1918. Returned to the US May 1919 and demobilized at Camp Dix, NJ.

**320th Machine Gun Bn**        Organized Sep 1917 at Camp Gordon, GA as component of 82nd Division (163rd Infantry Brigade). Moved overseas Apr 1918. Returned to the US May 1919 and demobilized at Camp Dix, NJ.

**321st Machine Gun Bn**        Organized Sep 1917 at Camp Gordon, GA as component of 82nd Division (164th Infantry Brigade). Moved overseas May 1918. Returned to the US May 1919 and demobilized at Camp Dix, NJ.

**322nd Machine Gun Bn**        Organized Sep 1917 at Camp Sherman, OH as component of 83rd Division. Moved overseas Jun 1918. Returned to the US Jan 1919. Demobilized Feb 1919 at Camp Sherman.

**323rd Machine Gun Bn**        Organized Sep 1917 at Camp Sherman, OH as component of 83rd Division (165th Infantry Brigade). Moved overseas Jun 1918. Returned to the US Jan 1919. Demobilized Mar 1919 at Camp Sherman.

**324<sup>th</sup> Machine Gun Bn**      Organized Sep 1917 at Camp Sherman, OH as component of 83<sup>rd</sup> Division (166<sup>th</sup> Infantry Brigade). Moved overseas Jun 1918. Returned to the US Feb 1919. Demobilized Mar 1919 at Camp Sherman.

**325<sup>th</sup> Machine Gun Bn**      Organized Aug 1917 at Camp Zachary Taylor, KY as component of 84<sup>th</sup> Division. Moved overseas Sep 1918. Skeletonized Nov 1918. Returned to the US Jan 1919. Demobilized Feb 1919 at Camp Zachary Taylor.

**326<sup>th</sup> Machine Gun Bn**      Organized Sep 1917 at Camp Zachary Taylor, KY as component of 84<sup>th</sup> Division (167<sup>th</sup> Infantry Brigade). Moved overseas Sep 1918. Skeletonized Nov 1918. Returned to the US Jan 1919. Demobilized Feb 1919 at Camp Zachary Taylor.

**327<sup>th</sup> Machine Gun Bn**      Organized Sep 1917 at Camp Zachary Taylor, KY as component of 84<sup>th</sup> Division (168<sup>th</sup> Infantry Brigade). Moved overseas Sep 1918. Skeletonized Nov 1918. Returned to the US Jan 1919. Demobilized Feb 1919 at Camp Zachary Taylor.

**328<sup>th</sup> Machine Gun Bn**      Organized Sep 1917 at Camp Custer, MI as component of 85<sup>th</sup> Division. Moved overseas Jul 1918. Returned to the US Apr 1919 and demobilized at Camp Custer.

**329<sup>th</sup> Machine Gun Bn**      Organized Sep 1917 at Camp Custer, MI as component of 85<sup>th</sup> Division (169<sup>th</sup> Infantry Brigade). Moved overseas Jul 1918. Returned to the US Apr 1919 and demobilized at Camp Custer.

**330<sup>th</sup> Machine Gun Bn**      Organized Sep 1917 at Camp Custer, MI as component of 85<sup>th</sup> Division (170<sup>th</sup> Infantry Brigade). Moved overseas Jul 1918. Returned to the US Apr 1919 and demobilized at Camp Custer.

**331<sup>st</sup> Machine Gun Bn**      Organized Sep 1917 at Camp Grant, IL as component of 86<sup>th</sup> Division. Moved overseas Sep 1918. Skeletonized Nov 1918. Returned to the US Jan 1919 and demobilized at Camp Grant.

**332<sup>nd</sup> Machine Gun Bn**      Organized Sep 1917 at Camp Grant, IL as component of 86<sup>h</sup> Division (171<sup>st</sup> Infantry Brigade). Moved overseas Sep 1918. Skeletonized Nov 1918. Returned to the US Jan 1919 and demobilized at Camp Grant.

**333<sup>rd</sup> Machine Gun Bn**      Organized Sep 1917 at Camp Grant, IL as component of 86<sup>th</sup> Division (172<sup>nd</sup> Infantry Brigade). Moved overseas Sep 1918. Skeletonized Nov 1918. Returned to the US Jan 1919 and demobilized at Camp Grant.

**334<sup>th</sup> Machine Gun Bn**      Organized Sep 1917 at Camp Pike, AR as component of 87<sup>th</sup> Division. Moved overseas Aug 1918. Returned to the US Mar 1919 and demobilized at Camp Dix, NJ.

**335th Machine Gun Bn**      Organized Sep 1917 at Camp Pike, AR as component of 87h Division (173rd Infantry Brigade). Moved overseas Aug 1918. Returned to the US Mar 1919 and demobilized at Camp Dix, NJ.

**336th Machine Gun Bn**      Organized Sep 1917 at Camp Pike, AR as component of 87th Division (174th Infantry Brigade). Moved overseas Aug 1918. Returned to the US Mar 1919 and demobilized at Camp Dix, NJ.

**337th Machine Gun Bn**      Organized Sep 1917 at Camp Dodge, IA as component of 88th Division. Moved overseas Aug 1918. Returned to the US May 1919. Demobilized Jun 1919 at Camp Dodge.

**338th Machine Gun Bn**      Organized Sep 1917 at Camp Dodge, IA as component of 88th Division (175th Infantry Brigade). Moved overseas Aug 1918. Returned to the US Jun 1919 and demobilized at Camp Dodge.

**339th Machine Gun Bn**      Organized Sep 1917 at Camp Dodge, IA as component of 88th Division (176th Infantry Brigade). Moved overseas Aug 1918. Returned to the US May 1919. Demobilized Jun 1919 at Camp Dodge.

**340th Machine Gun Bn**      Organized Sep 1917 at Camp Funston, KS as component of 89th Division. Moved overseas Jun 1918. Returned to the US May 1919. Demobilized Jun 1919 at Camp Funston.

**341st Machine Gun Bn**      Organized Sep 1917 at Camp Funston, KS as component of 89h Division (177th Infantry Brigade). Moved overseas Jun 1918. Returned to the US May 1919. Demobilized Jun 1919 at Camp Funston.

**342nd Machine Gun Bn**      Organized Sep 1917 at Camp Funston, KS as component of 89th Division (178th Infantry Brigade). Moved overseas Jun 1918. Returned to the US May 1919. Demobilized Jun 1919 at Camp Funston.

**343rd Machine Gun Bn**      Organized Sep 1917 at Camp Travis, TX as component of 90th Division. Moved overseas Jun 1918. Returned to the US Jun 1919 and demobilized at Camp Bowie, TX.

**344th Machine Gun Bn**      Organized Sep 1917 at Camp Travis, TX as component of 90h Division (179th Infantry Brigade). Moved overseas Jun 1918. Returned to the US Jun 1919 and demobilized at Camp Bowie, TX.

**345th Machine Gun Bn**      Organized Sep 1917 at Camp Travis, TX as component of 90th Division (180th Infantry Brigade). Moved overseas Jun 1918. Returned to the US Jun 1919 and demobilized at Camp Bowie, TX.

**346<sup>th</sup> Machine Gun Bn** Organized Sep 1917 at Camp Lewis, WA as component of 91<sup>st</sup> Division. Moved overseas Jul 1918. Returned to the US Apr 1919 and demobilized at Ft. D. A. Russell, WY.

**347<sup>th</sup> Machine Gun Bn** Organized Sep 1917 at Camp Lewis, WA as component of 91<sup>st</sup> Division (181<sup>st</sup> Infantry Brigade). Moved overseas Jul 1918. Returned to the US Apr 1919. Demobilized May 1919 at Camp Lewis, WA.

**348<sup>th</sup> Machine Gun Bn** Organized Sep 1917 at Camp Lewis, WA as component of 91<sup>st</sup> Division (182<sup>nd</sup> Infantry Brigade). Moved overseas Jul 1918. Returned to the US Apr 1919. Demobilized May 1919 at the Presidio of San Francisco, CA.

**349<sup>th</sup> Machine Gun Bn** Organized Dec 1917at Camp Funston, KS [with black enlisted personnel] as component of 92<sup>nd</sup> Division. Moved overseas Jun 1918. Returned to the US Mar 1919. Demobilized Apr 1919 at Camp Zachary Taylor, KY.

**350<sup>th</sup> Machine Gun Bn** Organized Nov 1917 at Camp Grant, IL [with black enlisted personnel] as component of 92<sup>nd</sup> Division (183<sup>rd</sup> Infantry Brigade). Moved overseas Jun 1918. Returned to the US Mar 1919 and demobilized at Camp Upton, NY.

**351<sup>st</sup> Machine Gun Bn** Organized Nov 1917 at Camp Upton, NY [with black enlisted personnel] as component of 92<sup>nd</sup> Division (184<sup>th</sup> Infantry Brigade). Moved overseas Jun 1918. Returned to the US Mar 1919 and demobilized at Camp Meade, MD

[352<sup>nd</sup> to 354<sup>th</sup> Machine Gun Bns would have gone to 93<sup>rd</sup> Division if it had been fully organized]

[355<sup>th</sup> to 357<sup>th</sup> Machine Gun Bns would have gone to 94<sup>th</sup> Division if it had been organized]

**358<sup>th</sup> Machine Gun Bn** Organized Oct 1918 at Camp Sherman, OH as component of 95<sup>th</sup> Division. Demobilized Dec 1918 at Camp Sherman.

**359<sup>th</sup> Machine Gun Bn** Organized Nov 1918 at Camp Sherman, OH as component of 95<sup>th</sup> Division (189<sup>th</sup> Infantry Brigade). Demobilized Dec 1918 at Camp Sherman.

**360<sup>th</sup> Machine Gun Bn** Organized Oct 1918 at Camp Sherman, OH as component of 95<sup>th</sup> Division. (190<sup>th</sup> Infantry Brigade) Demobilized Dec 1918 at Camp Sherman.

[361<sup>st</sup> and 362<sup>nd</sup> Machine Gun Bns constituted as components of 96<sup>th</sup> Division but never organized]

**363<sup>rd</sup> Machine Gun Bn** Organized Nov 1918 at Camp Wadsworth, SC as component of 96<sup>th</sup> Division (192<sup>nd</sup> Infantry Brigade). Demobilized Jan 1919 at Camp Wadsworth.

[364<sup>th</sup> and 365<sup>th</sup> Machine Gun Bns constituted as components of 97<sup>th</sup> Division but never organized]

**366<sup>th</sup> Machine Gun Bn** — Organized Oct 1918 at Camp Cody, NM as component of 97<sup>th</sup> Division (194<sup>th</sup> Infantry Brigade). Demobilized Dec 1918 at Camp Cody.

[367<sup>th</sup> to 381<sup>st</sup> Machine Gun Bns constituted as elements of 98<sup>th</sup> to 102<sup>nd</sup> Divisions but never organized]

*Anti-Aircraft Machine Gun Battalions*

**1<sup>st</sup> AA Machine Gun Bn** — Organized Jan 1918 at Camp Wadsworth, SC [Corps troops]. Moved overseas May 1918. Served with I Army Corps Aug 1918, First Army Sep-Nov 1918 and also with Second Army Nov 1918. Returned to the US May 1919 and demobilized at Camp Sherman, OH.

**2<sup>nd</sup> AA Machine Gun Bn** — Organized Jan 1918 at Camp Wadsworth, SC [Corps troops]. Moved overseas Jun 1918. Returned to the US Feb 1919 and demobilized at Camp Dix, NJ.

**3<sup>rd</sup> AA Machine Gun Bn** — Organized Jan 1918 at Camp Wadsworth, SC [Corps troops]. Moved overseas Aug 1918. Returned to the US May 1919 and demobilized at Camp Upton, NY.

**4<sup>th</sup> AA Machine Gun Bn** — Organized Jul 1918 at Camp Wadsworth, SC [Corps troops]. Moved overseas Sep 1918. Returned to the US Jan 1919 and demobilized at Camp Dodge, IA.

**5<sup>th</sup> AA Machine Gun Bn** — Organized Jul 1918 at Camp Wadsworth, SC [Corps troops]. Moved overseas Oct 1918. Returned to the US Jan 1919. Demobilized Feb 1919 at Camp Wadsworth.

**6<sup>th</sup> AA Machine Gun Bn** — Organized Oct 1918 at Camp Wadsworth, SC [Corps troops] and demobilized there Jan 1919.

# Field Artillery

*Field Artillery Brigades*[67]

**1st Field Artillery Brigade**   Organized Aug 1917 in the AEF as component of 1st Division. [5th, 6th and 7th FA and 1st TM Bty] Absent Aug to Oct 1917 for training.  Detached 24 Jul, 24-28 Aug, 13-31 Oct and 1-4 Nov 1918.  Returned to the US Sep 1919 and moved to Camp Zachary Taylor, KY.

**2nd Field Artillery Brigade**   Organized Jan 1918 in the AEF as component of 2nd Division. [12th, 15th and 17th FA and 2nd TM Bty]  Absent to Mar 1918 for training.  Detached 20-26 Jul, 19-22 Aug, 16-18 Sep, and 20-28 Oct 1918.  Returned to the US Aug 1919 and moved to Camp Travis, TX.

**3rd Field Artillery Brigade**   Organized Nov 1917 at Camp Stanley, TX as component of 3rd Division. [10th, 18th and 76th FA and 3rd TM Bty] Moved overseas Apr 1918.  Absent Apr to Jun 1918 for training. Detached 30 Jul to 2 Aug 1918.  Returned to the US Aug 1919 and moved to Camp Pike, AR.

**4th Field Artillery Brigade**   Organized Jan 1918 at Camp Greene, NC as component of 4th Division. [13th, 16th and 77th FA and 4th TM Bty] Moved overseas May 1918. A bsent May to Jul 1918 for training. Detached 3-17 Aug and 3-14 Sep 1918. Returned to the US Jul 1919 and moved to Camp Dodge, IA.

**5th Field Artillery Brigade**   Organized Dec 1917 at Camp Stanley, TX as component of 5th Division. [19th, 20th and 21st FA and 5th TM Bty] Moved overseas May 1918.  Absent Jun-Jul 1918 for training. Detached 17 Sep to 1 Dec 1918.  Returned to the US Jul 1919 and moved to Camp Bragg, NC.

---

[67] As with infantry, a field artillery brigade technically consists of the brigade headquarters. Assigned units have been shown. All of the brigades were detached on arrival in France and sent to camps for additional training. In part, this training was required by the decision to replace the US 3" guns with French 75mm guns; this eliminated the need to ship the US weapons to Europe. Many brigades never returned to. their parent division, and others were detached for extended periods of time.  These could serve as corps artillery, or in support of other divisions in place of that division's missing brigade.  In some cases, the trench mortar battery was detached from the brigade, especially when the latter served as corps troops.  Periods away from the parent division are shown, but no effort has been made here to indicate assignments in support of particular other divisions.

**6$^{th}$ Field Artillery Brigade**     Organized Apr 1918 at Ft. Sam Houston, TX as component of 6$^{th}$ Division. [3$^{rd}$, 11$^{th}$ and 78$^{th}$ FA and 6$^{th}$ TM Bty] Moved overseas Jul 1918.  Absent Jul to early Dec 1918.  Returned to the US Jun 1919 and moved to Camp Grant, IL.

**7$^{th}$ Field Artillery Brigade**     Organized Jan 1918 at Camp Wheeler, GA as component of 7$^{th}$ Division. [8$^{th}$, 79$^{th}$ and 80$^{th}$ FA and 7$^{th}$ TM Bty] Moved overseas Aug 1918.  Detached for training Sep 1918 to Feb 1919.  Returned to the US Jun 1919 and moved to Camp Funston, KS.

**8$^{th}$ Field Artillery Brigade**     Organized Feb 1918 at Camp Fremont, CA as component of 8$^{th}$ Division. [2$^{nd}$, 81$^{st}$ and 83$^{rd}$ FA and 8$^{th}$ TM Bty] Moved overseas Oct 1918.  Returned to the US Jan 1919 and moved to Camp Knox, KY.

**9$^{th}$ Field Artillery Brigade**     Organized Aug 1918 at Camp McClellan, AL as component of 9$^{th}$ Division and demobilized there Feb 1919. [25$^{th}$, 26$^{th}$ and 27$^{th}$ FA and 9$^{th}$ TM Bty]

**10$^{th}$ Field Artillery Brigade**     Organized Aug 1918 at Camp Funston, KS as component of 10$^{th}$ Division and demobilized there Feb 1919. [28$^{th}$, 29$^{th}$ and 30$^{th}$ FA and 10$^{th}$ TM Bty]

**11$^{th}$ Field Artillery Brigade**     Organized Aug 1918 at Camp Meade, MD as component of 11$^{th}$ Division.  Relieved Sep 1918 as corps artillery. [31$^{st}$, 32$^{nd}$ and 33$^{rd}$ FA and 11$^{th}$ TM Bty] Demobilized Dec 1918 at Camp Meade.

**12$^{th}$ Field Artillery Brigade**     Organized Aug 1918 at Camp McClellan, AL as component of 12$^{th}$ Division and demobilized there Feb 1919. [34$^{th}$, 35$^{th}$ and 36$^{th}$ FA and 12$^{th}$ TM Bty]

**13$^{th}$ Field Artillery Brigade**     Organized Aug 1918 at Camp Lewis, WA as component of 13$^{th}$ Division and demobilized there Mar 1919. [37$^{th}$, 38$^{th}$ and 39$^{th}$ FA and 13$^{th}$ TM Bty]

**14$^{th}$ Field Artillery Brigade**     Organized Aug 1918 at Camp Custer, MI as component of 14$^{th}$ Division and demobilized there Feb 1919. [40$^{th}$, 41$^{st}$ and 42$^{nd}$ FA and 14$^{th}$ TM Bty]

**15$^{th}$ Field Artillery Brigade**     Organized Sep 1918 at Camp Stanley, TX as component of 15$^{th}$ Division and demobilized there Feb 1919. [43$^{rd}$, 44$^{th}$ and 45$^{th}$ FA and 15$^{th}$ TM Bty]

**16$^{th}$ Field Artillery Brigade**     Organized Sep 1918 at Camp Kearney, CA as component of 16$^{th}$ Division and demobilized there Feb 1919. [46$^{th}$, 47$^{th}$ and 48$^{th}$ FA and 16$^{th}$ TM Bty]

**17$^{th}$ Field Artillery Brigade**     Organized Aug 1918 at Camp Bowie, TX as component of 17$^{th}$ Division and demobilized there Feb 1919. [49$^{th}$, 50$^{th}$ and 51$^{st}$ FA and 17$^{th}$ TM Bty]

**18$^{th}$ Field Artillery Brigade**     Organized Aug 1918 at Camp Travis, TX as component of 18$^{th}$ Division and demobilized there Feb 1919. [52$^{nd}$, 53$^{rd}$ and 54$^{th}$ FA and 18$^{th}$ TM Bty]

**19th Field Artillery Brigade**     Organized Aug 1918 at Camp Travis, TX as component of 19th Division and demobilized there Feb 1919. [55th, 56th and 57th FA and 19th TM Bty]

**20th Field Artillery Brigade**     Organized Nov 1918 at Camp Jackson, SC as component of 20th Division and demobilized there Feb 1919. [58th, 59th and 60th FA and 20th TM Bty]

**21st Field Artillery Brigade**     Organized Oct 1918 at Camp Sheridan, AL and demobilized there Dec 1918. [84th FA only component formed]

**22nd Field Artillery Brigade**     Organized Sep 1918 at Camp Meade, MD and demobilized there Dec 1918. [73rd FA only component formed]

**23rd Field Artillery Brigade**     Organized Oct 1918 at Camp Sheridan, AL and demobilized there Dec 1918. [74th FA only component formed] Intended as corps artillery.

**24th Field Artillery Brigade**     Organized Sep 1918 at Camp Knox, KY as component of 11th Division. [70th, 71st and 72nd FA and 24th TM Bty] Demobilized Feb 1919 at Camp Knox.

**51st Field Artillery Brigade**     Organized Aug 1917 at Boxford, MA as component of 26th Division. [101st, 102nd and 103rd FA and 101st TM Bty] Moved overseas Sep 1917.  Absent Sep 1917-Jan 1918 for training.  Detached 25 Jul-5 Aug, 8-11 Oct, and 17 Nov-20 Dec 1918. Returned to the US Apr 1919 and demobilized at Camp Devens, MA.

**52nd Field Artillery Brigade**     Organized Oct 1917 at Camp Wadsworth, SC as component of 27th Division (redesignated from Hq, 1st Field Artillery Brigade, NY NG). [104th, 105th and 106th FA and 102nd TM Bty] Moved overseas Jun 1918.  Absent for training Jul-Aug 1918. Detached 10 Sep-12 Dec 1918. Returned to the US Mar 1919 and demobilized Apr 1919 at Camp Upton, NY.

**53rd Field Artillery Brigade**     Organized Aug 1917 at Camp Hancock, GA as component of 28th Division (redesignated from Hq, Artillery Brigade, PA NG). [107th, 108th and 109th FA and 103rd TM Bty] Moved overseas May 1918.  Absent for training Jun 1918.  Detached 9-10 Oct, 30 Oct-4 Nov 1918, 10 Nov 1918-19 Mar 1919.  Returned to the US May 1919 and demobilized at Camp Dix, NJ.

**54th Field Artillery Brigade**     Organized Sep 1917 at Camp McClellan, AL as component of 29th Division. [110th, 111th and 112th FA and 104th TM Bty] Moved overseas Jun 1918.  Absent Jul-Dec 1918 for training. Returned to the US May 1919 and demobilized at Camp Lee, VA.

**55th Field Artillery Brigade**     Organized Sep 1917 at Camp Sevier, SC as component of 30th Division. [113th, 114th and 115th FA and 105th TM Bty] Moved overseas May 1918.  Absent Jun-Aug 1918 for training.  Detached 26 Aug-15 Sep, 23 Sep-8 Oct 1918, 11 Oct 1918-8 Jan 1919.  Returned to the US Mar 1919 and demobilized Apr 1919 at Ft. Oglethorpe, GA.

**56th Field Artillery Brigade**     Organized Sep 1917 at Camp Wheeler, GA as component of 31st Division. [116th, 117th and 118th FA and 106th TM Bty] Moved overseas Oct 1918.  Absent in training camp during time in Europe.  Returned to the US Dec 1918 and demobilized Jan 1919 at Camp Gordon, GA.

**57th Field Artillery Brigade**     Organized Sep 1917 at Camp MacArthur, TX as component of 32nd Division. [119th, 120th and 121st FA and 107th TM Bty] Moved overseas Feb 1918.  Absent Feb-early Jun 1918 for training.  Detached 7-24 Aug, 2-6 Sep, 22 Sep –6 Oct 1918, 20 Oct 1918-14 Jan 1919 (served with First Army, III Army Corps).  Returned to the US May 1919 and demobilized at Camp Devens, MA.

**58th Field Artillery Brigade**     Organized Sep 1917 at Camp Logan, TX as component of 33rd Division. [122nd, 123rd and 124th FA and 108th TM Bty] Moved overseas May 1918.  Absent Jun-Aug 1918 for training.  Detached 26 Aug-15 Sep, 26 Sep-11 Oct, 24 Oct-11 Nov 1918, 24 Nov 1918-18 Apr 1919 (served with First Army),.  Returned to the US May 1919 and demobilized Jun 1919 at Camp Grant, IL.

**59th Field Artillery Brigade**     Organized Oct 1917 at Camp Cody, NM as component of 34th Division. [125th, 126th and 127th FA and 109th TM Bty] Moved overseas Sep 1918.  Absent in training camp during time in Europe.  Returned to the US Jan 1919 and demobilized at Camp Dodge, IA.

**60th Field Artillery Brigade**     Organized Sep 1917 at Camp Doniphan, OK as component of 35th Division. [128th, 129th and 130th FA and 110th TM Bty] Moved overseas May 1918.  Absent Jun-Aug 1918 for training.  Detached 102 oct, 7 Nov-18 Dec 1918.  Returned to the US Apr 1919 and demobilized at Camp Pike, AR.

**61st Field Artillery Brigade**     Organized Oct 1917 at Camp Bowie, TX as component of 36th Division. [131st, 132nd and 133rd FA and 111th TM Bty] Moved overseas Jul 1918.  Absent in training camp during time in Europe.  Returned to the US Mar 1919 and demobilized at Camp Bowie.

**62nd Field Artillery Brigade**     Organized Sep 1917 at Camp Sheridan, AL as component of 37th Division. [134th, 135th and 136th FA and 112th TM Bty] Moved overseas Jun 1918.  Absent Jul-Sep 1918 for training.  Detached 26 Sep 1918-27 Jan 1919. Returned to the US Mar 1919 and demobilized Apr 1919 at Camp Sherman, OH.

**63rd Field Artillery Brigade**    Organized Oct 1917 at Camp Shelby, MS as component of 38th Division. [137th, 138th and 139th FA and 113th TM Bty]  Moved overseas Oct 1918.  Absent in training camp during time in Europe.  Returned to the US Dec 1918 and demobilized Jan 1919 at Ft. Benjamin Harrison, IN.

**64th Field Artillery Brigade**    Organized Dec 1917 at Camp Beauregard, AL as component of 39th Division. [140th, 141st and 142nd FA and 114th TM Bty]  Moved overseas Aug 1918. Detached when 39th Division became 5th Depot Division. Returned to the US Apr 1919 and demobilized May 1919 at Camp Shelby, MS.

**65th Field Artillery Brigade**    Organized Oct 1917 at Camp Kearny, CA as component of 40th Division. 143rd, 144th and 145th FA and 115th TM Bty]  Moved overseas Aug 1918.  Detached when 40th Division became 6th Depot Division.  Returned to the US Dec 1918 and demobilized Jan 1919 at Presidio of San Francisco, CA.

**66th Field Artillery Brigade**    Organized Oct 1917 at Camp Greene, NC as component of 41st Division. [146th, 147th and 148th FA and 116th TM Bty]  Moved overseas Aug 1918. Detached when 41st Division became 1st Depot Division.  Served as corps artillery from 8 Jul to 24 May 1919 (with First Army, I Army Corps, III Army Corps, V Army Corps, with Third Army (III Army Corps) on occupation of Germany).  Returned to the US Jun 1919 and demobilized at Camp Lewis, WA.

**67th Field Artillery Brigade**    Organized Sep 1917 at Camp Mills, NY as component of 42nd Division. [140th, 150th and 151st FA and 117th TM Bty]  Moved overseas Oct 1917.  Absent Nov 1917-Feb 1918 in camp. Detached 3-11 Aug, 7-12 Oct, 1-2 Nov 1918 (served with IV Army Corps).  Returned to the US Apr 1919 and demobilized May 1919 at Camp Grant, IL.

**151st Field Artillery Brigade**    Organized Aug 1917 at Camp Devens, MA as component of 76th Division. [301st, 302nd and 303rd FA and 301st TM Bty]  Moved overseas Jul 1918.  Detached when 76th Division became 3rd Depot Division.  In camp Sep-Oct 1918.  Served as corps troops (less 301st FA, which remained in camp) 2 Nov 1918-Mar 1919. Returned to the US Apr 1919 and demobilized May 1919 at Camp Devens.

**152nd Field Artillery Brigade**    Organized Sep 1917 at Camp Upton, NY as component of 77th Division. [304th, 305th and 306th FA and 302nd TM Bty]  Moved overseas Apr 1918.  Absent May-Jun 1918 in camp. Returned to the US Apr 1919 and demobilized May 1919 at Camp Upton.

**153rd Field Artillery Brigade**   Organized Oct 1917 at Camp Dix, NJ as component of 78th Division. [307th, 308th and 309th FA and 303rd TM Bty] Moved overseas May 1918.  Absent Jun-early Aug 1918 in camp. Detached 18 Aug-7 Dec 1918.  Returned to the US May 1919 and demobilized at Camp Dix, NJ.

**154th Field Artillery Brigade**   Organized Sep 1917 at Camp Meade, MD as component of 79th Division. [310th, 311th and 312th FA and 304th TM Bty] Moved overseas Jul 1918.  Returned to the US May 1919 and demobilized at Camp Dix, NJ.

**155th Field Artillery Brigade**   Organized Sep 1917 at Camp Lee, VA as component of 80th Division. [313th, 314th and 315th FA and 305th TM Bty] Moved overseas May 1918.  Returned to the US May 1919 and demobilized Jun 1919 at Camp Stuart, VA.

**156th Field Artillery Brigade**   Organized Sep 1917 at Camp Jackson, SC as component of 81st Division. [316th, 317th and 318th FA and 306th TM Bty] Moved overseas Aug 1918.  Absent in training camp during time in Europe.  Returned to the US Jun 1919 and demobilized at Camp Lee, VA.

**157th Field Artillery Brigade**   Organized Sep 1917 at Camp Gordon, GA as component of 82nd Division. [319th, 320th and 321st FA and 307th TM Bty] Moved overseas May 1918.  Absent Jun-Aug 1918 in camp. Detached 1-6 Nov, 10 Nov-16 Dec 1918.  Returned to the US May 1919 and demobilized at Camp Upton, NY.

**158th Field Artillery Brigade**   Organized Aug 1917 at Camp Sherman, OH as component of 83rd Division. [322nd, 323rd and 324th FA and 308th TM Bty] Moved overseas Jun 1918. Detached when 83rd Division became 2nd Depot Division.  In camp Jun-mid Sep 1918, then with other units 26-30 Sep 1918, 2 Oct 1918-19 Apr 1919.  Returned to the US May 1919 and demobilized at Camp Sherman.

**159th Field Artillery Brigade**   Organized Nov 1917 at Camp Zachary Taylor, KY as component of 84th Division. [325th, 326th and 327th FA and 309th TM Bty] Moved overseas Sep 1918. Absent in training camp during time in Europe.  Returned to the US Jan 1919 and demobilized at Camp Zachary Taylor.

**160th Field Artillery Brigade**   Organized Sep 1917 at Camp Custer, MI as component of 85th Division. [328th, 329th and 330th FA and 310th TM Bty] Moved overseas Jul 1918. Detached when 85th Division became 4th Depot Division.  Absent in training camp during time in Europe; intended as corps troops (some service with VI Army Corps). Returned to the US Apr 1919 and demobilized at Camp Custer.

**161st Field Artillery Brigade**   Organized Sep 1917 at Camp Grant, IL as component of 86th Division. [331st, 332nd and 333rd FA and 311th TM Bty]  Moved overseas Sep 1918.  Absent in training camp during time in Europe.  Returned to the US Jan 1919 and demobilized at Camp Grant.

**162nd Field Artillery Brigade**   Organized Sep 1917 at Camp Pike, AR as component of 87th Division. [334th, 335th and 336th FA and 312th TM Bty]  Moved overseas Aug 1918.  Absent in training camp or under SOS during time in Europe.  Returned to the US Feb 1919 and demobilized Mar 1919 at Camp Dix, NJ.

**163rd Field Artillery Brigade**   Organized Sep 1917 at Camp Dodge, IA as component of 88th Division. [337th, 338th and 339th FA and 313th TM Bty]  Moved overseas Aug 1918.  Absent in training camp during time in Europe.  Returned to the US Jan 1919 and demobilized at Camp Dodge.

**164th Field Artillery Brigade**   Organized Sep 1917 at Camp Funston, KS as component of 89th Division. [340th, 341st and 342nd FA and 314th TM Bty]  Moved overseas Jun 1918.  Absent Jul-mid Sep 1918 in camp. Detached 15-18 Sep, 7 Oct-11 Nov 1918.  Returned to the US May 1919 and demobilized Jun 1919 at Camp Upton, NY.

**165th Field Artillery Brigade**   Organized Aug 1917 at Camp Travis, TX as component of 90th Division. [343rd, 344th and 345th FA and 315th TM Bty]  Moved overseas Jun 1918.  Absent in training camp during time in Europe (but did have some service with IV Army Corps).  Returned to the US Jun 1919 and demobilized at Camp Bowie, TX.

**166th Field Artillery Brigade**   Organized Sep 1917 at Camp Lewis, WA as component of 91st Division. [346th, 347th and 348th FA and 316th TM Bty]  Moved overseas Jul 1918.  Absent Jul-Oct 1918 in camp. Detached 4 Nov 1918 to 10 Feb 1919 as corps troops (served with First Army).  Returned to the US Mar 1919 and demobilized Apr 1919 at Camp Kearny, CA.

**167th Field Artillery Brigade**   Organized Nov 1917 [with black enlisted personnel] at Camp Dix, NJ as component of 92nd Division. [349th, 350th and 351st FA and 3317th TM Bty]  Moved overseas  Jun 1918. Absent in training camp during time in Europe.  Returned to the US Feb 1919 and demobilized at Camp Meade, MD.

[168th and 169th Artillery Brigades would have gone to the 93rd and 94th Divisions had they been formed]

**170th Field Artillery Brigade**   Organized Sep 1918 at Camp Knox, KY as component of 95th Division and demobilized there Dec 1918. [67th, 68th and 69th FA and 23rd TM Bty]

**171st Field Artillery Brigade**  Organized Sep 1918 at Camp Camp Kearny, CA as component of 96th Division and demobilized there Dec 1918. [64th, 65th and 66th FA and 22nd TM Bty]

**172nd Field Artillery Brigade**  Organized Oct 1918 at Camp Jackson, SC as component of 96th Division and demobilized there Jan 1919. [61st, 62nd and 63rd FA and 21st TM Bty]

[173rd to 177th Field Artillery Brigades were constituted for the 98th to 102nd Divisions, but never organized]


*Regular Army Field Artillery Regiments*

**1st Field Artillery**  Apr 1917 station  the Hawaiian Islands.  Moved Dec 1917 to Ft. Sill, OK.

**2nd Field Artillery**  Apr 1917 station Philippine Islands.  Returned to the US Oct 1917 and moved to Camp Fremont, CA.  Assigned to 8th Division (8th FA Brigade) 31 Jan 1918 [155mm howitzer].  Moved overseas Oct 1918.  Returned to the US Jan 1919 and moved to Camp Zachary Taylor, KY.  Relieved from 8th Division 5 Sep 1919.

**3rd Field Artillery**  Apr 1917 station Ft. Sam Houston, TX.  Assigned 20 Mar 1917—1 Jun 1917 to Artillery Brigade, 1st Provisional Infantry Division.  Assigned to 6th Division (6th FA Brigade) 17 Nov 1917 [75mm gun].  Moved overseas Jul 1918.  Returned to the US Jun 1919 and moved to Camp Grant, IL.

**4th Field Artillery**  Apr 1917 station Camp Stewart, TX, but units stationed at various camps in the US and Panama Canal Zone until Jul 1918 when entire regiment assembled at Camp Logan, TX.  Assigned (less 2nd Bn) 20 Mar 1917—1 Jun 1917 to Artillery Brigade, 2nd Provisional Infantry Division.  (Bty D assigned 20 Mar 1917—1 Jun 1917 to Artillery Brigade, 1st Provisional Infantry Division.)  Moved Sep 1918 to Corpus Chrisi, TX and Jan 1919 to Camp Stanley, TX.

**5th Field Artillery**  Apr 1917 station Ft. Bliss, TX.  Assigned (less Btys D and F) 20 Mar 1917—1 Jun 1917 to Artillery Brigade, 2nd Provisional Infantry Division.  Assigned 8 Jun 1917 to 1st Expeditionary Division [later 1st Division] (1st FA Brigade) [155mm howitzer].  Moved overseas Jul 1917.  Returned to the US Sep 1919 and moved to Camp Zachary Taylor, KY.

**6<sup>th</sup> Field Artillery**   Apr 1917 station Douglas, AZ. Assigned (less Btys D and F) 20 Mar 1917—1 Jun 1917 to 3<sup>rd</sup> Provisional Infantry Division. (Btys D and F assigned 20 Mar 1917—1 Jun 1917 to Artillery Brigade, 1<sup>st</sup> Provisional Infantry Division.) Assigned 8 Jun 1917 to 1<sup>st</sup> Expeditionary Division [later 1<sup>st</sup> Division] (1<sup>st</sup> FA Brigade) [75mm gun]. Moved overseas Jul 1917. Returned to the US Sep 1919 and moved to Camp Zachary Taylor, KY.

**7<sup>th</sup> Field Artillery**   Apr 1917 station Ft. Sam Houston, TX. Assigned 20 Mar 1917—1 Jun 1917 to Artillery Brigade, 1<sup>st</sup> Provisional Infantry Division. Assigned 8 Jun 1917 to 1<sup>st</sup> Expeditionary Division [later 1<sup>st</sup> Division] (1<sup>st</sup> FA Brigade) [75mm gun]. Moved overseas Jul 1917. Returned to the US Sep 1919 and moved to Camp Zachary Taylor, KY.

**8<sup>th</sup> Field Artillery**   Apr 1917 station Ft. Bliss, TX. Assigned 20 Mar 1917—May 1917 to Artillery Brigade, 2<sup>nd</sup> Provisional Infantry Division. Moved May 1917 to Camp Robinson, WI and Nov 1917 to Camp Wheeler, GA. Assigned to 7<sup>th</sup> Division (7<sup>th</sup> FA Brigade) 6 Dec 1917 [155mm howitzer]. Moved overseas Aug 198. Returned to the US Jun 1991 and moved to Camp Funston, KS.

**9<sup>th</sup> Field Artillery**   Apr 1917 station the Hawaiian Islands. Moved Jan 1918 to Ft. Sill, OK.

**10<sup>th</sup> Field Artillery**   Organized 1 Jun 1917 at Douglas, AZ. Assigned 12 Nov 1917 to 3<sup>rd</sup> Division (3<sup>rd</sup> FA Brigade) [75mm gun]. Moved overseas Apr 1918. Returned to the US Aug 1919 and moved to Camp Pike, AR.

**11<sup>th</sup> Field Artillery**   Organized 1 Jun 1917 at Douglas, AZ. Assigned to 6<sup>th</sup> Division (6<sup>th</sup> FA Brigade) in Nov 1917 [155mm howitzer]. Moved overseas Jul 1918. Returned to the US Jun 1919 and moved to Camp Grant, IL.

**12<sup>th</sup> Field Artillery**   Organized 7 Jun 1917 at Ft. Myer, VA as component of to 2<sup>nd</sup> Division (2<sup>nd</sup> FA Brigade) [75mm gun]. Moved overseas Jan 1918. Returned to the US Aug 1919 and moved to Camp Travis, TX.

**13<sup>th</sup> Field Artillery**   Organized 1 Jun 1917 at Camp Stewart, TX; moved Jul 1917 to Ft. Bliss, TX and Dec 1917 to Camp Greene, NC. Assigned 10 Dec 1917 to 4<sup>th</sup> Division (4<sup>th</sup> FA Brigade) [155mm howitzer]. Moved overseas May 1918. Returned to the US Jul 1919 and moved to Camp Dodge, IA.

**14<sup>th</sup> Field Artillery**   Organized 1 Jun 1917 at Ft. Sill, OK. Remained in the US throughout the war.

**15<sup>th</sup> Field Artillery**   Organized 1 Jun 1917 at Syracuse, NY and moved Aug 1917 to Pine Camp, NY. Assigned 21 Sep 1917 to 2<sup>nd</sup> Division (2<sup>nd</sup> FA Brigade) [75mm gun]. Moved overseas Dec 1917. Returned to the US Aug 1919 and moved to Camp Travis, TX.

**16<sup>th</sup> Field Artillery**    Organized 21 May 1917 at Camp Robinson, WI; moved Oct 1917 to Plattsburg Barracks, NY and Nov 1917 to Camp Greene, NC.  Assigned 19 Nov 1917 to 4<sup>th</sup> Division (4<sup>th</sup> FA Brigade) [75mm gun].  Moved overseas May 1918.  Returned to the US Jul 1919 and moved to Camp Dodge, IA.

**17<sup>th</sup> Field Artillery**    Organized 6 Jun 1917 at Camp Robinson, WI.  Assigned 21 Sep 1917 to 2<sup>nd</sup> Division (2<sup>nd</sup> FA Brigade) [155mm howitzer].  Moved overseas Dec 1917.  Returned to the US Aug 1919 and moved to Camp Travis, TX.

**18<sup>th</sup> Field Artillery**    Organized 1 Jun1917 at Ft. Bliss, TX.  Assigned 12 Nov 1917 to 3<sup>rd</sup> Division (3<sup>rd</sup> FA Brigade) [155mm howitzer].  Moved overseas Apr 1918.  Returned to the US Aug 1919 and moved to Camp Pike, AR.

**19<sup>th</sup> Field Artillery**    Organized 1 Jun 1917 at Camp Wilson, TX; moved Jul 1917 to Ft. Sam Houston, TX and Nov 1917 to Camp Stanley, TX.  Assigned 12 Dec 1917 to 5<sup>th</sup> Division (5<sup>th</sup> FA Brigade) [75mm gun].  Moved overseas May 1918.  Returned to the US Jul 1919 and moved to Camp Bragg, NC.

**20<sup>th</sup> Field Artillery**    Organized 1 Jun 1917 at Ft. Sam Houston, TX; moved Jun 1917 to Camp Funston, TX.  Assigned Dec 1917 to 5<sup>th</sup> Division (5<sup>th</sup> FA Brigade) [75mm gun].  Moved overseas May 1918.  Returned to the US Jul 1919 and moved to Camp Bragg, NC.

**21<sup>st</sup> Field Artillery**    Organized 1 Jun 1917 at Camp Wilson, TX; moved Jul 1917 to Camp Funston, TX.  Assigned 12 Dec 1917 to 5<sup>th</sup> Division (5<sup>th</sup> FA Brigade) [155mm howitzer].  Moved overseas May 1918.  Returned to the US Jul 1919 and moved to Camp Bragg, NC.

[Numbers 22 to 24 not used]

[Numbers 25 to 75 allotted to National Army regiments assigned to Regular Army and National Army divisions[68]]

**76<sup>th</sup> Field Artillery**    Organized 1 Nov 1917 at Ft. Ethan Allen, VT by conversion and redesignation of 18<sup>th</sup> Cavalry and then moved to Camp Shelby, MS.  Assigned 12 Nov 1917 to 3<sup>rd</sup> Division (3<sup>rd</sup> FA Brigade) [75mm gun].  Moved overseas Apr 1918.  Returned to the US Aug 1919 and moved to Camp Pike, AR.

**77<sup>th</sup> Field Artillery**    Organized 1 Nov 1917 at Ft. Ethan Allen, VT by conversion and redesignation of 19<sup>th</sup> Cavalry; moved then to Camp Shelby, MS and Dec 1917 to Camp Greene, NC.  Assigned 19 Nov 1917 to 4<sup>th</sup> Division (4<sup>th</sup> FA Brigade) [75mm gun].  Moved overseas May 1918.  Returned to the US Jul 1919 and moved to Camp Dodge, IA.

---

[68] Newly-constituted regiments in the Coast Artillery Corps had numbers in this gap, thus avoiding duplication between the two artillery branches in 1917.  The formation of additional National Army regiments in both arms altered this.

**78th Field Artillery**     Organized 18 Nov 1917 at Camp Logan, TX by conversion and redesignation of 20th Cavalry as component of to 6th Division (6th FA Brigade) [75mm gun]. Moved overseas Jul 1918. Returned to the US Jun 1919 and moved to Camp Grant, IL.

**79th Field Artillery**     Organized 1 Nov 1917 at Camp Logan, TX by conversion and redesignation of 21st Cavalry. Assigned 6 Dec 1917 to 7th Division (7th FA Brigade) [75mm gun]. Moved overseas Aug 1918. Returned to the US Jun 1919 and moved to Camp Funston, KS.

**80th Field Artillery**     Organized 1 Nov 1917 at Ft. Oglethorpe, GA by conversion and redesignation of 22nd Cavalry. Assigned 6 Dec 1917 to 7th Division (7th FA Brigade) [75mm gun]. Moved Feb 1918 to Camp MacArthur, TX. Moved overseas Aug 1918. Returned to the US Jun 1919 and moved to Camp Funston, KS.

**81st Field Artillery**     Organized 3 Nov 1917 at Ft. Oglethorpe, GA by conversion and redesignation of 23rd Cavalry; moved Feb 1918 to Camp Fremont, CA. Assigned 18 Feb 1918 to 8th Division (8th FA Brigade) [75mm gun]. Moved overseas Nov 1918. Returned to the US Jan 1919 and moved to Camp Knox, KY. Relieved 5 Sep 1919 from 8th Division.

**82nd Field Artillery**     Organized 1 Nov 1917 at Camp Logan, TX by conversion and redesignation of 24th Cavalry as component of 15th Cavalry Division [75mm gun]. Moved Dec 1917 to Ft. Bliss, TX. Relieved from 15th Cavalry Division in May 1918.

**83rd Field Artillery**     Organized 1 Nov 1917 at Ft. D. A. Russell, WY by conversion and redesignation of 25th Cavalry. Assigned 17 Dec 1917 to 8th Division (8th FA Brigade) [75mm gun]. Moved Feb to Camp Fremont, CA. Moved overseas Oct 1918. Returned to the US Jan 1919 and moved to Camp Knox, KY. Relieved 5 Sep 1919 from 8th Division.

[Numbers 84 and 85 allotted to National Army regiments]

*National Guard Field Artillery Regiments*[69]

**101st Field Artillery**    Organized 18-22 Aug 1917 at Boxford, MA as component of 26th Division (51st FA Brigade) [75mm gun] (formed from 1st Field Artillery, MA NG).  Moved overseas Sep 1917.  Returned to the US Apr 1919 and demobilized 29 Apr 1919 at Camp Devens, MA.

**102nd Field Artillery**    Organized 22 Aug 1917 at Boxford, MA as component of 26th Division (51st FA Brigade) [75mm gun] (formed from 2nd Field Artillery, MA NG).  Moved overseas Sep 1917.  Returned to the US Apr 1919 and demobilized 29 Apr 1919 at Camp Devens, MA.

**103rd Field Artillery**    Organized Aug 1917 at Boxford, MA as component of 26th Division (51st FA Brigade) (formed from 1st Separate Bn, Field Artillery, RI NG [1st Bn], troop, 1st Sep Sqn Cavalry, RI NG, Btys E and F, Field Artillery, CT NG, and Bty A, Field Artillery, NH NG) [155mm howitzer].  Moved overseas Sep 1917.  Returned to the US Apr 1919 and demobilized 29 Apr 1919 at Camp Devens, MA.

**104th Field Artillery**    Organized 1 Oct 1917 at Camp Wadsworth, SC as component of 27th Division (52nd FA Brigade) [75mm gun] (formed from 1st Field Artillery, NY NG and personnel from 12th Infantry, NY NG).  Moved overseas Jun 1918.  Returned to the US Mar 1919.  Demobilized 3 Apr 1919 at Camp Upton, NY.

**105th Field Artillery**    Organized 1 Oct 1917 at Camp Wadsworth, SC as component of 27th Division (52nd FA Brigade) [75mm gun] (formed from 2nd Field Artillery, NY NG and personnel from 14th Infantry NY NG).  Moved overseas Jun 1918.  Returned to the US Mar 1919.  Demobilized 3 Apr 1919 at Camp Upton, NY.

**106th Field Artillery**    Organized 1 Oct 1917 at Camp Wadsworth, SC as component of 27th Division (52nd FA Brigade) (formed from 3rd Field Artillery, NY NG and personnel from 1st, 71st and 74th Infantry, NY NG) [155mm howitzer].  Moved overseas Jun 1918.  Returned to the US Mar 1919.  Demobilized 31 Mar 1919 at Camp Upton, NY.

---

[69] As with the infantry, some National Guard field artillery units were simply redesignations of existing regiments and some were formed by consolidation or conversion. All are simply shown as "organized" as of the date they were given the new numbers. Nomenclature of the state units has been standardized; many included "regiment" in their official title and could have other variations as well. Thus, the 1st Regiment, North Carolina Field Artillery (Light) is shown as 1st Field Artillery (Light), NC NG.

**107<sup>th</sup> Field Artillery**   Organized 11 Oct 1917 at Camp Hancock, GA as component of 28<sup>th</sup> Division (53<sup>rd</sup> FA Brigade) [75mm gun] (formed from 1<sup>st</sup> Field Artillery, PA NG and detachments from 1<sup>st</sup> Cavalry, PA NG).  Moved overseas May 1918.  Returned to the US May 1919 and demobilized 21 May 1919 at Camp Dix, NJ.

**108<sup>th</sup> Field Artillery**   Organized 11 Oct 1917 at Camp Hancock, GA as component of 28<sup>th</sup> Division (53<sup>rd</sup> FA Brigade) (formed from 2<sup>nd</sup> Field Artillery, PA NG and three troops plus detachments from 1<sup>st</sup> Cavalry, PA NG) [155mm howitzer].  Moved overseas May 1918.  Returned to the US May 1919 and demobilized at Camp Dix, NJ.

**109<sup>th</sup> Field Artillery**   Organized 11 Oct 1917 at Camp Hancock, GA as component of 28<sup>th</sup> Division (53<sup>rd</sup> FA Brigade) [75mm gun] (formed from 3<sup>rd</sup> Field Artillery, PA NG and detachments from 1<sup>st</sup> Cavalry, PA NG).  Moved overseas May 1918.  Returned to the US May 1919 and demobilized 17 May 1919 at Camp Dix, NJ.

**110<sup>th</sup> Field Artillery**   *See* 112<sup>th</sup> Field Artillery

**110<sup>th</sup> Field Artillery**   Organized 18 Sep 1917 at Camp McClellan, AL as 112<sup>th</sup> Field Artillery as component of 29<sup>th</sup> Division (54<sup>th</sup> FA Brigade) [75mm gun] (formed from Btys A, B and C, Field Artillery, MD NG, Btys A and B, Field Artillery, DC NG, 1<sup>st</sup> Sqn Cavalry, DC NG, and two companies 5<sup>th</sup> Infantry MD NG).  Redesignated 27 Nov 1917 as 110<sup>th</sup> Field Artillery.  Moved overseas Jun 1918.  Returned to the US May 1919. Demobilized 4 Jun 1919 at Camp Lee, VA.

**111<sup>th</sup> Field Artillery**   Organized 15 Sep 1917 at Camp McClellan, AL as component of 29<sup>th</sup> Division (54<sup>th</sup> FA Brigade) [75mm gun] (formed from 1<sup>st</sup> Field Artillery, VA NG and two companies 4<sup>th</sup> Infantry, VA NG).  Moved overseas Jun 1918.  Returned to the US Jun 1919 and demobilized 2 Jun 1919 at Camp Lee, VA.

**112<sup>th</sup> Field Artillery**   *See* 110<sup>th</sup> Field Artillery

**112<sup>th</sup> Field Artillery**   Organized 15 Sep 1918 at Camp McClellan, AL as 110<sup>th</sup> Field Artillery as component of 29<sup>th</sup> Division (54<sup>th</sup> FA Brigade) (formed from 1<sup>st</sup> Field Artillery, NJ NG and two troops, 1<sup>st</sup> Separate Sqn Cavalry, NJ NG) [155mm howitzer].  Redesignated 27 Nov 1917 as 112<sup>th</sup> Field Artillery.  Moved overseas Jun 1918.  Returned to the US May 1919 and demobilized 31 May 1919 at Camp Dix, NJ.

**113<sup>th</sup> Field Artillery**   Organized 12 Sep 1917 at Camp Sevier, SC as component of 30<sup>th</sup> Division (55<sup>th</sup> FA Brigade) [75mm gun] (formed from 1<sup>st</sup> Field Artillery (Light), NC NG).  Moved overseas May 1918.  Returned to the US Mar 1919 and demobilized 28 Mar 1919 at Camp Jackson, SC.

**114th Field Artillery**    Organized Sep 1917 at Camp Sevier, SC as component of 30th Division (55th FA Brigade) [75mm gun] (formed from 1st Field Artillery, TN NG).  Moved overseas May 1918.  Returned to the US Mar 1919 and demobilized Apr 1919 at Ft. Oglethorpe, GA.

**115th Field Artillery**    Organized Sep 1917 at Camp Sevier, SC as component of 30th Division (55th FA Brigade) [155mm howitzer] (formed from 1st Infantry, TN NG and personnel 2nd Bn, 2nd Infantry, TN NG).  Moved overseas May 1918.  Returned to the US Mar 1919 and demobilized Apr 1919 at Ft. Oglethorpe, GA.

**116th Field Artillery**    Organized 1 Oct-1 Nov 1917 at Camp Wheeler, GA as component of 31st Division (56th FA Brigade) [75mm gun] (formed from personnel from 1st Infantry, FL NG, five troops 1st Cavalry, AL NG, and 1st Bn (-), Field Artillery, GA NG).  Moved overseas Oct 1918 and returned to the US Dec 1918.  Demobilized 16 Jan 1919 at Camp Gordon, GA.

**117th Field Artillery**    Organized Oct 1917 at Camp Wheeler, GA as component of 31st Division (56th FA Brigade) [75mm gun] (formed from Bty A, 1st Bn, Field Artillery, GA NG, personnel from 1st Infantry, FL NG, and 1st Cavalry (- seven troops), 1st Cavalry, AL NG).  Moved overseas Oct 1918 and returned to the US Dec 1918.  Demobilized Jan 1919 at Camp Gordon, GA.

**118th Field Artillery**    Organized 23 Sep 1917 at Camp Wheeler, GA as component of 31st Division (56th FA Brigade) [155mm howitzer] (formed from 1st Infantry (- seven companies), GA NG and personnel from 1st Infantry, FL NG).  Moved overseas Oct 1918 and returned to the US Dec 1918.  Demobilized 14-18 Jan 1919 at Camp Gordon, GA.

**119th Field Artillery**    Organized 22 Sep 1917 at Camp MacArthur, TX as component of 32nd Division (57th FA Brigade) [75mm gun] (1st Bn, Field Artillery, MI NG [1st Bn], 1st Sqn, Cavalry, MI NG, and some personnel from 31st Infantry, MI NG).  Moved overseas Feb 1918.  Returned to the US May 1919 and demobilized 16 May 1919 at Camp Custer, MI.

**120th Field Artillery**    Organized 28 Sep 1917 at Camp MacArthur, TX as component of 32nd Division (57th FA Brigade) [75mm gun] (formed from 1st Cavalry, WI NG).  Moved overseas Mar 1918.  Returned to the US May 1919 and demobilized 16 May 1919 at Camp Grant, IL.

**121st Field Artillery**    Organized 19 Sep 1917 at Camp MacArthur, TX as component of 32nd Division (57th FA Brigade) [155mm howitzer] (formed from 1st Field Artillery, WI NG and personnel from 6th Infantry, WI NG).  Moved overseas Mar 1918.  Returned to the US May 1919 and demobilized 17 May 1919 at Camp Grant, IL.

**122<sup>nd</sup> Field Artillery**    Organized 21 Sep 1917 at Camp Logan, TX as component of 33<sup>rd</sup> Division (58<sup>th</sup> FA Brigade) [75mm gun] (formed from 2<sup>nd</sup> Field Artillery, IL NG).  Moved overseas May 1918.  Returned to the US May 1919.  Demobilized 10 Jun 1919 at Camp Grant, IL.

**123<sup>rd</sup> Field Artillery**    Organized 19 Sep 1917 at Camp Logan, TX as component of 33<sup>rd</sup> Division (58<sup>th</sup> FA Brigade) [155mm howitzer] (formed from 6<sup>th</sup> Infantry, IL NG).  Moved overseas May 1918.  Returned to the US May 1919.  Demobilized 9 Jun 1919 at Camp Grant, IL.

**124<sup>th</sup> Field Artillery**    Organized Sep 1917 at Camp Logan, TX as component of 33<sup>rd</sup> Division (58<sup>th</sup> FA Brigade) [75mm gun] (formed from 3<sup>rd</sup> Field Artillery, IL NG).  Moved overseas May 1918.  Returned to the US May 1919.  Demobilized Jun 1919 at Camp Grant, IL.

**125<sup>th</sup> Field Artillery**    Organized 1 Oct 1917 at Camp Cody, NM as component of 34<sup>th</sup> Division (59<sup>th</sup> FA Brigade) [3" horse-drawn, then 6" motorized, and finally 155mm howitzer] (formed from 3<sup>rd</sup> Infantry, MN NG).  Moved overseas Sep 1918.  Returned to the US Jan 1919 and demobilized 23 Jan 1919 at Camp Dodge, IA.

**126<sup>th</sup> Field Artillery**    Organized 1 Oct 1917 at Camp Cody, NM as component of 34<sup>th</sup> Division (59<sup>th</sup> FA Brigade) [75mm gun] (formed from 1<sup>st</sup> Field Artillery, IA NG).  Moved overseas Sep 1918.  Returned to the US Jan 1919 and demobilized 20 Jan 1919 at Camp Dodge, IA.

**127<sup>th</sup> Field Artillery**    Organized Oct 1917 at Camp Cody, NM as component of 34<sup>th</sup> Division (59<sup>th</sup> FA Brigade) [155mm howitzer] (formed from 4<sup>th</sup> Infantry, NE NG).  Moved overseas Sep 1918.  Returned to the US Jan 1919 and demobilized Jan 1919 at Camp Dodge, IA.

**128<sup>th</sup> Field Artillery**    Organized 1 Oct 1917 at Camp Doniphan, OK as component of 35<sup>th</sup> Division (60<sup>th</sup> FA Brigade) [75mm gun] (formed from 1<sup>st</sup> Field Artillery, MO NG).  Moved overseas May 1918.  Returned to the US Apr 1919.  Demobilized 19 May 1919 at Ft. Riley, KS.

**129<sup>th</sup> Field Artillery**    Organized 1 Oct 1917 at Camp Doniphan, OK as component of 35<sup>th</sup> Division (60<sup>th</sup> FA Brigade) [75mm gun] (formed from 2<sup>nd</sup> Field Artillery, MO NG and Trp B, Cavalry, MO NG).  Moved overseas May 1918.  Returned to the US Apr 1919.  Demobilized 6 May 1919 at Camp Funston, KS.

**130<sup>th</sup> Field Artillery**    Organized 1 Oct 1917 at Camp Doniphan, OK as component of 35<sup>th</sup> Division (60<sup>th</sup> FA Brigade) [155mm howitzer] (formed from 1<sup>st</sup> Field Artillery, KS NG).  Moved overseas May 1918.  Returned to the US Apr 1919.  Demobilized 11 May 1919 at Camp Funston, KS.

**131st Field Artillery**     Organized 1 Oct 1917 at Camp Bowie, TX as component of 36th Division (61st FA Brigade) [75mm gun] (formed from 2nd Field Artillery, TX NG). Moved overseas Jul 1918. Returned to the US Mar 1919. Demobilized 2 Apr 1919 at Camp Travis, TX.

**132nd Field Artillery**     Organized 15 Oct 1917 at Camp Bowie, TX as component of 36th Division (61st FA Brigade) [75mm gun] (formed from 1st Cavalry (-), TX NG). Moved overseas Jul 1918. Returned to the US Mar 1919. Demobilized 10 Apr 1919 at Camp Bowie, TX.

**133rd Field Artillery**     Organized 15 Oct 1917 at Camp Bowie, TX as component of 36th Division (61st FA Brigade) [155mm howitzer] (formed from 1st Field Artillery, TX NG). Moved overseas Jul 1918. Returned to the US Mar 1919. Demobilized 2 Apr 1919 at Camp Bowie, TX.

**134th Field Artillery**     Organized 15 Sep 1917 at Camp Sheridan, AL as component of 37th Division (62nd FA Brigade) [75mm gun] (formed from 1st Field Artillery, OH NG and personnel from 6th Infantry, OH NG). Moved overseas Jun 1918. Returned to the US Mar 1919. Demobilized 9 Apr 1919 at Camp Sherman, OH.

**135th Field Artillery**     Organized 15 Sep 1917 at Camp Sheridan, AL as component of 37th Division (62nd FA Brigade) [75mm gun] (formed from 2nd Field Artillery, OH NG and personnel from 6th Infantry, OH NG). Moved overseas Jun 1918. Returned to the US Mar 1919. Demobilized 10 Apr 1919 at Camp Sherman, OH.

**136th Field Artillery**     Organized 15 Sep 1917 at Camp Sheridan, AL as component of 37th Division (62nd FA Brigade) [155mm howitzer] (formed from 3rd Field Artillery, OH NG and personnel from 6th Infantry, OH NG). Moved overseas Jun 1918. Returned to the US Mar 1919. Demobilized 10 Apr 1919 at Camp Sherman, OH.

**137th Field Artillery**     Organized Oct 1917 at Camp Shelby, MS as component of 38th Division (63rd FA Brigade) [75mm gun] (formed from 3rd Infantry, IN NG). Moved overseas Oct 1918 and returned to the US Dec 1918. Demobilized Jan 1919 at Ft. Benjamin Harrison, IN.

**138th Field Artillery**     Organized 9 Oct 1917 at Camp Shelby, MS as component of 38th Division (63rd FA Brigade) [75mm gun] (formed from 1st Infantry (- five companies), KY NG). Moved overseas Oct 1918 and returned to the US Dec 1918. Demobilized 8 Jan 1919 at Camp Taylor, KY.

**139th Field Artillery**     Organized 1 Oct 1917 as component of 38th Division (63rd FA Brigade) [155mm howitzer] (formed from 4th Infantry (- 3 companies), IN NG and Trp B, Sqn Cavalry, IN NG). Moved overseas Oct 1918 and returned to the US Dec 1918. Demobilized 16 Jan 1919 at Ft. Benjamin Harrison, IN.

**140th Field Artillery**    Organized Sep 1917 at Camp Jackson, MS as component of 39th Division (64th FA Brigade) [75mm gun] (formed from 1st Field Artillery, MS NG).  Moved Nov 1917 to Camp Beauregard, LA.  Moved overseas Aug 1918.  Returned to the US Jun 1919 and demobilized at Camp Shelby, MS.

**141st Field Artillery**    Organized 27 Sep 1917 at Camp Nicholls, LA as component of 39th Division (64th FA Brigade) [75mm gun] (formed from 1st Field Artillery, LA NG).  Moved Oct 1917 to Camp Beauregard, LA.  Moved overseas Aug 1918.  Returned to the US Apr 1919.  Demobilized 3 May 1919 at Camp Shelby, MS.

**142nd Field Artillery**    Organized Nov 1917 at Ft. Logan H. Roots, AR as component of 39th Division (64th FA Brigade) [155mm howitzer] (formed from 2nd Infantry, AR NG).  Moved Nov 1917 to Camp Beauregard, LA.  Moved overseas Aug 1918.  Returned to the US Jun 1919 and demobilized at Camp Pike, AR.

**143rd Field Artillery**    Organized 24 Sep 1917 at the Presidio of San Francisco, CA as component of 40th Division (65th FA Brigade) [75mm gun] (formed from 1st Field Artillery, CA NG).  Moved Oct 1917 to Camp Kearny, CA.  Moved overseas Aug 1918.  Returned to the US Dec 1918.  Demobilized 28 Jan 1919 at the Presidio of San Francisco.

**144th Field Artillery**    Organized Oct 1917 at Camp Kearney, CA as component of 40th Division (65th FA Brigade) [155mm howitzer] (formed from 2nd Field Artillery, CA NG).  Moved overseas Aug 1918.  Returned to the US Jan 1919 and demobilized at the Presidio of San Francisco, CA.

**145th Field Artillery**    Organized 3 Oct 1917 at Ft. Douglas, UT as component of 40th Division (65th FA Brigade) [4.7" gun] (formed from 1st Field Artillery, UT NG).  Moved Oct 1917 to Camp Kearny, CA.  Moved overseas Aug 1918.  Returned to the US Jan 1919 and demobilized 21-29 Jan 1919 at Logan, UT.

**146th Field Artillery**    Organized 19 Sep 1917 at Camp Greene, NC as component of 41st Division (66th FA Brigade) [3" horse-drawn; 155mm howitzer in France] (formed from 1st Bn, Field Artillery, WA NG; Bty A, Field Artillery, NM, NG; and 1st Bn and other elements, 2nd Infantry, Idaho NG).  Moved overseas Dec 1917.  Returned to the US Jun 1919 and demobilized 26 Jun 1919 at Ft. D. A. Russell, WY.

**147th Field Artillery**    Organized 3 Oct 1917 at Camp Greene, NC as component of 41st Division (66th FA Brigade) [75mm gun] (formed from elements 4th Infantry, SD NG).  Moved overseas Jan 1918.  Returned to the US May 1919 and demobilized 24 May 1919 at Camp Dodge, IA.

**148<sup>th</sup> Field Artillery**    Organized 19 Sep 1917 at Camp Greene, NC as component of 41<sup>st</sup> Division (66<sup>th</sup> FA Brigade) [155mm howitzer] (formed from 1<sup>st</sup> Separate Bn, Field Artillery, CO NG [1<sup>st</sup> Bn], Separate Sqn Cavalry, OR NG, and 1<sup>st</sup> Bn, 3<sup>rd</sup> Infantry, WY NG).  Moved overseas Jan 1918.  Returned to the US Jun 1919 and demobilized 29 Jun 1919 at Ft. D. A. Russell, WY.

**149<sup>th</sup> Field Artillery**    Organized Aug 1917 at Ft. Sheridan, IL as component of 42<sup>nd</sup> Division (67<sup>th</sup> FA Brigade) [75mm gun] formed from 1<sup>st</sup> Field Artillery, ID NG).  Moved overseas Oct 1917.  Returned to the US Apr 1919.  Demobilized May 1919 at Camp Grant, IL.

**150<sup>th</sup> Field Artillery**    Organized 14 Aug 1917 at Ft. Benjamin Harrison, IN as component of 42<sup>nd</sup> Division (67<sup>th</sup> FA Brigade) [155mm howitzer] (formed from 1<sup>st</sup> Field Artillery, IN NG).  Moved overseas Oct 1917.  Returned to the US Apr 1919.  Demobilized 9 May 1919 at Camp Zachary Taylor, KY.

**151<sup>st</sup> Field Artillery**    Organized 18 Aug 1917 at Ft. Snelling, MN as component of 42<sup>nd</sup> Division (67<sup>th</sup> FA Brigade) [75mm gun] (formed from 1<sup>st</sup> Field Artillery, MN NG).  Moved overseas Oct 1917.  Returned to the US Apr 1919.  Demobilized 10 May 1919 at Camp Dodge, IA.

*National Army Field Artillery Regiments*

[Numbers below 100 were supposed to be allotted to the Regular Army, but many of them were given to field artilleryregiments constituted in the National Army.  Numbers in the 40s and 50s had originally gone to new regiments in the Coast Artillery Corps; the creation of new regiments in summer 1918 led to a duplication of numbers between the two branches.]

**25<sup>th</sup> Field Artillery**    Organized 2 Aug 1918 at Camp McClellan, AL, as component of 9<sup>th</sup> Division (9<sup>th</sup> FA Brigade). Demobilized 8 Feb 1919 at Camp McClellan.

**26<sup>th</sup> Field Artillery**    Organized 2 Aug 1918 at Camp McClellan, AL, as component of 9<sup>th</sup> Division (9<sup>th</sup> FA Brigade). Demobilized 9 Feb 1919 at Camp McClellan.

**27<sup>th</sup> Field Artillery**    Organized 2 Aug 1918 at Camp McClellan, AL, as component of 9<sup>th</sup> Division (9<sup>th</sup> FA Brigade). Demobilized 8 Feb 1919 at Camp McClellan.

**28<sup>th</sup> Field Artillery**    Organized 10 Aug 1918 at Camp Funston, KS, as component of 10<sup>th</sup> Division (10<sup>th</sup> FA Brigade). Demobilized 7 Feb 1919 at Camp Funston.

**29th Field Artillery**    Organized 11 Aug 1918 at Camp Funston, KS, as component of 10th Division (10th FA Brigade). Demobilized 4 Feb 1919 at Camp Funston.

**30th Field Artillery**    Organized 10 Aug 1918 at Camp Funston, KS, as component of 10th Division (10th FA Brigade). Demobilized 5 Feb 1919 at Camp Funston.

**31st Field Artillery**    Organized 6 Aug 1918 at Camp George G. Meade, MD, as component of 11th Division (11th FA Brigade). Relieved 30 Sep 1918 from 11th Division. Demobilized 9 Dec 1918 at Camp George G. Meade.

**32nd Field Artillery**    Organized 5 Aug 1918 at Camp George G. Meade, MD, as component of 11th Division (11th FA Brigade). Demobilized 13 Dec 1918 at Camp George G. Meade.

**33rd Field Artillery**    Organized 5 Aug 1918 at Camp George G. Meade, MD, as component of 11th Division (11th FA Brigade). Demobilized 12 Dec 1918 at Camp George G. Meade.

**34th Field Artillery**    Organized 7 Aug 1918 at Camp McClellan, AL, as component of 12th Division (12th FA Brigade). Demobilized 6 Feb 1919 at Camp McClellan, AL.

**35th Field Artillery**    Organized 9 Aug 1918 at Camp McClellan, AL, as component of 12th Division (12th FA Brigade). Demobilized 8 Feb 1919 at Camp McClellan, AL.

**36th Field Artillery**    Organized 7 Aug 1918 at Camp McClellan, AL, as component of 12th Division (12th FA Brigade). Demobilized 8 Feb 1919 at Camp McClellan, AL.

**37th Field Artillery**    Organized 17 Aug 1918 at Camp Lewis, WA, as component of 13th Division (13th FA Brigade). Demobilized 11 Feb 1919 at Camp Lewis.

**38th Field Artillery**    Organized 17 Aug 1918 at Camp Lewis, WA, as component of 13th Division (13th FA Brigade). Demobilized 10 Feb 1919 at Camp Lewis.

**39th Field Artillery**    Organized 9 Aug 1918 at Camp Lewis, WA, as component of 13th Division (13th FA Brigade). Demobilized 26 Feb 1919 at Camp Lewis.

**40th Field Artillery**    Organized 10 Aug 1918 at Camp Custer, MI, as component of 14th Division (14th FA Brigade). Demobilized 6 Feb 1919 at Camp Custer.

**41st Field Artillery**    Organized 10 Aug 1918 at Camp Custer, MI, as component of 14th Division (14th FA Brigade). Demobilized 6 Feb 1919 at Camp Custer.

**42nd Field Artillery**    Organized 10 Aug 1918 at Camp Custer, MI, as component of 14th Division (14th FA Brigade). Demobilized 7 Feb 1919 at Camp Custer.

**43<sup>rd</sup> Field Artillery**     Organized 15 Aug 1918 by conversion and redesignation of elements 304<sup>th</sup> Cavalry; assigned 15<sup>th</sup> Division (15<sup>th</sup> FA Brigade).  Demobilized 17 Feb 1919 at Camp Stanley, TX.

**44<sup>th</sup> Field Artillery**     Organized 27 Aug 1918 by conversion and redesignation of elements 305<sup>th</sup> Cavalry; assigned 15<sup>th</sup> Division (15<sup>th</sup> FA Brigade).  Demobilized 17 Feb 1919 at Camp Stanley, TX.

**45<sup>th</sup> Field Artillery**     Organized 27 Aug 1918 by conversion and redesignation of elements 305<sup>th</sup> Cavalry; assigned 15<sup>th</sup> Division (15<sup>th</sup> FA Brigade).  Demobilized 17 Feb 1919 at Camp Stanley, TX.

**46<sup>th</sup> Field Artillery**     Organized 27 Aug 1918 by conversion and redesignation of elements 301<sup>st</sup> Cavalry; assigned 16<sup>th</sup> Division (16<sup>th</sup> FA Brigade).  Demobilized 15 Feb 1919 at Camp Kearny, CA.

**47<sup>th</sup> Field Artillery**     Organized 27 Aug 1918 by conversion and redesignation of elements 301<sup>st</sup> Cavalry; assigned 16<sup>th</sup> Division (16<sup>th</sup> FA Brigade).  Demobilized 15 Feb 1919 at Camp Kearny, CA.

**48<sup>th</sup> Field Artillery**     Organized 26 Aug 1918 by conversion and redesignation of elements 302<sup>nd</sup> Cavalry; assigned 16<sup>th</sup> Division (16<sup>th</sup> FA Brigade).  Demobilized in Feb 1919 at Camp Kearny, CA.

**49<sup>th</sup> Field Artillery**     Organized 20 Aug 1918 by conversion and redesignation of elements 306<sup>th</sup> Cavalry; assigned 17<sup>th</sup> Division (17<sup>th</sup> FA Brigade).  Demobilized 8 Feb 1919 at Ft. Sill, OK.

**50<sup>th</sup> Field Artillery**     Organized 20 Aug 1918 by conversion and redesignation of elements 306<sup>th</sup> Cavalry; assigned 17<sup>th</sup> Division (17<sup>th</sup> FA Brigade).  Demobilized 8 Feb 1919 at Ft. Sill, OK.

**51<sup>st</sup> Field Artillery**     Organized 17 Aug 1918 by conversion and redesignation of elements 307<sup>th</sup> Cavalry; assigned 18<sup>th</sup> Division (18<sup>th</sup> FA Brigade).  Demobilized  8 Feb 1919 at Ft. Sill, OK.

**52<sup>nd</sup> Field Artillery**     Organized 14 Aug 1918 by conversion and redesignation of elements 303<sup>rd</sup> Cavalry; assigned 18<sup>th</sup> Division (18<sup>th</sup> FA Brigade).  Demobilized 13 Feb 1919 at Camp Travis, TX.

**53<sup>rd</sup> Field Artillery**     Organized 14 Aug 1918 by conversion and redesignation of elements 303<sup>rd</sup> Cavalry; assigned 18<sup>th</sup> Division (18<sup>th</sup> FA Brigade).  Demobilized 13 Feb 1919 at Camp Travis, TX.

**54<sup>th</sup> Field Artillery**     Organized 15 Aug 1918 by conversion and redesignation of elements 304<sup>th</sup> Cavalry; assigned 18<sup>th</sup> Division (18<sup>th</sup> FA Brigade).  Demobilized 13 Feb 1919 at Camp Travis, TX.

**55<sup>th</sup> Field Artillery**     Organized 17 Aug 1918 by conversion and redesignation of elements 307<sup>th</sup> Cavalry; assigned 19<sup>th</sup> Division (19<sup>th</sup> FA Brigade).  Demobilized  10 Feb 1919 at Ft. Sill, OK.

**56<sup>th</sup> Field Artillery**     elements 309<sup>th</sup> Cavalry; assigned 19<sup>th</sup> Division (19<sup>th</sup> FA Brigade).  Demobilized 7 Feb 1919 at Ft. Sill, OK.

**57<sup>th</sup> Field Artillery**      Organized 18 Aug 1918 by conversion and redesignation of elements 309<sup>th</sup> Cavalry; assigned 19<sup>th</sup> Division (19<sup>th</sup> FA Brigade). Demobilized 10 Feb 1919 at Ft. Sill, OK.

**58<sup>th</sup> Field Artillery**      Organized 18 Oct 1918 by conversion and redesignation of elements 310<sup>th</sup> Cavalry; assigned 20<sup>th</sup> Division (20<sup>th</sup> FA Brigade). Demobilized 10 Feb 1919 at Camp Jackson, SC.

**59<sup>th</sup> Field Artillery**      Organized 18 Oct 1918 by conversion and redesignation of elements 310<sup>th</sup> Cavalry; assigned 20<sup>th</sup> Division (20<sup>th</sup> FA Brigade). Demobilized 10 Feb 1919 at Camp Jackson, SC.

**60<sup>th</sup> Field Artillery**      Organized 13 Aug 1918 by conversion and redesignation of Ft. Myer, VA elements 312<sup>th</sup> Cavalry; assigned 20<sup>th</sup> Division (20<sup>th</sup> FA Brigade). Demobilized 10 Feb 1919 at Camp Jackson, SC.

**61<sup>st</sup> Field Artillery**      Organized 14 Aug 1918 by conversion and redesignation of Ft. Sheridan, IL elements 312<sup>th</sup> Cavalry; assigned 97<sup>th</sup> Division (172<sup>nd</sup> FA Brigade). Demobilized in Jan 1919 at Camp Jackson, SC.

**62<sup>nd</sup> Field Artillery**      Organized 18 Oct 1918 by conversion and redesignation of elements 314<sup>th</sup> Cavalry; assigned 97<sup>th</sup> Division (172<sup>nd</sup> FA Brigade). Demobilized 19 Jan 1919 at Camp Jackson, SC.

**63<sup>rd</sup> Field Artillery**      Organized 18 Oct 1918 by conversion and redesignation of elements 314<sup>th</sup> Cavalry; assigned 97<sup>th</sup> Division (172<sup>nd</sup> FA Brigade). Demobilized 17 Jan 1919 at Camp Jackson, SC.

**64<sup>th</sup> Field Artillery**      Organized 26 Aug 1918 by conversion and redesignation of elements 302<sup>nd</sup> Cavalry; assigned 96<sup>th</sup> Division (171<sup>st</sup> FA Brigade). Demobilized 20 Dec 1918 at Camp Kearny, CA.

**65<sup>th</sup> Field Artillery**      Organized 13 Sep 1918 by conversion and redesignation of elements 308<sup>th</sup> Cavalry; assigned 96<sup>th</sup> Division (171<sup>st</sup> FA Brigade). Demobilized 22 Dec 1918 at Camp Kearny, CA.

**66<sup>th</sup> Field Artillery**      Organized 13 Sep 1918 by conversion and redesignation of elements 308<sup>th</sup> Cavalry; assigned 96<sup>th</sup> Division (171<sup>st</sup> FA Brigade). Demobilized 22 Dec 1918 at Camp Kearny, CA.

**67<sup>th</sup> Field Artillery**      Organized 1 Sep 1918 by conversion and redesignation of elements 311<sup>th</sup> Cavalry; assigned 95<sup>th</sup> Division (170<sup>th</sup> FA Brigade). Demobilized 22 Dec 1918 at Camp Knox, KY.

**68<sup>th</sup> Field Artillery**      Organized 1 Sep 1918 by conversion and redesignation of elements 311<sup>th</sup> Cavalry; assigned 95<sup>th</sup> Division (170<sup>th</sup> FA Brigade). Demobilized 22 Dec 1918 at Camp Knox, KY.

**69<sup>th</sup> Field Artillery**      Organized 23 Aug 1918 by conversion and redesignation of elements 313<sup>th</sup> Cavalry; assigned 95<sup>th</sup> Division (170<sup>th</sup> FA Brigade). Demobilized 21 Dec 1918 at Camp Knox, KY.

**70<sup>th</sup> Field Artillery**     Organized 23 Aug 1918 by conversion and redesignation of elements 313<sup>th</sup> Cavalry; assigned 24<sup>th</sup> FA Brigade. Demobilized 21 Dec 1918 at Camp Knox, KY.

**71<sup>st</sup> Field Artillery**     Organized 19 Aug 1918 by conversion and redesignation of elements 315<sup>th</sup> Cavalry; assigned 24<sup>th</sup> FA Brigade. Demobilized 30 Jan 1919 at Camp Knox, KY.

**72<sup>nd</sup> Field Artillery**     Organized 19 Aug 1918 by conversion and redesignation of elements 315<sup>th</sup> Cavalry; assigned 24<sup>th</sup> FA Brigade. Demobilized 30 Jan 1919 at Camp Knox, KY.

**73<sup>rd</sup> Field Artillery**     Organized 12 Oct 1918 at Camp Jackson, SC. Demobilized 28 Dec 1918 at Camp Jackson.

**75<sup>th</sup> Field Artillery**     Organized 7 Oct 1918 at Camp Sheridan, AL. Demobilized 11 Dec 1918 at Camp Sheridan.

[Numbers 76 to 83 allotted to Regular Army regiments]

**84<sup>th</sup> Field Artillery**     Partially organized 3 Oct 1918 at Camp Sheridan, AL. Demobilized 13 Dec 1918 at Camp Sheridan.


**301<sup>st</sup> Field Artillery**     Organized 29 Aug 1917 at Camp Devens, MA, as component of 76<sup>th</sup> Division (151<sup>st</sup> FA Brigade) [75mm gun].  Moved overseas Jul 1918.  (Did not serve with brigade in Europe.)  Returned to the US Jan 1919 and demobilized 20 Jan 1919 at Camp Devens.

**302<sup>nd</sup> Field Artillery**     Organized Aug 1917 at Camp Devens, MA, as component of 76<sup>th</sup> Division (151<sup>st</sup> FA Brigade) [4.7" gun].  Moved overseas Jul 1918.  Returned to the US Apr 1919.  Demobilized 7 May 1919 at Camp Devens.

**303<sup>rd</sup> Field Artillery**     Organized 29 Aug 1917 at Camp Devens, MA, as component of 76<sup>th</sup> Division (151<sup>st</sup> FA Brigade) [155mm howitzer]. Moved overseas Jul 1918.  Returned to the US Apr 1919.  Demobilized 1 May 1919 at Camp Devens.

**304<sup>th</sup> Field Artillery**     Organized Aug-Sep 1917 at Camp Upton, NY, as component of 77<sup>th</sup> Division (152<sup>nd</sup> FA Brigade) [75mm gun].  Moved overseas Apr 1918.  Returned to the US Apr 1919. Demobilized 19 May 1919 at Camp Upton.

**305<sup>th</sup> Field Artillery**     Organized Sep 1917 at Camp Upton, NY, as component of 77<sup>th</sup> Division (152<sup>nd</sup> FA Brigade) [75mm gun]. Moved overseas Apr 1918. Returned to the US Apr 1919. Demobilized 10 May 1919 at Camp Upton.

**306<sup>th</sup> Field Artillery**     Organized 17 Sep 1917 at Camp Upton, NY, as component of 77<sup>th</sup> Division (152<sup>nd</sup> FA Brigade) [155mm howitzer]. Moved overseas Apr 1918.  Returned to the US Apr 1919. Demobilized 10 May 1919 at Camp Upton.

**307<sup>th</sup> Field Artillery**     Organized Sep 1917 at Camp Dix, NJ, as component of 78<sup>th</sup> Division (153<sup>rd</sup> FA Brigade) [75mm gun]. Moved overseas May 1918.  Returned to the US May 1919 and demobilized 17 May 1919 at Camp Dix.

**308<sup>th</sup> Field Artillery**     Organized Sep 1917 at Camp Dix, NJ, as component of 78<sup>th</sup> Division (153<sup>rd</sup> FA Brigade) [75mm gun]. Moved overseas May 1918.  Returned to the US May 1919 and demobilized 27 May 1919 at Camp Dix.

**309<sup>th</sup> Field Artillery**     Organized Sep 1917 at Camp Dix, NJ, as component of 78<sup>th</sup> Division (153<sup>rd</sup> FA Brigade) [155mm howitzer].  Moved overseas May 1918.  Returned to the US May 1919 and demobilized 14 May 1919 at Camp Dix.

**310<sup>th</sup> Field Artillery**     Organized 29 Aug 1917 at Camp Meade, MD, as component of 79<sup>th</sup> Division (154<sup>th</sup> FA Brigade) [75mm gun].  Moved overseas Jul 1918.  Returned to the US May 1919 and demobilized 29 May 1919 at Camp Dix, NJ.

**311<sup>th</sup> Field Artillery**     Organized 30 Aug 1917 at Camp Meade, MD, as component of 79<sup>th</sup> Division (154<sup>th</sup> FA Brigade) [75mm gun].  Moved overseas Jul 1918.  Returned to the US May 1919. Demobilized 3 Jun 1919 at Camp Dix, NJ.

**312<sup>th</sup> Field Artillery**     Organized 29 Aug 1917 at Camp Meade, MD, as component of 79<sup>th</sup> Division (154<sup>th</sup> FA Brigade) [155mm howitzer].  Moved overseas Jul 1918.  Returned to the US May 1919 and demobilized 31 May 1919 at Camp Dix, NJ.

**313<sup>th</sup> Field Artillery**          Organized Aug-Sep 1917 at Camp Lee, VA, as component of 80<sup>th</sup> Division (155<sup>th</sup> FA Brigade) [75mm gun].  Moved overseas May 1918.  Returned to the US May 1919.  Demobilized 6 Jun 1919 at Camp Lee.

**314<sup>th</sup> Field Artillery**     Organized Aug 1917 at Camp Lee, VA, as component of 80<sup>th</sup> Division (155<sup>th</sup> FA Brigade) [75mm gun]. Moved overseas May 1918. Returned to the US May 1919. Demobilized 7 Jun 1919 at Camp Lee.

**315<sup>th</sup> Field Artillery**     Organized Sep 1917 at Camp Lee, VA, as component of 80<sup>th</sup> Division (155<sup>th</sup> FA Brigade) [155mm howitzer].  Moved overseas May 1918.  Returned to the US May 1919. Demobilized 10 Jun 1919 at Camp Lee.

**316<sup>th</sup> Field Artillery**     Organized 31 Aug-4 Sep 1917 at Camp Jackson, SC, as component of 81<sup>st</sup> Division (156<sup>th</sup> FA Brigade) [155mm howitzer].  Moved overseas Aug 1918.  Returned to the US Jun 1919 and demobilized 13 Jun 1919 at Camp Lee, VA.

**317th Field Artillery**    Organized Sep 1917 at Camp Jackson, SC, as component of 81st Division (156th FA Brigade) [75mm gun]. Moved overseas Aug 1918.  Returned to the US Jun 1919 and demobilized 13 Jun 1919 at Camp Morrison, VA.

**318th Field Artillery**    Organized Sep 1917 at Camp Jackson, SC, as component of 81st Division (156th FA Brigade) [75mm gun]. Moved overseas Aug 1918.  Returned to the US Jun 1919 and demobilized 16 Jun 1919 at Ft. Oglethorpe, GA.

**319th Field Artillery**    Organized 2 Sep 1917 at Camp Gordon, GA, as component of 82nd Division (157th FA Brigade) [155mm howitzer]. Moved overseas May 1918.  Returned to the US May 1919 and demobilized 18 May 1919 at Camp Dix, NJ.

**320th Field Artillery**    Organized 29 Aug 1917 at Camp Gordon, GA, as component of 82nd Division (157th FA Brigade) [75mm gun].  Moved overseas May 1918.  Returned to the US May 1919 and demobilized 12 May 1919 at Camp Dix, NJ.

**321st Field Artillery**    Organized 2 Sep 1917 at Camp Gordon, GA, as component of 82nd Division (157th FA Brigade) [75mm gun].  Moved overseas May 1918.  Returned to the US May 1919 and demobilized 26 May 1919 at Camp Dix, NJ.

**322nd Field Artillery**    Organized  Sep 1917 at Camp Sherman, OH, as component of 83rd Division (158th FA Brigade) [75mm gun].  Moved overseas Jun 1918.  Returned to the US May 1919. Demobilized 2 Jun 1919 at Camp Sherman.

**323rd Field Artillery**    Organized  30 Aug 1917 at Camp Sherman, OH, as component of 83rd Division (158th FA Brigade) [75mm gun].  Moved overseas Jun 1918.  Returned to the US May 1919 and demobilized 21 May 1919 at Camp Sherman.

**324th Field Artillery**    Organized  30 Aug 1917 at Camp Sherman, OH, as component of 83rd Division (158th FA Brigade) [155mm howitzer]. Moved overseas Jun 1918.  Returned to the US May 1919. Demobilized 5 Jun 1919 at Camp Sherman.

**325th Field Artillery**    Organized  26 Aug 1917 at Camp Zachary Taylor, KY, as component of 84th Division (159th FA Brigade) [75mm gun].  Moved overseas Sep 1918.  Returned to the US Feb 1919. D emobilized 1 Mar 1919 at Camp Sherman, OH.

**326th Field Artillery**    Organized  Aug 1917 at Camp Zachary Taylor, KY, as component of 84th Division (159th FA Brigade) [75mm gun].  Moved overseas Sep 1918.  Returned to the US Feb 1919.  Demobilized 8 Mar 1919 at Camp Zachary Taylor.

**327th Field Artillery**    Organized 25 Aug 1917 at Camp Zachary Taylor, KY, as component of 84th Division (159th FA Brigade) [155mm howitzer]. Moved overseas Sep 1918.  Returned to the US Feb 1919 and demobilized 21 Feb 1919 at Camp Grant, IL.

**328th Field Artillery**    Organized 1 Sep 1917 at Camp Custer, MI, as component of 85th Division (160th FA Brigade) [75mm gun].  Moved overseas Jul 1918.  Returned to the US Apr 1919 and demobilized 1 Apr 1919 at Camp Custer.

**329th Field Artillery**    Organized Sep 1917 at Camp Custer, MI, as component of 85th Division (160th FA Brigade) [75mm gun]. Moved overseas Jul 1918.  Returned to the US Apr 1919 and demobilized 24 Apr 1919 at Camp Custer.

**330th Field Artillery**    Organized Sep 1917 at Camp Custer, MI, as component of 85th Division (160th FA Brigade) [155mm howitzer]. Moved overseas Jul 1918.  Returned to the US Apr 1919 and demobilized at Camp Custer.

**331st Field Artillery**    Organized Aug 1917 at Camp Grant, IL, as component of 86th Division (161st FA Brigade) [75mm gun]. Moved overseas Sep 1918.  Returned to the US Feb 1919 and demobilized 22 Feb 1919 at Camp Grant.

**332nd Field Artillery**    Organized Aug 1917 at Camp Grant, IL, as component of 86th Division (161st FA Brigade) [75mm gun]. Moved overseas Sep 1918.  Returned to the US Feb 1919 and demobilized 28 Feb 1919 at Camp Grant.

**333rd Field Artillery**    Organized 25 Aug 1917 at Camp Grant, IL, as component of 86th Division (161st FA Brigade) [155mm howitzer]. Moved overseas Sep 1918.  Returned to the US Jan 1919 and demobilized 23 Jan 1919 at Camp Grant.

**334th Field Artillery**    Organized Sep 1917 at Camp Pike, AR, as component of 87th Division (162nd FA Brigade) [75mm gun]. Moved overseas Aug 1918.  Returned to the US Feb 1919. Demobilized 4 Mar 1919 at Camp Dix, NJ.

**335th Field Artillery**    Organized Sep 1917 at Camp Pike, AR, as component of 87th Division (162nd FA Brigade) [75mm gun]. Moved overseas Aug 1918.  Returned to the US Mar 1919 and demobilized 16 Mar 1919 at Camp Dix, NJ.

**336th Field Artillery**    Organized Sep 1917 at Ft. Logan H. Roots, AR, as component of 87th Division (162nd FA Brigade) [155mm howitzer]. Moved overseas Aug 1918.  Returned to the US Mar 1919 and demobilized 17 Mar 1919 at Camp Dix, NJ.

**337th Field Artillery**    Organized 25 Aug 1917 at Camp Dodge, IA, as component of 88th Division (163rd FA Brigade) [75mm gun, then 155mm howitzer]. Moved overseas Aug 1918. Returned to the US Jan 1919 and demobilized 31 Jan 1919 at Camp Dodge.

**338th Field Artillery**    Organized 25 Aug 1917 at Camp Dodge, IA, as component of 88th Division (163rd FA Brigade) [75mm gun]. Moved overseas Aug 1918. Returned to the US Jan 1919 and demobilized Jan 1919 at Camp Dodge.

**339th Field Artillery**    Organized Sep 1917 at Camp Dodge, IA, as component of 88th Division (163rd FA Brigade) [155mm howitzer]. Moved overseas Aug 1918. Returned to the US Jan 1919. Demobilized 17 Feb 1919 at Camp Dodge.

**340th Field Artillery**    Organized Sep 1917 at Camp Funston, KS, as component of 89th Division (164th FA Brigade) [75mm gun]. Moved overseas Jun 1918. Returned to the US May 1919. Demobilized 11 Jun 1919 at Ft. Bliss, TX.

**341st Field Artillery**    Organized Sep 1917 at Camp Funston, KS, as component of 89th Division (164th FA Brigade) [75mm gun]. Moved overseas Jun 1918. Returned to the US May 1919. Demobilized 10 Jun 1919 at Ft. D. A. Russell, WY.

**342nd Field Artillery**    Organized 5 Sep 1917 at Camp Funston, KS, as component of 89th Division (164th FA Brigade) [155mm howitzer]. Moved overseas Jun 1918. Returned to the US May 1919. Demobilized 10 Jun 1919 at Camp Funston.

**343rd Field Artillery**    Organized 29 Aug 1917 at Camp Travis, TX, as component of 90th Division (165th FA Brigade) [75mm gun]. Moved overseas Jun 1918. Returned to the US Jun 1919 and demobilized 19 Jun 1919 at Camp Pike, AR.

**344th Field Artillery**    Organized Aug 1917 at Camp Travis, TX, as component of 90th Division (165th FA Brigade) [75mm gun]. Moved overseas Jun 1918. Returned to the US Jun 1919 and demobilized 27 Jun 1919 at Camp Bowie, TX.

**345th Field Artillery**    Organized 29 Aug 1917 at Camp Travis, TX, as component of 90th Division (165th FA Brigade) [155mm howitzer]. Moved overseas Jun 1918. Returned to the US Jun 1919 and demobilized 23 Jun 1919 at Camp Bowie, TX.

**346th Field Artillery**    Organized Sep 1917 at Camp Lewis, WA, as component of 91st Division (166th FA Brigade) [4.7" gun]. Moved overseas Jul 1918. Returned to the US Jan 1919. Demobilized 8 Feb 1919 at Camp Lewis.

**347th Field Artillery**     Organized Sep 1917 at Camp Lewis, WA, as
component of 91st Division (166th FA Brigade) [4.7" gun]. Moved
overseas Jul 1918.  Returned to the US Mar 1919. Demobilized 29 Apr
1919 at the Presidio of San Francisco, CA.

**348th Field Artillery**     Organized Sep 1917 at Camp Lewis, WA, as
component of 91st Division (166th FA Brigade) [155mm howitzer].
Moved overseas Jul 1918.  Returned to the US Mar 1919.  Demobilized
20 Apr 1919 at Ft. D. A. Russell, WY.

**349th Field Artillery**     Organized 2 Nov 1917 with black enlisted personnel at
Camp Dix, NJ, as component of 92nd Division (167th FA Brigade)
[75mm gun].  Moved overseas Jun 1918.  Returned to the US Mar
1919 and demobilized 18 Mar 1919 at Camp Dix.

**350th Field Artillery**     Organized 2 Nov 1917 with black enlisted personnel at
Camp Dix, NJ, as component of 92nd Division (167th FA Brigade)
[75mm gun].  Moved overseas Jun 1918.  Returned to the US Mar
1919 and demobilized 12 Mar 1919 at Camp Dix.

**351st Field Artillery**     Organized 26 Oct 1917 with black enlisted personnel
at Camp Meade, MD, as component of 92nd Division (167th FA
Brigade) [155mm howitzer].  Moved overseas Jun 1918.  Returned to
the US Feb 1919.  Demobilized 6 Mar 1919 at Camp Meade.

[Numbers 352 to 354 and 355 to 357 would have gone to 93rd and 94th
Divisions, neither of which were formed]

[Numbers 358 to 366 would have gone to 95th to 97th Divisions, but their field
artillery brigades used National Army regiments formed in the 61 to 69 series]

[367th to 381st Field Artillery were constituted for the 98th to 102nd Divisions
(173rd to 177th FA Brigades) but never organized]

*Field Artillery Battalion*

**Separate Bn of Mountain Artillery**               Organized 10 Jul 1918 at
Corozal, Panama CZ.

## Trench Artillery

*Trench Mortar Battalions*

**1st Trench Mortar Bn**               Organized Dec 1917 at Jackson Barracks, LA
[Corps troops] (Bty B formed from 5th Coy, CD of Mobile).
Moved overseas Mar 1918.  Served with I and IV Army Corps.
Returned to the US Feb 1919. Demobilized Mar 1919 at Camp
Upton, NY.

**2<sup>nd</sup> Trench Mortar Bn**      Organized Jan 1918 at Ft. Monroe, VA[Corps troops]. Moved overseas May 1918. Served with IV Army Corps. Returned to the US Apr 1919 and demobilized at Camp Upton, NY.

**3<sup>rd</sup> Trench Mortar Bn**      Organized Apr 1918 at Ft. Crockett, TX [Corps troops]. Moved overseas Jul 1918. Returned to the US Jan 1919 and demobilized at Ft. DuPont, DE.

**4<sup>th</sup> Trench Mortar Bn**      Organized Jun 1918 at Camp Eustis, VA [Corps troops]. Moved overseas Oct 1918. Returned to the US Jan 1919. Demobilized Feb 1919 at Ft. Howard, MD.

**5<sup>th</sup> Trench Mortar Bn**      Organized Aug 1918 at Ft. Hancock, NJ [Corps troops]. Moved overseas Sep 1918. Returned to the US Jan 1919 and demobilized at Ft. Hamilton, NY.

**6<sup>th</sup> Trench Mortar Bn**      Organized Oct 1918 at Ft. Caswell, NC [Corps troops]. Moved overseas Nov 1918. Returned to the US Jan 1919 and demobilized at Ft. Monroe, VA.

**7<sup>th</sup> Trench Mortar Bn**      Organized Oct 1918 at Ft. DuPont, DE [Corps troops]. Moved overseas Oct 1918. Returned to the US Jan 1919 and demobilized at Ft. Monroe, VA.

**8<sup>th</sup> Trench Mortar Bn**      Organized Nov 1918 at Ft. Moultire, SC and demobilized there Dec 1918.

**9<sup>th</sup> Trench Mortar Bn**      Organized Nov 1918 at Camp Nicholls, LA and demobilized there Dec 1918.

*Trench Mortar Batteries*[70]

**1<sup>st</sup> Trench Mortar Bty**      Organized Jun 1917 at Ft. DuPont, DE and assigned 1<sup>st</sup> Division (1<sup>st</sup> FA Brigade) (formed from 5<sup>th</sup> Coy, Ft. DuPont, CAC). Moved overseas Aug 1917. Returned to the US Apr 1919. Demobilized May 1919 at Camp Upton, NY.

**2<sup>nd</sup> Trench Mortar Bty**      Organized Oct 1917 at Gettysburg, PA and assigned 2<sup>nd</sup> Division (2<sup>nd</sup> FA Brigade). Moved overseas Dec 1917. Returned to the US Apr 1919 and demobilized at Camp Dix, NJ.

**3<sup>rd</sup> Trench Mortar Bty**      Organized Nov 1917 at Camp Stanley, TX and assigned 3<sup>rd</sup> Division (3<sup>rd</sup> FA Brigade). Moved overseas Apr 1918. Returned to the US Mar 1919 and demobilized at Camp Stuart, VA.

**4<sup>th</sup> Trench Mortar Bty**      Organized Dec 1917 at Camp Greene, NC and assigned 4<sup>th</sup> Division (4<sup>th</sup> FA Brigade). Moved overseas May 1918. Returned to the US Apr 1919 and demobilized at Camp Dix, NJ.

---

[70] The 1<sup>st</sup> to 8<sup>th</sup> were probably constituted in the Regular Army; 9<sup>th</sup> to 26<sup>th</sup> probably in the National Army (15<sup>th</sup> to 26<sup>th</sup> certainly so); 101<sup>st</sup> to 117<sup>th</sup> in the National Guard; and 301<sup>st</sup> on up in the National Army.

**5<sup>th</sup> Trench Mortar Bty**       Organized Dec 1917 at Camp Stanley, TX and assigned 5<sup>th</sup> Division (5<sup>th</sup> FA Brigade). Moved overseas Jun 1918. Returned to the US Mar 1919 and demobilized at Camp Upton, NY.

**6<sup>th</sup> Trench Mortar Bty**       Organized Feb 1918 at Camp McClellan, AL and assigned 6<sup>th</sup> Division (6<sup>th</sup> FA Brigade). Moved overseas Jul 1918. Returned to the US Apr 1919 and demobilized at Camp Dix, NJ.

**7<sup>th</sup> Trench Mortar Bty**       Organized Apr 1918 at Camp Wheeler, BA and assigned 7<sup>th</sup> Division (7<sup>th</sup> FA Brigade). Moved overseas Aug 1918. Returned to the US Jan 1919 and demobilized at Camp Merritt, NJ.

**8<sup>th</sup> Trench Mortar Bty**       Organized May 1918 at Camp Fremont, CA and assigned 8<sup>th</sup> Division (8<sup>th</sup> FA Brigade). Moved overseas Oct 1918. Returned to the US Jan 1919. Demobilized Feb 1919 at Camp Knox, KY.

**9<sup>th</sup> Trench Mortar Bty**       Organized Aug 1918 at Camp McClellan, AL and assigned 9<sup>th</sup> Division (9<sup>th</sup> FA Brigade). Demobilized Feb 1919 at Camp McClellan.

**10<sup>th</sup> Trench Mortar Bty**       Organized Aug 1918 at Camp Funston, KS and assigned 10<sup>th</sup> Division (10<sup>th</sup> FA Brigade). Demobilized Jan 1919 at Camp Funston.

**11<sup>th</sup> Trench Mortar Bty**       Organized Aug 1918 at Camp Meade, MD and assigned 11<sup>th</sup> Division (11<sup>th</sup> FA Brigade). Demobilized Dec 1918 at Camp Meade.

**12<sup>th</sup> Trench Mortar Bty**       Organized Aug 1918 at Camp McClellan, AL and assigned 12<sup>th</sup> Division (12<sup>th</sup> FA Brigade). Demobilized Jan 1919 at Camp McClellan.

**13<sup>th</sup> Trench Mortar Bty**       Organized Aug 1918 at Camp Lewis, WA and assigned 13<sup>th</sup> Division (13<sup>th</sup> FA Brigade). Demobilized Feb 1919 at Camp Lewis.

**14<sup>th</sup> Trench Mortar Bty**       Organized Aug 1918 at Camp Custer, MI and assigned 14<sup>th</sup> Division (14<sup>th</sup> FA Brigade). Demobilized Feb 1919 at Camp Custer.

**15<sup>th</sup> Trench Mortar Bty**       Organized 27 Aug 1918 at Camp Stanley, TX by conversion and redesignation of element 305<sup>th</sup> Cavalry; assigned 15<sup>th</sup> Division (15<sup>th</sup> FA Brigade). Demobilized 17 Feb 1919 at Camp Stanley.

**16<sup>th</sup> Trench Mortar Bty**       Organized 27 Aug 1918 at Camp Kearny by conversion and redesignation of element 301<sup>st</sup> Cavalry; assigned 16<sup>th</sup> Division (16<sup>th</sup> FA Brigade). Demobilized 15 Feb 1919 at Camp Kearny.

**17<sup>th</sup> Trench Mortar Bty**       Organized 20 Aug 1918 at Camp Bowie, TX by conversion and redesignation of element 306<sup>th</sup> Cavalry; assigned 17<sup>th</sup> Division (17<sup>th</sup> FA Brigade). Moved Nov 1918 to Ft. Sill OK and demobilized there 8 Feb 1919.

**18<sup>th</sup> Trench Mortar Bty**        Organized 14 Aug 1918 at Camp Travis, TX by conversion and redesignation of element 303<sup>rd</sup> Cavalry; assigned 18<sup>th</sup> Division (18<sup>th</sup> FA Brigade).  Demobilized 13 Feb 1919 at Camp Travis.

**19<sup>th</sup> Trench Mortar Bty**        Organized 18 Aug 1918 at Camp Bowie, TX by conversion and redesignation of element 309<sup>th</sup> Cavalry; assigned 19<sup>th</sup> Division (19<sup>th</sup> FA Brigade).  Moved Oct 1918 to Ft. Sill, OK and demobilized there 12 Feb 1919.

**20<sup>th</sup> Trench Mortar Bty**        Organized 18 Oct 1918 at Ft. Ethan Allen, VT by conversion and redesignation of element 310<sup>th</sup> Cavalry; assigned 20<sup>th</sup> Division (20<sup>th</sup> FA Brigade).  Moved Nov 1918 to Camp Jackson, SC and demobilized there 10 Feb 1919.

**21<sup>st</sup> Trench Mortar Bty**        Organized 18 Oct 1918 at Ft. Bliss, TX by conversion and redesignation of element 314<sup>th</sup> Cavalry; assigned 97<sup>th</sup> Division (172<sup>nd</sup> FA Brigade).  Demobilized 2 Jan 1919 at Camp Jackson, SC.

**22<sup>nd</sup> Trench Mortar Bty**        Organized 13 Sep 1918 at Camp Kearny, CA by conversion and redesignation of element 308<sup>th</sup> Cavalry; assigned 96<sup>th</sup> Division (171<sup>st</sup> FA Brigade).  Demobilized 21 Dec 1918 at Camp Kearny.

**23<sup>rd</sup> Trench Mortar Bty**        Organized 1 Sep 1918 by conversion and redesignation of element 311<sup>th</sup> Cavalry; assigned 95<sup>th</sup> Division (170<sup>th</sup> FA Brigade).  Demobilized 22 Dec 1918 at Camp Knox, KY.

**24<sup>th</sup> Trench Mortar Bty**        Organized 19 Aug 1918 at Camp Knox, KY by conversion and redesignation of element 315<sup>th</sup> Cavalry; assigned 24<sup>th</sup> FA Brigade.  Demobilized 30 Jan 1919 at Camp Knox.

**25<sup>th</sup> Trench Mortar Bty**        Organized 15 Aug 1918 at Camp Stanley, TX by conversion and redesignation of element 304<sup>th</sup> Cavalry; assigned 100<sup>th</sup> Division (175<sup>th</sup> FA Brigade), but never joined.  Demobilized 11 Dec 1918 at Camp Stanley.

**26<sup>th</sup> Trench Mortar Bty**        Organized 23 Aug 1918 at Camp Knox, KY by conversion and redesignation of element 313<sup>th</sup> Cavalry; assigned 98<sup>th</sup> Division (173<sup>rd</sup> FA Brigade) but never joined it.  Demobilized 21 Dec 1918 at Camp Knox.

**27<sup>th</sup> Trench Mortar Bty**        Organized 17 Aug 1918 at Camp Bowie, TX by conversion and redesignation of element 307<sup>th</sup> Cavalry; assigned 101<sup>st</sup> Division (176<sup>th</sup> FA Brigade) but never joined it.  Demobilize 4 Dec 1918 at Camp Bowie.

**28<sup>th</sup> Trench Mortar Bty**        Organized 14 Aug 1918 at Ft. Sheridan, IL by conversion and redesignation of Ft. A. D. Russell, WY element 312<sup>th</sup> Cavalry; assigned 99<sup>th</sup> Division (174<sup>th</sup> FA Brigade) but never joined it. Moved Oct 1918 to Camp Jackson, SC and demobilized there 17 Dec 1918.

**29ᵗʰ Trench Mortar Bty**     Organized 26 Aug 1918 at Camp Kearny, CA by conversion and redesignation of element 302ⁿᵈ Cavalry; assigned 102ⁿᵈ Division (177ᵗʰ FA Brigade) but never joined it. Demobilized 20 Dec 1918 at Camp Kearny.

**101ˢᵗ Trench Mortar Bty**     Organized Aug 1917 at Brunswick, ME as component of 26ᵗʰ Division (51ˢᵗ FA Brigade) (formed with personnel from 1ˢᵗ Heavy Field Artillery, ME NG). Moved overseas Oct 1917. Returned to the US Mar 1919 and demobilized at Camp Devens, MA.

**102ⁿᵈ Trench Mortar Bty**     Organized Oct 1917 at Camp Wadsworth, SC as component of 27ᵗʰ Division (52ⁿᵈ FA Brigade) (formed from one troop and other personnel, 1ˢᵗ Cavalry, NY NG). Moved overseas Jun 1918. Returned to the US Jan 1919. Demobilized Feb 1919 at Camp Upton, NY.

**103ʳᵈ Trench Mortar Bty**     Organized Dec 1917 at Camp Hancock, GA as component of 28ᵗʰ Division (53ʳᵈ FA Brigade) (formed with personnel from 1ˢᵗ Cavalry, PA NG). Moved overseas May 1918. Returned to the US Mar 1919. Demobilized Apr 1919 at Camp Dix, NJ.

**104ᵗʰ Trench Mortar Bty**     Organized Sep 1917 at Camp McClellan, AL as component of 29ᵗʰ Division (54ᵗʰ FA Brigade) (formed from a battery, Field Artillery, NJ NG). Moved overseas Jul 1918. Returned to the US Mar 1919 and demobilized at Camp Dix, NJ.

**105ᵗʰ Trench Mortar Bty**     Organized Sep 1917 at Camp Sevier, SC as component of 30ᵗʰ Division (55ᵗʰ FA Brigade) (formed from troop, 1ˢᵗ Sqn, Cavalry, TN NG). Moved overseas May 1918. Returned to the US Mar 1919 and demobilized at Ft. Oglethorpe, GA.

**106ᵗʰ Trench Mortar Bty**     Organized Sep 1917 at Camp Wheeler, GA as component of 31ˢᵗ Division (56ᵗʰ FA Brigade) (formed from troop, 1ˢᵗ Cavalry, AL NG). Moved overseas Oct 1918. Returned to the US Jan 1919 and demobilized at Camp Gordon, GA.

**107ᵗʰ Trench Mortar Bty**     Organized Oct 1917 at Camp MacArthur, TX as component of 32ⁿᵈ Division (57ᵗʰ FA Brigade) (formed with personnel from 4ᵗʰ Infantry, WI NG). Moved overseas Feb 1918. Returned to the US May 1919 and demobilized at Camp Grant, IL.

**108ᵗʰ Trench Mortar Bty**     Organized Oct 1917 at Camp Logan, TX as component of 33ʳᵈ Division (58ᵗʰ FA Brigade) (formed from company, 6ᵗʰ Infantry, IL NG). Moved overseas May 1918. Returned to the US Mar 1919 and demobilized at Camp Grant, IL.

**109ᵗʰ Trench Mortar Bty**     Organized Oct 1917 at Camp Cody, NM as component of 34ᵗʰ Division (59ᵗʰ FA Brigade) (formed from elements 2ⁿᵈ Infantry, IA NG). Moved overseas Sep 1918. Returned to the US Jan 1919 and demobilized at Camp Dodge, IA.

**110$^{th}$ Trench Mortar Bty**        Organized Oct 1917 at Camp Doniphan, OK as component of 35$^{th}$ Division (60$^{th}$ FA Brigade) (formed from elements 2$^{nd}$ Infantry, MO NG).  Moved overseas May 1918.  Returned to the US Apr 1919.  Demobilized May 1919 at Camp Funston, KS.

**111$^{th}$ Trench Mortar Bty**        Organized Oct 1917 at Camp Bowie, TX as component of 36$^{th}$ Division (61$^{st}$ FA Brigade) (formed from troop, 1$^{st}$ Cavalry, TX NG).  Moved overseas Aug 1918.  Returned to the US Mar 1919.  Demobilized Apr 1919 at Camp Travis, TX.

**112$^{th}$ Trench Mortar Bty**        Organized Sep 1917 at Camp Sheridan, AL as component of 37$^{th}$ Division (62$^{nd}$ FA Brigade) (formed from elements 10$^{th}$ Infantry, OH NG).  Moved overseas Jun 1918.  Returned to the US Apr 1919.  Demobilized May 1919 at Camp Sherman, OH.

**113$^{th}$ Trench Mortar Bty**        Organized Oct 1917 at Camp Shelby, MS as component of 38$^{th}$ Division (63$^{rd}$ FA Brigade) (formed from company, 1$^{st}$ Infantry, KY NG).  Moved overseas Oct 1918.  Returned to the US Jan 1919 and demobilized at Camp Zachary Taylor, KY.

**114$^{th}$ Trench Mortar Bty**        Organized Nov 1917 at Camp Beauregard, LA as component of 39$^{th}$ Division (64$^{th}$ FA Brigade) (formed with personnel from 1$^{st}$ Field Artillery, LA NG).  Moved overseas Aug 1918.  Returned to the US Jan 1919.  Demobilized Feb 1919 at Camp Beauregard.

**115$^{th}$ Trench Mortar Bty**        Organized Oct 1917 at Camp Kearny, CA as component of 40$^{th}$ Division (65$^{th}$ FA Brigade) (formed from company, 2$^{nd}$ Infantry, CO NG).  Moved overseas Aug 1918.  Returned to the US Jan 1919 and demobilized at the Presidio of San Francisco, CA.

**116$^{th}$ Trench Mortar Bty**        Organized Oct 1917 at Camp Greene, NC as component of 41$^{st}$ Division (66$^{th}$ FA Brigade) (formed from company, 2$^{nd}$ Infantry, ND NG).  Moved overseas Jan 1918.  Returned to the US Mar 1919 and demobilized at Camp Dodge, IA.

**117$^{th}$ Trench Mortar Bty**        Organized Sep 1917 at Camp Mills, NY as component of 42$^{nd}$ Division (67$^{th}$ FA Brigade) (formed from two coast artillery companies, MD NG).  Moved overseas Oct 1917.  Returned to the US Apr 1919.  Demobilized May 1919 at Camp Meade, MD.

**301$^{st}$ Trench Mortar Bty**        Organized Aug 1917 at Camp Devens, MA as component of 76$^{th}$ Division (151$^{st}$ FA Brigade).  Moved overseas Jul 1918.  Returned to the US Jan 1919.  Demobilized Feb 1919 at Camp Devens.

**302$^{nd}$ Trench Mortar Bty**        Organized Sep 1917 at Camp Upton, NY as component of 77$^{th}$ Division (152$^{nd}$ FA Brigade).  Moved overseas Apr 1918.  Returned to the US Feb 1919.  Demobilized Mar 1919 at Camp Upton.

**303<sup>rd</sup> Trench Mortar Bty**    Organized Sep 1917 at Camp Dix, NJ as component of 78th Division (153rd FA Brigade).  Moved overseas May 1918.  Returned to the US Apr 1919.  Demobilized May 1919 at Camp Dix.

**304<sup>th</sup> Trench Mortar Bty**    Organized Sep 1917 at Camp Meade, MD as component of 79th Division (154th FA Brigade).  Moved overseas Jul 1918.  Returned to the US Mar 1919 and demobilized at Camp Dix, NJ.

**305<sup>th</sup> Trench Mortar Bty**    Organized Sep 1917 at Camp Lee, VA as component of 80th Division (155th FA Brigade).  Moved overseas May 1918.  Returned to the US Feb 1919.  Demobilized Mar 1919 at Camp Lee.

**306<sup>th</sup> Trench Mortar Bty**    Organized Sep 1917 at Camp Jackson, SC as component of 81st Division (156th FA Brigade).  Moved overseas Jul 1918.  Returned to the US Mar 1919.  Demobilized Apr 1919 at Camp Lee, Va.

**307<sup>th</sup> Trench Mortar Bty**    Organized Sep 1917 at Camp Gordon, GA as component of 82nd Division (157th FA Brigade).  Moved overseas May 1918.  Returned to the US Mar 1919 and demobilized at Camp Dix, NJ.

**308<sup>th</sup> Trench Mortar Bty**    Organized Sep 1917 at Camp Sherman, OH as component of 83rd Division (158th FA Brigade).  Moved overseas Jun 1918.  Returned to the US Apr 1919.  Demobilized May 1919 at Camp Sherman.

**309<sup>th</sup> Trench Mortar Bty**    Organized Aug 1917 at Camp Zachary Taylor, KY as component of 84th Division (159th FA Brigade).  Moved overseas Sep 1918.  Returned to the US Jan 1919 and demobilized at Camp Zachary Taylor.

**310<sup>th</sup> Trench Mortar Bty**    Organized Nov 1917 at Camp Custer, MI as component of 85th Division (160th FA Brigade).  Moved overseas Jul 1918.  Returned to the US Mar 1919 and demobilized at Camp Custer.

**311<sup>th</sup> Trench Mortar Bty**    Organized Sep 1917 at Camp Grant, IL as component of 86th Division (161st FA Brigade).  Moved overseas Sep 1918.  Returned to the US Jan 1919 and demobilized at Camp Stuart, Va.

**312<sup>th</sup> Trench Mortar Bty**    Organized Sep 1917 at Camp Pike, AR as component of 87th Division (162nd FA Brigade).  Moved overseas Aug 1918.  Returned to the US Mar 1919 and demobilized at Camp Dodge, IA.

**313<sup>th</sup> Trench Mortar Bty**    Organized Sep 1917 at Camp Dodge, IA as component of 88th Division (163rd FA Brigade).  Moved overseas Aug 1918.  Returned to the US Jan 1919 and demobilized at Camp Dodge.

**314th Trench Mortar Bty**    Organized Sep 1917 at Camp Funston, KS as component of 89th Division (164th FA Brigade). Moved overseas Jun 1918. Returned to the US Mar 1919 and demobilized at Camp Dodge, IA.

**315th Trench Mortar Bty**    Organized Sep 1917 at Camp Travis, TX as component of 90th Division (165th FA Brigade). Moved overseas Jun 1918. Returned to the US Mar 1919. Demobilized Apr 1919 at Camp Bowie, TX.

**316th Trench Mortar Bty**    Organized Oct 1917 at Camp Lewis, WA as component of 91st Division (166th FA Brigade). Moved overseas Jul 1918. Returned to the US Mar 1919 and demobilized at Camp Lewis.

**317th Trench Mortar Bty**    Organized May 1918 [with black enlisted personnel] at Camp Dix, NJ as component of 92nd Division (167th FA Brigade). Moved overseas Jun 1918. Returned to the US Feb 1919. Demobilized Mar 1919 at Camp Shelby, MS.

[Numbers 318 and 319 would have gone to 93rd and 94th Divisions had they been organized]

[Numbers 320 to 327 would have gone to the 95th to 102nd Divisions, but the 21st, 23rd and 25th to 29th Trench Mortar Btys were organized and assigned instead]


# Coast Artillery[71]

*Artillery Brigades*

**1st Expeditionary Brigade**    *See* 30th Separate Artillery Brigade

**30th Separate Artillery Brigade (Railway)**    Organized Jul 1917 at Ft. Adams, RI as 1st Expeditionary Brigade, CAC. Moved overseas Aug 1917. Redesignated Sep 1917 as 1st Brigade, CAC. Redesignated Mar 1918 as 30th Separate Artillery Brigade (Railway). First Army Sep-Oct 1918 then Railway Artillery Reserve, AEF. Returned to the US Jan 1919 and moved to Camp Eustis, VA.

**31st Heavy Artillery Brigade**    Organized Jan 1918 at Key West, FL. Moved overseas Mar 1918. III Army Corps Aug 1918. First Army Oct-Nov 1918. Returned to the US Feb 1919 and moved to Camp Lewis, WA.

---

[71] The Coast Artillery Corps was a distinct branch from the Field Artillery. Many of its units were separate companies, assigned to various posts on coast defence duties. The regimental numbers originally used (from 41 up) had not been used by Field Artillery; however, the creation of new field artillery regiments in 1918 resulted in a duplication of regimental numbers between the two branches. The heavy artillery for the AEF came from the Coast Artillery Corps because it was used to guns of large caliber and the Field Artillery had no interest in them.

**32nd Artillery Brigade** Organized Jan 1918 at Key West, FL. Moved overseas Mar 1918. First Army Sep-Nov 1918. Returned to the US Dec 1918 and demobilized Jan 1919 at Camp Hill, VA.

**33rd Artillery Brigade** Organized Mar 1918 at Ft. Winfield Scott, CA. Moved overseas Jul 1918. Returned to the US Feb 1919 and demobilized at Ft. Monroe, VA.

**34th Artillery Brigade** Organized Feb 1918 at Ft. Adams, RI. Moved overseas Jul 1918. Returned to the US Feb 1919 and demobilized at Ft. Wadsworth, NY.

**35th Artillery Brigade** Organized Ft. Hunt, VA. Moved overseas Aug 1918. Returned to the US Mar 1919 and demobilized at Ft. Totten, NY.

**36th Artillery Brigade** Organized Jun 1918 at Ft. DuPont, DE. Moved overseas Aug 1918. Returned to the US Mar 1919 and demobilized at Ft. Totten, NY.

**37th Artillery Brigade** Organized Oct 1918 at Camp Eustis, VA. Moved overseas Nov 1918. Returned to the US Feb 1919 and demobilized at Ft. Totten, NY.

**38th Artillery Brigade** Organized Sep 1918 at Camp Eustis, VA. Moved overseas Oct 1918. Returned to the US Feb 1919 and demobilized at Ft. Monroe, VA.

**39th Artillery Brigade** Organized Aug 1918 in the AEF. First Army Sep-Oct and then Second Army Oct-Nov 1918. Moved to the US Jan 1919 and moved to Camp Jackson, SC.

**40th Artillery Brigade** Organized Aug 1918 at Ft. Hamilton, NY. Moved overseas Sep 1918. Railway Artillery Reserve, AEF. Returned to the US Dec 1918 and demobilized at Ft. Hamilton.

**41st Artillery Brigade** Organized Sep 1918 at Ft. Totten, NY. Demobilized Dec 1918 at Ft. Wadsworth, NY.

**42nd Artillery Brigade** Organized Oct 1918 at Ft. Strong, MA. Demobilized Dec 1918 at Camp Eustis, VA.

**43rd Artillery Brigade** Organized Oct 1918 at Ft. Hamilton, NY. Demobilized Dec 1918 at Camp Eustis, VA.

**44th Artillery Brigade** Organized Nov 1918 at Ft. Monroe, VA. Demobilized Dec 1918 at Ft. Monroe.

**45th Artillery Brigade** Organized Nov 1918 at Ft. Strong, MA. Demobilized Dec 1918 at Ft. Revere, MA.

[46th to 48th Artillery Brigades were authorized but never organized]

*Coast Artillery Regiments*[72]

**Howitzer Regiment, 30<sup>th</sup> Brigade, CAC**      *See* 44<sup>th</sup> Artillery (Coast
Artillery Corps)

**6<sup>th</sup> Provisional Regiment, CAC**      *See* 51<sup>st</sup> Artillery (Coast Artillery
Corps)

**7<sup>th</sup> Provisional Regiment, CAC**      *See* 52<sup>nd</sup> Artillery (Coast Artillery
Corps)

**8<sup>th</sup> Provisional Regiment, CAC**      *See* 53<sup>rd</sup> Artillery (Coast Artillery
Corps)

**15<sup>th</sup> Artillery (Coast Artillery Corps)**      Organized Oct 1918 at Ft.
Crockett, TX.  Demobilized Nov 1918 at Ft. Crockett.

**17<sup>th</sup> Artillery (Coast Artillery Corps)**      Organized Oct 1918 at Ft.
Monroe, VA.  Demobilized Jan 1919 at Ft. Monroe.

**18<sup>th</sup> Artillery (Coast Artillery Corps)**      Organized Oct 1918 at Ft.
Winfield Scott, CA.[73]  Demobilized Dec 1918 at Ft. Winfield Scott.

**19<sup>th</sup> Artillery (Coast Artillery Corps)**      Organized Oct 1918 at Ft.
MacArthur, CA.[74]  Demobilized Dec 1918 at Ft. MacArthur.

**20<sup>th</sup> Artillery (Coast Artillery Corps)**      Organized Oct 1918 at Ft.
Crockett, TX.  Demobilized Nov 1918 at Ft. Crockett

**21<sup>st</sup> Artillery (Coast Artillery Corps)**      Organized Nov 1918 at Ft.
Pickens, FL.  Demobilized Dec 1918 at Ft. Pickens.

**25<sup>th</sup> Artillery (Coast Artillery Corps)**      Organized Oct 1918 at Ft.
Rosecrans, CA.[75]  Demobilized Dec 1918 at Ft. Rosecrans.

**26<sup>th</sup> Artillery (Coast Artillery Corps)**      Organized Nov 1918 at Ft.
Screven, GA.  Demobilized Dec 1918 at Ft. Screven.

**27<sup>th</sup> Artillery (Coast Artillery Corps)**      Organized Oct 1918 at Ft.
Stevens, OR.  Demobilized Dec 1918 at Camp Eustis, VA.

**28<sup>th</sup> Artillery (Coast Artillery Corps)**      Organized Nov 1918 at Ft.
Strong, MA.  Demobilized Dec 1918 at Ft. Revere, MA.

**29<sup>th</sup> Artillery (Coast Artillery Corps)**      Organized Nov 1918 at Ft.
Williams, ME.  Demobilized Dec 1918 at Ft. Williams.

---

[72] While officially designated as "Artillery (Coast Artillery Corps)" the regiments were commonly referred to as "Coast Artillery."

[73] 12<sup>th</sup>, 16<sup>th</sup>, 19<sup>th</sup> 27<sup>th</sup> and 45<sup>th</sup> Coys, C.D. of San Francisco (27<sup>th</sup> ex CA NG) formed Btys A, B, C, D and F, 18<sup>th</sup> CA.

[74] 13<sup>th</sup>, 11<sup>th</sup>, 14<sup>th</sup>, 18<sup>th</sup>, 19<sup>th</sup> and 20<sup>th</sup> Coys, C.D. of Los Angeles formed Btys B, A, C, D, E, and F, 19<sup>th</sup> CA. Some reverted to former designations on demobilization of the regiment.

[75] 4<sup>th</sup>, 6<sup>th</sup>, 7<sup>th</sup> and 8<sup>th</sup> Coys, C.D. of San Diego (all but 4<sup>th</sup> ex CA NG) formed Btys A, E, B and F, respectively, of 25<sup>th</sup> CA.

**30th Artillery (Coast Artillery Corps)**  Organized Nov 1918 at Ft. H. G. Wright, NY. Demobilized Dec 1918 at Camp Eustis, VA.

**31st Artillery (Coast Artillery Corps)**  Organized Oct 1918 at Ft. Hancock, NJ. Demobilized Dec 1918 at Camp Eustis, VA.

**32nd Artillery (Coast Artillery Corps)**  Organized Oct 1918 at Ft. Hamilton, NY. Demobilized Dec 1918 at Camp Eustis, VA.

**33rd Artillery (Coast Artillery Corps)**  Organized Sep 1918 at Ft. Strong, MA. Demobilized Dec 1918 at Camp Eustis, VA.

**34th Artillery (Coast Artillery Corps)**  Organized Oct 1918 at Ft. Totten, NY. Demobilized Dec 1918 at Camp Eustis, VA.

**35th Artillery (Coast Artillery Corps)**  Organized Nov 1918 at Ft. DuPont, DE. Demobilized Dec 1918 at Ft. DuPont.

**36th Artillery (Coast Artillery Corps)**  Organized Sep 1918 at Ft. Moultrie, SC. Demobilized Dec 1918 at Ft. Monroe.

**37th Artillery (Coast Artillery Corps)**  Organized Sep 1918 at Ft. Hanckock, NJ. Demobilized Dec 1918 at Ft. Hancock.

**38th Artillery (Coast Artillery Corps)**  Organized Sep 1918 at Ft. Hamilton, NY. Demobilized Dec 1918 at Ft. Hamilton.

**39th Artillery (Coast Artillery Corps)**  Organized Sep 1918 at Ft. Worden, OR. Demobilized Dec 1918 at  Camp Grant, IL.

**40th Artillery (Coast Artillery Corps)**  Organized Sep 1918 at Ft. Winfield Scott, CA.[76] Demobilized Jan 1919 at Presidio of San Francisco, CA.

**41st Artillery (Coast Artillery Corps)**  Organized 1 Oct 1918 at Ft. Monroe, VA. Demobilized 22 Dec 1918 at Ft. Monroe.

**42nd Artillery (Coast Artillery Corps)**  Organized 7 Aug 1918 in France from existing Regular Army units. Railway artillery unit [24cm] with 30th Brigade. (With 32nd Brig early Sep 1918.) Moved to the US Feb 1919 and moved to Camp Eustis, VA.

**43rd Artillery (Coast Artillery Corps)**  Organized 7 Aug 1918 in France from existing Regular Army units and one New York NG company. Railway artillery unit [19cm] with 30th Brigade. (With 32nd Brig early Sep 1918.) Moved to the US Dec 1918 and moved to Camp Eustis, VA. (NG company demobilized in Feb 1919; regiment continued on active status.)

---

[76] 2nd, 4th 15th and 29th Coys, C.D. of San Francisco (29th ex CA NG) formed Btys A, B, D and F, 40th CA. 6th and 18th Coys, C.D. of San Francisco formed Bty C, 40th CA.

**44th Artillery (Coast Artillery Corps)** Organized 26 Mar 1918 in France from existing Regular Army units as the Howitzer Regiment, 30th Brigade, CAC. [8" howitzers] Redesignated 7 Aug 1918 as 44th Artillery (CAC). Served with 32nd Brig and then 39th Brig, including support of IV Army Corps. Moved to the US Feb 1919 and moved to Ft. Totten, NY

**45th Artillery (Coast Artillery Corps)** Organized Jul 1918 at Camp Eustis, VA. Moved overseas Oct 1918. Returned to the US Jan 1919 and demobilized Feb 1919 at Camp Dix, NJ.

**46th Artillery (Coast Artillery Corps)** Organized Jul 1918 at Camp Eustis, VA. Moved overseas Oct 1918. Returned to the US Feb 1919 and demobilized Mar 1919 at Camp Dix, NJ.

**47th Artillery (Coast Artillery Corps)** Organized Jul 1918 at Camp Eustis, VA. Moved overseas Oct 1918. Returned to the US Feb 1919 and demobilized at Camp Eustis.

**48th Artillery (Coast Artillery Corps)** Organized Jul 1918 at Camp Eustis, VA. Moved overseas Oct 1918. Returned to the US Mar 1919 and demobilized at Camp Grant, IL.

**49th Artillery (Coast Artillery Corps)** Organized Jul 1918 at Camp Eustis, VA. Moved overseas Oct 1918. Returned to the US Mar 1919 and demobilized at Camp Grant, IL.

**50th Artillery (Coast Artillery Corps)** Organized Jul 1918 at Camp Eustis, VA. Moved overseas Oct 1918. Returned to the US Feb 1919 and demobilized Mar 1919 at Camp Dix, NJ.

**51st Artillery (Coast Artillery Corps)** Organized 21 Jul 1917 at Ft. Adams, RI from existing Regular Army units as 6th Provisional Regiment, CAC [240mm and 8" howitzer].[77] Moved overseas Aug 1917. Redesignated 5 Feb 1918 as 51st Artillery (CAC). Served with 32nd Brig and then 39th Brig, including support of IV Army Corps. Returned to the US Feb 1919 and moved to Camp Jackson, SC.

**52nd Artillery (Coast Artillery Corps)** Organized 22 Jul 1917 at Ft. Adams, RI from existing Regular Army units as 7th Provisional Regiment, CAC.[78] Moved overseas Aug 1917. Redesignated 5 Feb 1918 as 52nd Artillery (CAC). Railway artillery unit [32cm] with 30th Brigade. Returned to the US Jan 1919 and moved to Camp Eustis, VA.

---

[77] 2nd, 3rd and 4th Coys, Ft. Andrews, BO; 1st Coy, Ft. Baker, ME; 2nd Coy, Ft. Grable, RI; 1st and 5th Coys, Ft. McKinley, ME; 1st coy, Ft. Preble, ME; 3rd Coy, Ft. Strong, MA; and 2nd, 3rd and 4th Coys, Ft. William, ME were redesignated, respectively, as Btys I, L, M, K, B, A, D, E, C, H, G and F of 6th Provisional Regiment CAC.

[78] 2nd and 4th Coys, Ft. Adams, RI; 4th and 6th Coys, Ft. Hamilton, NY; 2nd Coy, Ft. Schuyler, NY; 2nd and 6th Coys, Ft. Terry, NY; 2nd and 6th Coys, Ft. totten, NY; and 1st, 2nd and 6th Coys, Ft. H. G. Wright, NY were redesignated, respectively, as Btys K, I, M, L, F,C, B, G, H, A, E and D of 7th Provisional Regiment CAC.

**53rd Artillery (Coast Artillery Corps)**          Organized Jul 1917 from existing Regular Army units as 8th Provisional Regiment, CAC.[79] Moved overseas Aug 1917. Redesignated 5 Feb 1918 as 53rd Artillery (CAC). Railway artillery unit [19cm, 340mm, 400mm] with 30th Brigade. Returned to the US Mar 1919 and moved to Camp Eustis, VA.

**54th Artillery (Coast Artillery Corps)**          Organized Jan 1918 at Coast Defenses of Portland (Hq at Ft. Williams, ME).[80] Moved overseas Mar 1918. Reorganized Sep 1918 into replacement battalions for heavy artillery. Regiment reformed Dec 1918 in AEF. Returned to the US Mar 1919 and demobilized at Camp Devens, MA.

**55th Artillery (Coast Artillery Corps)**          Organized 1 Dec 1917 at Boston, MA from existing Regular Army units and MA and RI NG companies [155mm gun].[81] Moved overseas Mar 1918. Served with 31st Brig, including support of III and V Army Corps. Returned to the US Jan 1919 and moved later to Camp Lewis, WA. (NG companies demobilized in Feb 1919; regiment continued on active status.)

**56th Artillery (Coast Artillery Corps)**          Organized Dec 1917 at Boston, MA from existing Regular Army units and CT NG companies [155mm gun].[82] Moved overseas Mar 1918. Served with 31st Brig, including support of III and V Army Corps. Returned to the US Jan 1919 and moved later to Camp Jackson, SC. (NG companies demobilized 20 Jan-1 Feb 1919 at St. Schuyler, NY.)

---

[79] 2nd Coy, Ft. Ceswell, NC; 3rd Coy, Ft. Hamilton, NY; 10th, 11th and 12th Coys, Ft. Monroe, VA; 2nd Coy, Ft. Moultrie, SC; 3rd Coy, Rockaway Beach, NY; 3rd Coy, Ft. Screven, GA; and 3rd Coy, Ft. Wadsworth, NY were redesignated, respectively, as Btys I, F, D, B, C, H, G, M, and E of 8th Provisional Regiment CAC.

[80] 18th and 19th Coys, C.D. of Portland, formed Bty B; 13th and 16th Coys, C.D. of Portland, formed Bty C; 8th, 22nd and 29th Coys, C.D. of Portland, formed Bty D; 24th and 27th Coys, C.D. of Portland, formed Bty E; and 25th and 26th Coys, C.D. of Portland, formed Bty F, 54th CA.

[81] 1st and 8th Coys, C.D. of Boston formed Btys A and C, 55th CA. 18th and 19th Coys, C.D. of Boston (ex MA NG) and 29th Coy, C.D. of Boston (ex RI NG) became Btys F, D and E, respectively, of 55th CA.

[82] 13th, 16th and 3rd Coys, C.D. of Long Island Sound formed Btys A, B and C, 56th Ca. 27th, 29th, 37th and 38th Coys, C.D. of Long Island Sound (all ex CT NG) became Btys F, E, B and D, 56th CA.

**57<sup>th</sup> Artillery (Coast Artillery Corps)**          Organized 11 Jan 1918 at Ft. Hancock, NJ from new and existing Regular Army units and NY NG companies [155mm gun].[83] Moved overseas Mar 1918. Served with 32<sup>nd</sup> and then 31<sup>st</sup> Brig, including support of V Army Corps. Returned to the US Jan 1919 and moved later to Camp Lewis, WA. (NG companies demobilized in Feb 1919; regiment continued on active status.)

**58<sup>th</sup> Artillery (Coast Artillery Corps)**          Organized Feb 1918 at Ft. Totten, NY[84] [8" howitzer]. Moved overseas Mar 1918. Served with 32<sup>nd</sup> Brig, including support of IV Army Corps. Returned to the US Apr 1919 and demobilized May 1919 at Camp Upton, NY.

**59<sup>th</sup> Artillery (Coast Artillery Corps)**          Organized 1 Jan 1918 at Ft. Hamilton, NY from existing Regular Army units and NY NG companies [8" howitzer].[85] Moved overseas Mar 1918. Served with 32<sup>nd</sup> Brig, including support of I and IV Army Corps. Returned to the US Jan 1919 and later moved to Camp Lewis, WA. (NG companies demobilized in Jan-Feb 1919; regiment continued on active status.)

**60<sup>th</sup> Artillery (Coast Artillery Corps)**          Organized 23 Dec 1917 at Ft. Monroe, VA from existing Regular Army units and NG companies from VA and DC [155mm gun].[86] Moved overseas Mar 1918. Served with 32<sup>nd</sup> and then 39<sup>th</sup> Brig, including support of I and III Army Corps. Returned to the US Feb 1919 and demobilized 24 Feb 1919 at Ft. Washington, MD.

**61<sup>st</sup> Artillery (Coast Artillery Corps)**          Organized 9 Mar 1918 at Ft. Moultrie, SC from existing Regular Army units and NG companies from GA and SC.[87] Moved overseas Jul 1918. Returned to the US Feb 1919 and demobilized 28 Feb 1919 at Camp Upton, NY.

**62<sup>nd</sup> Artillery (Coast Artillery Corps)**          Organized Jan 1918 at Coast Defenses of San Francisco (Hq at Ft. Winfield Scott, CA). Moved overseas Jul 1918. Returned to the US Feb 1919 and demobilized Mar 1919 at Camp Eustis, VA.

---

[83] NY NG coast artillery companies formed Btys E and F, and contributed personnel to Btys B and D as well.

[84] 5<sup>th</sup> Coy, C.D. of Baltimore formed Bty E, 58<sup>th</sup> CA. Personnel from MD NG coast artillery units helped to form Bty F.

[85] 2<sup>nd</sup> and 4<sup>th</sup> Coys, C.D. of Southern New York formed Btys C and A, 59<sup>th</sup> CA. 3<sup>rd</sup> and 4<sup>th</sup> CD Coys, NY NG formed Btys E and F, 59<sup>th</sup> CA and 6<sup>th</sup> CD Coy, NYNG was absorbed by the new regiment.

[86] 4<sup>th</sup> Coy, C.D. of Delaware became Bty A and 6<sup>th</sup> Coy, C.D. of Chesapeake Bay became Bty E, 60<sup>th</sup> CA. 1<sup>st</sup> CA Coy, DC NG became Bty D, 60<sup>th</sup> CA.

[87] 3<sup>rd</sup> Coy, C.D. of Savannah became Bty C, 61<sup>st</sup> CA.

**63<sup>rd</sup> Artillery (Coast Artillery Corps)** Organized Dec 1917 at Coast Defenses of Puget Sound (Hq at Ft. Worden, WA).[88] Moved overseas Jul 1918. Returned to the US Feb 1919 and demobilized Mar 1919 at Camp Lewis, WA.

**64<sup>th</sup> Artillery (Coast Artillery Corps)** Organized Jan 1918 at Coast Defenses of Tampa (Hq at Ft. Dade, FL). Moved overseas Jul 1918. Returned to the US Feb 1919 and demobilized Apr 1919 at Camp Eustis, VA.

**65<sup>th</sup> Artillery (Coast Artillery Corps)** Organized (less 1<sup>st</sup> Bn) 26 Dec 1917 at Ft. Stevens, OR from existing Regular Army units and a CA NG company.[89] (1<sup>st</sup> Bn organized 1 Jan 1918 at Ft. Rosecrans CA) [9.2"]. Moved overseas Mar 1918. Served with 32<sup>nd</sup> Brig, including support of I and V Army Corps. Returned to the US Jan 1919 and demobilized 28 Feb 1919 at Camp Lewis, WA.

**66<sup>th</sup> Artillery (Coast Artillery Corps)** Organized Mar 1918 at Coast Defenses of Narragansett Bay (Hq at Ft. Adams, RI). Moved overseas Jul 1918. Returned to the US Mar 1919 and demobilized at Camp Upton, NY.

**67<sup>th</sup> Artillery (Coast Artillery Corps)** Organized 21 May 1918 at Ft. Winfield Scott, CA from existing Regular Army units and CA NG companies.[90] Moved overseas Aug 1918. Returned to the US Mar 1919. Demobilized 23 Apr 1919 at the Presidio of San Francisco, CA.

**68<sup>th</sup> Artillery (Coast Artillery Corps)** Organized 1 Jun 1918 at Ft. Terry, NY. Moved overseas Aug 1918. Returned to the US Feb 1919 and demobilized 1 Mar 1919 at Ft. Wadsworth, NY.

**69<sup>th</sup> Artillery (Coast Artillery Corps)** Organized May 1918 at Coast Defenses of Puget Sound (Hq at Ft. Worden, WA). Moved overseas Aug 1918. Returned to the US Feb 1919 and demobilized at Camp Eustis, VA.

**70<sup>th</sup> Artillery (Coast Artillery Corps)** Organized Jun 1918 at Ft. Hamilton, NY. Moved overseas Jul 1918. Returned to the US Feb 1919 and demobilized Mar 1919 at Camp Sherman, OH.

**71<sup>st</sup> Artillery (Coast Artillery Corps)** Organized 12 May 1918 in the Coast Defenses of Boston (Hq at Ft. Strong, MA). Moved overseas Jul 1918. Returned to the US Feb 1919 and demobilized 6 Mar 1919 at Camp Devens, MA.

---

[88] WA NG coast artillery contributed personnel to Btys B, D and F.

[89] 2<sup>nd</sup> Coy, C.D. of San Diego formed Bty A, 65<sup>th</sup> CA. 6<sup>th</sup> Coy, C.D. of San Diego (ex CA NG) formed Bty B, 65<sup>th</sup> CA. OR NG coast artillery also contributed personnel to the regiment, especially to Bty C; WA NG coast artillery also contributed to Bty F.

[90] 13<sup>th</sup>, 14<sup>th</sup>, 17<sup>th</sup>, 26<sup>th</sup>, 28<sup>th</sup> and 7<sup>th</sup> Coys, C.D. of San Francisco (26<sup>th</sup>, 28<sup>th</sup> and 7<sup>th</sup> ex CA NG) formed Btys A, E, F, B, D, and C, 67<sup>th</sup> CA.

**72<sup>nd</sup> Artillery (Coast Artillery Corps)**          Organized Jun 1918in the
          Coast Defenses of Portland (Hq and Ft. Williams, ME).  Moved
          overseas Aug 1918.  Returned to the US Mar 1919 and demobilized
          Apr 1919 at Camp Grant, IL.

**73<sup>rd</sup> Artillery (Coast Artillery Corps)**          Organized Jul 1918 at Ft.
          Banks, MA.  Moved overseas Sep 1918.  Railway artillery unit with
          40<sup>th</sup> Brigade.  Returned to the US Dec 1918 and demobilized Jan 1919
          at Camp Devens, MA.

**74<sup>th</sup> Artillery (Coast Artillery Corps)**          Organized Jun 1918 at Ft.
          Schuyler, NY.  Moved overseas Sep 1918.  Railway artillery unit with
          40<sup>th</sup> Brigade.  Returned to the US Dec 1918 and demobilized Jan 1919
          at Ft. Totten, NY.

**75<sup>th</sup> Artillery (Coast Artillery Corps)**          Organized Sep 1918 at Ft.
          Moultrie, SC.  Moved overseas Oct 1918.  Railway artillery unit with
          40<sup>th</sup> Brigade.  Returned to the US Mar 1919 and demobilized at Camp
          Grant, IL.

*Coast Defense Commands*[91]

Continental US

| | |
|---|---|
| C.D. of Baltimore | 7 companies [2 companies MD NG] |
| C.D. of Boston | 32 companies [12 companies MA NG; 5 |
| companies RI NG] | |
| C.D. of The Cape Fear | 12 companies [6 companies NC NG] |
| C.D. of  Charleston | 12 companies [5 companies SC NG] |
| C.D. of  Chesapeake Bay | 17 companies [5 companies VA NG] |
| C.D. of  The Columbia | 23 companies [12 companies OR NG] |
| C.D. of  The Delaware | 11 companies [1 company NJ NG] |
| C.D. of  Eastern New York | 13 companies |
| C.D. of  Galveston | 14 companies [5 companies TX NG] |
| C.D. of  Key West | 4 companies [1 company FL NG] |

---

[91] Prior to 1916, companies of the Coast Artillery Corps were numbered in a single series. In 1916, they were numbered sequentially by garrison (e.g., 1<sup>st</sup> Company, Ft. Washington). In 1917 they were numbered in sequence within the new coast defense commands (established Jul 1917) (e.g., 3<sup>rd</sup> Company, C.D. of Portsmouth).  In the section above, the total number of companies authorized for each C.D. command is shown; some were formed from National Guard coast artillery companies. In some cases, a company could be redesignated and another company formed with the same number. (Higher-numbered companies sometimes were redesignated with lower numbers to fill in these gaps.)  The various coast defense commands built up to these strengths during 1917 and 1918, and in a few cases new companies were added in 1919.

| | |
|---|---|
| C.D. of Long Island Sound | 38 companies[92] [13 companies CT NG] |
| C.D. of Los Angeles | 37 companies[93] [8 companies CA NG] |
| C.D. of Mobile | 6 companies |
| C.D. of Narragansett Bay | 32 companies [14 companies RI NG] |
| C.D. of New Bedford | 5 companies [1 company RI NG] |
| C.D. of New Orleans | 15 companies |
| C.D. of Pensacola | 20 companies [1 company FL NG] |
| C.D. of Portland | 29 companies [13 companies ME NG] |
| C.D. of Portsmouth | 10 companies [4 companies NH NG] |
| C.D. of The Potomac | 8 companies [1 company DC NG] |
| C.D. of Puget Sound | 41 companies [12 companies WA NG] |
| C.D. of San Diego | 13 companies [5 companies CA NG] |
| C.D. of San Francisco | 60 companies[94] [10 companies CA NG] |
| C.D. of Sandy Hook | 24 companies [12 companies NY NG] |
| C.D. of Savannah | 14 companies [4 companies GA NG] |
| C.D. of Southern New York | 45 companies [13 companies NY NG] |
| C.D. of Tampa | 6 companies [1 company FL NG] |

Overseas

| | |
|---|---|
| C.D. of Balboa | 11 companies |
| C.D. of Cristobal | 11 companies |
| C.D. of Manila and Subic Bays | 21 companies |
| C.D. of Oahu | 14 companies |

## Anti Aircraft Units[95]

**1st AA Sector** — Organized Nov 1917 at Ft. Winfield Scott, CA as AA Bn (San Francisco).[96] Redesignated Dec 1917 as 1st AA Bn and moved overseas. Redesignated Nov 1918 as 1st AA Sector. Returned to the US Mar 1919 and demobilized at Presidio of San Francisco, CA.

[2nd AA Bn was never reorganized as 2nd AA Sector]

**3rd AA Sector** — Organized Apr 1918 at Ft Morgan, AL as 3rd AA Bn. Moved overseas Aug 1918. Redesignated Nov 1918 as 3rd AA Sector. Returned to the US Jan 1919 and demobilized at Ft. Monroe, VA.

---

[92] The 25th Coy, C.D. of Long Island Sound, was authorized but never organized.

[93] The 16th, 17th, and 21st to 28th Coys, C.D. of Los Angeles, were authorized but never organized.

[94] The 54th to 56th Coys, C.D. of San Francisco, were authorized but never organized.

[95] These form part of the Coast Artillery Corps. There were also AA machine gun battalions, which are listed under Machine Gun Units.

[96] 14th and 16th Coys, C.D. of San Francisco formed Btys D and C, 1st AA Bn.

**4th AA Sector** Organized Jun 1918 as 4th AA Bn. Moved overseas Oct 1918. Redesignated Nov 1918 as 4th AA Sector. Returned to the US Jan 1919 and demobilized at Ft. Totten, NY.

**5th AA Sector** Organized Sep 1918 as 5th AA Bn. Moved overseas Oct 1918. Redesignated Nov 1918 as 5th AA Sector. Returned to the US Jan 1919 and demobilized at Camp Devens, MA.

**6th AA Sector** Organized Sep 1918 as 6th AA Bn. Moved overseas Sep 1918. Redesignated Nov 1918 as 6th AA Sector. Returned to the US Jan 1919 and demobilized Feb 1919 at Ft. Wadsworth, NY.

**7th AA Sector** Organized Oct 1918 as 7th AA Bn. Moved overseas Oct 1918. Redesignated Nov 1918 as 7th AA Sector. Returned to the US Jan 1919 and demobilized at Ft. Monroe, VA.

**8th AA Sector** Organized Nov 1918 in the AEF. Returned to the US Jan 1919 and demobilized at Ft. Totten, NY.

**9th AA Sector** Organized Nov 1918 in the AEF. Returned to the US Jan 1919 and demobilized at Camp Eustis, VA.

**10th AA Sector** Organized Nov 1918 in the AEF. Returned to the US Mar 1919 and demobilized at Camp Lee, VA.

**11h AA Sector** Organized Nov 1918 in the AEF. Demobilized Dec 1918 in Europe.

**12th AA Sector** Organized Nov 1918 in the AEF. Returned to the US Jan 1919 and demobilized Feb 1919 at Ft. Wadsworth, NY.

**13th AA Sector** Organized Nov 1918 in the AEF. Returned to the US Dec 1918 and demobilized Jan 1919 at Camp Eustis, VA.

[14th AA Sector authorized but never organized]

**15th AA Sector** Organized Oct 1918 at Camp Eustis, VA as 8th AA Bn. Redesignated Nov 1918 as 15th AA Sector. Demobilized Dec 1918 at Camp Eustis.

**16th AA Sector** Organized Nov 1918 at Camp Eustis, VA and demobilized there Dec 1918.

**17th AA Sector** Organized Nov 1918 at Ft. Hancock, NJ. Moved to Camp Eustis, VA and demobilized there Dec 1918..

**18th AA Sector** Organized Nov 1918 at Ft. Dade, FL as 9th AA Bn and redesignated same month as 19th AA Sector. Demobilized Dec 1918 at Ft. Dade.

**19th AA Sector** Organized Oct 1918 at Ft. Morgan, AL as 10th AA Bn. Redesignated Nov 1918 as 19th AA Sector. Demobilized Dec 1918 at Ft. Morgan.

[20th AA Sector authorized but never organized]

**1st AA Bn** *See* 1st AA Sector

**2<sup>nd</sup> AA Bn** Organized Jan 1918 at Ft. MacArthur, CA.[97] Moved overseas Jun 1918. Returned to the US Dec 1918 and demobilized Jan 1919 at Camp Dix, NJ.

**3<sup>rd</sup> AA Bn** *See* 3<sup>rd</sup> AA Sector

**4<sup>th</sup> AA Bn** *See* 4<sup>th</sup> AA Sector

**5<sup>th</sup> AA Bn** *See* 5<sup>th</sup> AA Sector

**6<sup>th</sup> AA Bn** *See* 6<sup>th</sup> AA Sector

**7<sup>th</sup> AA Bn** *See* 7<sup>th</sup> AA Sector

**8<sup>th</sup> AA Bn** *See* 15<sup>th</sup> AA Sector

**9<sup>th</sup> AA Bn** *See* 18<sup>th</sup> AA Sector

**10<sup>th</sup> AA Bn** *See* 19<sup>th</sup> AA Sector

[11<sup>th</sup> to 23<sup>rd</sup> AA Bns authorized but never organized]

# Tank Corps

*Tank Centers*

**301<sup>st</sup> Tank Center** Organized overseas Mar 1918 as 2<sup>nd</sup> Heavy Tank Center and the same month as [first] 302<sup>nd</sup> Tank Center; redesignated Jun 1918 as 301<sup>st</sup> Tank Center. GHQ unit with AEF Nov 1918. Moved to the US Mar 1919 and demobilized Apr 1919 at Camp Meade, MD.

**302<sup>nd</sup> Tank Center** Organized overseas Feb 1918 as 1<sup>st</sup> Light Tank Center; redesignated Jun 1918 as 311<sup>th</sup> Tank Center and Sep 1918 as [second] 302<sup>nd</sup> Tank Center. GHQ unit with AEF Nov 1918. Moved to the US Apr 1919 and then to Camp Meade, MD.

**303<sup>rd</sup> Tank Center** Organized Jun 1918 at Camp Colt, PA. Moved overseas Sep 1918 and redesignated Oct 1918 as 303<sup>rd</sup> Tank Center. Redesignated 6 Nov 1918 as 307<sup>th</sup> Tank Brigade.

**303<sup>rd</sup> Tank Center** Organized Sep 1918 at Camp Colt, PA as 304<sup>th</sup> Tank Center. Moved overseas Oct 1918 and redesignated Nov 1918 as 303<sup>rd</sup> Tank Center. Returned to the US May 1919 and demobilized at Camp Meade, MD.

**304<sup>th</sup> Tank Center** *See* [second] 303<sup>rd</sup> Tank Center

**309<sup>th</sup> Tank Center** Organized Oct 1918 at Camp Colt, PA. Demobilized Dec 1918 at Camp Dix, NJ.

---

[97] 4<sup>th</sup> and 5<sup>th</sup> Coys, C.D. of Los Angeles (5<sup>th</sup> ex CA NG) formed Btys C and D, 2<sup>nd</sup> AA Bn.

**310th Tank Center** — Organized Oct 1918 at Camp Colt, PA. Demobilized Dec 1918 at Camp Dix, NJ.

**314th Tank Center** — *See* [first] 303rd Tank Center

*Tank Brigades*

**304th Tank Brigade** — Formed Aug 1918 in the AEF as 1st Provisional Tank Brigade. Served with First Army Sep-Nov 1918 [with IV Army Corps at St. Mihiel and I and V Army Corps in Meuse-Argonne]. Redesignated 6 Nov 1918 as 304th Tank Brigade. GHQ unit with AEF Nov 1918. Moved to the US Mar 1919 and moved to Camp Meade, MD.

**305th Tank Brigade** — Formed Oct 1918 in the AEF as 2nd Provisional Tank Brigade. Redesignated 6 Nov 1918 as 305th Tank Brigade. Moved to the US Mar 1919 and moved to Camp Meade, MD.

**306th Tank Brigade** — Formed Oct 1918 in the AEF as 3rd Provisional Tank Brigade. Under V Army Corps in Meuse-Argonne. Hq with First Army by Nov 1918. Redesignated 6 Nov 1918 as 306th Tank Brigade. Moved to the US Mar 1919 and demobilized Sep 1919 at Camp Meade, MD.

**307th Tank Brigade** — Formed Oct 1918 in the AEF as 4th Provisional Tank Brigade.[98] Served with II Army Corps.[99] Redesignated 6 Nov 1918 as 307th Tank Brigade. GHQ unit with AEF Nov 1918. Moved to the US May 1919 and demobilized at Camp Meade, MD.

*Tank Battalions*[100]

The Tank Service, National Army, was authorized Feb 1918 and the original tank battalions in the US were formed as elements of the 65th Engineers, which had a Heavy Tank Section and a Light Tank Section. In Mar and Apr 1918, its units became numbered battalions in the Tank Service (a branch separated from the Engineers in Mar 1918), and later in Apr 1918 (with new numbers), battalions in the Tank Corps. Independently of this, General Pershing created a

---

[98] Note that the Army source shows the original 303rd Tank Center redesignated Nov 1918 as 307th Tank Brigade as well. Perhaps Hq 4th Provisional Tank Brigade and Hq 303rd Tank Center were merged, or the latter redesignated as the former before becoming Hq 307th Tank Brigade.

[99] Controlled British 1st and 4th Bns, Tank Corps, along with US 301st Bn.

[100] The 344th and 345th [light] Tank Bns entered combat on 12 Sep 1918 and the 331st in Nov 1918. The 301st [heavy] Tank Bn entered combat 29 Sep 1918 (it served with II Army Corps in the British area and was equipped with British tanks) These were the only US tank units to receive campaign participation credit in World War I.

Tank Corps in the AEF.  With units created in three locations (US, England, and France) there was some initial duplication of numbers.

> 1st Separate Bn, Heavy Tank Service, 65th Engineers organized Feb 1918 at Camp Upton, NY and moved overseas Mar 1918.
>
> 2nd Separate Bn, Heavy Tank Service, 65th Engineers organized Feb 1918 (initially Coy D only, at Camp Meade, MD; remainder of battalion organized Mar 1918).
>
> 1st Separate Bn, Light Tank Service, 65th Engineers organized Feb 1918 at Camp Upton, NY.
>
> 2nd Separate Bn, Light Tank Service, 65th Engineers organized Feb 1918 at Camp Upton, NY.

The 1st Separate Bn, Heavy Tank Service, 65th Engineers was redesignated 16 Mar 1918 as 1st Heavy Bn, Tank Service; 16 Apr 1918 as 41st Heavy Bn, Tank Corps; and its final number (301st) on 25 Apr 1918.[101]  I have not seen the intermediate designations for the other three battalions formed in the 65th Engineers.  Battalions numbered 301—308 were nominally heavy and 326 up were light.

**301st Tank Bn**    Organized Apr 1918 overseas by redesignation of 41st Heavy Bn, Tank Corps [old 1st Separate Bn, Heavy Tank Section, 65th Engineers].  Served with II Army Corps; GHQ unit with AEF Nov 1918.  Moved to the US Mar 1919 and moved to Camp Meade, MD.

**302nd Tank Bn**    *See* 306th Tank Bn

**302nd Tank Bn**    Organized Apr 1918 by redesignation of old 2nd Separate Bn, Heavy Tank Section, 65th Engineers.  Moved overseas Sep 1918.  GHQ unit with AEF Nov 1918.  Returned to the US May 1919 and demobilized at Camp Meade, MD.

**303rd Tank Bn**    Organized May 1918 at Camp Colt, PA.  Moved overseas Aug 1918.  GHQ unit with AEF Nov 1918.  Returned to the US Mar 1919 and moved to Camp Meade, MD.

**304th Tank Bn**    Organized Jun 1918 at Camp Colt, PA.  Moved overseas Oct 1918.  GHQ unit with AEF Nov 1918.  Returned to the US May 1919 and demobilized at Camp Meade, MD.

**305th Tank Bn**    Organized Jun 1918 at Camp Colt, PA.  Moved overseas Sep 1918.  Returned to the US Dec 1918 and demobilized at Camp Greene, NC.

**306th Tank Bn**    Organized Jun 1918 in the AEF as 302nd Tank Bn; redesignated Sep 1918 as 302nd Provisional Tank Bn and Oct 1918 as 306th Tank Bn.  GHQ unit with AEF Nov 1918.  Returned to the US Mar 1919 and demobilized Oct 1919 at Camp Meade, MD.

---

[101] This is per the official lineage.  The World War I order of battle volume omits the temporary two-digit number and only shows the redesignation as 301st in Apr 1918.

**307th Tank Bn**   Organized Oct 1918 at Camp Polk, NC. Demobilized Dec 1918 at Camp Greene, NC.

**308th Tank Bn**   Organized in the AEF Nov 1918. Moved to the US Dec 1918 and demobilized at Camp Greene, NC.

[numbers 309 to 325 not used]

**326th Tank Bn**   *See 344th Tank Bn*

**326th Tank Bn**   Organized Apr 1918 by redesignation of old 1st Separate Bn, Light Tank Section, 65th Engineers. Moved overseas Sep 1918. GHQ unit with AEF Nov 1918. Returned to the US May 1919 and demobilized at Camp Meade, MD.

**327th Tank Bn**   *See 345th Tank Bn*

**327th Tank Bn**   Organized Apr 1918 by redesignation of old 2nd Separate Bn, Light Tank Section, 65th Engineers. Moved overseas Sep 1918. GHQ unit with AEF Nov 1918. Returned to the US May 1919 and demobilized at Camp Meade, MD.

**328th Tank Bn**   Organized Apr 1918 at Camp Colt, PA. Moved overseas Aug 1918. GHQ unit with AEF Nov 1918. Returned to the US Mar 1919.

**329th Tank Bn**   Organized May 1918 at Camp Colt, PA. Moved overseas Aug 1918. GHQ unit with AEF Nov 1918. Returned to the US Mar 1919.

**330th Tank Bn**   Organized Jun 1918 at Camp Colt, PA. Moved overseas Aug 1918. GHQ unit with AEF Nov 1918. Returned to the US Mar 1919. Demobilized Oct 1919 at Camp Meade, MD.

**331st Tank Bn**   Organized Jun 1918 at Camp Colt, PA. Moved overseas Aug 1918. Under 3rd [306th] Tank Brigade. Returned to the US Mar 1919. Demobilized Oct 1919 at Camp Meade, MD.

**332nd Tank Bn**   Organized Aug 1918 at Camp Colt, PA. Moved overseas Sep 1918. GHQ unit with AEF Nov 1918. Returned to the US May 1919 and demobilized at Camp Meade, MD.

**333rd Tank Bn**   Organized Aug 1918 at Camp Colt, PA. Demobilized Dec 1918 at Camp Dix, NJ.

**334th Tank Bn**   Organized Aug 1918 at Camp Colt, PA. Demobilized Dec 1918 at Camp Dix, NJ.

**335th Tank Bn**   Organized Sep 1918 at Camp Colt, PA. Moved overseas Oct 1918. GHQ unit with AEF Nov 1918. Returned to the US May 1919 and demobilized at Camp Meade, MD.

**336th Tank Bn**   Organized Oct 1918 at Camp Colt, PA. Moved overseas Oct 1918. GHQ unit with AEF Nov 1918. Returned to the US May 1919 and demobilized at Camp Meade, MD.

**337th Tank Bn**   Organized Oct 1918 at Camp Colt, PA. Moved overseas Oct 1918. GHQ unit with AEF Nov 1918. Returned to the US May 1919 and demobilized at Camp Meade, MD.

**338th Tank Bn**       Organized Oct 191 at Camp Colt, PA. Demobilized Dec 1918 at Camp Dix, NJ.

**339th Tank Bn**       Organized Oct 1918 at Camp Colt, PA. Demobilized Dec 1918 at Camp Dix, NJ.

**340th Tank Bn**       Organized Nov 1918 at Camp Polk, NC. Demobilized Dec 1918 at Camp Greene, NC.

**341st Tank Bn**       Organized Nov 1918 at Camp Polk, NC. Demobilized Dec 1918 at Camp Greene, NC.

**342nd Tank Bn**       Organized Nov 1918 at Camp Polk, NC. Demobilized Dec 1918 at Camp Greene, NC.

**343rd Tank Bn**       Organized Nov 1918. at Camp Polk, NC. Demobilized Dec 1918 at Camp Greene, NC.

**344th Tank Bn**       Organized Jun 1918 in the AEF as 326th Tank Bn and renumbered 1 Sep 1918 as 344th. Served with First Army Sep-Nov 1918 (under 1st Brigade). GHQ unit with AEF Nov 1918. Returned to the US Mar 1919.

**345th Tank Bn**       Organized Jun 1918 in the AEF as 327th Tank Bn and renumbered 12 Sep 1918 as 345th. Served with First Army Sep-Nov 1918 (under 1st Brigade and also with 3rd Brigade). Returned to the US Mar 1919.

**346th Tank Bn**       Organized Oct 1918 at Camp Colt, PA. Demobilized Dec 1918 at Camp Dix, NJ.


## Chemical Warfare Service

**1st Gas Regiment**       Organized Oct 1917 as 30th Engineer Regiment (Gas and Flame). [Coy A organized Oct 1917 at Camp American University, DC; Coys B, C and D organized Nov (B) and Dec (C and D) 1917 at Camp American University, DC; Coys E and F organized Jan and Mar 1918 at Ft. Myer, VA. Coys A and B moved overseas Dec 1917, C and D Feb 1918, and E and F Jun 1918.] Redesignated 13 Jul 1918 as 1st Gas Regiment. [Coys G, H, I, K, L and M organized Oct 1918 at Camp Sherman, OH and demobilized there Dec 1918. Coy Q organized Aug 1918 in the AEF and demobilized there Jan 1919. Coys A to F returned to the US Feb 1919 and demobilized at Camp Kendrick, NJ.]

# Engineers[102]

*Regular Army Engineer Regiments*

**1st Engineers**  Sapper regiment stationed Apr 1917 at Washington Barracks, DC. However, moved (less Co D) to Camp Wilson, TX and assigned 1st Provisional Infantry Division ca. Apr—1 Jun 1917. [Expanded 15 May 1917 to form 1st, 6th and 7th Engineers.] Assigned ca. Aug 197 to 1st Division and moved overseas. Returned to the US Aug 1919 and moved to Camp Zachary Taylor, KY.[103]

**2nd Engineers**  Sapper regiment stationed Apr 1917 at El Paso, TX. Assigned 20 Mar 1917—1 Jun 1917 to 2nd Provisional Infantry Division. [Expanded 21 May—20 Jun 1917 to form 2nd, 4th and 5th Engineers.) Assigned ca. Sep 1917 to 2nd Division and moved overseas. Returned to the US Aug 1919 and moved to Camp Travis, TX.

**3rd Engineers**  Sapper regiment stationed Apr 1917 in the Philippine Islands (1st Bn there and 2nd Bn in Panama). Moved Oct 1917 to Territory of Hawaii.

**4th Engineers**  Sapper regiment organized Jun 1917 at Vancouver Barracks, WA (from elements of 2nd Engineers). Assigned 1 Jan 1918 to 4th Division. Moved overseas Apr 1918. Returned to the US Jul 1919 and moved to Camp Dodge, IA.

**5th Engineers**  Sapper regiment organized 21 May 1917 at Camp Newton D. Baker, TX (from elements of 2nd Engineers). Assigned 6 Dec 1917 to 7th Division. Moved overseas Jul 1918. Returned to the US Feb 1919 and moved to Camp A. A. Humphreys, VA.

---

[102] The *Order of Battle* volumes list all Corps of Engineers units—regiment, battalion, or company—simply as "Engineers" and then give a parenthetical designation with size and type of unit. That convention has been adapted here; however, it appears that it is primarily accurate only for regiments, and possibly only for the sapper regiments (what would later be combat engineer units), which were redesignated in Aug 1917 from "regiment of engineers" to "engineers" (matching arms like infantry and field artillery, which had eliminated "regiment" from the official designation of regiments). The two mounted battalions, surprisingly enough, had different designations: 8th Engineer Bn (Mounted) and 9th Engineers. Some battalions were designated as such. Two units with current descendants had official 1917 designations of 42nd Engineer Bn [an auxiliary forestry unit] and 47th Engineer Railway Maintenance-of-Way Bn. But other battalions were—like the regiments—simply designated engineers.

[103] Coy A remained in Germany 1919, and Coys A, B and D were there in 1920.

**6th Engineers**  Sapper regiment organized 15 May 1917 at Washington Barracks, DC (from elements 1st Engineers). Assigned Nov 1917 to 3rd Division. Moved overseas Dec 1917. Returned to the US Aug 1919 and moved to Camp Pike, AR.

**7th Engineers**  Sapper regiment organized 15 May 1917 at Washington Barracks, DC (from elements 1st Engineers). Assigned Dec 1917 to 5th Division. Moved overseas Mar 1918. Returned to the US Jul 1919 and moved to Camp Gordon, GA.

*National Guard Engineer Regiments*

**101st Engineers** Sapper regiment organized Aug 1917 at Boston, MA as component of 26th Division (formed from 1st Engineers, MA NG). Moved overseas Sep 1917. Returned to the US Apr 1919 and demobilized at Camp Devens, MA.

**102nd Engineers**  Sapper regiment organized Aug 1917 at Camp Wadsworth, SC as component of 27th Division (formed from 22nd Engineers, NY NG, and personnel from 1st, 12th, 14gh, 71st and 74th Infantry, NY NG). Moved overseas May 1918. Returned to the US Mar 1919 and demobilized Apr 1919 at Camp Upton, NY.

**103rd Engineers**  Sapper regiment organized Aug 1917 at Camp Hancock, GA as component of 28th Division (formed from 1st Engineers, PA NG, and five troops from 1st Cavalry, PA NG). Moved overseas May 1918. Returned to the US May 1919 and demobilized at Camp Dix, NJ.

**104th Engineers**  Sapper regiment organized Aug 1917 at Camp McClellan, AL as component of 29th Division(formed from 1st Bn Engineers, NJ NG [1st Bn] and companies from 1st, 2nd, 3rd, 4th and 5th Infantry, NJ NG; regiment completed 6 Oct 1917 with personnel from 1st, 2nd, 3rd, 4th and 5th Infantry, New Jersey NG). Moved overseas Jun 1918. Returned to the US and demobilized at Camp Dix, NJ.

**105th Engineers**  Sapper regiment organized Sep 1917 at Camp Sevier, SC as component of 30th Division (1st Bn formed from 1st Separate Bn Engineers, NC NG; 2nd Bn formed from 1st Bn, 1st Infantry, NC NG). Moved overseas May 1918. Returned to the US Apr 1919 and demobilized at Camp Jackson, SC.

**106th Engineers**  Sapper regiment organized Sep 1917 at Camp Wheeler, GA as component of 31st Division (formed from Coy A, Engineers, GA NG and new units, largely formed from personnel of 1st Infantry, FL NG). Moved overseas Sep 1918. Returned to the US Jul 1919 and demobilized at Camp Jackson, SC.

**107th Engineers**      Sapper regiment organized Sep 1917 at Camp MacArthur, TX as component of 32nd Division (formed from 1st Bn, Engineers MI NG; Bn Engineers, WI NG, and personnel from 5th and 6th Infantry, WI NG). Moved overseas Jan 1918. Returned to the US May 1919 and demobilized at Camp Custer, MI.

**108th Engineers**      Sapper regiment organized Aug 1917 at Chicago, IL as component of 33rd Division (formed from 1st Engineers, IL NG). Moved overseas May 1918. Returned to the US May 1919 and demobilized Jun 1919 at Camp Grant, IL.

**109th Engineers**      Sapper regiment organized Sep 1917 at Camp Cody, NM as component of 34th Division (formed from 1st Separate Bn, Engineers, IA NG and 2nd Bn (plus other elements), 6th Infantry, NE NG). Moved overseas Sep 1918. Returned to the US Jun 1919 and demobilized Jul 1919 at Camp Dodge, IA.

**110th Engineers**      Sapper regiment organized Sep 1917 at Camp Doniphan, OK as component of 35th Division (1st Bn formed from Bn, Engineers, MO NG; 2nd Bn formed from 1st Separate Bn, Engineers, KS NG). Moved overseas May 1918. Returned to the US Apr 1919 and demobilized at Camp Funston, KS.

**111th Engineers**      Sapper regiment organized Aug 1917 at Camp Bowie, TX as component of 36th Division (1st Bn formed from Bn Engineers, TX NG; 2nd Bn formed from 1st Bn, Engineers, OK NG). Moved overseas Jul 1918. Returned to the US May 1919 and demobilized Jun 1919 at Camp Bowie.

**112th Engineers**      Sapper regiment organized Aug 1917 at Camp Sheridan, AL as component of 37th Division (formed from 1st Engineers, OH NG, and elements 6th Infantry, OH NG). Moved overseas Jun 1918. Returned to the US Apr 1919 and demobilized at Camp Sherman, OH.

**113th Engineers**      Sapper regiment organized Sep 1917 at Camp Shelby, MS as component of 38th Division (formed from 1st Separate Bn, Engineers, IN NG and company, 3rd Infantry, KY NG and two companies 1st Infantry, WV NG). Moved overseas Sep 1918. Returned to the US Jun 1919 and demobilized at Camp Sherman, OH.

**114th Engineers**      Sapper regiment organized Aug 1917 at Camp Beauregard, LA as component of 39th Division (formed from Coy A, Engineers, MS NG and new units formed from personnel 1st Infantry, LA NG and 2nd Infantry, MS NG). Moved overseas Aug 1918. Returned to the US May 1919 and demobilized at Camp Shelby, MS.

**115th Engineers**      Sapper regiment organized Aug 1917 at Camp Kearny, CA as component of 40th Division (formed from 1st Bn, Engineers, CO NG and troop, 1st Cavalry, CO NG). Moved overseas Aug 1918. Served as corps troops. Returned to the US Jun 1919 and demobilized Jul 1919 at Ft. D. A. Russell, WY.

**116th Engineers**      Sapper regiment organized Aug 1917 at Camp Greene, NC as component of 41st Division (formed from Separate Bn, Engineers OR NG and 2nd Bn, 2nd Infantry, ID NG). Moved overseas Nov 1917. Returned to the US Mar 1919 and demobilized at Camp Dix, NJ.

**117th Engineers**      Sapper regiment organized Aug 1917 at Camp Mills, NY as component of 42nd Division (formed from 1st Bn, Engineers SC NG [1st Bn] and 1st Separate Bn, Engineers, CA NG [2nd Bn]). Moved overseas Oct 1917. Returned to the US Apr 1919 and demobilized May 1919 at Camp Jackson, SC.

*Wartime Engineer Regiments*[104]

**10th Engineers**      Forestry regiment organized Aug 1917 at American University, Washington, DC. Moved overseas Sep 1917. Absorbed Oct 1918 by 20th Engineers.

**11th Engineers**      Standard gauge railway construction regiment [SOS troops] organized Jun 1917 at Ft. Totten, NY from 1st Engineers, NA. Moved overseas Jul 1917. With First Army Sep-Nov 1918. Returned to the US Apr 1919 and demobilized May 1919 at Camp Upton, NY.

**12th Engineers**      Standard gauge railway operation regiment [army troops] organized May 1917 at St. Louis, MO from 2nd Reserve Engineers. Moved overseas Jul 1917. With First Army Sep-Nov 1918. Returned to the US Apr 1919 and demobilized May 1919 at Camp Funston, KS.

**13th Engineers**      Standard gauge railway operation regiment [army troops] organized May 1917 at Chicago, IL from 3rd Reserve Engineers. Moved overseas Jul 1917. Returned to the US Apr 1919 and demobilized May 1919 at Camp Grant, IL.

**14th Engineers**      Standard gauge railway operation regiment [army troops] organized Jun 1917 at Camp Rockingham, NH from 4th Reserve Engineers. Moved overseas Jul 1917. With First Army Sep-Nov 1918. Returned to the US Apr 1919 and demobilized May 1919 at Camp Devens, MA.

---

[104] These were all presumably constituted in the National Army.

**15<sup>th</sup> Engineers**  Standard gauge railway construction regiment [army troops] organized May 1917 at Oakmont, PA from 5<sup>th</sup> Reserve Engineers. Moved overseas Jul 1917. With First Army Sep-Nov 1918. Returned to the US Apr 1919 and demobilized May 1919 at Camp Sherman, OH.

**16<sup>th</sup> Engineers**  Standard gauge railway construction regiment [SOS troops] organized May 1917 at Detroit, MI from 6<sup>th</sup> Reserve Engineers. Moved overseas Jul 1917. With First Army Sep-Nov 1918. Returned to the US Apr 1919 and demobilized May 1919 at Camp Custer, MI.

**17<sup>th</sup> Engineers**  Standard gauge railway construction regiment [SOS troops] organized May 1917 at Atlanta, GA from 7<sup>th</sup> Reserve Engineers. Moved overseas Jul 1917. Returned to the US Mar 1919 and demobilized Apr 1919 at Camp Gordon, GA.

**18<sup>th</sup> Engineers**  Standard gauge railway construction regiment [SOS troops] organized May 1917 at American Lake, WA from 8<sup>th</sup> Reserve Engineers. Moved overseas Aug 1917. Returned to the US Apr 1919 and demobilized May 1919 at Camp Lewis, WA.

**19<sup>th</sup> Engineers**  Standard gauge railway shop regiment organized May 1917 at Philadelphia, PA from 9<sup>th</sup> Reserve Engineers. Moved overseas Aug 1917. Converted Sep 1918 to 19<sup>th</sup> Regiment TC.

**20<sup>th</sup> Engineers**  Forestry regiment [SOS troops] organized Sep 1917 at American University, Washington, DC. Moved overseas Nov 1917. Absorbed other forestry units Oct 1918.[105] Returned to the US Jul 1919 and demobilized at Camp Grant, IL.

**21<sup>st</sup> Engineers**  Light railway operation regiment [army troops] organized Aug 1917 at Camp Grant, IL. Moved overseas Dec 1917. With First Army Sep-Nov 1918. Returned to the US Jun 1919 and demobilized at Camp Devens, MA.

**22<sup>nd</sup> Engineers**  Light railway construction regiment [army troops] organized Mar 1918 at Camp Sheridan, AL. Moved overseas Mar 1918. With First Army Sep-Nov 1918. Returned to the US Jun 1919 and demobilized Jul 1919 at Camp Zachary Taylor, KY.

**23<sup>rd</sup> Engineers**  Highway regiment [army troops] organized Sep 1917 at Camp Meade, MD. Moved overseas Mar 1918. With First Army Sep-Nov 1918. Returned to the US Jun 1919 and demobilized at Camp Devens, MA.

**24<sup>th</sup> Engineers**  Supply and shop regiment [army troops] organized Nov 1917 at Camp Dix, NJ. Moved overseas Mar 1918. With First Army Sep-Nov 1918. Returned to the US May 1919 and demobilized at Camp Jackson, SC.

---

[105] The regiment was originally formed with 10 battalions of three companies each. At its peak, it was authorized 29 battalion headquarters and 145 companies.

**25th Engineers**    General construction regiment [army troops] organized Sep 1917 at Camp Devens, MA. Moved overseas Feb 1918. With First Army Sep-Nov 1918. Returned to the US May 1919 and demobilized at Camp Upton, NY.

**26th Engineers**    Water supply regiment [army troops] organized Oct 1917 at Camp Meade, MD. Moved overseas Jun 1918. With First Army Sep-Nov 1918. Returned to the US Mar 1919 and demobilized at Camp Dix, NJ.

**27th Engineers**    Mining regiment [army troops] organized Oct 1917 at Camp Meade, MD. Moved overseas Jun 1918. With First Army Sep-Nov 1918. Returned to the US Mar 1919 and demobilized Apr 1919 at Camp Grant, IL.

**28th Engineers**    Quarry regiment [army troops] organized Nov 1917 at Camp Meade, MD. Moved overseas Aug 1918. With First Army Sep-Nov 1918. Returned to the US Jul 1919 and demobilized at Camp Devens, MA.

**29th Engineers**    Regiment came into existence beginning Sep 1917 but no regimental headquarters formed. Regiment organized Sep 1917 to Nov 1918 at various stations. Battalions and companies were attached to armies and corps primarily for surveying and printing duties. (2nd Bn redesignated 1 Dec 1918 as 1st Bn, 74th Engineers.) [Coy H with GHQ, AEF.] Demobilized 13 Jul—2 Sep 1919 at Camp Upton, NY and Camp Humphreys, VA.

**30th Engineers**    *See* 1st Gas Regiment under Chemical Warfare Service

**31st Engineers**    Standard gauge railway operation and maintenance regiment organized Feb 1918 at Ft. Leavenworth, KS. Moved overseas Jun 1918. *Converted Sep 1918 into 31st Regiment, TC.*

**32nd Engineers**    Standard gauge railway construction regiment [SOS troops] organized Jan 1918 at Camp Grant, IL. Moved overseas Jun 1918. Returned to the US Jun 1919 and demobilized at Camp Grant, IL.

**33rd Engineers**    General construction regiment [army troops] organized Jan 1918 at Camp Devens, MA. Moved overseas Jul 1918. Returned to the US Jul 1919 and demobilized at Camp Grant, IL.

**34th Engineers**    Supply and shop regiment [SOS troops] organized Feb 1918 at Camp Dix, NJ. Moved overseas Aug 1918. Returned to the US Aug 1919 and demobilized at Newport News, VA.

**35th Engineers**    Railway shop regiment organized Oct 1917 at Camp Grant, IL. Moved overseas Jan 1918. With First Army Sep-Nov 1918. Converted Sep 1918 into 35th Regiment, TC.

**37<sup>th</sup> Engineers**  Electrical and mechanical regiment [Army troops] organized Jan 1918 at Ft. Myer, VA. Moved overseas Jun 1918. With First Army Sep-Nov 1918. Returned to the US Mar 1919 and demobilized Apr 1919 at Camp Stuart, VA (2<sup>nd</sup> Bn demobilized Mar 1919 at Camp Upton, NY).

**55<sup>th</sup> Engineers**  Standard gauge railway construction regiment [SOS troops] organized Mar 1918 at Camp Custer, MI. Moved overseas Jun 1918. Returned to the US Jul 1919 and demobilized at Camp Dodge, IA.

**56<sup>th</sup> Engineers**  Searchlight regiment [Army troops] organized Jan 1918 at Washington Barracks, DC. Moved overseas May 1918. With First Army Sep-Nov 1918. Returned to the US Apr 1919 and demobilized Sep 1919 at Camp A. A. Humphreys, VA.

**57<sup>th</sup> Engineers**  Inland waterway regiment organized Apr 1918 at Camp Laurel, MD. Moved overseas Jun 1918. Converted Sep 1918 into 57<sup>th</sup> Regiment, TC.

**65<sup>th</sup> Engineers**  *See* Tank Corps

**66<sup>th</sup> Engineers**  Standard gauge railway operation regiment organized Apr 1918 at Camp Laurel, MD. Moved overseas Jun 1918. Converted Sep 1918 into 66<sup>th</sup> Regiment, TC.

**71<sup>st</sup> Engineers**  Domestic AA searchlight operation regiment organized Sep 1918 at Washington Barracks, DC, and demobilized there Jan 1919.

**73<sup>rd</sup> Engineers**  Searchlight regiment organized Oct 1918 at Washington Barracks, DC, and demobilized there Dec 1918.

**97<sup>th</sup> Engineers**  Supply regiment organized Sep 1918 at Camp Leach, DC and demobilized there Dec 1918.

**118<sup>th</sup> Engineers**  Standard gauge railway operation regiment organized Sep 1918 at Ft. Benjamin Harrison, IN. Moved overseas Sep 1918 and absorbed Dec 1918 into Transportation Corps.

**120<sup>th</sup> Engineers**  Standard gauge railway shop regiment organized Sep 1918 at Ft. Benjamin Harrison, IN and demobilized there Dec 1918.

**138<sup>th</sup> Engineers**  Railway construction regiment organized Nov 1918 at Ft. Benjamin Harrison, IN and demobilized there Dec 1918.

**139<sup>th</sup> Engineers**  Dock construction regiment organized Nov 1918 at Camp Shelby, MS and demobilized there Dec 1918.

**140<sup>th</sup> Engineers**  General construction regiment organized Nov 1918 at Camp Shelby, MS and demobilized there Dec 1918.

**145<sup>th</sup> Engineers**  Light railway and shop regiment organized Nov 1918 at Ft. Leavenworth, KS and demobilized there Jan 1919.

**147<sup>th</sup> Engineers**  Railway operation regiment organized Nov 1918 at Ft. Benjamin Harrison, IN and demobilized there Dec 1918.

**149th Engineers**    Electrical and mechanical regiment organized Nov 1918 at Camp Shelby, MS and demobilized there Dec 1918.

**150th Engineers**    General construction regiment organized Nov 1918 at Camp Shelby, MS and demobilized there Dec 1918.

**209th Engineers**    Sapper regiment organized Aug 1918 at Camp Forrest, GA as component of 9th Division. Moved Sep 1918 to Camp Sheridan, AL and demobilized there Jan 1919.

**210th Engineers**    Sapper regiment organized Aug 1918 at Camp Forrest, GA as component of 10th Division. Moved twice before going to Camp A. A. Humphreys, VA Jan 1919 and demobilized there Mar 1919.

**211th Engineers**    Sapper regiment organized Aug 1918 at Camp Forrest, GA as component of 11th Division. Moved Oct 1918 to Camp Meade, MD and demobilized there Feb 1919.

**212th Engineers**    Sapper regiment organized Aug 1918 at Camp Forrest, GA as component of 12th Division. Moved Aug 1918 to Camp Devens, MA and demobilized there Jan 1919.

**213th Engineers**    Sapper regiment organized Aug 1918 at Camp Forrest, GA as component of 13th Division. Moved Oct 1918 to Camp Lewis, WA and demobilized there Feb 1919.

**214th Engineers**    Sapper regiment organized Aug 1918 at Camp Forrest, GA as component of 14th Division. Moved Oct 1918 to Camp Custer, MI and demobilized there Feb 1919.

**215th Engineers**    Sapper regiment organized Sep 1918 at Camp A. A. Humphreys, VA as component of 15th Division. Moved Nov 1918 to Camp Logan, TX and demobilized there Feb 1919.

**216th Engineers**    Sapper regiment organized Sep 1918 at Camp A. A. Humphreys, VA as component of 16th Division. Moved Oct 1918 to Camp Kearny, CA and demobilized there Feb 1919.

**217th Engineers**    Sapper regiment organized Sep 1918 at Camp A. A. Humphreys, VA as component of 17th Division. Moved Nov 1918 to Camp Beauregard, LA and demobilized there Jan 1919.

**218th Engineers**    Sapper regiment organized Sep 1918 at Camp A. A. Humphreys, VA as component of 18th Division. Moved Nov 1918 to Camp Travis, TX and demobilized there Feb 1919.

**219th Engineers**    Sapper regiment organized Sep 1918 at Camp A. A. Humphreys, VA as component of 19th Division. Moved Nov 1918 to Camp Dodge, IA and demobilized there Jan 1919.

**220th Engineers**    Sapper regiment organized Sep 1918 at Camp A. A. Humphreys, VA as component of 20th Division. Moved Oct 1918 to Camp Sevier, SC and Dec 1918 to Washington Barracks, DC, where demobilized Jun 1919.

**301<sup>st</sup> Engineers**      Sapper regiment organized Aug 1917 at Camp Devens, MA as component of 76<sup>th</sup> Division. Moved overseas Jul 1918. Served with IV Army Corps Aug-Nov 1918. Returned to the US Jun 1919 and demobilized at Camp Devens.

**302<sup>nd</sup> Engineers**      Sapper regiment organized Aug 1917 at Camp Upton, NY as component of 77<sup>th</sup> Division. Moved overseas Mar 1918. Returned to the US May 1919 and demobilized at Camp Upton.

**303<sup>rd</sup> Engineers**      Sapper regiment organized Sep 1917 at Camp Dix, NJ as component of 78<sup>th</sup> Division. Moved overseas May 1918. Returned to the US Jun 1919 and demobilized at Camp Dix.

**304<sup>th</sup> Engineers**      Sapper regiment organized Aug 1917 at Camp Meade, MD as component of 79<sup>th</sup> Division. Moved overseas Jul 1918. Returned to the US May 1919 and demobilized at Camp Dix, NJ.

**305<sup>th</sup> Engineers**      Sapper regiment organized Sep 1917 at Camp Lee, VA as component of 80<sup>th</sup> Division. Moved overseas May 1918. Returned to the US Jun 1919 and demobilized at Camp Dix, NJ.

**306<sup>th</sup> Engineers**      Sapper regiment organized Aug 1917 at Camp Jackson, SC as component of 81<sup>st</sup> Division. Moved overseas Jul 1918. Returned to the US Jun 1919 and demobilized at Camp Jackson.

**307<sup>th</sup> Engineers**      Sapper regiment organized Aug 1917 at Camp Gordon, GA as component of 82<sup>nd</sup> Division. Moved overseas May 1918. Returned to the US May 1919 and demobilized at Camp Dix, NJ .

**308<sup>th</sup> Engineers**      Sapper regiment organized Sep 1917 at Camp Sherman, OH as component of 83<sup>rd</sup> Division. Moved overseas Jun 1918. Served as Corps troops (I Army Corps Jul-Aug 1918; III Army Corps Aug-Nov 1918). Returned to the US Jun 1919 and demobilized Jul 1919 at Camp Sherman.

**309<sup>th</sup> Engineers**      Sapper regiment organized Aug 1917 at Camp Zachary Taylor, KY as component of 84<sup>th</sup> Division. Moved overseas Sep 1918. Returned to the US Jul 1919 and demobilized at Camp Sherman, OH.

**310<sup>th</sup> Engineers**      Sapper regiment organized Aug 1917 at Camp Custer, MI as component of 85<sup>th</sup> Division. Moved overseas Jul 1918. Returned to the US Jul 1919 and demobilized at Camp Sherman, OH.

**311<sup>th</sup> Engineers**      Sapper regiment organized Aug 1917 at Camp Grant, IL as component of 86<sup>th</sup> Division. Moved overseas Sep 1918. Returned to the US Jun 1919 and demobilized Jul 1919 at Camp Grant.

**312<sup>th</sup> Engineers**      Sapper regiment organized Aug 1917 at Camp Pike, AR as component of 87<sup>th</sup> Division. Moved overseas Aug 1918. Returned to the US Jun 1919 and demobilized at Camp Dix, NJ.

**313<sup>th</sup> Engineers**      Sapper regiment organized Sep 1917 at Camp Dodge, IA as component of 88<sup>th</sup> Division. Moved overseas Aug 1918. Returned to the US Jun 1919 and demobilized at Camp Doge.

**314<sup>th</sup> Engineers**    Sapper regiment organized Sep 1917 at Camp Funston, KS as component of 89<sup>th</sup> Division. Moved overseas Jun 1918. Returned to the US May 1919 and demobilized Jun 1919 at Camp Funston.

**315<sup>th</sup> Engineers**    Sapper regiment organized Aug 1917 at Camp Travis, TX as component of 90<sup>th</sup> Division. Moved overseas Jun 1918. Returned to the US Jun 1919 and demobilized at Camp Dodge, IA.

**316<sup>th</sup> Engineers**    Sapper regiment organized Aug 1917 at Camp Lewis, WA as component of 91<sup>st</sup> Division. Moved overseas Jul 1918. Returned to the US Apr 1919 and demobilized May 1919 at Presidio of San Francisco, CA.

**317<sup>th</sup> Engineers**    Sapper regiment organized Nov 1917 [with black enlisted personnel] at Camp Sherman, OH as component of 92<sup>nd</sup> Division. Moved overseas Jun 1918. Returned to the US Mar 1919 and demobilized at Camp Sherman.

**318<sup>th</sup> Engineers**    Sapper regiment organized Dec 1917 at Vancouver Barracks, WA as component for 6<sup>th</sup> Division.[106] Moved overseas May 1918. Returned to the US Jun 1919 and moved to Camp Grant, IL.

**319<sup>th</sup> Engineers**    Sapper regiment organized Jan 1918 at Camp Fremont, CA as component for 8<sup>th</sup> Division.[107] Moved overseas Sep 1918. Returned to the US Aug 1919 and demobilized Sep 1919 at Presidio of San Francisco, CA.

[320<sup>th</sup> to 327<sup>th</sup> Engineers constituted for 95<sup>th</sup> to 102<sup>nd</sup> Divisions but never organized]

**472<sup>nd</sup> Engineers**    Military mapping regiment organized May 1918 at Washington DC and demobilized there Apr 1919.

**601<sup>st</sup> Engineers** Sapper regiment organized Mar 1918 at Camp Laurel, MD [Corps troops]. Moved overseas Jun 1918. Returned to the US Jul 1919 and demobilized at Camp Dix, NJ.

**602<sup>nd</sup> Engineers**    Sapper regiment organized Mar 1918 at Camp Devens, MA [Corps troops]. Moved overseas Jul 1918. With First Army Sep 1918. Returned to the US Jun 1919 and demobilized at Camp Grant, IL.

**603<sup>rd</sup> Engineers**    Sapper regiment organized Apr 1918 at Ft. Benjamin Harrison, IN [Corps troops]. Moved overseas Aug 1918. With First Army Sep-Nov 1918. Returned to the US Jun 1919 and demobilized at Camp Grant, IL.

---

[106] Note that in the normal numbering scheme, this regiment would have been a component of the 93<sup>rd</sup> Division, which was only partially formed.

[107] Note that in the normal numbering scheme, this regiment would have been a component of the 94<sup>th</sup> Division, which was never formed.

**604th Engineers**      Sapper regiment organized Apr 1918 at Vancouver Barracks, WA [Corps troops]. Moved overseas Aug 1918. With First Army Sep-Nov 1918. Returned to the US Jun 1919 and demobilized Jul 1919 at Camp Grant, IL.

**605th Engineers**      Sapper regiment organized Jun 1918 at Camp Forrest GA [Corps troops]. Moved overseas Sep 1918. Returned to the US Jun 1919 and demobilized at Camp Dix, NJ.

**606th Engineers**      Sapper regiment organized Oct 1918 at Camp A. A. Humphreys, VA and demobilized there Jan 1919.

*Pontoon Units*[108]

**401st Engineers**      Pontoon park [Army troops] organized Jul 1918 at Camp Forrest, GA. Moved overseas Sep 1918. Returned to the US Mar 1919 and demobilized at Camp Mead, MD.

**464th Engineers**      Pontoon train [Corps troops] organized Jan 1918 at Washington Barracks, DC. Moved overseas Jul 1918. With First Army Sep-Nov 1918. Returned to the US Apr 1919 and demobilized May 1919 at Camp Sherman, OH.

**465th Engineers**      Pontoon train [Corps troops] organized Mar 1918 at Washington Barracks, DC. Moved overseas Aug 1918. With First Army Sep-Nov 1918. Returned to the US May 1919 and demobilized at Camp Dix, NJ.

**466th Engineers**      Pontoon train [Corps troops] organized May 1918 at Washington Barracks, DC. Moved overseas Sep 1918. Returned to the US Jan 1919 and demobilized Feb 1919 at Camp A. A. Humphreys, VA.

**467th Engineers**      Pontoon train [Corps troops] organized Jul 1918 at Camp Forrest, GA. Moved overseas Sep 1918. Returned to the US Mar 1919 and demobilized at Camp Mead, MD.

**468th Engineers**      Pontoon train [Corps troops] organized Jul 1918 at Camp Forrest, GA. Moved overseas Sep 1918. Returned to the US Mar 1919 and demobilized at Camp Dodge, IA.

**480th Engineers**      Pontoon train organized Oct 1918 at Washington Barracks, DC and demobilized there Jan 1919.

---

[108] All are war-formed units, and presumably National Army.

*Regular Army Engineer Battalions*

**8th Engineers**       1st Bn, Mounted Engineers organized 21 May 1917 at Camp Stewart, TX. [109] Reorganized and redesignated 29 Jul 1917 as 8th Engr Bn (Mounted). Moved Nov 1917 to Camp Newton D. Baker, TX. Assigned 27 Nov 1917—12 May 1918 to 15th Cavalry Division.

**9th Engineers**       Mounted battalion organized 21 May 1917 at Camp Newton D. Baker, TX as 2nd Bn, Mounted Engineers. Redesignated 29 Jul 1917 as 9th Engineers. Moved May 1917 to Camp Stewart, TX and Oct 1917 to Camp Courcheane, TX. Assigned to 15th Cavalry Division 27 Nov 1917—22 May 1919 [sic]. Moved Jan 1919 to Camp Cody, NM.

*Wartime Engineer Battalions*[110]

**36th Engineers**       Railway transportation battalion organized Mar 1918 at Camp Grant, IL. Moved overseas Jun 1918. Converted Sep 1918 into 36th Regiment, TC.

**38th Engineers**       Crane operating battalion organized Oct 1917 at Ft. Myer, VA. Moved overseas Feb 1918. Converted Sep 1918 into 38th Regiment, TC.

**39th Engineers**       Standard gauge railway operation battalion organized 18 Feb 1918 at Camp Upton, NY. Moved overseas Jun 1918. Converted 7 Sep 1918 into 39th Regiment, TC.

**40th Engineers**       Camouflage battalion organized Dec 1917 at Camp Leach, DC. Moved overseas Jan 1918. With First Army Sep-Nov 1918. Returned to the US Jan 1919 and demobilized Feb 1919 at Washington Barracks, DC.

**41st Engineers**       Auxiliary forestry battalion organized Jan 1918 at American University, Washington, DC. Moved overseas Feb 1918. Absorbed Oct 1918 into 20th Engineers.

**42nd Engineers**       Auxiliary forestry battalion organized 7 Feb1918 at American University, Washington, DC. Moved overseas May 1918. Absorbed 18 Oct 1918 into 20th Engineers.

**43rd Engineers** A       uxiliary forestry battalion organized Jan 1918 at American University, Washington, DC. Moved overseas May 1918. Absorbed Oct 1918 into 20th Engineers.

---

[109] The battalion was constituted 1 Jul 1916, but only Coy A was actually filled with personnel and formed (20 Aug 1916); Headquarters and Coys B and C were organized 21 May 1917.

[110] These are probably all National Army units.

**44<sup>th</sup> Engineers**       Standard gauge railway maintenance of way battalion organized May 1918 at Ft. Benjamin Harrison, IN. Moved overseas Jul 1918. Converted Sep 1918 into 44<sup>th</sup> Regiment, TC.

**45<sup>th</sup> Engineers**       Railway maintenance of way battalion organized Mar 1918 at Camp Meade, MD. Moved overseas Jul 1918. Converted Sep 1918 into 45<sup>th</sup> Regiment, TC.

**46<sup>th</sup> Engineers**       Railway maintenance of way battalion organized Mar-Apr 1918 at Camp Sheridan, AL. Moved overseas Jul 1918. Converted 18 Sep 1918 into 46<sup>th</sup> Regiment, TC.

**47<sup>th</sup> Engineers**       Railway maintenance of way battalion organized 31 Mar 1918 at Camp Sheridan, AL. Moved overseas Jul 1918. Converted 7 Sep 1918 into 47<sup>th</sup> Regiment, TC.

**48<sup>th</sup> Engineers**       Standard gauge railway maintenance of way battalion organized May 1918 at Ft. Benjamin Harrison, IN. Moved overseas Jul 1918. Converted Sep 1918 into 48<sup>th</sup> Regiment, TC.

**49<sup>th</sup> Engineers**       Railway shop, maintenance of equipment battalion organized Mar 1918 at Ft. Myer, VA. Moved overseas Jul 1918. Converted Sep 1918 into 49<sup>th</sup> Regiment, TC.

**50<sup>th</sup> Engineers**       Railway maintenance of equipment battalion organized Apr 1918 at Camp Laurel, MD. Moved overseas Jul 1918. Converted Sep 1918 into509<sup>th</sup> Regiment, TC.

**51<sup>st</sup> Engineers**       Trades and shopkeepers battalion organized Mar 1918 at Camp Lee, VA. Moved overseas Jul 1918. Converted Sep 1918 into 51<sup>st</sup> Regiment, TC.

**52<sup>nd</sup> Engineers**       Standard gauge railway operation battalion organized Feb 1918 at Camp Upton, NY. Moved overseas Jul 1918. Converted Sep 1918 into 52<sup>nd</sup> Regiment, TC.

**53<sup>rd</sup> Engineers**       Standard gauge railway operation battalion organized Mar 1918 at Camp Dix, NJ. Moved overseas Jul 1918. Converted Sep 1918 into 53<sup>rd</sup> Regiment, TC.

**54<sup>th</sup> Engineers**       Standard gauge railway operation battalion organized Mar 1918 at Camp Dix, NJ. Moved overseas Jul 1918. Converted Sep 1918 into 54<sup>th</sup> Regiment, TC.

**58<sup>th</sup> Engineers**       Standard gauge railway operation battalion organized Jun 1918 in the AEF. Converted Sep 1918 into 58<sup>th</sup> Regiment, TC.

**59<sup>th</sup> Engineers**       Standard gauge railway operation battalion organized Jun 1918 in the AEF. Converted Sep 1918 into 59<sup>th</sup> Regiment, TC.

**60<sup>th</sup> Engineers**       Standard gauge railway operation battalion organized May 1918 at Ft. Benjamin Harrison, IN. Moved overseas Jun 1918. Converted Sep 1918 into 60<sup>th</sup> Regiment, TC.

**61<sup>st</sup> Engineers**       Standard gauge railway operation battalion organized May 1918 at Ft. Benjamin Harrison, IN. Moved overseas Jul 1918. Converted Sep 1918 into 61<sup>st</sup> Regiment, TC.

**62<sup>nd</sup> Engineers**        Standard gauge railway operation battalion organized May 1918 at Ft. Benjamin Harrison, IN.  Moved overseas Jul 1918.  Converted Sep 1918 into 62<sup>nd</sup> Regiment, TC.

**63<sup>rd</sup> Engineers**        Standard gauge railway operation battalion organized May 1918 at Ft. Benjamin Harrison, IN.  Moved overseas Jul 1918.  Converted Sep 1918 into 63<sup>rd</sup> Regiment, TC.

**64<sup>th</sup> Engineers**        Standard gauge railway operation battalion organized Jun 1918 in the AEF.  Converted Sep 1918 into 64<sup>th</sup> Regiment, TC.

**65<sup>th</sup> Engineers**[111]        Standard gauge railway operation battalion organized Jun 1918 in the AEF.  Converted Sep 1918 into 64<sup>th</sup> Regiment, TC.

**66<sup>th</sup> Engineers**        Standard gauge railway operation battalion organized Apr 1918 at Camp Laurel, MD.  Moved overseas Jun 1918.  Converted Sep 1918 into 66<sup>th</sup> Regiment, TC.

**67<sup>th</sup> Engineers**        Standard gauge railway operation battalion organized Jun 1918 in the AEF.  Converted Sep 1918 into 67<sup>th</sup> Regiment, TC.

**68<sup>th</sup> Engineers**        Standard gauge railway operation battalion organized Jul 1918 at Camp Leach, DC.  Moved overseas Dec 1918 and converted into TC companies.

**69<sup>th</sup> Engineers**        Standard gauge railway operation battalion organized Jul 1918 Ft. Myer, VA.  Moved overseas Dec 1918 and converted into TC companies.

**70<sup>th</sup> Engineers**        Railway construction battalion organized Aug 1918 at Ft. Douglas, UT.  Moved Nov 1918 to Camp A. A. Humphreys, VA and demobilized there Jan 1919.

**72<sup>nd</sup> Engineers**        Standard gauge railway construction battalion organized Nov 1918 in the AEF.  Returned to the US Jul 1919 and demobilized at Camp Dix, NJ.

**74<sup>th</sup> Engineers**        Sound and flash ranging battalion organized Dec 1918 in the AEF (formed from 2<sup>nd</sup> Bn, 29<sup>th</sup> Engineers).  Returned to the US Mar 1919 and demobilized at Camp Dix, NJ.

**75<sup>th</sup> Engineers**        Battalion organized Oct 1918 at Ft. Benjamin Harrison, IN.  Demobilized there Nov 1918 (absorbed by 70<sup>th</sup> and 138<sup>th</sup> Engineers).

**76<sup>th</sup> Engineers**        General construction battalion organized Oct 1918 at Ft. Myer VA and demobilized Dec 1918 at Camp Leach, DC.

**77<sup>th</sup> Engineers**        General construction battalion organized Oct 1918 at Ft. Myer VA and demobilized Dec 1918 at Camp Leach, DC.

**78<sup>th</sup> Engineers**        General construction battalion organized Oct 1918 at Camp Leach, DC and demobilized there Dec 1918.

**79<sup>th</sup> Engineers**        General construction battalion organized Oct 1918 at Camp Leach, DC and demobilized there Dec 1918.

---

[111] Repeats number of earlier 65<sup>th</sup> Engineers, the tank service regiment.

**81st Engineers**          Locomotive repair battalion organized Sep 1918 at Ft. Benjamin Harrison, IN and demobilized there Dec 1918.

**87th Engineers**          Car repair battalion organized Oct 1918 at Ft. Benjamin Harrison, IN. Demobilized Jan 1919 at Camp A. A. Humphreys, VA.

**93rd Engineers**          Standard gauge railway maintenance of way battalion organized Oct 1918 at Ft. Benjamin Harrison, IN and demobilized there Dec 1918.

**98th Engineers**          Road battalion organized Sep 1918 at Camp Leach, DC and demobilized there Dec 1918.

**99th Engineers**          Battalion organized Sep 1918 at Ft. Myer, VA and demobilized Dec 1918 at Camp Leach, DC.

**121st Engineers**          Standard gauge railway construction battalion organized Nov 1918 in the AEF. Returned to the US Jul 1919 and demobilized at Camp Dix, NJ.

**122nd Engineers**          Standard gauge railway construction battalion organized Nov 1918 in the AEF. Returned to the US Jul 1919 and demobilized at Camp Dix, NJ.

**124th Engineers**          Dock construction battalion organized Nov 1918 at Camp Forrest, GA and demobilized there Jan 1919.

**125th Engineers**          Dock construction battalion organized Nov 1918 at Camp Forrest, GA and demobilized there Jan 1919.

**126th Engineers**          General construction battalion organized Nov 1918 in the AEF. Returned to the US Jul 1919 and demobilized at Camp Dix, NJ.

**127th Engineers**          General construction battalion organized Nov 1918 in the AEF. Returned to the US Jul 1919 and demobilized at Camp Dix, NJ.

**128th Engineers**          General construction battalion organized Nov 1918 in the AEF. Returned to the US Jul 1919 and demobilized at Camp Dix, NJ.

**129th Engineers**          General construction battalion organized Nov 1918 in the AEF. Returned to the US Jul 1919 and demobilized at Camp Dix, NJ.

**130th Engineers**          General construction battalion organized Nov 1918 in the AEF. Returned to the US Jul 1919 and demobilized at Camp Dix, NJ.

**131st Engineers**          General construction battalion organized Nov 1918 in the AEF. Returned to the US Jul 1919 and demobilized at Camp Sherman, OH.

**132nd Engineers**          Road battalion organized Apr 1919 at Camp Mills, NY and demobilized Jul 1919 at Camp Grant, IL.

188

**134th Engineers**     Road battalion organized Nov 1918 and demobilized Dec 1918 overseas.

**135th Engineers**     Road battalion organized Dec 1918 and demobilized Dec 1918 overseas.

**136th Engineers**     Water supply battalion organized Nov 1918 and demobilized Dec 1918 overseas.

**137th Engineers**     Electrical and mechanical battalion organized Dec 1918 in the AEF. Returned to the US Jul 1919 and demobilized at Camp Dix, NJ.

**141st Engineers**     Road battalion organized Nov 1918 at Camp Shelby, MS and demobilized there Dec 1918.

**142nd Engineers**     Road battalion organized Nov 1918 at Camp Shelby, MS and demobilized there Dec 1918.

**143rd Engineers**     Water supply battalion organized Nov 1918 at Camp Shelby, MS and demobilized there Dec 1918.

**144th Engineers**     Electrical and mechanical battalion organized Nov 1918 at Camp Shelby, MS and demobilized there Dec 1918.

**153rd Engineers**     Dock construction battalion organized Nov 1918 at Camp Shelby, MS and demobilized there Dec 1918.

**154th Engineers**     General construction battalion organized Nov 1918 at Camp Shelby, MS and demobilized there Dec 1918.

**469th Engineers**     Transportation corps battalion organized Feb 1918 at Ft. Slocum, NY. Moved overseas Apr 1918. Converted into TC units Nov 1918.

**501st Engineers**     Service battalion[112] organized Sep 1917 at Washington, DC. Moved overseas [SOS troops] Nov 1917. Returned to the US Jun 1919 and demobilized at Camp Upton, NY.

**502nd Engineers**     Service battalion organized Sep 1917 at Washington, DC. Moved overseas [SOS troops] Nov 1917. Returned to the US Jun 1919 and demobilized at Camp Upton, NY.

**503rd Engineers**     Service battalion organized Sep 1917 at Camp Grant, IL. Moved overseas [SOS troops] Nov 1917. Absorbed Oct 1918 by 20th Engineers.

**504th Engineers**     Service battalion organized Oct 1917 at Camp Merritt, NJ. Moved overseas [SOS troops] Nov 1917. Returned to the US Jun 1919 and demobilized at Camp Devens, MA.

**505th Engineers**     Service battalion organized [with black enlisted personnel] Oct 1917 at Camp Lee, VA. Moved overseas [Army troops] Dec 1917. With First Army Sep-Nov 1918. Returned to the US May 1919 and demobilized Jun 1919 at Camp Meade, MD.

---

[112] The *Order of Battle* volume shows the 501st to 504th as "(white service battalion)" and the remainder as "(colored service battalion)."

**506<sup>th</sup> Engineers**    Service battalion organized [with black enlisted personnel] Oct 1917 at Camp Lee, VA. Moved overseas [SOS troops] Nov 1917. Returned to the US May 1919 and demobilized Jun 1919 at Camp Meade, MD.

**507<sup>th</sup> Engineers**    Service battalion organized [with black enlisted personnel] Nov 1917 at Camp Travis, TX. Moved overseas Feb 1918. Absorbed Oct 1918 by 20<sup>th</sup> Engineers.

**508<sup>th</sup> Engineers**    Service battalion organized [with black enlisted personnel] Oct 1917 at Camp Pike, AR. Moved overseas [Army troops] Jan 1918. With First Army Sep-Nov 1918. Returned to the US Jun 1919 and demobilized at Camp Shelby, MS.

**509<sup>th</sup> Engineers**    Service battalion organized [with black enlisted personnel] Oct 1917 at Camp Travis, TX. Moved overseas [SOS troops] Feb 1918. Returned to the US Jun 1919 and demobilized at Camp Travis, TX.

**510<sup>th</sup> Engineers**    Service battalion organized [with black enlisted personnel] Jan 1918 at Camp Lee, VA. Moved overseas [SOS troops] Mar 1918. Returned to the US Jun 1919 and demobilized at Camp Lee, Va.

**511<sup>th</sup> Engineers**    Service battalion organized [with black enlisted personnel] Jan 1918 at Camp Lee, VA. Moved overseas [SOS troops] Mar 1918. Returned to the US Jun 1919 and demobilized at Camp Lee, Va.

**512<sup>th</sup> Engineers**    Service battalion organized [with black enlisted personnel] Jan 1918 at Camp Pike, AR. Moved overseas [SOS troops] Apr 1918. Returned to the US Jun 1919 and demobilized at Camp Pike.

**513<sup>th</sup> Engineers**    Service battalion organized [with black enlisted personnel] Jan 1918 at Camp Travis, TX. Moved overseas [Army troops] Apr 1918. Returned to the US Jun 1919 and demobilized at Camp Bowie, TX.

**514<sup>th</sup> Engineers**    Service battalion organized [with black enlisted personnel] Feb 1918 at Camp Gordon, GA. Moved overseas [SOS troops] Apr 1918. Returned to the US Jun 1919 and demobilized at Camp Gordon.

**515<sup>th</sup> Engineers**    Service battalion organized [with black enlisted personnel] Jan 1918 at Camp Zachary Taylor, KY. Moved overseas [SOS troops] May 1918. R eturned to the US Jul 1919 and demobilized at Camp Zachary Taylor.

**516<sup>th</sup> Engineers**    Service battalion organized [with black enlisted personnel] Apr 1918 at Camp Gordon, GA. Moved overseas [Army troops] Jul 1918. Returned to the US Jun 1919 and demobilized at Camp Gordon.

**517<sup>th</sup> Engineers**      Service battalion organized [with black enlisted personnel] Apr 1918 at Camp Gordon, GA. Moved overseas [SOS troops] Jul 1918. Absorbed Oct 1918 by 20<sup>th</sup> Engineers.

**518<sup>th</sup> Engineers**      Service battalion organized [with black enlisted personnel] May 1918 at Camp Gordon, GA. Moved overseas [SOS troops] Sep 1918. Converted Dec 1918 into TC units.

**519<sup>th</sup> Engineers**      Service battalion organized [with black enlisted personnel] Apr 1918 at Camp Devens, MA. Moved overseas [SOS troops] Jul 1918. Absorbed Oct 1918 by 20<sup>th</sup> Engineers.

**520<sup>th</sup> Engineers**      Service battalion organized [with black enlisted personnel] Apr 1918 at Camp Devens, MA. Moved overseas [SOS troops] Aug 1918. Returned to the US Jun 1919 and demobilized at Camp Sherman, OH.

**521<sup>st</sup> Engineers**      Service battalion organized [with black enlisted personnel] Apr 1918 at Camp Meade. MD. Moved overseas [SOS troops] Aug 1918. Returned to the US Jun 1919 and demobilized at Camp Jackson, SC.

**522<sup>nd</sup> Engineers**      Service battalion organized [with black enlisted personnel] Mar 1918 at Camp Meade. MD. Moved overseas [Army troops] Aug 1918. With First Army Sep-Nov 1918. Returned to the US Jun 1919 and demobilized at Camp Bowie, TX.

**523<sup>rd</sup> Engineers**      Service battalion organized [with black enlisted personnel] Mar 1918 at Camp Pike, AR. Moved overseas [SOS troops] Jul 1918. Absorbed Oct 1918 by 20<sup>th</sup> Engineers.

**524<sup>th</sup> Engineers**      Service battalion organized [with black enlisted personnel] Apr 1918 at Camp Pike, AR. Moved overseas [Army troops] Jul 1918. With First Army Sep-Nov 1918. Returned to the US Jun 1919 and demobilized Jul 1991 at Camp Jackson, SC.

**525<sup>th</sup> Engineers**      Service battalion organized [with black enlisted personnel] Apr 1918 at Camp Pike, AR. Moved overseas [SOS troops] Jul 1918. Returned to the US Jul 1919 and demobilized at Camp Shelby, MS.

**526<sup>th</sup> Engineers**      Service battalion organized [with black enlisted personnel] May 1918 at Camp Pike, AR. Moved overseas [SOS troops] Jul 1918. Returned to the US Jul 1919 and demobilized at Camp Shelby, MS.

**527<sup>th</sup> Engineers**      Service battalion organized [with black enlisted personnel] Mar 1918 at Camp Dodge, IA. Moved overseas [Army troops] Jun 1918. Served with V Army Corps Aug-Sep 1918. With First Army Sep-Nov 1918. Returned to the US Jun 1919 and demobilized at Camp Gordon, GA.

**528th Engineers** Service battalion organized [with black enlisted personnel] Apr 1918 at Camp Dodge, IA. Moved overseas [Army troops] Jul 1918. W ith First Army Sep-Nov 1918. Returned to the US Jun 1919 and demobilized at Camp Gordon, GA.

**529th Engineers** Service battalion organized [with black enlisted personnel] Apr 1918 at Camp Funston, KS. Moved overseas [Army troops] Jun 1918. Returned to the US Jun 1919 and demobilized at Camp Upton, NY.

**530th Engineers** Service battalion organized [with black enlisted personnel] Apr 1918 at Camp Funston, KS. Moved overseas [Army troops] Jul 1918. With First Army Sep-Nov 1918. Returned to the US Jun 1919 and demobilized at Camp Upton, NY.

**531st Engineers** Service battalion organized [with black enlisted personnel] Apr 1918 at Camp Travis, TX. Moved overseas [SOS troops] Jun 1918. Absorbed Oct 1918 by 20th Engineers.

**532nd Engineers** Service battalion organized [with black enlisted personnel] May 1918 at Camp Zachary Taylor, KY. Moved overseas [Army troops] Jul 1918. Returned to the US Jul 1919 and demobilized at Camp Zachary Taylor.

**533rd Engineers** Service battalion organized [with black enlisted personnel] Jun 1918 at Camp Pike, AR. Moved overseas [SOS troops] Aug 1918. Absorbed Oct 1918 by 20th Engineers.

**534th Engineers** Service battalion organized [with black enlisted personnel] May 1918 at Camp Jackson, SC. Moved overseas [Army troops] Aug 1918. Returned to the US Jul 1919 and demobilized at Camp Devens, MA.

**535th Engineers** Service battalion organized [with black enlisted personnel] May 1918 at Camp Lee, VA. Moved overseas [Army troops] Aug 1918. With First Army Sep-Nov 1918. Returned to the US Jun 1919 and demobilized at Camp Upton, NY.

**536th Engineers** Service battalion organized [with black enlisted personnel] May 1918 at Camp Custer, MI. Moved overseas [SOS troops] Aug 1918. Returned to the US Jul 1919 and demobilized at Camp Jackson, SC.

**537th Engineers** Service battalion organized [with black enlisted personnel] May 1918 at Camp Travis, TX. Moved overseas [Army troops] Jul 1918. With First Army Sep-Nov 1918. Returned to the US Jul 1919 and demobilized at Camp Bowie, TX.

**538th Engineers** Service battalion organized [with black enlisted personnel] May 1918 at Camp Meade. MD. Moved overseas [SOS troops] Aug 1918. Converted Dec 1918 into TC units.

**539th Engineers**  Service battalion organized [with black enlisted personnel] May 1918 at Camp Gordon, GA. Moved overseas [Army troops] Sep 1918. Returned to the US Jun 1919 and demobilized Jul 1919 at Camp Gordon, GA.

**540th Engineers**  Service battalion organized [with black enlisted personnel] Aug 1918 at Camp A. A. Humphreys, VA. Moved overseas [SOS troops] Oct 1918. Returned to the US Jun 1919 and demobilized at Camp Lee, VA.

**541st Engineers**  Service battalion organized [with black enlisted personnel] Aug 1918 at Camp A. A. Humphreys, VA. Moved overseas [Army troops] Sep 1918. Returned to the US Jul 1919 and demobilized at Camp Dix, NJ.

**542nd Engineers**  Service battalion organized [with black enlisted personnel] Aug 1918 at Camp A. A. Humphreys, VA. Moved overseas [Army troops] Sep 1918. Served with Second Army Oct-Nov 1918. Returned to the US Jun 1919 and demobilized at Camp Dix, NJ.

**543rd Engineers**  Service battalion organized [with black enlisted personnel] Aug 1918 at Camp A. A. Humphreys, VA. Moved overseas [Army troops] Sep 1918. Served with Second Army Oct-Nov 1918. Returned to the US Jun 1919 and demobilized Jul 1919 at Camp Lee, VA.

**544th Engineers**  Service battalion organized [with black enlisted personnel] Aug 1918 at Camp A. A. Humphreys, VA. Moved overseas [Army troops] Sep 1918. With First Army Sep-Nov 1918. Returned to the US Jul 1919 and demobilized at Norfolk, VA.

**545th Engineers**  Service battalion organized [with black enlisted personnel] Aug 1918 at Camp A. A. Humphreys, VA. Moved overseas [SOS troops] Oct 1918. With First Army Oct-Nov 1918. Returned to the US Jun 1919 and demobilized at Camp Meade, MD.

**546th Engineers**  Service battalion organized [with black enlisted personnel] Sep 1918 at Camp A. A. Humphreys, VA. Moved overseas [Army troops] Sep 1918. With First Army Sep-Nov 1918. Returned to the US Jun 1919 and demobilized at Camp Jackson, SC.

**547th Engineers**  Service battalion organized [with black enlisted personnel] Sep 1918 at Camp A. A. Humphreys, VA. Moved overseas [SOS troops] Oct 1918. Returned to the US Jul 1919 and demobilized at Camp Lee, VA.

**548th Engineers**  Service battalion organized [with black enlisted personnel] Sep 1918 at Camp A. A. Humphreys, VA. Moved overseas [SOS troops] Oct 1918. Returned to the US Jul 1919 and demobilized at Camp Gordon, GA.

**549th Engineers**     Service battalion organized [with black enlisted personnel] Sep 1918 at Camp A. A. Humphreys, VA. Moved overseas [SOS troops] Nov 1918. Returned to the US Jul 1919 and demobilized at Camp Lee, VA.

**550th Engineers**     Service battalion organized [with black enlisted personnel] Sep 1918 at Camp A. A. Humphreys, VA. Moved overseas [SOS troops] Nov 1918. Returned to the US Jul 1919 and demobilized at Camp Gordon, GA.

**551st Engineers**     Service battalion organized [with black enlisted personnel] Oct 1918 at Camp A. A. Humphreys, VA and demobilized there Jan 1919.

**552nd Engineers**     Service battalion organized [with black enlisted personnel] Oct 1918 at Camp A. A. Humphreys, VA and demobilized there Jan 1919.

**553rd Engineers**     Service battalion organized [with black enlisted personnel] Oct 1918 at Camp A. A. Humphreys, VA and demobilized there Jan 1919.

**554th Engineers**     Service battalion organized [with black enlisted personnel] Oct 1918 at Camp A. A. Humphreys, VA and demobilized there Nov 1918.

[555th Engineers (presumably service battalion) authorized but never organized]

**556th Engineers**     Service battalion organized [with black enlisted personnel] Oct 1918 at Camp A. A. Humphreys, VA and demobilized there Nov 1918.

**564th Engineers**     Service battalion organized [with black enlisted personnel] Nov 1918 at Camp Shelby, MS and demobilized there Dec 1918.

**565th Engineers**     Service battalion organized [with black enlisted personnel] Oct 1918 at Camp Shelby, MS and demobilized there Dec 1918.

**566th Engineers**     Service battalion organized [with black enlisted personnel] Oct 1918 at Camp Shelby, MS and demobilized there Dec 1918.

**567th Engineers**     Service battalion organized [with black enlisted personnel] Oct 1918 at Camp Shelby, MS and demobilized.Dec 1918 at Camp Wheeler, GA.

[568th to 600th Engineers (presumably service battalion) authorized but never organized]

**701st Engineers**     Stevedore battalion organized Sep 1918 at Camp Alexander, VA. Moved overseas Oct 1918 and converted into TC units Dec 1918.

**702<sup>nd</sup> Engineers**       Stevedore battalion organized Oct 1918 Camp Alexander, VA.  Moved overseas Nov 1918 and converted into TC units Dec 1918.

# Appendix 1: Division Components

## Infantry Divisions

*Units entered in italics were constituted but never actually organized.*
Units in brackets are US Marine Corps.

| Div | Inf Bde | Inf Rgt | Inf Rgt | MG Bn | Inf Bde | Inf Rgt | Inf Rgt | MG Bn | MG Bn |
|---|---|---|---|---|---|---|---|---|---|
| 1 | 1 | 16 | 18 | 2 | 2 | 26 | 28 | 3 | 1 |
| 2 | 3 | 9 | 23 | 5 | [4] | [5] | [6] | [6] | 4 |
| 3 | 5 | 4 | 7 | 8 | 6 | 30 | 38 | 9 | 7 |
| 4 | 7 | 39 | 47 | 11 | 8 | 58 | 59 | 12 | 10 |
| 5 | 9 | 6 | 11 | 14 | 10 | 60 | 61 | 15 | 13 |
| 6 | 11 | 51 | 52 | 17 | 12 | 53 | 54 | 18 | 16 |
| 7 | 13 | 35 | 55 | 20 | 14 | 56 | 64 | 21 | 19 |
| 8 | 15 | 8 | 12 | 23 | 16 | 13 | 62 | 24 | 22 |
| 9 | 17 | 45 | 67 | 26 | 18 | 46 | 68 | 27 | 25 |
| 10 | 19 | 41 | 69 | 29 | 20 | 20 | 70 | 30 | 28 |
| 11 | 21 | 17 | 71 | 32 | 22 | 63 | 72 | 33 | 31 |
| 12 | 23 | 36 | 73 | 35 | 24 | 42 | 74 | 36 | 34 |
| 13 | 25 | 1 | 75 | 38 | 26 | 44 | 76 | 39 | 37 |
| 14 | 27 | 10 | 77 | 41 | 28 | 40 | 78 | 42 | 40 |
| 15 | 29 | 43 | 79 | 44 | 30 | 57 | 80 | 45 | 43 |
| 16 | 31 | 21 | 81 | 47 | 32 | 32 | 82 | 48 | *46* |
| 17 | *33* | 5 | 83 | 50 | 34 | 29 | 84 | 51 | 49 |
| 18 | 35 | 19 | 85 | 53 | 36 | 35 | 86 | 54 | 52 |
| 19 | 37 | 14 | 87 | 56 | 38 | 2 | 88 | 57 | 55 |
| 20 | 39 | 48 | 89 | 59 | 40 | 50 | 90 | 60 | 58 |
| 26 | 51 | 101 | 102 | 102 | 52 | 103 | 104 | 103 | 101 |
| 27 | 53 | 105 | 106 | 105 | 54 | 107 | 108 | 106 | 104 |
| 28 | 55 | 109 | 110 | 108 | 56 | 111 | 112 | 109 | 107 |
| 29 | 57 | 113 | 114 | 111 | 58 | 115 | 116 | 112 | 110 |
| 30 | 59 | 117 | 118 | 114 | 60 | 119 | 120 | 115 | 113 |
| 31 | 61 | 121 | 122 | 117 | 62 | 123 | 124 | 118 | 116 |
| 32 | 63 | 125 | 126 | 120 | 64 | 127 | 128 | 121 | 119 |
| 33 | 65 | 129 | 130 | 123 | 66 | 131 | 132 | 124 | 122 |
| 34 | 67 | 133 | 134 | 126 | 68 | 135 | 136 | 127 | 125 |
| 35 | 69 | 137 | 138 | 129 | 70 | 139 | 140 | 130 | 128 |
| 36 | 71 | 141 | 142 | 132 | 72 | 143 | 144 | 133 | 131 |
| 37 | 73 | 145 | 146 | 135 | 74 | 147 | 148 | 136 | 134 |
| 38 | 75 | 149 | 150 | 138 | 76 | 151 | 152 | 139 | 137 |
| 39 | 77 | 153 | 154 | 141 | 78 | 155 | 156 | 142 | 140 |
| 40 | 79 | 157 | 158 | 144 | 80 | 159 | 160 | 145 | 143 |
| 41 | 81 | 161 | 162 | 147 | 82 | 163 | 164 | 148 | 146 |

| Div | Inf Bde | Inf Rgt | Inf Rgt | MG Bn | Inf Bde | Inf Rgt | Inf Rgt | MG Bn | MG Bn |
|---|---|---|---|---|---|---|---|---|---|
| 42 | 83 | 165 | 166 | 150 | 84 | 167 | 168 | 151 | 149 |
| 76 | 151 | 301 | 302 | 302 | 152 | 303 | 304 | 303 | 301 |
| 77 | 153 | 305 | 306 | 305 | 154 | 307 | 308 | 306 | 304 |
| 78 | 155 | 309 | 310 | 308 | 156 | 311 | 312 | 309 | 307 |
| 79 | 157 | 313 | 314 | 311 | 158 | 315 | 316 | 312 | 310 |
| 80 | 159 | 317 | 318 | 314 | 160 | 319 | 320 | 315 | 313 |
| 81 | 161 | 321 | 322 | 317 | 162 | 323 | 324 | 318 | 316 |
| 82 | 163 | 325 | 326 | 320 | 164 | 327 | 328 | 321 | 319 |
| 83 | 165 | 329 | 330 | 323 | 166 | 331 | 332 | 324 | 322 |
| 84 | 167 | 333 | 334 | 326 | 168 | 335 | 336 | 327 | 325 |
| 85 | 169 | 337 | 338 | 329 | 170 | 339 | 340 | 330 | 328 |
| 86 | 171 | 341 | 342 | 332 | 172 | 343 | 344 | 333 | 331 |
| 87 | 173 | 345 | 346 | 335 | 174 | 347 | 348 | 336 | 334 |
| 88 | 175 | 349 | 350 | 338 | 176 | 351 | 352 | 339 | 337 |
| 89 | 177 | 353 | 354 | 341 | 178 | 355 | 356 | 340 | 340 |
| 90 | 179 | 357 | 358 | 344 | 180 | 359 | 360 | 345 | 343 |
| 91 | 171 | 361 | 362 | 347 | 182 | 363 | 364 | 348 | 346 |
| 92 | 183 | 365 | 366 | 350 | 184 | 367 | 368 | 351 | 349 |
| 93[113] | 185 | 369 | 370 | .. | 186 | 371 | 372 | .. | .. |
| 94[114] | 187 | 373 | 374 | .. | 188 | 375 | 376 | .. | .. |
| 95 | 189 | 377 | 378 | 359 | 190 | 379 | 380 | 360 | 358 |
| 96 | 191 | 381 | 382 | 362 | 192 | 383 | 384 | 363 | 361 |
| 97 | 193 | 385 | 386 | 365 | 194 | 387 | 388 | 366 | 364 |
| 98 | 195 | 389 | 390 | 368 | 196 | 395 | 396 | 372 | 367 |
| 99 | 197 | 393 | 394 | 371 | 198 | 395 | 396 | 372 | 370 |
| 100 | 199 | 397 | 398 | 374 | 200 | 399 | 400 | 375 | 373 |
| 101 | 201 | 401 | 402 | 377 | 202 | 403 | 404 | 378 | 376 |
| 102 | 203 | 405 | 406 | 380 | 204 | 407 | 408 | 381 | 379 |

| Div | FA Bde | FA Rgt | FA Rgt | FA Rgt | TM Bty | Eng Rgt | FS Bn |
|---|---|---|---|---|---|---|---|
| 1 | 1 | 5 | 6 | 7 | 1 | 1 | 2 |
| 2 | 2 | 12 | 15 | 17 | 2 | 2 | 1 |
| 3 | 3 | 10 | 18 | 76 | 3 | 6 | 5 |
| 4 | 4 | 13 | 16 | 77 | 4 | 4 | 8 |
| 5 | 5 | 19 | 20 | 21 | 5 | 7 | 9 |
| 6 | 6 | 3 | 11 | 78 | 6 | 318 | 6 |
| 7 | 7 | 8 | 79 | 80 | 7 | 5 | 10 |
| 8 | 8 | 2 | 81 | 83 | 8 | 319 | 320 |

[113] 93rd Division was never formed, although the infantry brigades and regiments (and a small headquarters) were.
[114] 94th Division was never formed, although three infantry regiments were given designations that fell within its sequence.

| Div | FA Bde | FA Rgt | FA Rgt | FA Rgt | TM Bty | Eng Rgt | FS Bn |
|-----|--------|--------|--------|--------|--------|---------|-------|
| 9  | 9   | 25  | 26  | 27  | 9   | 209 | 209 |
| 10 | 10  | 28  | 29  | 30  | 10  | 210 | 210 |
| 11 | 11  | 31  | 32  | 33  | 11  | 211 | 211 |
| 12 | 12  | 34  | 35  | 36  | 12  | 212 | 212 |
| 13 | 13  | 37  | 38  | 39  | 13  | 213 | 213 |
| 14 | 14  | 40  | 41  | 42  | 14  | 214 | 214 |
| 15 | 15  | 43  | 44  | 45  | 15  | 215 | 215 |
| 16 | 16  | 46  | 47  | 48  | 16  | 216 | 216 |
| 17 | 17  | 49  | 50  | 51  | 17  | 217 | 217 |
| 18 | 18  | 52  | 53  | 54  | 18  | 218 | 218 |
| 19 | 19  | 55  | 56  | 57  | 19  | 219 | 219 |
| 20 | 20  | 58  | 59  | 60  | 20  | 220 | 220 |
| 26 | 51  | 101 | 102 | 103 | 101 | 101 | 101 |
| 27 | 52  | 104 | 105 | 106 | 102 | 102 | 102 |
| 28 | 53  | 107 | 108 | 109 | 103 | 103 | 103 |
| 29 | 54  | 110 | 111 | 112 | 104 | 104 | 104 |
| 30 | 55  | 113 | 114 | 115 | 105 | 105 | 105 |
| 31 | 56  | 116 | 117 | 118 | 106 | 106 | 106 |
| 32 | 57  | 119 | 120 | 121 | 107 | 107 | 107 |
| 33 | 58  | 122 | 123 | 124 | 108 | 108 | 108 |
| 34 | 59  | 125 | 126 | 127 | 109 | 109 | 109 |
| 35 | 60  | 128 | 129 | 130 | 110 | 110 | 110 |
| 36 | 61  | 131 | 132 | 133 | 111 | 111 | 111 |
| 37 | 62  | 134 | 135 | 136 | 112 | 112 | 112 |
| 38 | 63  | 137 | 138 | 139 | 113 | 113 | 113 |
| 39 | 64  | 140 | 141 | 142 | 114 | 114 | 114 |
| 40 | 65  | 143 | 144 | 145 | 115 | 115 | 115 |
| 41 | 66  | 146 | 147 | 148 | 116 | 116 | 116 |
| 42 | 67  | 149 | 150 | 151 | 117 | 117 | 117 |
| 76 | 151 | 301 | 302 | 303 | 301 | 301 | 301 |
| 77 | 152 | 304 | 305 | 306 | 302 | 302 | 302 |
| 78 | 153 | 307 | 308 | 309 | 303 | 303 | 303 |
| 79 | 154 | 310 | 311 | 312 | 304 | 304 | 304 |
| 80 | 155 | 313 | 314 | 315 | 305 | 305 | 305 |
| 81 | 156 | 316 | 317 | 318 | 306 | 306 | 306 |
| 82 | 157 | 319 | 320 | 321 | 307 | 307 | 307 |
| 83 | 158 | 322 | 323 | 324 | 308 | 308 | 308 |
| 84 | 159 | 325 | 326 | 327 | 309 | 309 | 309 |
| 85 | 160 | 328 | 329 | 330 | 310 | 310 | 310 |
| 86 | 161 | 331 | 332 | 333 | 311 | 311 | 311 |
| 87 | 162 | 334 | 335 | 336 | 312 | 312 | 312 |
| 88 | 163 | 337 | 338 | 339 | 313 | 313 | 313 |
| 89 | 164 | 340 | 341 | 342 | 314 | 314 | 314 |
| 90 | 165 | 343 | 344 | 345 | 315 | 315 | 315 |

| Div | FA Bde | FA Rgt | FA Rgt | FA Rgt | TM Bty | Eng Rgt | FS Bn |
|-----|--------|--------|--------|--------|--------|---------|-------|
| 91 | 166 | 346 | 347 | 348 | 316 | 316 | 316 |
| 92 | 167 | 349 | 350 | 351 | 317 | 317 | 317 |
| 93[115] | .. | .. | .. | .. | .. | .. | .. |
| 94[116] | .. | .. | .. | .. | .. | .. | .. |
| 95 | 170 | 67 | 68 | 69 | 23 | 320 | 620 |
| 96 | 171 | 64 | 65 | 66 | 22 | 321 | 621 |
| 97 | 172 | 61 | 62 | 63 | 21 | 322 | 622 |
| 98 | 173 | 367 | 368 | 369 | 26 | 323 | 623 |
| 99 | 174 | 370 | 371 | 372 | 28 | 324 | 624 |
| 100 | 175 | 373 | 374 | 375 | 25 | 325 | 625 |
| 101 | 176 | 376 | 377 | 378 | 27 | 326 | 626 |
| 102 | 177 | 379 | 380 | 381 | 29 | 327 | 627 |

## Cavalry Division

The only division formed was the 15th.

| Cav Bde | Cav Rgt | Cav Rgt | Cav Rgt | Cav Bde | Cav Rgt | Cav Rgt | Cav Rgt |
|---------|---------|---------|---------|---------|---------|---------|---------|
| 1 | 6 | 14 | 16 | 2 | 5 | 7 | 8 |

| Cav Bde | Cav Rgt | Cav Rgt | Cav Rgt | FA Rgt | Eng Bn | Aero Sqn | FS Bn |
|---------|---------|---------|---------|--------|--------|----------|-------|
| 3 | 1 | 15 | 17 | 82 | 8 | 2 | 7 |

---

[115] 93rd Division was never formed, although the infantry brigades and regiments (and a small headquarters) were.
[116] 94th Division was never formed, although three infantry regiments were given designations that fell within its sequence.

# Appendix 2: World War I Campaigns

The US Army credited a number campaigns in World War I. Color-bearing units receiving campaign credit were entitled to a streamer (rainbow-colored, similar to the Victory Medal's ribbon) with the name of the campaign emblazoned. Not every campaign had at least one division receive credit; details are given here only for units from army to division. In some cases, a unit not entitled to any campaign credit could receive a streamer without inscription, reflecting overseas service during the war.

An anomaly in this system are certain campaign credits listed in the official lineages (such as Ile de France 1918) which are not contained in the master list of campaign streamers for the US Army.[117] In unit lineages, these are always listed after any other campaign participation credits. The *Order of Battle* volumes refer to them as sector participation. While not part of the Army's current 174 campaign streamers, the units themselves are entitled to the streamers for these campaigns.

Campaigns (US Army Campaigns, Streamer Awarded)

**Cambrai** (20 Nov-4 Dec 1917)

**Somme Defensive** (21 Mar-6 Apr 1918)

**Lys** (9-27 Apr 1918)

**Aisne** (27 May-5 Jun 1918)

> 2nd Division, 3rd Division

**Montdidier-Noyon** (9-13 Jun 1918)

> 1st Division

**Champagne-Marne** (18 Jul-6 Aug 1918)

> I Army Corps
> 3rd Division, 26th Division, 28th Division, 42nd Division

---

[117] This situation is not unique to World War I, as earlier wars have similar campaign credits that are not part of the official list of named campaigns. It appears that the practice ended with World War I, though.

**Aisne-Marne** (15-18 Jul 1918)

I Army Corps, III Army Corps
1$^{st}$ Division, 2$^{nd}$ Division, 3$^{rd}$ Division, 4$^{th}$ Division, 26$^{th}$ Division, 28$^{th}$
Division, 32$^{nd}$ Division, 42$^{nd}$ Division

**Somme Offensive** (8 Aug-11 Nov 1918)

II Army Corps
27$^{th}$ Division, 30$^{th}$ Division, 33$^{rd}$ Division, 80$^{th}$ Division

**Oise-Aisne** (18 Aug-11 Nov 1918)

III Army Corps
28$^{th}$ Division, 32$^{nd}$ Division, 77$^{th}$ Division

**Ypres-Lys** (19 Aug-11 Nov 1918)

27$^{th}$ Division, 28$^{th}$ Division [FA only], 30$^{th}$ Division, 37$^{th}$ Division, 91$^{st}$
Division [less FA]

**St. Mihiel** (12-16 Sep 1918)

First Army, I Army Corps, III Army Corps, IV Army Corps, V Army
Corps
1$^{st}$ Division, 2$^{nd}$ Division, 3$^{rd}$ Division, 4$^{th}$ Division, 5$^{th}$ Division, 26$^{th}$
Division, 33$^{rd}$ Division, 42$^{nd}$ Division, 78$^{th}$ Division, 82$^{nd}$
Division, 89$^{th}$ Division, 90$^{th}$ Division

**Meuse-Argonne** (26 Sep-11 Nov 1918)

First Army, I Army Corps, V Army Corps
1$^{st}$ Division, 2$^{nd}$ Division, 3$^{rd}$ Division, 4$^{th}$ Division, 5$^{th}$ Division, 6$^{th}$
Division, 26$^{th}$ Division, 28$^{th}$ Division, 29$^{th}$ Division, 32$^{nd}$
Division, 33$^{rd}$ Division, 35$^{th}$ Division, 36$^{th}$ Division, 37$^{th}$
Division, 42$^{nd}$ Division, 77$^{th}$ Division, 78$^{th}$ Division, 79$^{th}$
Division, 80$^{th}$ Division, 81$^{st}$ Division, 82$^{nd}$ Division, 89$^{th}$
Division, 90$^{th}$ Division, 91$^{st}$ Division [less FA], 92$^{nd}$ Division
[less FA]

**Vittoria Veneto** (24 Oct-4 Nov 1918)

**Streamer without inscription**

VII Army Corps
8th Division, 31st Division, 34th Division, 38th Division, 39th Division, 40th Division, 41st Division, 76th Division, 83rd Division, 84th Division, 85th Division, 86th Division, 87th Division

Campaigns (Streamer Awarded to Units Only)

**Lorraine 1917**

1st Division

**Alsace 1918**

5th Division, 6th Division, 29th Division, 32nd Division, 35th Division, 88th Division

**Flanders 1918**

30th Division

**Ile de France 1918**

I Army Corps
2nd Division, 26th Division

**Champagne 1918**

I Army Corps, III Army Corps
3rd Division, 4th Division, 28th Division, 42nd Division, 77th Division

**Lorraine 1918**

I Army Corps, III Army Corps, IV Army Corps, V Army Corps, VI Army Corps
1st Division, 2nd Division, 4th Division, 5th Division, 7th Division, 26th Division, 28th Division, 33rd Division, 35th Division, 37th Division, 42nd Division, 77th Division, 78th Division, 79th Division, 81st Division, 82nd Division, 89th Division, 91st Division, 92nd Division

**Picardy 1918**

        1<sup>st</sup> Division, 33<sup>rd</sup> Division

**Russia**

**Siberia 1918**

**Siberia 1919**

**Venetia 1918**

# Appendix 3: Selected Tables of Organization and Equipment

Infantry Division Components
as of 30 Jun 1918

## Infantry Regiment

Personnel:[118]   112 officers and 3720 enlisted personnel (3832 aggregate)

Weapons:   1200 pistols, 3200 rifles, 192 automatic rifles, 3 1-pounder guns, 16 heavy machine guns, 6 3" Stokes mortars

Transport:[119]   1 motor car, 2 motorcycles with side cars 65 riding horses, 315 draft mules, 10 riding mules 57 4-mule wagons[120]

An infantry battalion had 27 officers and 1000 enlisted personnel (1027 aggregate). Its personnel only had small arms (295 pistols, 940 rifles, and 64 automatic rifles)[121]. For transport it had (if provided) 3 riding horses and 60 draft mules.

## Infantry Machine Gun Battalion [four companies, for the infantry brigades]

Personnel:   28 officers and 748 enlisted personnel (776 aggregate)

Weapons:   721 pistols, 40 rifles, 64 heavy machine guns

Transport:[122]   38 riding horses, 187 draft mules, 13 riding mules, 17 4-mule wagons

---

[118] Because of heavy causalities in the AEF, Gen Pershing cut the enlisted strength of rifle companies from 250 to 175. This would have eliminated 300 men from each battalion, 900 from the regiment, and 3600 from a division.

[119] The TOE is annotated "Animals not furnished until further orders." It is unlikely that the regiments ever had the numbers of animals indicated (or possibly, any at all), given the inability to either ship or procure locally the required numbers of horses and mules for the AEF.

[120] Throughout these TOEs, wagons/trucks totals include "rolling kitchens."

[121] All heavier weapons were either in the regimental machine gun company or in the headquarters company.

[122] This TOE is also annotated "Animals not furnished until further orders."

**Machine Gun Battalion** [motorized; two companies, at division level]

Personnel:          16 officers and 377 enlisted personnel (393 aggregate)
Weapons:          386 pistols, 32 heavy machine guns
Transport:          43 motor cars, 14 trucks, 12 motorcycles, 29 motorcycles with side cars

**Regiment of Light Artillery** [3" field gun; two battalions]

Personnel:          64 officers and 1501 enlisted personnel (1566 aggregate)
Weapons:          1451 pistols, 87 rifles, 12 anti-aircraft machine guns, 24 3" guns[123]
Transport:[124]   1 motor car, 2 trucks, 3 motorcycles with side cars 72 caissons (6-horse),   442 riding horses, 726 draft horses, 8 riding mules, 164 draft mules, 46 wagons (horse or mule-drawn)

**Regiment of Heavy Artillery** [4.7" guns or 6" howitzers, motorized; three battalions]

Personnel:          72 officers and 1608 enlisted personnel (1680 aggregate)
Weapons:          597 pistols, 1045 rifles, 12 anti-aircraft machine guns, 24 howitzers (6" or 155mm) or guns (4.7")
Transport:          20 motor cars, 108 motorcycles with side cars 36 caissons, 64 ordnance tractors, 150 trucks

The original version of this TOE was horse-drawn. It had a personnel strength of 71 officers and 1772 enlisted personnel (1843 aggregate). It would have had 1444 horses (482 riding and 962 draft) and 186 mules (8 riding and 178 draft). Vehicles included 1 motor car, 4 motorcycles with side cars, and 2 trucks. There were also 72 caissons and 51 wagons. The regiment carried 2016 rounds of ammunition for its 24 6" howitzers. The shortage of draft animals in the AEF led to a decision to motorize the heavy artillery regiments, but only 11 were so converted by war's end.

---

[123] In France these regiments were primarily outfitted with the French 75mm gun.
[124] The TOE is annotated "Animals not furnished until further orders" for the draft mules only. The shortage of draft animals led to a plan to motorize one light regiment in each division, but this had not begun by the time of the Armistice.

**Regiment of Engineers** (sappers)

| | |
|---|---|
| Personnel: | 51 officers and 1646 enlisted personnel (1697 aggregate) |
| Weapons: | 179 pistols, 1487 rifles |
| Transport:[125] | 1 motor car, 16 motorcycles with side cars 44 4-mule wagons, 94 riding horses, 108 draft horses, 48 pack mules, 104 draft mules |

Army and Corps Troops

**Cavalry Regiment**  [20 Aug 1918; Corps Troops]

| | |
|---|---|
| Personnel: | 95 officers and 1807 enlisted personnel (1902 aggregate) |
| Weapons: | 1866 pistols, 1478 rifles, 48 automatic rifles, 1462 sabers, 8 heavy machine guns |
| Transport: | 1 motor car, 2 motorcycles with side cars 1804 cavalry horses, 21 riding mules, 75 pack mules, 348 draft mules, 69 wagons (4-mule) |

**Pioneer Infantry Regiment**  [8 Oct 1918; Army or Corps Troops]

| | |
|---|---|
| Personnel: | 101 officers and 3450 enlisted personnel (3551 aggregate) |
| Weapons: | 977 pistols, 3142 rifles, 192 automatic rifles |
| Transport:[126] | 1 motor car, 2 motorcycles with side cars 59 riding horses, 7 riding mules, 245 draft mules, 48 wagons (4-mule) |

**Anti-Aircraft Sector**  [11 Oct 1918; Army Artillery]

| | |
|---|---|
| Personnel: | 17 officers and 438 enlisted personnel (455 aggregate) |
| Weapons: | 151 pistols, 292 rifles, 8 3" guns |
| Transport: | 6 motor cars, 23  motorcycles with side cars, 8 gun trailers, 49 trucks, 1 artillery tractor |

---

[125] The TOE is annotated "Animals not furnished until further orders" for the pack mules only.

[126] The entry for the draft mules is annotated "Animals not furnished until further orders."

This TOE shows a sector with Headquarters, Headquarters and Supply Company, and four AA batteries. The number of batteries per sector could vary.

A basic AA battery [11 Oct 1918 TOE] had 3 officers and 92 enlisted personnel (95 aggregate), with 2 3" (or 75mm) guns. The men were armed with 29 pistols and 66 rifles. Battery vehicles were 1 motor car, 4 motorcycles with sidecars, 2 gun trailers, and 10 trucks.

There was also a semi-mobile (75mm gun) AA battery [3 Oct 1918 TOE] with 2 officers and 66 enlisted personnel (68 aggregate), with 2 75mm guns and 2 60" motorized Engineer searchlights. The men were armed with 25 pistols and 43 rifles. Battery vehicles were 1 motor car, 4 motorcycles with sidecars, 2 trailers (gun and caisson), and 4 trucks.

**Anti-Aircraft Machine Gun Battalion** [20 Jul 1918]

Personnel: 28 officers and 737 enlisted personnel (765 aggregate)
Weapons: 750 pistols, 64 anti-aircraft machine guns
Transport: 85 motor cars, 24 motorcycles, 53 motorcycles with sidecars, 27 trucks

**Regiment of Engineers** (sappers) [Corps or Army Troops]

Personnel: 52 officers and 1697 enlisted personnel (1749 aggregate)
Weapons: 231 pistols, 1487 rifles
Transport:[127] 1 motor car, 16 motorcycles with sidecars
94 riding horses, 108 draft horses, 48 pack mules, 104 draft mules, 24 wagons (4-horse), 20 wagons (4-mule)

---

[127] The entry for the draft mules is annotated "Animals not furnished until further orders."

## Appendix 4: Departments (Zone of the Interior and Overseas)

On 1 May 1917 the existing departments in the continental United States changed from four (Eastern, Central, Southern and Western) to the six detailed below. These lasted until 20 Aug 1920 when the departments in the US were discontinued and succeeded by nine corps areas. Departments were responsible for most troops and stations within their areas andfor calling into service the National Guard within their areas.

### Northeastern Department

The Department was established 1 May 1917, containing the states of Maine, New Hampshire, Vermont, Massachusetts, Rhode Island, and Connecticut. Headquarters was at Boston, MA.

Department Commanders[128]

| | |
|---|---|
| 1 May 1917 | Brig Gen [Maj Gen 22 Aug 1917] Clarence R. Edwards |
| 1 Sep 1917 | Brig Gen John A. Johnston |
| 23 May 1918 | Maj Gen John W.Ruckman |
| 21 Jul 1918 | Maj Gen William Crozier |
| 1 Dec 1918 | Maj Gen Clarence R. Edwards |

The department also contained the North Atlantic Coast Artillery District (headquarters also at Boston, MA). The District embraced the coast defenses of Portland, Portsmouth, Boston, New Bedford, and Narragansett Bay.

### Eastern Department

An existing department, reorganized 1 May 1917 to cover the states of New York, New Jersey, Pennsylvania, Delaware, Maryland, Virginia, and the District of Columbia, along with the Canal Zone, and the island of Puerto Rico. On 1 Jul 1, 1917 the Canal Zone was separated and constituted the Panama Canal Department. Headquarters was at Governors Island, NY.

Department Commanders

| | |
|---|---|
| 6 Apr 1917 | Maj Gen Leonard Wood |
| 1 May 1917 | Maj Gen J Franklin Bell |
| 25 Aug 1917 | Brig Gen Eli D. Hoyle |
| 16 Jan 1918 | Maj Gen William A. Mann |
| 31 Jul 1918 | Col John C. F. Tillson (interim) |
| 1 Aug 1918 | Maj Gen J Franklin Bell |

---

[128] For all departments, the last commander shown remained through at least 20 Jun 1919, and commanders appointed after that date are not given. For existing departments, 6 Apr 1917 indicates the commander on the date the US declared war, not the actual date of appointment.

| 9 Jan 1919 | Col John C. F. Tillson (interim) |
| 15 Jan 1919 | Maj Gen Thomas H. Barry |

The department also contained the Middle Atlantic Coast Artillery District (headquarters at Ft Totten, NY). The District embraced the coast defenses of Long Island Sound, Eastern New York, Southern New York, Sandy Hook, The Delaware, Baltimore, The Potomac, Chesapeake Bay, and San Juan, Puerto Rico.

## Southeastern Department
The Department was established 1 May 1917, containing the states of Tennessee, North Carolina, South Carolina, Georgia, Florida, Alabama, Mississippi, Louisiana, and Arkansas, together with the Coast Defenses of Galveston. Headquarters was at Charleston, SC.

Department Commander

| 1 May 1917 | Maj Gen Leonard Wood |
| 22 Aug 1917 | Brig Gen John W. Ruckman (interim) |
| 28 Aug 1917 | Col James N. Pickering (interim) |
| 29 Aug 1917 | Maj Gen WilliamP. Duvall |
| 6 Jan 1918 | Maj Gen William L. Sibert |
| 17 May 1918 | Brig Gen William R. Dashiell (interim) |
| 21 May 1917 | Col Thomas Ridgway (interim) |
| 14 Jun 1918 | Maj Gen Henry C. Sharpe |
| 28 May 1919 | Brig Gen Clarence H. McNeil (interim) |
| 16 Jun 1919 | Col Charles A. Bennett (interim) |

The department also contained the South Atlantic Coast Artillery District The District embraced the coast defenses of The Cape Fear, Charleston, Savannah, Tampa, Key West, Pensacola, Mobile, New Orleans, and Galveston.

## Central Department
An existing department, which on 1 May 1917, contained the states of West Virginia, Kentucky, Ohio, Michigan, Indiana, Illinois, Wisconsin, Minnesota, North Dakota, South Dakota, Iowa, Missouri, Kansas, Nebraska, and Colorado. Headquarters was at Chicago, IL.

Department Commanders

| 6 Apr 1917 | Maj Gen Thomas H. Barry |
| 27 Aug 1917 | Maj Gen William H. Carter |
| 21 Mar 1918 | Maj Gen Thomas H. Barry |
| 14 Jan 1919 | Col William A. Shunk |
| 15 Jan 1919 | Maj Gen Leonard Wood |

**Southern Department**
An existing department which, on 1 May 1917, contained the states of Texas (except the Coast Defenses of Galveston), Oklahoma, New Mexico, and Arizona.  Headquarters was at Ft Sam Houston, TX.

Department Commanders
| | |
|---|---|
| 6 Apr 1917 | Maj Gen John J. Pershing |
| 8 May 1917 | Brig Gen James Parker (interim) |
| 30Aug 1917 | Maj Gen John W. Ruckman |
| 4 May 1918 | Maj Gen Willard A. Holbrook |
| 24 Sep 1918 | Brig Gen [May Gen 12 Oct 1918] DeRosey C. Cabell |

In addition to the normal duties of a department, Southern Department had the responsibility for patrolling most of the border with Mexico.  From 1916 it had the bulk of the tactical units of the Regular Army, along with much of the National Guard.  On 20 Mar 1917 the Regulars were organized into divisions (1st to 3rd Provisional Infantry and 1st Provisional Cavalry Divisions).  These provisional divisions were given territorial assignments to border districts, which had been maintained since the Mexican border mobilization.  When the provisional divisions were discontinued 1 Jun 1917, the border area was reorganized into four districts: Brownsville, Laredo, El Paso and Arizona (Hq at Douglas).  On 18 Nov 1917 the Laredo District subdivided into the Laredo and Eagle Pass Districts, and the El Paso District into the El Paso and Big Bend (Hq at Marfa) Districts.

**Western Department**
An existing department which on 1 May 1917, the Department contained the states of Washington, Oregon, Idaho, Montana, Wyoming, California, Nevada, Utah, and the Territory of Alaska.  Headquarters was at San Francisco, CA.

Department Commanders
| | |
|---|---|
| 6 Apr 1917 | Maj Gen J. Franklin Bell |
| 24 Apr 1917 | Brig Gen William L. Sibert (interim) |
| 15 May 1917 | Maj Gen Hunter Liggett |
| 6 Sep 1917 | Maj Gen Arthur Murray |
| 8 May 1918 | Brig Gen Charles G. Treat |
| 18 Jun 1918 | Maj Gen John F. Morrison |

The department also had the Southern California District for patrolling the state's border with Mexico.

The Pacific Coast Artillery District was discontinued 1 May 1917 and superseded by two new districts within the department.  The North Pacific

Coast Artillery District (Hq at Seattle) controlled the coast defenses of Puget Sound and The Columbia. The South Pacific Coast Artillery District (Hq at Ft Miley, CA) controlled the coast defenses of San Diego, San Francisco, and Los Angeles.

## Panama Canal Department

This department was established 1 Jul 1917 (Hq at Ancon, CZ); prior to that date US Troops, Canal Zone, came under the Eastern Department.

Department Commanders
| | |
|---|---|
| 1 Jul 1917 | Brig Gen Edward H. Plummer[129] |
| 14 Aug 1917 | Brig Gen Adelbert Cronkhite |
| 31 Aug 1917 | Col George F. Landers (interim) |
| 28 Feb 19187 | Brig Gen Richard M. Blatchford |
| 28 Apr 1918 | Maj Gen Chase W. Kennedy |

The department also controlled the Panama Coast Artillery District (Hq at Ancon to 16 May 1918 then Ft Amador, CZ). The District embraced the coast defenses of Balboa and Cristobal.

The department was just over 11,000 troops when the war began and generally ran in the 10- to 12,000 range until Mar 1919 when it fell to 7500 and was gradually reduced from there.

## Hawaiian Department

An existing department with headquarters at Honolulu, Oahu.

Department Commanders
| | |
|---|---|
| 6 Apr 1917 | Brig. Gen. Frederick S. Strong |
| 6 Jul 1917 | Brig. Gen. Charles J. Treat (interim) |
| 16 Aug 1917 | Col. Lucien G. Berry (interim) |
| 3 Sep 1917 | Brig. Gen. Andrew Hero, Jr. (interim) |
| 5 Sep 1917 | Col. Lucius L. Durfee (interim) |
| 14 Sep 1917 | Brig. Gen. John P. Wiser |
| 21 May 1918 | Brig. Gen. Augustus P. Blocksom |
| 10 Nov 1918 | Brig. Gen. John W. Heard (interim) |
| 24 Mar 1919 | Brig. Gen. Henry C. Hodges, Jr. |
| 29 May 1919 | Col. Thomas Ridgwsy (interim) |

---

[129] Plummer was the existint commander of US Troops, CZ when the new department was established.

The department contained the coast defenses of Oahu.

The Hawaiian Department had just over 10,000 men when war began, and went as high as just over 13,000 some months, it was at 10,000 in Oct 1918 and then began to reduce.

## Philippine Department

An existing department, which also controlled US troops in China. Headquarters was at Manila.

Department Commanders
| | |
|---|---|
| 6 Apr 1917 | Maj. Gen. Hunter Liggett |
| 16 Apr 1917 | Brig. Gen. Charles J. Bailey |
| 8 Aug 1917 | Brig. Gen. Robert K. Evane |
| 7 Aug 1918 | Brig. Gen. Henry A. Greene |
| 7 Dec 1918 | Col. Edwin A. Root (interim) |
| 21 Jan 1919 | Col. Samuel E. Allen (interim) |
| 17 Feb 1919 | Brig. Gen. Francis H. French |

The department controlled the Coast Defenses of Manila and Subic Bays.

The department had some 19,700 men when war began, and settled in at a normal strength of 14,000 to 17,000 during the course of the war, remaining over 13,000 even with peace.

## Apendix 5: Provisional Divisions 1917

On 20 Mar 1917 troops in the Southern Department were organized into four provisional divisions, which also served as border districts for patrolling the border with Mexico. These were discontinued 1 Jun1917 and replaced by districts. Apr 1917 locations are shown. Some assigned units had already begun to depart for other stations during May.

1st Provisional Infantry Division (Camp Wilson, TX)
Brig Gen James Parker
 1st Brigade
   4th Infantry Brownsville, TX
   26th Infantry Harlinger, TX
   28th Infantry Ft. Ringgold, TX
 2nd Brigade
   9th Infantry Camp Wilson, TX[130]
   19th Infantry Ft. Sam Houston, TX
   37th Infantry Ft. McIntosh, TX
 3rd Brigade
   3rd Infantry Camp Eagle Pass, TX
   30th Infantry Camp Eagle Pass, TX[131]
   36th Infantry Ft. Clark, TX
 Artillery Brigade
   3rd Field Artilery Ft. Sam Houston, TX
   7th Field Artilery Ft. Sam Houston, TX
   Btys D & F, 6th Field Artillery
   Bty. D, 4th Field Artilery
 Divisional Cavalry
   14th Cavalry Camp Del Rio, TX
 1st Engineers (less Coy D) Camp Wilson, TX[132]
 8th Aero Sqn Kelly Field, TX
 2nd Field Sig Bn Brownsville, TX
1st Provisional Cavalry Brigade – attached to 1st Prov Inf Div
   3rd Cavalry Ft. Sam Houston, TX
   16th Cavalry Lilano Grande, TX

---

[130] Moved May 1917 to Syracuse, NY.
[131] Moved May 1917 to Syracuse, NY.
[132] Permanent station Washington Barracks, DC; reorganized 15 May 1917 into 1st, 6th and 7th Engineers.

2nd Provisional Infantry Division (El Paso, TX)
Brig Gen George Bell, Jr
       1st Brigade
              7th Infantry  Camp Ft. Bliss, TX
              17th Infantry[133]
              23rd Infantry  Camp Cotton, TX[134]
       2nd Brigade
              6th Infantry  Camp Newton D. Baker, TX[135]
              16th Infantry  Camp Newton D. Baker, TX
              20th Infantry  Camp Ft. Bliss, TX[136]
       3rd Brigade
              24th Infantry  Camp Furlong, NM
              34th Infantry  Marfa, TX
       Artillery Brigade
              4th Field Artillery (less 2nd Bn.)  Camp Stewart, TX[137]
              5th Field Artillery (less Btys. D and F)  Ft. Bliss,TX
              8th Field Artillery  Ft. Bliss,TX
       Divisional Cavalry
              6th Cavalry  Marfa, TX
              12th Cavalry (less 1st Sqn), attached  Columbus, NM
       2nd Engineers (less Coys. E and F)  El Paso, TX[138]
       1st Aero Sqn  Columbus, NM
       1st Field Sig Bn  Camp Ft. Bliss, TX

---

[133] However, there is no record that the regiment moved from its Apr 1917 station at Ft. McPherson, GA to join the division.
[134] Moved May 1917 to Syracuse, NY.
[135] Moved May 1917 to Chickamauga Park, GA.
[136] Moved May 1917 to Ft. Douglas, UT.
[137] Moved May 1917 to Syracuse, NY.
[138] Reorganized May-Jun 1917 into 2nd, 4th and 5th Engineers.

3rd Provisional Infantry Division (Douglas, AZ)
Brig Gen Thomas F. Davis
      1st Brigade
            12th Infantry  Nogales, AZ[139]
            14th Infantry. (less 1st Bn)  Yuma, AZ
            35th Infantry  Nogales, AZ
      2nd Brigade
            11th Infantry  Douglas, AZ[140]
            18th Infantry  Camp Harry J. Jones, Douglas, AZ
            22nd Infantry[141]
      6th Field Artilery  Douglas, AZ
      Divisional Cavalry
            10th Cavalry (less one troop)  Ft. Huachuca, AZ
            1st Cavalry (less four troops) attached   Camp Harry J. Jones,
Douglas, AZ


1st Provisional Cavalry Division (El Paso, TX)
Brig Gen Eben Swift
      1st Brigade
            8th Cavalry  Ft. Bliss, TX
            17th Cavalry  Ft. Bliss, TX
      2nd Brigade
            7th Cavalry  Camp Stewart, TX
            13th Cavalry (less one troop)  Camp Stewart, TX
      3rd Brigade
            5th Cavalry  Camp Stewart, TX
            11th Cavalry  Camp Stewart, TX

---

[139] Moved May 1917 to the Presidio of San Francisco.
[140] Moved May 1917 to Chickamauga Park, GA.
[141] However, there is no record that the regiment left its Apr 1917 station of Ft. Jay, NY.

# Appendix 6: Major Camps and Cantonments

The Apr 1917 Army had housing for about 124,000 personnel at the various camps, posts and stations throughout the US. Before any of the mobilization recounted in earlier sections could be accomplished, there had to be someplace to house the additional personnel. Within six months, the Army had completed 32 new camps, each capable of holding at least one division. Sixteen were created for National Guard divisions, and largely located in the south. An additional 16 were built for National Army divisions, and these were spread more widely. In addition to other problems, the change in the size and organization of divisions between May and early Aug 1917, with construction already underway, required makeshift adaptations in the use of barracks. In addition to the 32 divisional cantonments, a number of other camps were constructed for training of support units or other special purposes. Prior to World War I, the US Army had no permanent divisions and thus no need for divisional camps. The reader familiar with current Army posts will note that many of the existing forts (division homes or training centers) began as these World War I camps.

Principal World War I camps, their planned maximum capacity, and division tenants are shown below.

## National Guard Camps[142]

Beauregard (Alexandria, LA)     29,100
     39th Division organized Aug 1917—Jul 1918
     17th Division organized and demobilized Aug 1918—Feb 1919
     39th Division demobilized Dec 1918—Jan 1919
Bowie (Fort Worth, TX)     41,800
     36th Division organized Aug 1917—Jun 1918
     100th Division began organization and then demobilized Oct— Nov 1918
     36th Division demobilized Jun 1919
     90th Division demobilized Jun 1919
Cody (Deming, NM)     44,900
     34th Division organized Aug 1917—Jul 1918
     97th Division partially organized and demobilized Sep—
        Dec 1918

---

[142] National Guard divisions are taken as beginning organization in Aug 1917, although some division headquarters were formed later and renumbering and reorganization of National Guard units below division level could occur as late as Oct 1917. For divisions, the last month of organization is shown as the month before they reported to a camp for embarkation.

Doniphan (Fort Sill, OK)                46,100
    35th Division organized Aug 1917—Mar 1918
Fremont (Palo Alto, CA)                30,000
    8th Division organized Jan—Oct 1918
Greene (Charlotte, NC)[143]            48,300
    3rd Division organized here and elsewhere Nov 1917—Mar 1918
    4th Division organized here and elsewhere Nov 1917—Apr 1918
    41st Division organized Aug—Oct 1917[144]
Hancock (Augusta, GA)        45,000
    28th Division organized Aug 1917—Mar 1918
Kearney (Linda Vista, CA)            32,000
    40th Division organized Aug 1917—Jul 1918
    16th Division organized and demobilized Aug 1918—Mar 1919
    40th Division demobilized Mar—Apr 1919
Logan (Houston, TX)                44,800
    5th Division organized here and elsewhere Dec 1917—Apr 1918
    33rd Division organized Aug 1917—Apr 1918
    15th Division organized and demobilized Aug 1918—Feb 1919
MacArthur (Waco, TX)        45,000
    32nd Division organized Aug—Dec 1917
McClellan (Anniston, AL)            57,700
    6th organized here and elsewhere Nov 1917—Mar 1918
    29th Division organized Aug 1917—May 1918
    98th Division began organization and then demobilized Oct—
    Nov 1918
Sevier (Greenville, SC)        41,600
    30th Division organized Aug 1917—Apr 1918
    20th Division organized and demobilized Aug 1918—Feb 1919
Shelby (Hattiesburg, MS)            36,000
    38th Division organized Aug 1917—Aug 1918
    101st Division slated for organization Nov 1918
Sheridan (Montgomery, AL)            41,500
    37th Division organized Aug 1917—Apr 1918
    9th Division organized and demobilized Jul 1918—Feb 1919

---

[143] 26th Division was to be organized at Camp Greene; however it was instead concentrated at various locations in New England and marked for early shipment overseas.

[144] 41st Division was to have been organized at Camp Fremont, CA. However, construction delays there result in a change to Camp Greene, which was available when the 26th Division was organized elsewhere.

Wadsworth (Spartanburg, SC)          56,200
      27th Division organized Aug 1917—Apr 1918
      96th Division partially organized and demobilized Oct 1918—
      Jan 1919
Wheeler (Macon, GA)          43,000
      31st Division organized Aug 1917—Aug 1918
      7th Division organized here and elsewhere Jan—May 1918
      99th Division began organization and then demobilized Oct—
         Nov 1918


National Army Cantonments

Custer (Battle Creek, MI)          49,000
      85th Division organized Aug 1917—Jul 1918
      14th Division organized and demobilized Jul 1918—Feb 1919
      85th Division demobilized Mar—Apr 1919
      32nd Division demobilized May 1919
Devens (Ayer, MA)          36,800
      76th Division organized Aug 1917—Jul 1918
      12th Division organized and demobilized Jul 1918—Feb 1919
      76th Division demobilized Dec 1918—Jan 1919
      26th Division demobilized Apr—May 1919
Dodge (Des Moines, IA)          49,200
      88th Division organized Aug 1917—Jul 1918
      19th Division organized and demobilized Sep 1918—Feb 1919
      88th Division demobilized Jun 1919
      4th Division peacetime garrison from Aug 1919
Dix (Wrightstown, NJ)          42,800
      78th Division organized Aug 1917—Apr 1918
      102nd Division slated for organization Nov 1918
      87th Division demobilized Jan—Feb 1919
      41st Division demobilized Feb 1919
      28th Division demobilized Apr—May 1919
      29th Division demobilized May 1919
      42nd Division demobilized May 1919
      79th Division demobilized May—Jun 1919
      78th Division demobilized Jun 1919
      8th Division demobilized Sep 1919[145]

---

[145] While the division headquarters lasted this long, the remainder of the division had been demobilized or relieved by about Feb 1919.

Funston (Fort Riley, KS)       42,800
>89th Division organized Aug 1917—Apr 1918
>10th Division organized and demobilized Aug 1918—Feb 1919
>35th Division demobilized Apr—May 1919
>89th Division demobilized May—Jul 1919
>7th Division peacetime garrison from Jun 1919

Gordon (Atlanta, GA)       46,600
>82nd Division organized Aug 1917—Apr 1918
>31st Division demobilized Dec 1918—Jan 1919
>5th Division peacetime garrison from Jul 1919

Grant (Rockford, IL)       62,600
>86th Division organized Aug 1917—Jun 1918
>86th Division demobilized Jan 1919
>34th Division demobilized Jan—Feb 1919
>33rd Division demobilized May—Jun 1919
>6th Division peacetime garrison from Jun 1919

Jackson (Columbia, SC)     44,000
>81st Division organized Aug 1917—Apr 1918
>30th Division demobilized Apr—May 1919

Lee (Petersburg, VA)       60,300
>80th Division organized Aug 1917—Apr 1918
>80th Division demobilized May—Jun 1919

Lewis (American Lake, WA)   46,200
>91st Division organized Aug 1917—May 1918
>13th Division organized and demobilized Jul 1918—Mar 1919

Meade (Admiral, MD)       52,500
>79th Division organized Aug 1917—Jun 1918
>11th Division organized and demobilized Aug 1918—Feb 1919
>92nd Division demobilized Feb 1919

Pike (Little Rock, AR)     55,000
>87th Division organized Aug 1917—May 1918
>3rd Division peacetime garrison from Aug 1919

Sherman (Chillicothe, OH)   49,100
>83rd Division organized Aug 1917—Apr 1918
>95th Division partially organized and demobilized Sep—
>>Dec 1918
>83rd Division demobilized Jan—Oct 1919[146]
>37th Division demobilized Apr—Jun 1919

---

[146] While the division headquarters lingered, the bulk of the division was demobilized much earlier.

Zachary Taylor (Louisville, KY)                45,400
       84th Division organized Aug 1917—May 1918
       38th Division demobilized Dec 1918—Jan 1919
       84th Division demobilized Jan—Jul 1919
       1st Division peacetime garrison from Sep 1919
Travis (San Antonio, TX)                42,800
       90th Division organized Aug 1917—May 1918
       18th Division organized and demobilized Aug 1918—Feb 1919
       2nd Division peacetime garrison from Aug 1919
Upton (Yaphank, NY)                43,500
       77th Division organized Aug 1917—Feb 1918
       27th Division demobilized Mar—Apr 1919
       77th Division demobilized Apr—May 1919
       82nd Division demobilized May 1919

### Special Camps Constructed During the War

| Camp | Capacity | Branch |
|---|---|---|
| Benning (Columbus, GA) | 5,000 | Infantry School |
| Bragg (Fayetteville, NC) | 11,800 | Field Artillery |
| Colt (Gettysburg, PA) | 4,000 | Tank Corps |
| Eustis (Lee Hall, VA) | 17,000 | Coast Artillery |
| Forrest (Ft. Oglethorpe, GA) | 24,400 | Engineers |
| Franklin (Camp Meade, MD) | 11,000 | Signal Corps |
| Holabird (Baltimore, MD) | 7,500 | Motor Transport |
| Humphreys (Belvoir, VA) | 32,400 | Engineers |
| Johnston (Jacksonville, FL) | 18,200 | Quartermaster |
| Knox (Stithton, KY) | 27,800 | Field Artillery |
| Las Casas (San Juan, PR) | 13,200 | Training |
| Meigs (Washington, DC) | 3,700 | Quartermaster |
| Merritt (Dumont, NJ) | 39,000 | Embarkation |
| Mills (Garden City, NY) | 25,000 | Embarkation |
| Polk (Raleigh, NC) | 4,800 | Tank Corps |
| Raritan (Metuchen, NJ) | 6,200 | Ordnance |
| Stuart (Newport News, VA) | 30,000 | Embarkation |

220

## Appendix 7: Abbreviations

| | |
|---|---|
| AA | Anti-aircraft |
| AEF | American Expeditionary Forces |
| AF in F | American Forces in France |
| AF in G | American Forces in Germany |
| Art | Artillery |
| Bn | Battalion |
| Brig | Brigade |
| Brig Gen | Brigadier General |
| Bty | Battery |
| CA | Coast Artillery |
| CAC | Coast Artillery Corps |
| Cav | Cavalry |
| Col | Colonel |
| Coy(s) | Company (companies) |
| Div | Division |
| Engr | Engineer |
| FA | Field Artillery |
| FSB | Field Signal Battalion |
| Ft. | Fort |
| Gen | General |
| GHQ | General Headquarters |
| Hq | Headquarters |
| Inf | Infantry |
| Lt Col | Lieutenant Colonel |
| MG | Machine Gun |
| MP | Military Police |
| NG | National Guard |
| Regt | Regiment |
| SOS | Services of Supply |
| Sqn | Squadron |
| TC | Transport Corps |
| USMC | United States Marine Corps |

For brevity, the official postal abbreviations for US states have been used throughout, both for locations and for states when identifying National Guard units.

# Sources

The basic source is *Order of Battle of the United States Land Forces in the World War (1917—19)*. 3 volumes published in 5 (Volume 3 in three parts) (Washington, DC, Government Printing Office, 1931—49; reprinted 1988).

This was supplemented by available lineage information from the following sources:[147]

McKenney, Janice F. *Air Defense Artillery*. ARMY LINEAGE SERIES. (Washington, DC: Center of Military History, US Army, 1983)
    _____. *Field Artillery: Regular Army and Army Reserve*. ARMY LINEAGE SERIES. (Washington, DC: Center of Military History, US Army, 1985)
Sawicki, James A. *Field Artillery Battalions of the US Army*. 2 vols (Dumfries, VA: Centaur Publications, 1977 and 1978)
    _____. *Infantry Regiments of the US Army*. (Dumfries, VA: Wyvern Publications, 1981)
    _____. *Cavalry Regiments of the US Army*. (Dumfries, VA: Wyvern Publications, 1985)
Stubbs, Mary Lee and Stanley Russell Connor. *Armor-Cavalry. Part I: Regular Army and Army Reserve*. ARMY LINEAGE SERIES. (Washington, DC: Office of the Chief of Military History, US Army, 1969)
    _____. *Armor-Cavalry. Part II: Army National Guard*. ARMY LINEAGE SERIES. (Washington, DC: Office of the Chief of Military History, US Army, 1972)
US Army Center for Military History, Lineage and Honors Information (www.army.mil/cmh-pg/lineage/LH.htm)
Wilson, John B. *Armies, Corps, Divisions and Separate Brigades*. ARMY LINEAGE SERIES. (Washington, DC: Center of Military History, US Army, 1993)
    _____. *Armies, Corps, Divisions and Separate Brigades*. ARMY LINEAGE SERIES. (Washington, DC: Center of Military History, US Army, 1999)[148]

---

[147] The Center for Military History is, for obvious reasons, most interested in units that are still active, and (because of their extreme complexity and frequent reorganizations) no longer posts any Army National Guard lineages in its on-line pages. Anyone interested in Army lineages thus owes gratitude to James Sawicki. Even his volumes, however, do not include all World War I elements, especially in the field artillery, which is built around those units created or surviving as battalions after regiments disappeared as tactical units. There are some conflicts between lineage information in the Sawicki volumes and the material from the Militia Bureau in the *Order of Battle* volumes on which National Guard units were used to form wartime regiments.

222

Introductory and other explanatory material is based on the following:

*The Army Almanac: A Book of Facts Concerning the Army of the United States*.
  ([Department of the Army] Washington, DC: Government Printing
  Office, 1950)
Kreidberg, Lt Col Marvin A. and 1st Lt Merton G. Henry. *History of Military
  Mobilization in the United States Army, 1775—1945*. Department of
  the Army Pamphlet No. 20-212 (Department of the Army, Jun 1955)
THE UNITED STATES ARMY IN THE WORLD WAR, 1917-1919. Volume 1:
  *Organization of the American Expeditionary Forces*. (Washington,
  DC: Center of Military History, US Army, 1988 reprint)
Wilson, John B. *Maneuver and Firepower: The Evolution of Divisions and
  Separate Brigades*. ARMY LINEAGE SERIES. (Washington, DC: Center
  of Military History, US Army, 1998)

Information on the US Marine Corps is primarily from:

McClellan, Maj (USMC) Edwin N., *The United States Marine Corps in the
  World War* (Published 1920 by Headquarters, US Marine Corps, Office
  of the Commandant, Washington, DC) and available online at
  http://www.au.af.mil/au/awc/awcgate/usmchist/war.txt

---

[148] The two volumes together contain more information than either does apart, because lineage is traced via the headquarters. Thus, for example, the Headquarters, 36th Infantry Division was disbanded in 1980 (as Headquarters, 36th Airborne Brigade) and then reconstituted in 1988 (as Headquarters, 36th Brigade, 49th Armored Division). Since the 1993 volume was actually completed in 1986, you would search it in vain for any record of the 36th Infantry Division. All of the World War I divisions can now be accounted for between the two volumes.

# Index

Officers below the rank of Maj Gen and units below division are not included. The main entry for an organization is indicated by a bold page number.

224

Printed in the United States
72775LV00003B/68